THE RADICAL MONK
Social and Political Philosophy of Swami Vivekanand

Books by B.N. Ray

Tradition and Innovation in Indian Political Thought
Political Theory : Interrogations and Interventions
Critical Theory : The Marx-Marcuse Encounter
Liberalism and the Communitarian Challenge
John Rawls and the Agenda of Social Justice
C.B. Macpherson and Liberalism
Contemporary Political Thinking
Nietzsche After Hundred Years
Citizenship in a Globalising World
Gandhigiri
Reading Gandhi
Political Theory and Thought
Indian Political Thought
Foundations of Western Political Thought
Political Philosophy

THE RADICAL MONK
Social and Political Philosophy of Swami Vivekanand

B.N. Ray

Kaveri Books
New Delhi - 110 002

First Published in 2017

ISBN: 978-81-7479-162-7

Published by
Kaveri Books
4832/24, Ansari Road
New Delhi - 110 002 (India)
Ph.: 011-4707 2321
E-mail: info@kaveribooks.com
Email: kaveribooks@gmail.com
Website: www.kaveribooks.com

Laser Typesetting by
Aarati Computers, Delhi - 110 009

PRINTED IN INDIA

Dedicated to

Dr. Achyuta Samanta
Founder, KISS & KIIT
A True *Karmayogi* like
Swami Vivekananda

Foreword

Swami Vivekananda's inspiring personality was well known both in India and in America during the last decade of the nineteenth century and the first decade of the twentieth century. The unknown monk of India suddenly leapt into fame at the Parliament of Religions held in Chicago in 1893, at which he represented Hinduism. His vast knowledge of Eastern and Western culture as well as his deep spiritual insight, magical eloquence, brilliant conversation, broad human empathy, colourful personality, and handsome figure made an irresistible appeal to the many types of Americans who came in contact with him. People who saw or heard him even once still cherish his memory after a lapse of more than half a century.

In America Vivekananda's mission was the interpretation of India's spiritual genius, especially in its Vedantic setting. He also tried to enrich the religious consciousness of the Americans through the rational and humanistic teachings of the Vedanta philosophy. In America he became India's spiritual ambassador and pleaded eloquently for better understanding between India and the New World in order to create a healthy synthesis of East and West, of religion and science.

In his own motherland Vivekananda is regarded as the patriot-saint of modern India and an inspirer of her dormant national consciousness. To the Hindus he preached the ideal of a strength-giving and man-making religion. Service to man as the visible manifestation of the Godhead was the special form of worship he advocated for the Indians, devoted as they were to the rituals and myths of their ancient faith. Many political leaders of India have publicly acknowledged their indebtedness to Swami Vivekananda.

His mission was both national and international. A lover of humankind, he strove to promote peace and human brotherhood on the spiritual foundation of the Vedantic Oneness of existence. A mystic of the highest order, Vivekananda had a direct and intuitive experience of Reality. He derived his ideas from that unfailing source of wisdom and often presented them in the soul-stirring language of poetry.

The natural tendency of Vivekananda's mind, like that of his Master, Ramakrishna, was to soar above the world and forget itself in contemplation of the Absolute. But another part of his personality bled at the sight of human suffering in East and West alike. It might appear that his mind seldom found a point of rest in its oscillation between contemplation of God and service to man. Be that as it may, he chose, in obedience to a higher call, service to man as his mission on earth; and this choice has endeared him to people in the West, Americans in particular.

In the course of a short life of thirty-nine years, of which only ten were devoted to public activities — and those, too, in the midst of acute physical suffering — he left for posterity his four classics: *Jnana-Yoga, Bhakti-Yoga, Karma-Yoga,* and *Raja-Yoga,* all of which are outstanding treatises on Hindu philosophy. In addition, he delivered innumerable lectures, wrote inspired letters in his own hand to his many friends and disciples, composed numerous poems, and acted as spiritual guide to the many seekers who came to him for instruction. He also organized the Ramakrishna Order of monks, which is the most outstanding religious organization of modern India. It is devoted to the propagation of the Hindu spiritual culture not only in the Swami's native land, but also in America and in other parts of the world.

Swami Vivekananda once spoke of himself as a 'condensed India.' His life and teachings are of inestimable value to the West for an understanding of the mind of Asia. William James, the Harvard philosopher, called the Swami the 'paragon of Vedantists.' Max Müller and Paul Deussen, the famous Orientalists of the nineteenth century, held him in genuine respect and affection.

Swami Vivekananda was thoroughly convinced by his intimate knowledge of the Indian people that the life-current of the nation, far from being extinct, was only submerged under the dead weight of ignorance and poverty. India still produced great saints whose message of the Spirit was sorely needed by the Western world. But the precious jewels of spirituality discovered by them were hidden, in the absence of a jewel-box, in a heap of filth. The West had created the jewel-box, in the form of a healthy society, but it did not have the jewels. Further, it took him no long time to understand that a materialistic culture contained within it the seeds of its own destruction. Again and again he warned the West of its impending danger. The bright glow on the Western horizon might not be the harbinger of a new dawn; it might very well be the red flames of a huge funeral pyre. The Western world was caught in the maze of its incessant activity — interminable movement without any goal. The hankering for material comforts, without a higher spiritual goal and a feeling of universal sympathy, might flare up among the nations of the West into jealousy and hatred, which in the end would bring about their own destruction.

Swami Vivekananda was a lover of humanity. Man is the highest manifestation of God, and this God was being crucified in different ways in the East and the West. Thus he had a double mission to perform in America. He wanted to obtain from the Americans money, scientific knowledge, and technical help for the regeneration of the Indian masses, and, in turn, to give to the Americans the knowledge of the Eternal Spirit to endow their material progress with meaning. No false pride could prevent him from learning from America the many features of her social superiority; he also exhorted the Americans not to allow racial arrogance to prevent them from accepting the gift of spirituality from India. Through this policy of acceptance and mutual respect he dreamt of creating a healthy human society for the ultimate welfare of man's body and soul.

The commemorative festivities for the 150th birth anniversary of Swami Vivekananda are continuing throughout the country since the past two years. The great amount of reverence and admiration that this young monk still commands is superbly amazing. No other personality belonging to the last two centuries could arguably match the impact which Vivekanada still has upon his countrymen. This is to great extent is so because he was a matchless dreamer; and is able to inspire people with what he once dreamt. In the formative days as a monk he crisscrossed the country mostly on foot and keenly observed both his country and the people residing within. The misery of the poor and degraded people took him to tears and gave him a burning dream – to ameliorate their wretched condition. With this dream and an unwavering determination he left India for America. Rest of the story needs no recapitulation. What he said on the opening day of the Parliament of Religions is smeared with unmistakable love for his country. "I am proud to belong to a nation which has sheltered the persecuted and the refugees of all religions and all nations of the earth," he said.

When he came back, he once said in Madras, "We have become real earthworms, crawling at the feet of everyone who dares to put his foot on us. Therefore, my friends, as one of your blood, as one that lives and dies with you, let me tell you that we want strength, strength, and every time strength". Thus he began to lead his people to rise; and love, as well. "Give up being a slave. For the next 50 years this alone shall be our keynote – this, our great Mother India. Let all other vain gods disappear for the time from our minds. This is the only god that is awake, our own race – everywhere his hands, everywhere his feet, everywhere his ears, he covers everything.. The first gods we have to worship are our countrymen".

The essence of his message, the crux of his great life was to bring highest morality and ethics to his people through religion, and then make morality and ethics the highest religion. His utterance betrays this aim: "The enjoyment of advantage over another is privilege, and throughout ages, the aim of morality has been its destruction. This is the work which tends towards sameness, towards unity, without destroying variety".

But Vivekanada never let anything taken for granted and, hence, raised questions too. "Why should a man be moral and pure? Because this straightness his will. Everything that strengthens the will by revealing the real nature is moral. Everything that does the reverse is immoral". What he said time and again has the distinct mark of highest catholicity. "Throughout all religious systems and ideals is the same morality; one thing only is preached: "Be unselfish, love others". And to put more meaning to such words, he adds elsewhere, "If there is power in hate there is infinitely more power in love." His dominant interest is visible when he said, "it is grand and good to know the laws that govern the stars and planets; it is infinitely grander and better to know the laws that govern the passions, the feelings, the will, of mankind". He realised that the art of living resides in the art of giving.

His counteractive weapon for all sorts of social ills was education. His experience prompted him to say, "From the day when education and culture etc. began to spread gradually from patricians to plebeians, grew the distinction between the modern civilization as of Western countries, and that of ancient civilisations as of India, Egypt, Rome etc. I see it before my eyes". His heart always wept for the hardship of people and the long tradition of relief work by the Ramakrishna Mission bears witness to that; still he pointed out the crippling effect of perpetual help: "We may convert every house in the country into a charity asylum". Therefore, his highest ideal became man-thinking, and he took education as the only means to achieve his aim. He argued that "a nation is advanced in proportion as education and intelligence spread among the masses. The chief cause of India's ruin and decline has been the monopolizing of the whole education and intelligence of the land, by dint of pride and royal authority, among a handful of men. If we are to rise again, we shall have to do it in the same way, i.e. by spreading education among the masses". He knew the hurdle too. "The great difficulty in the way of educating the poor [in India] is that the poor boys would rather help their fathers in the fields, or otherwise try to make a living, than come to the school... If the poor boy cannot come to education, education must go to him".

Vivekanada permitted no space for compromise. "Intelligence must not remain the monopoly of the cultured few; it will be disseminated from higher to lower classes. The immense power of our people for work must be utilized. India's potentialities are great and will be called forth".

His close friends and followers observed in Vivekananda his inconsistency, for which he appeared to show no particular concern or anger/anxiety. Neither did he try to reconcile his often contradictory points of view. The inconsistencies frequently apparent in his statements may be explained in two ways. In the first place, it has to be accepted that Vivekananda was a multi-layered personality, speaking from multiple reference points. He also grew irritable in his later life and was given to enormous mood-swings. Moreover, he was always an eager learner, never ashamed to admit that he had either changed or outgrown his earlier views. His active public life brought him in contact with a wide variety of people and cultures and he was constantly reframing and reformulating his ideas in the light of new revelations and experiences. The social environment in which he lived and worked was itself riddled with many incongruities and contradictions.

By the mid-nineteenth century, the educated Indian had become sufficiently aware of both his rich historical heritage and abject state of his current existence. Nostalgia and a sense of racial identity grew as Indians gradually perceived the oppressiveness of alien rule. In the early nineteenth century Orientalist scholars associated with the Fort William College, Calcutta, helped considerably to unearth several obscure Indian texts and traditions, thereby also creating a new awareness and sensitivity among Indians about their cultural heritage.

My friend Bichitrananda Ray has asked me to write the foreword for his book "The Radical Monk". I feel greatly honoured by his request. We studied together Political Science in the then Ravenshaw College. For our M.A. I went to BHU and he went to Delhi University. Over the last forty years of his teaching career in Delhi University and Pondicherry Central University he has established himself as a bright scholar. He was student of great political theorist C B Macpherson at the University of Toronto, Canada. He has published 15 books and hope this book on Swami Vivekananda will add another feather to his cap. I am sure this book will be of great help to students, scholars, teachers and the public to understand Hinduism and Modern India in a new perspective.

Soumya Ranjan Patnaik

Editor, The Sambad

Preface

From the time I decided to write a book on Vivekananda I have come to see it as a personal tribute to an outstanding fellow Indian, whose vivacity and compassion have impacted my life. Insight, not objectivity, is the key to the understanding of a life as multi-layered as that of Vivekananda and in the course of writing this book, I have often felt intimidated by the realization that a political theorist may not always be a good biographer. I have also been perplexed by the several inconsistencies and paradoxes of his life, and only by bringing these out more sharply, I felt, one could consciously depart from the hagiography that permeates biographical work on him. It is impossible to reach an understanding of a personality as complex as Vivekananda's without studying his ambiguities and shifting positions on various issues. In trying to integrate these in a holistic manner. I have largely followed his advice - judge a man ultimately by his strengths, not his weaknesses. Nothing could convey better Vivekananda's thoughts and personality than his own powerful language which I have liberally borrowed.

Swami Vivekananda remains the most influential figure in modern Hinduism. He revitalised the religion within and outside India. He was the principal reason behind the enthusiastic reception of yoga, transcendental meditation and other forms of Indian spiritual self-improvement in the West. It is true that ...modern Hindus derive their knowledge of Hinduism from Vivekananda, directly or indirectly. He espoused the idea that all sects within Hinduism and, indeed, all religions, are different paths to the same goal.

In the background of germinating nationalism in the British-ruled India, Vivekananda crystallised the nationalistic ideal. In the words of the social reformer Charles Freer Andrews, "The Swami's intrepid patriotism gave a new colour to the national movement throughout India. More than any other single individual of that period Vivekananda had made his contribution to the new awakening of India." Vivekananda drew the attention towards the prevalence of poverty in the country, and maintained that addressing such poverty was prerequisite for the national awakening. His nationalistic thoughts influenced scores of Indian thinkers and leaders and a whole generation of freedom fighters such as Gandhi, Netaji Subhas Chandra Bose, Aurobindo Ghose, Bal Gangadhar Tilak and Bagha Jatin.

Subhas Chandra Bose paying tribute to Vivekananda said "His personality was rich, profound and complex... Reckless in his sacrifice, unceasing in his activity, boundless in his love, profound and versatile in his wisdom, exuberant in his emotions, merciless in his attacks but yet simple as a child, he was a rare personality in this world of ours." Aurobindo Ghose considered Vivekananda as his spiritual mentor, saying "Vivekananda was a soul of puissance if ever there was one, a very lion among men..." At the Belur Math, Mahatma Gandhi was heard to say that his whole life was an effort to bring into action the ideas of Vivekananda. Many years after Vivekananda's death, Rabindranath Tagore told French Nobel Laureate Romain Rolland, "If you want to know India, study Vivekananda. In him everything is positive and nothing negative." Rolland himself wrote that "His words are great music, phrases in the style of Beethoven, stirring rhythms like the march of Händel choruses. I cannot touch these sayings of his, scattered as they are through the pages of books, at thirty years' distance, without receiving a thrill through my body like an electric shock. And what shocks, what transports, must have been produced when in burning words they issued from the lips of the hero!"

Though belonging to an ancient order of monks, Vivekananda was no ordinary sanyasi. Even as a world-renouncer, he embraced the world with all its beauty and ugliness and retained a deep interest in pressing everyday social problems. Second, Vivekananda's life and work appear to coincide with modern India rediscovering itself. His enduring message to his countrymen, and more generally to all oppressed people in the world, was to recover the innate potentialities and self-belief in man that had been eroded by certain historical reasons and circumstances. In this sense, Vivekananda seems to have employed cultural hermeneutics and innovative philosophical thinking to overturn history. For him, Vedanta was not simply a closed system of philosophical belief but a worldview that could be transformed into active social and political praxis. No Vedantin declared 'man-making' to be his primary goal in life as did Vivekananda.

Vivekananda anticipated Gandhi in preferring to closely identify with the everyday life of the people and taking stock of their pressing problems before eking to any ambitious reformist agenda. His aim was to arrive at 'root and branch' reform, not attempts at cosmetically changing appearances. He understood self-awakening in man to be not simply the furtherance of our material lives but also spiritualizing the material. Our everyday lives, Vivekananda claimed, turned meaningful only when we realized the unity of all life and its foundations in the Spirit. Though a Vedantin, he never overemphasized the traditional Hindu quest for personal salvation. Rather, the collective, in his view, had to realize itself in the individual and the individual in the collective. It was thus, he believed, that a nation is truly born.

Looking back at his life and work, it appears as though Vivekananda's overarching mission in life was to restore to man his lost dignity and selfhood. In doing this he often over-reached himself, only so that his countrymen and humanity at large could find greater bliss and self-realization. Vivekananda passed away when barely forty but his legacy lives on and surfaces every time we look beyond ourselves to problems persistently confronting humanity.

Jamsetji Tata was influenced by Vivekananda to establish the Indian Institute of Science—one of India's best known research universities. Abroad, Vivekananda had interactions with Max Müller. Scientist Nikola Tesla was one of those influenced by the Vedic philosophy teachings of Vivekananda. On 11 November 1995, a section of Michigan Avenue, one of the most prominent streets in downtown Chicago, was formally renamed "Swami Vivekananda Way". National Youth Day in India is observed on his birthday, 12 January. He is projected as a role model for youth by the Indian government as well as non-government organisations. In September 2010, India's Finance Ministry highlighted the relevance of teachings and values of Swami Vivekananda in the modern competitive environment. The former Union Finance Minister, and presently

President of India Shri Pranab Mukherjee, approved in principle the "Swami Vivekananda Values Education Project" at the cost of 100 crore with the objectives such as involving the youth through competitions, essays, discussions and study circles and publishing Swami Vivekananda's complete work in different languages.

For centuries to come people everywhere will be inspired by Swami Vivekananda's message: O man! first realize that you are one with Brahman — *aham Brahmasmi* — and then realize that the whole universe is verily the same Brahman — *sarvam khalvidam Brahma*.

This nation is currently celebrating the 150th birth anniversary of Vivekananda and the Government of India has decided to join in the celebrations by organizing seminars, opening chairs in hs same and declaring his birthday as National Youth Day. There is an added cause for happiness. In recent times, academic and quasi-academic writing, especially on spiritual figures in India, has been the subject of fierce and protracted controversy. In his lifetime and thereafter, the life and work of Vivekananda himself has often been superficially understood and ideologically appropriated. Thus, one has heard of the Left interpreting sanyas as parasitic and the Right quite indefensibly treating some of ideas as the building blocks for Hindutva. The new danger that now seems to have arisen is from the institution that has hitherto closely and ably guarded his legacy: the Ramakrishna Mission itself, which, is getting increasingly selective about which aspects of his life and work to project and in what manner.

This biography was written with a non-specialist reader in mind and any comparison with works of scholarship would be quite unwarranted. Over the years, I have come to realize that readers prefer handling short critical works to those that appear somewhat intimidating on account of their lengths, citations, quotations or rigorous academic. This would explain the decision of generally keep out detailed notes and citations as a part of this text. For the benefit of the reader who seeks to go beyond this book, I have given a list though, again, this is by no means exhaustive.

I claim here no great originality in writing this book. Instead, I have digested the existing literature on the subject and written the book with my own focus on Vivekananda as an icon of mass churning and upsurge in the society, to make Indians rise above their petty local, linguistic and caste loyalities and to commit ourselves into a vedantic society.

BN Ray
Senior Professor
KISS, KIIT University Campus-10
Bhubaneshwar, Odisha

Contents

1

Introduction

Swami Vivekananda (1863-1902) is a figure of great importance in the development of a modern Hindu self-understanding and in formulating the West's view of Hinduism. He was a key figure in the introduction of Indian philosophies of Vedanta and Yoga to the western world, and was credited with raising interfaith awareness, bringing Hinduism to the status of a major world religion in the late 19th century. He was a major force in the revival of Hinduism in India, and contributed to the notion of nationalism in colonial India. He was the chief disciple of the 19th century saint Ramakrishna and the founder of the Ramakrishna Math and the Ramakrishna Mission. He is perhaps best known for his inspiring speech beginning with "Sisters and Brothers of America," through which he introduced Hinduism at the Parliament of the Religions in Chicago in 1893.

Swami Vivekananda whose pre-monkhood name was Narendra Nath Datta or Naren for short, belonged to an aristocratic section of the Kshatriya caste of Bengal. The Dattas displayed several of the traditional characteristics of the Kshatriyas, including a faith in leading an ostentatious life, but also producing an occasional "*Sannyasin*". Naren's father Visvanath Datta, a solicitor in the Calcutta High Court, was known for his varied interests and activities, and being conscious of his own superior position in the society, he exhibited a broad outlook on social and cultural matters, including a feeling of indifference to caste. Naren's mother, Bhuvaneswari Devi, was a highly educated woman of regal majesty, whose heroic spirit had been nurtured on the great Hindu epics. During private conversation with his disciples in America, Vivekananda later acknowledged the deep influence of his mother and said, "It is my mother who has been the constant inspiration of my life and work."

Swami Vivekananda was born as Narendranath Dutta in Calcutta, the capital of British India, on Monday 12 January 1863 during the Makar Sankranti festival. He belonged to a traditional Bengali Kayastha family. There was precedence of ascetics in his family—Narendra's grandfather Durga Charan Datta renounced the world and became a monk at the age of twenty five. Narendra's father Vishwanath Datta was an attorney of Calcutta High Court. Vishwanath Datta had a liberal, progressive outlook on social and religious matters. Narendra's mother, Bhuvaneswari Devi, was a pious woman. Before the birth of Narendra, she prayed for a son and asked a relative at Varanasi to make religious offerings to the god Shiva. According to traditional accounts, Bhuvaneswari Devi had a dream in which Shiva said that he would be born as her son. Bhuvaneswari Devi accepted the child as a boon from Shiva and named him Vireswara, meaning "powerful god" in Bengali. The rational approach of his father and the religious temperament of his mother helped shape young Narendra's thinking and personality. He learnt the power of self-control from his mother. In later life, Narendra often quoted a saying of his mother, "Remain pure all your life; guard your own honour and never transgress the honour of others. Be very tranquil, but when necessary, harden your heart." He was adept in meditation and could enter the state of samadhi (a higher level of concentrated meditation). He would often visualise a light while falling asleep and had a vision of Gautama Buddha during his meditation. During his childhood, he was fascinated by the wandering ascetics and monks.

Narendra had a wide range of scholarship in philosophy, religion, history, the social sciences, arts, literature, and other subjects. He evinced interest in the Hindu scriptures such as the Vedas, the Upanishads, the Bhagavad Gita, the Ramayana, the Mahabharata and the Puranas. He was trained in Indian classical music under two *Ustads* (maestro), Beni Gupta and Ahamad Khan. He regularly participated in physical exercise, sports, and organisational activities. Even when he was young, he questioned the validity of superstitious customs and discrimination based on caste and refused to accept anything without rational proof and pragmatic test. Narendra joined the Metropolitan Institution of Ishwar Chandra Vidyasagar in 1871 and studied there till 1877 when his family moved to Raipur. His family returned to Calcutta two years later.

In 1879 after his family moved back to Calcutta, Narendra passed the entrance examination from the Presidency College, Calcutta. He subsequently studied western logic, western philosophy and history of European nations in the General Assembly's Institution (now known as the Scottish Church College). In 1881 he passed the Fine Arts examination and in 1884 he completed a Bachelor of Arts degree.

Narendra studied the works of David Hume, Immanuel Kant, Johann Gottlieb Fichte, Spinoza, Hegel, Arthur Schopenhauer, Auguste Comte, Herbert Spencer, John Stuart Mill, and Charles Darwin. Narendra became fascinated with the evolutionism of Herbert Spencer and had correspondence with him; he translated Spencer's book Education (1861) into Bengali. Alongside his study of Western philosophers, he was thoroughly acquainted with Indian Sanskrit scriptures and many Bengali works. According to his professors, Narendra was a student prodigy. Dr. William Hastie, principal of General Assembly's Institution, wrote, "Narendra is really a genius. I have travelled far and wide but I have never come across a lad of his talents and possibilities, even in German universities, among philosophical students." He was regarded as a srutidhara—a man with prodigious memory.

Narendra became the member of a Freemason's lodge and of a breakaway faction of the Brahmo Samaj led by Keshub Chandra Sen. His initial beliefs were shaped by Brahmo concepts, which included belief in a formless God and deprecation of the worship of idols. Not satisfied with his knowledge of philosophy, he wondered if God and religion could be made a part of one's growing experiences and deeply internalised. Narendra went about asking prominent residents of contemporary Calcutta whether they had come "face to face with God" but could not get answers which satisfied him. His first introduction to the saint Ramakrishna occurred in a literature class in General Assembly's Institution, when he heard Hastie lecturing on William Wordsworth's poem The Excursion. While explaining the word "trance" in the poem, Hastie suggested his students to visit Ramakrishna of Dakshineswar to know the real meaning of trance. This prompted some of his students, including Narendra, to visit Ramakrishna. Narendra's meeting with Ramakrishna in November 1881 proved to be a turning point in his life. Narendra said about this first meeting:

"Ramakrishna looked just like an ordinary man, with nothing remarkable about him. He used the most simple language and I thought 'Can this man be a great teacher?'. I crept near to him and asked him the question which I had been asking others all my life: 'Do you believe in God, Sir?' 'Yes', he replied. 'Can you prove it, Sir?' 'Yes'. 'How?' 'Because I see Him just as I see you here, only in a much intenser sense.' That impressed me at once. I began to go to that man, day after day, and I actually saw that religion could be given. One touch, one glance, can change a whole life."

He further said : "The magic touch of the Master that day immediately brought a wonderful change over my mind. I was astounded to find that really there was nothing in the universe but God! ... everything I saw appeared to be Brahman. ... I realized that I must have had a glimpse of the Advaita state. Then it struck me that the words of the scriptures were not false. Thenceforth I could not deny the conclusions of the Advaita philosophy."

Though Vevekanand did not accept Ramakrishna as his guru initially and revolted against his ideas, he was attracted by his personality and visited him frequently. He initially looked upon Ramakrishna's ecstasies and visions as "mere figments of imagination", "mere hallucinations". As a member of Brahmo Samaj, he revolted against idol worship and polytheism, and Ramakrishna's worship of Kali. He even rejected the Advaitist Vedantism of identity with absolute as blasphemy and madness and often made fun of the concept. Though at first Narendra could not accept Ramakrishna and his visions, he did not neglect him. Instead, he tested Ramakrishna, who faced all of his arguments and examinations with patience—"Try to see the truth from all angles" was his Master's reply. During the course of five years of his training under Ramakrishna, he was increasingly ready to renounce everything for the sake of realising God. In time, he accepted Ramakrishna as his guru and completely surrendered as disciple.

In 1885, Ramakrishna developed throat cancer and he was transferred to Calcutta and later to Cossipore. Narendra and Ramakrishna's other disciples took care of him during his final days. Vivekananda's spiritual education under Ramakrishna continued. At Cossipore, he reportedly experienced Nirvikalpa Samadhi. During Ramakrishna's last days, he and some of the other disciples received the ochre (monastic robes) from Ramakrishna, forming the first monastic order of Ramakrishna. He was taught that service to men was the most effective worship of God. When young he doubted Ramakrishna's claim of avatar, Ramakrishna said, "He who was Rama, He who was Krishna, He himself is now Ramakrishna in this body." During his final days, Ramakrishna asked Vivekananda to take care of other monastic disciples and in turn asked them to look upon Vivekananda as their leader. Ramakrishna died in the early morning hours of 16 August 1886 at his garden house in Cossipore. According to his disciples, this was *Mahasamadhi*.

After the death of Ramakrishna, many of his disciples returned home and were inclined towards a *Grihastha* (family-oriented) life. Such *Grihastha* disciples financially helped the monastic disciples led by Vivekananda to form fellowship at a derelict house at Baranagar on the river Ganges. The house became the first building of the Ramakrishna Math—the monastery of the first monastic order of Ramakrishna. The dilapidated house was chosen because of its low rent and proximity to the Cossipore burning-ghat where Ramakrishna was cremated. Vivekananda and other members of the Math spent their time in meditation, discussing the philosophies and teachings of spiritual teachers including Ramakrishna, Adi Sankara, Ramanuja, and Jesus Christ. In January 1899 the Baranagar Math was transferred to Belur in the Howrah district, now known as the Belur Math.

In January 1887, he and eight other disciples took formal monastic vows. He took the name of Swami Vividishananda. Later he was crowned with the name Vivekananda by Ajit Singh, the Maharaja of Khetri. It is not out of place to say a few words about the name Vivekananda through which, he became famous. Name and fame are the last obstacles of monastic life; A monk is supposed to transcend name and fame and be absorbed in Brahman. Vivekananda renounced his family name when he took his monastic vows and became 'Swami Vivekananda'. During his itinerant days, he frequently changed his name so that he could remain incognito; sometimes he was Vividishananda, and sometimes Sachidananda.

The history behind the name 'Vivekananda' was told by Munshi Jagmohanlal to Pandit Jhabarmal Sharma. During his visit in Khetri, one day Vivekananda was seated with Raja Ajit Singh. Raja said to him smilingly: 'Maharaj, you r name Vividishananda is very difficult.

Without the help of a commentator, ordinary people will not understand its meaning, and it is not easy to pronounce either. Moreover, the time of vividisha [the desire to know] in your life is over.' Listening to Raja rational suggestion, he asked, 'What name do you suggest?' Raja answered, 'I think your right and meaningful name is "Vivekananda" he who finds bliss discriminating between the real and the unreal". From then on, at the request of Raja, he used the name "Vivekananda".

Now the question is: When did Swamiji get this name? According to Jagmohan's account, Swamiji got the name during his first visit to Khetri; however, all main biographers of Vivekananda agree that he got the name during his last visit. After his first visit to Khetri, he travelled all over South India as Swami Sachchidananda. This indicates that he received the name "Vivekananda" during his last visit; otherwise it seems unreasonable that he would accept and then abandon the name which his beloved disciple Raja Ajit Singh had given to him.

While he and his friends were at Bombay together, they said to him: "Swami, you. are going to America; time is very precious there. You must have a. watch.' 'All right; buy me one,' was his quick answer. 'You should also have some visiting cards.' 'Very well, have one hundred printed.' At that time he was known as Sachchidananda — but when he asked, 'What name has to put on the cards?' he replied, 'Swami Vivekananda.' It was the first time that he used that name.

Sometimes we may wonder why Swami Vivekananda is usually seen in his images dressed more like a maharaja in saffron, than a sanyasi? The majestic turban and robe are, in fact, so inseparable from the image of the Swami that most people, perhaps, would not recognise the great Indian monk without them. But what is much less known is that both his famous attire and his name Vivekananda were not bestowed to the Swami by his Guru, as convention would dictate, but instead by his disciple — Maharaja Ajit Singh of Khetri in erstwhile Rajputana in Jhunjhunu district, Shekhawati — the man Vivekananda claimed was his "only friend on Earth".

Khetri was known for its enlightened rulers who were pioneers in various fields. Incidentally, it was also the place where Rajasthan's first branch of the Brahmo Samaj, the new brand of reformist Hinduism established by prolific Bengali social reformers of the time, was established in 1886, five years before Vivekananda's visit to Khetri.

As a young 28-year-old wandering monk on a pilgrimage to understand his motherland and discover his vision in life, Vivekananda travelled to Rajasthan as well. It was in Maharaja Ajit Singh's summer palace in Mt. Abu that they first met. The Maharaja's first question to him was, "What is life?" to which he replied, "Life is the unfolding and development of a being under circumstances tending to press it down." He spent five months with the Maharaja, who was perhaps his age, and accompanied him to Khetri.

The Maharaja dedicated himself to him as a benefactor, disciple, and philosopher-friend. He provided him with not just the means to fulfil his grand vision, but also the all-important gift of a lasting friendship. He, in one of his letters, went to the extent of saying that "I have not the least shame in opening my mind to you", and could indeed, because of the Maharaja's "steadiness of purpose", as he himself said, depend on him at any time.

The two conversed mostly in English, and sometimes, interestingly, in Sanskrit too. They not only conversed, but participated in hunting expeditions and musical sessions where Vivekananda sang and the Maharaja, also a skilled veena player, accompanied him on the harmonium.

Once, upon learning that he was uncomfortable with the heat, the Maharaja advised him to wear the turban long silk robe and taught him how to wear it — an art that he soon mastered and took away with him the dress as a prominent Rajasthani custom. He assumed the name of Vivekananda for good at the suggestion of the Maharaja, just before leaving for America. He previously roamed about India assuming various 'monastic' names such as Sachchidananda or Vividishananda — successfully fulfilling his aim of breaking all ties by concealing his identity.

He would say, "As for Rajaji, his love for me is simply without limit." Interestingly, although he formally initiated the Maharaja as his spiritual disciple, he gave him lessons not just in the deepest philosophy of vedanta, but also in material sciences such as physics and chemistry, for which a special lab was constructed. He also gave him lessons in law, and even astronomy.

His discourses to the Maharaja carried on even while he was away, through lengthy letters. In one such letter, he writes, "And when I think of you, Raja Ajit Singh...I cannot help believing in the glorious renaissance of the religion eternal, when such hands are willing to rebuild it again." And the Maharaja...would rise in the middle of the night to carry out the humbling services of a devotee, pressing his feet, or fanning him, despite the Swami's fervent protests.

Once, the Maharaja, celebrating the birth of a son with his guru, had arranged a nautch performance one evening, and requested him to join him, who, being a monk, felt it inappropriate and refused. The nautch singer was deeply hurt by this dismissal, and sang aloud in agony, a devotional Surdas song that matched her emotions perfectly, elaborating Vivekananda how the Lord sees all with the same-sighted vision. Vivekananda was touched profoundly by this deep vedantic insight of oneness, joined the party, and later recollected how this incident "removed the scales from his eyes".

It was Ajit Singh's contribution that was a prominent source of funding for his first historic trip to America. The Maharaja provided him with resources not only for his own work, but also a fixed monthly amount for the upkeep of his widowed mother and younger brothers.

The Maharaja's support indeed continued lifelong, and he also provided Vivekananda with a large sum of money towards establishing his visionary project, the Belur Math. He articulated lucidly in a letter to Jagmohanlal, "Certain men are born in certain periods to perform certain actions in combination. Ajit Singh and myself are two such souls — born to help each other in a big work for the good of mankind.... We are as supplement and complement."

One of the most captivating illustrations of his teachings also happened to take place in Rajasthan, in Alwar, in the presence of its anglicised Maharaja, Mangal Singh. When the Maharaja proclaimed that he did not believe in image worship, Vivekananda boldly asked his Dewan to take down a portrait of the Maharaja and spit on it, whose shocked refusal to spit on a "likeness" of their revered Maharaja provoked a breathtaking discourse by him on how, similarly, the image represents God to many Hindus, who worship the "ideal" behind the idol, and the material, stone or metal is not worshipped itself. This incident completely transformed the sceptical outlook of the Maharaja, who claimed that Vivekananda had indeed opened his eyes. In order to celebrate Swamiji's 150th birth anniversary, and as an attempt to keep their relationship intact and ever-growing, the Ramakrishna Mission's centre in Khetri, housed in the Maharaja's palace, Fateh-Bilass, renamed as 'Vivekananda Smriti-Mandir', is at the moment trying to restrengthen its roots by refurbishing this historical heritage property, also in its 150th year.

In 1888, Vivekananda left the monastery as a Parivrâjaka—the Hindu religious life of a wandering monk, without fixed abode, without ties, independent and strangers wherever they go. His sole possessions were a kamandalu (water pot), staff, and his two favourite books—*Bhagavad Gita* and *The Imitation of Christ*. Vivekananda travelled extensively in India for five years, visiting centres of learning, acquainting himself with the diverse religious traditions and different patterns of social life. He developed a sympathy for the suffering and poverty of the masses and resolved to uplift the nation. Living mainly on *bhiksha* (alms), Vivekananda travelled on foot and railway tickets bought by his admirers whom he met during the travels. During these travels he made acquaintance and stayed with Indians from all walks of life and religions—scholars, dewans, Rajas, Hindus, Muslims, Christians, pariahs and government officials.

In 1888, Vivekananda's first destination was the city of Varanasi, where he met the learned Bengali writer, Bhudev Mukhopadhyay and the saint Trailanga Swami. He also met Babu Pramadadas Mitra, the noted Sanskrit scholar, with whom he corresponded on the interpretation of the Hindu scriptures. After Varanasi he visited Ayodhya, Lucknow, Agra, Vrindavan, Hathras and Rishikesh. At Hathras, he met Sharat Chandra Gupta, a railway station master who later became one of his earliest disciples as Sadananda. Between 1888 and 1890, he visited Vaidyanath and Allahabad. From Allahabad, he went on to Ghazipur, where he met Pavhari Baba, a Advaita Vedanta ascetic who spent most of his time in meditation. During this period, Vivekananda returned to Baranagar Math a few times, because of ill health and to arrange for monetary funds.

In July 1890, accompanied by the fellow monk Swami Akhandananda a disciple of Ramakrishna, Vivekananda visited the Himalayas. This constituted the first phase of his journey that would encompass the West. He visited Nainital, Almora, Srinagar and Dehradun, Rishikesh and Haridwar. During these travels, he met Swami Brahmananda, Saradananda, Turiyananda, Akhandananda and Advaitananda. They stayed at Meerut for some days engaged in meditation, prayer and study of scriptures. At the end of January 1891, Vivekananda left his fellows and journeyed to Delhi.

After visiting historical sites at Delhi, Vivekananda journeyed towards Alwar in Rajputana. Later he journeyed to Jaipur, where he studied Panini's Ashtadhyayi with a Sanskrit scholar. He next travelled to Ajmer, where he visited the palace of Akbar and the Dargah Sharif. At Mount Abu, he met Raja Ajit Singh of Khetri, who became his ardent devotee and supporter.

Vivekananda visited Ahmedabad, Wadhra and Limbdi. At Ahmedabad, he completed his studies of Islamic and Jain culture. At Limbdi, he met Thakur Saheb Jaswant Singh, who had himself been to England and America. From Thakur Saheb, he first got the idea of going to the West to preach Vedanta. He later visited Junagadh, where he was the guest of Haridas Viharidas Desai, the Diwan of the State. The Diwan who was so charmed with his company that every evening he, with all the State officials, used to meet him and converse with him until late at night. Vivekananda also visited Girnar, Kutch, Porbander, Dwaraka, Palitana, Nadiad, and Baroda. At Porbander, he stayed three quarters of a year, furthering his philosophical and Sanskrit studies with learned pandits.

Vivekananda's next destinations included Mahabaleshwar, Pune, Khandwa and Indore. At Kathiawar, he heard of the Parliament of the World's Religions and was urged by his followers there to attend it. After a brief stay in Bombay in July 1892, he met Bal Gangadhar Tilak during a train journey. After staying with Tilak for a few days in Pune, he travelled to Belgaum in October 1892 and to Panaji and Margao in Goa. He spent three days in the Rachol Seminary, the oldest convent of Goa, where rare religious literature in manuscripts and printed works in Latin were preserved. There, he studied Christian theological works.

Later Vivekananda travelled to Bangalore, where he became acquainted with K. Seshadri Iyer, the Dewan of the Mysore state, and stayed at the palace as a guest of the Maharaja of Mysore,

Chamaraja Wodeyar. Regarding Vivekananda's learning, Seshadri remarked on "a magnetic personality and a divine force which were destined to leave their mark on the history of his country." The Maharaja provided him a letter of introduction to the Dewan of Cochin and got him a railway ticket.

From Bangalore, he visited Trichur, Kodungalloor, and Ernakulam. At Ernakulam, he met Chattampi Swamikal, contemporary of Narayana Guru, in early December 1892. From Ernakulam, he travelled to Trivandrum, Nagercoil and reached Kanyakumari on foot during the Christmas Eve of 1892. At Kanyakumari, he meditated on the "last bit of Indian rock", famously known later as the Vivekananda Rock Memorial, for three days. At Kanyakumari, Vivekananda had the "Vision of one India", also commonly called "The Kanyakumari resolve of 1892". He wrote,

"At Cape Camorin sitting in Mother Kumari's temple, sitting on the last bit of Indian rock—I hit upon a plan: We are so many sanyasis wandering about, and teaching the people metaphysics—it is all madness. Did not our Gurudeva use to say, 'An empty stomach is no good for religion?' We as a nation have lost our individuality and that is the cause of all mischief in India. We have to raise the masses."

From Kanyakumari he visited Madurai, where he met the Raja of Ramnad, Bhaskara Sethupathi, to whom he had a letter of introduction. The Raja became his disciple and urged him to go to the Parliament of Religions at Chicago. From Madurai, he visited Rameswaram, Pondicherry and Madras and there he met some his most devoted disciples, who played important roles in collecting funds for his voyage to America and later in establishing the Ramakrishna Mission in Madras. With the aid of funds collected by his Madras disciples and Rajas of Mysore, Ramnad, Khetri, Dewans and other followers, Vivekananda left for Chicago on 31 May 1893 from Bombay assuming the name Vivekananda—the name suggested by the Maharaja of Khetri, Ajit Singh.

On his way to Chicago, Vivekananda visited Japan in 1893. He first reached the port city of Nagasaki, and then boarded a steamer to Kobe. From here he took the land route to Yokohama, visiting along the way the three big cities of Osaka, Kyoto and Tokyo. He called the Japanese "one of the cleanest people on earth", and was impressed not only by neatness of their streets and dwellings but also by their movements, attitudes and gestures, all of which he found to be 'picturesque'.

This was a period of rapid military build-up in Japan—a prelude to the Sino-Japanese War and the Russo-Japanese War. These preparations did not escape the attention of Vivekananda, who wrote: "The Japanese seem now to have fully awakened themselves to the necessity of the present times. They have now a thoroughly organised army equipped with guns which one of their own officers has invented and which is said to be second to none. Then, they are continually increasing their navy." About the industrial progress he observed, "The match factories are simply a sight to see, and they are bent upon making everything they want in their own country."

Contrasting the rapid progress of Japan with the situation back in India, he urged his countrymen—the "offspring of centuries of superstition and tyranny" —to come out of their narrow holes and have a look abroad:

"Only I want that numbers of our young men should pay a visit to Japan and China every year. Especially to the Japanese, India is still the dreamland of everything high and good. And you, what are you? ... talking twaddle all your lives, vain talkers, what are you? Come, see these people, and then go and hide your faces in shame. A race of cowards, you lose your caste if you come out! Sitting down these hundreds of years with an ever-increasing load of crystallized superstition on your heads, for hundreds of years spending all your energy upon discussing the touchableness or untouchableness of this food or that, with all humanity crushed out of you by the continuous social tyranny of ages—what are you? And what are you doing now? ... promenading the sea-shores with books in your hands—repeating undigested stray bits of European brainwork, and the whole soul bent upon getting a thirty rupee clerkship, or at best becoming a lawyer—the height of young India's ambition—and every student with a whole brood of hungry children cackling at his heels and asking for bread! Is there not water enough in the sea to drown you, books, gowns, university diplomas, and all?"

A number of philosophic as well as practical questions arose in Naren's mind and he sought answers to such questions by consulting senior college students like Brajendra Nath Seal as well as leaders of the Brahmo Samaj, including Devendranath Tagore.

The advice that Naren received through such consultation naturally varied, and each piece of advice seemed to provide partial help to Naren in his "search for truth." Bajendra Nath Seal put forward the merits of rationalism, and he even spoke in terms of the "God of Reason." Romain Rolland describes how Brajendra's viewpoint could satisfy only Naren's "intellect" but not his "heart":

Brajendra's rationalism was of a peculiar kind in that it claimed to be an amalgamation of the pure monism of the Vedanta, the Hegelian dialectic of the Absolute Idea, and the Gospel of the French Revolution: Liberty, Equality and Fraternity. He believed that the principle of individualism was "the evil", and Universal Reason "the good"... Brajendra's rationalism appealed to some sides of Naren's domineering nature, but the latter's tumultuous personality was not to be confined within such limits. Although his intellect certainly wished to accept or impose the sovereignty of universal reason and to make the foundation of morality an imperious negation of individualism, his life would not agree. . . Naren's heart and senses looked for the living revelation, the realization of the Absolute, God-made man—some holy Guru, who could say to him, "I have seen Him, I have touched Him, I have been He."

Naren joined the movement of young Brahmos in Bengal for the education and unity of the Indian masses without distinction of caste, race or religion. Some of them attacked orthodox Hinduism even more bitterly than did the Christian missionaries. Romain Rolland describes why the Brahmo spirit also failed to satisfy Naren's "heart":

Naren's free and living intelligence quickly realised the unintelligent narrowness of the Brahmos, who were not free from irrational fanaticism, and Naren's spirit no less than his national pride was, wounded by them. He could not subscribe to the abdication of Indian wisdom before the badly assimilated knowledge of the West. Although Naren continued to attend the meetings of the Brahmo Samaj, in his heart he was not at rest.

As a last attempt to seek answers to the questions that made him live in great turmoil of soul, Naren went to Devendranath Tagore and asked him: "Sir, Have you seen God?" Although Tagore recognized the depth of feeling and sincerity that prompted Naren to raise such fundamental issues, he gave no direct reply to his question and only said, "My boy, you have the eyes of a yogi. You should practise meditation." Naren returned unsatisfied, and his inability to achieve the reconciliation of his mental struggles started showing up in the form of dreams, as he himself recalled in later days:

"From my youth up, every night just as I fell asleep, two dreams took shape. In one I saw myself among the great ones of the earth, the possessor of riches, honours, power, and glory; and I felt that the capacity to attain all these was in me. But the next instant I saw myself renouncing all worldly things, dressed in a simple loin-cloth, living on alms, sleeping at the foot of a tree; and I thought that I was capable also of living thus, like the *Rishis* of old. Of these two pictures, the second took the upper hand and I felt that only thus could a man attain supreme bliss...And I fell asleep in the foretaste of that bliss...And each night it was renewed..."

A friend persuaded him to come and meet Ramakrishna. Ramakrishna immediately recognized to him as the incarnation of Narayana, the Highest God, who had come to redeem humankind from suffering. In a strange ritual Ramakrishna placed his foot on Narendra's body – and the power to see God was communicated to him. Narendra now saw God everywhere and no longer took interest in anything else. When his father died, the young man had to take responsibility for his family. He encountered much difficulty in finding employment. His mother scolded him for his 'God madness', exclaiming: 'If God is good, why are millions dying for want of food?' Narendra agreed and became an 'atheist'. However, falling exhausted on his bed after another frustrating day searching for employment, he had a vision: he saw how God's love and justice, providence and suffering each had its place in the world. From now on he knew that his true calling was to renounce the world and devote his life to the service of God. His only worldly concern was to see his mother provided for. He went to Dakshineshwar to pray to Kali for money. Three times he tried, and three times he went into an ecstasy before her image, praying only for 'knowledge and devotion'. Like Ramakrishna, he realized that 'everything that is, is Mother'.

Such was the condition of Naren in November 1880 when a friend of his, Surendranath Mitra, a rich gentleman converted to Christianity, asked Naren to sing a religious hymn, in the presence of Sri Ramakrishna who had by that time been widely recognized as a great spiritual leader.

Sri Ramakrishna, whose pre-sainthood name was Gadadhar, was born in 1836 in a poor Brahmin family of a Bengal village. His father, Khudiram Chattopadhyaya, had been deprived of all he possessed, because he had refused to bear witness to the advantage of the great landowner who was his neighbour. Khudiram died when Gadadhar was seven years old, and the latter had to depend on whatever his elder brother Ramkumar could earn as a teacher. Ramkumar tried to keep Gadadhar into school but without much success. Rather, the inner urge of Gadadhar's life was expressed in artistic emotions, so much so that a beautiful sight of snow-white cranes flying at the edge of a dark cloud made him lose his consciousness. Shortly thereafter, at the age of eight, Gadadhar was again seized with ecstasy when, playing the part of Siva in the village festivities, he was carried away by devotional music and the sight of artistic images.

Poor family circumstances forced Ramkumar in 1855 to accept the paid office of a priest in a new temple, founded by Rani Rasmani, a rich woman belonging to a low caste. This temple was dedicated to the Great Goddess, the Divine Mother, Kali, and was located at Dakshineshwar, on the banks of the Ganga river near Calcutta. When Ram kumar died in 1856, his younger brother Gadadhar, the future Sri Ramakrishna, began his astounding career of spiritual disciplines and attainments, as a temple priest and devotee of Mother Kali.

Of the total period of thirty years that Sri Ramakrishna spent at Dakshineshwar, the first half was devoted by him in personally verifying the efficacy of the diverse mode of sadhana or spiritual discipline prescribed by the various religions. He was first initiated into the Tantric mode of *sadhana*. He practised it for two years, and passed successfully through all the stages till he was in a position to obtain from Mother Kali answers to all his questions on many occasions. He then followed the mode of sadhana laid down by the Vaisnava cult, and is said to have obtained a vision of Sri Krisna. He was next formally initiated into ascetic life by Totapuri, a great saint who had realized in his life the highest truths of Vedanta, and practised the Vedantic sadhana. Sri Ramakrishna was then initiated into the Sufi doctrine of Islam and followed all the rites preacribed by that religion. He ate and dressed like a Muslim, offered regular prayers to Allah, ceased to visit Hindu temples, and in three days, obtained the vision of God. Later, he practised similar sadhana according to Christian rites, and on the third day obtained the vision of Jesus Christ.

Sri Ramakrishna made his own life a laboratory for the thesis of different systems of religion—a wonderful synthesis of higher forms of spiritual discipline with rituals and ceremonies—of *sakara* (God with form) with *nirakara* (God without form); of Vedanta with devotion; of rationalism with emotion and intuition; of asceticism with social and domestic life. Another great distinguishing characteristic of Sri Ramakrishna's spiritual attainments was the spontaneity and depth of feeling with which he wanted to serve the poor. In 1868, when he travelled to holy cities like Varanasi and Allahabad with Mathur Babu, the master of his temple, the sight of human suffering aroused so much sympathy in his heart that he compelled his rich companion to do his best to alleviate at least a part of such suffering. Sri Ramakrishna's insistence on "sharing the fate" of the poor creatures brought about a change in Mathur Babu as well. When Sri Ramakrishna arrived at Deoghar with his rich companion, (Mathur Babu), he saw its almost naked inhabitants, the Santhals, emaciated and dying of hunger: for a terrible famine was ravaging the land. He told Mathur Babu that he must feed these unfortunates. Mathur Babu objected that he was not rich enough to support the misery of the whole world. Ramakrishna thereupon sat down among the poor creatures and wept, declaring that he would not move from thence, but would share their fate. Babu1 was obliged to submit and to do the will of his poor priest.

During the summer of 1870 Mathur Babu made the mistake of taking Ramaktlshna in the course of another journey to one of his estates at the time of the payment of dues. The harvests had failed for two years running and the tenants were reduced to extreme misery. Ramakrishna told Mathur Babu to remand their dues, to distribute help to them and to give them a sumptuous feast. Mathur Babu protested but Ramakrishna was adamant.

"You are only the steward of the Mother," Ramakrishna said to the rich proprietor. "They are the Mother's tenants. You must spend the Mother's money. When they are suffering, how can you refuse to help them? You must do so."

Swami Shivananda recalls how Sri Ramakrishna set a unique example of the most humble service that he himself rendered to a pariah. Sri Ramakrishna, a Brahmin, went to a pariah's house and asked permission to clean it. The pariah, overcome by the proposal, a criminal one in the eyes of an orthodox Hindu, which might have exposed his visitor and himself to the worst reprisals, refused to allow it. So Ramakrishna went to his house at night when all were asleep and wiped the floor with his long hair. He prayed: "O Mother, make me the servant of the pariah!"

Although Naren's singing of a religious hymn at Surendranath Mitra's house in November 1880 drew Sri Ramakrishna's attention, the latter had the capacity to peep into the "depth of Naren's unsatisfied soul", and he asked Naren to come and see him at Dakshineswar. At their next meeting, Naren's song moved the master deeply, and he started the process of obtaining Naren's participation in his mission, to which Naren initially resisted. In later years, Naren recalled this occasion and described it thus: Sri Ramakrishna said, "Ah! you have come so late. Why have you been so unkind as to make me wait so long? My ears are tired of hearing the futile words of other men. Oh! how I have longed to pour out my spirit into the breast of somebody fitted to receive my inner experiences!..". He continued thus, sobbing the while. Then standing before me with folded hands he said, "Lord, I know that you are the ancient sage Nara, the incarnation of Narayana, reborn on the earth, to take away the misery of humanity". I was amazed. "What have I come to see?" I thought. "He ought to be put in a straitjacket! Why, I am the son of Visvanath Datta. How dare he speak thus to me? But I remained outwardly unmoved and let him talk."

A few minutes later, when the Master and Naren joined the group of friends assembled in the larger room, Naren heard the Master say "God can be realized. One can see Him and speak to Him as I speak to and see you. But who takes the trouble to do so? People will shed tears for a wife, children, or possessions. But who weeps for the love of God? Yet if a man weeps sincerely for Him, He will manifest Himself to him."

Naren gradually felt that Sri Ramakrishna was "worthy of respect," but the former also wanted to be on his guard to escape the latter's eccentric behaviour. The type of conflict between his "intellect" and "heart" that Naren had earlier experienced in his relations with Brajendranath Seal, now seemed to reappear, but in a reverse form, as Romain Rolland describes:

"Naren was struck by the incomprehensible power of Ramakrishna. It attracted him, as a magnet attracts iron, but he himself was made of stern metal. His reason would not submit to domination.

If in his recent relations with the rationalist Brajendra Seal it had been his heart that strove against his intellect, now his intellect mistrusted his heart. He was resolved to maintain his independence, and to accept nothing from the Master except what could be rigorously controlled by his own reason. The uncritical faith of the others roused his contempt".

Although several important developments took place to bring Naren and the Master closer and closer, a special mention needs to be made of what happened after Naren's father suddenly died in early 1884, leaving the family heavily indebted and facing starvation. In spite of the B.A. degree, Naren could not get any job and was hard put to it to maintain his widowed mother and younger brothers. At last, unable to bear the distress of the family, and in sheer desperation, he fell at the feet of Sri Ramakrishna and requested him to approach Mother Kali on his behalf.

Ramakrishna asked Naren to go himself and ask the favour of the deity. Naren went to the temple, but as soon as he stood before Kali, he found in her the Mother Goddess in a living visible form. He forgot the worldly affairs and, prostrating himself before her, prayed that he might be ended with true knowledge and a spirit of devotion and renunciation. When on his return he was questioned by Ramakrishna, he remembered that he had forgotten to pray to the Mother to remove his misery. He was sent back, and again a third time, but with no better result... He was assured by Ramakrishna that his family would not be wanting in bare necessities of life, and so it turned out, as Naren could secure some jobs.

Sri Ramakrishna gradually prepared Naren to be the head of the group of sincere devotees who would carry out the Master's Mission after he himself passed away. He never concealed his feelings about Naren's future destiny. When Naren implored the Master to show him the way to nirvikalpa samadhi— the attainment of final bliss after sundering all earthly ties—he was administered a sharp rebuke. "Fie on you!" exclaimed Sri Ramakrishna, "I never thought you so mean as to be anxious for your own salvation only whereas you have powers to do much good to mankind." At his insistent request the Master one day gave him a glimpse of it and said, "Just as a treasure is locked up in a box, so the realization of the supreme bliss will be locked up and the key shall remain with me. You have work to do."

Sri Ramakrishna also taught Naren that the proper way of doing good to mankind was to view it as worship to God, and that it was sheer arrogance if any feeling of superiority were to be associated with compassion. As the Master put it, "Compassion! Who are you to be compassionate? God alone can have compassion for the mortal. But service to man should be done as worship to God—Jiva is none else than Siva." Naren understood what the master had in mind, and he told his friends, "Today I have heard a new Truth of great significance. In time I shall broadcast this for humanity."

A mysterious incident symbolizing the transmittal of special powers from Sri Ramakrishna to Naren, occured as confirmed by Vivekananda himself. Knowing that his end was imminent, the Master, in order to endow Naren with the spiritual wealth which he himself had acquired after years of superhuman efforts and unprecedented austerities, called him to his side only three or four days before his mahasamadhi. Having seated him in front and looking intently into the eyes of his dear disciple, he fell into a deep trance. Naren felt the powerful impact of a tremendous force passing into his own body and soon lost all body consciousness. When, after a while, Naren came to himself, the Master was found shedding tears. When interrogated, Sri Ramakrishna softly replied, 'Oh Naren, today I have given you my all and have become a fakir (beggar). By the force of the power transmitted by me, great things will be done by you; only after that, will you go to whence you came."

Naren also learnt from the Master the supreme lesson that it is more glorious to help even one man than to be freed from the cycle of birth and death. In the pre-Ramakrishna Hindu tradition as commonly understood personal salvation or Mukti was viewed as the highest attainment, and taking birth was considered a symbol of imperfection. Ram Srikrishna, by his own example, helped revive the social service-oriented Hindu view, which was close to the Bodhtsattva ideal of putting the salvation of all above one's own salvation. In the closing days of his worldly life, Sri Ramakrishna permitted visitors to seek his guidance on spiritual matters, even though doctors wanted him to take complete rest. As Romain Rolland puts it: He never turned to anybody He said, "Let me be condemned to be born over and over again, even in the form of a dog, if so I can be of help to a single soul !"

And again, "I will give up twenty thousand such bodies to help one man. It is glorious to help even one man!"

He even reproached himself for his ecstasies, because they took time that might otherwise have been given to others: "O Mother, stop me from enjoying them! Let me stay in my normal state, so that I can be of more use in the world."

Sri Ramakrishna also explained to Naren and to other disciples, the secret of reconciling worldly life with spiritual development, which, in the Bhagavad Gita, has been identified as the technique of non-attachment or renunciation of the egoistic feeling of doership. One of the parables which Sri Ramakrishna used to clarify his teaching on this subject was the following:

"As a wet-nurse in a rich family brings up the child of her master, loving the baby as if it were her own, but knows well that she has no claim upon it; so think also that you are but trustees and guardians of your children whose real father is the Lord God in Heaven."

Vivekananda revolutionized the traditional image of Sannyasins by making social service an integral part of their fife. Although a formal shape to his new ideas was given by Vivekananda in 1897, all his activities from 1886 onward helped prepare the ground for introducing so radical a change. A firsthand observation of the miseries of the poor in the various parts of the country culminated in what is commonly called 'The Kanyakumari Resolve of' 1892", and about which Vivekananda himself wrote in a letter from America:

"At Cape Comorin, sitting in Mother Kumari's temple, sitting on the last bit of Indian rock, I hit upon a plan. We are so many *sannyasins* wandering about and teaching the people metaphysics—it is all madness. Did not our Gurudeva use to say, 'An empty stomach is no good for religion'? That these poor people are leading a life of brutes is simply due to ignorance. Suppose some disinterested sannyasins, bent on doing good to others, go from village to village, disseminating education and seeking in various ways to better the condition of all down to the Chandala, through oral teaching and by means of maps, cameras, globes and such other accessories – can't that bring forth good in time? We as a nation have lost our individuality and that is the cause of all mischief in India. We have to give back to the nation its lost individuality and raise the masses."

After the death of his guru, Vivekananda became a wandering monk, extensively touring the Indian subcontinent and acquiring first-hand knowledge of conditions in India. He later travelled to the United States and represented India as a delegate in the 1893 Parliament of World Religions. He conducted hundreds of public and private lectures and classes, disseminating tenets of Hindu philosophy in America, England and Europe. He established the Vedanta societies in America and England.

In America Vivekananda became India's spiritual ambassador. His mission there was the interpretation of India's spiritual culture and heritage. He also tried to enrich the religious consciousness of Americans through the teachings of the Vedanta philosophy.

In America he preached a doctrine unity of all religions and tolerance; that there should be recognized of universality and that there is value in diversity, furthermore, that India did not need missionaries to convert its people to Christianity, nor chruches, but material support to stop starvation. Vivekananda is partly to blame for the commonly held belief that the East is spiritual while the West is materialistic. He was convinced of the spiritual superiority of the East, while acknowledging the material, technological and scientific superiority of the West. This dichotomy has tended to reinforce the image of India as the West's other'; the reality being more complex as both cultures contain strong spiritual and material features.

Vivekananda stayed in the West to promote his ideas and founded the Vedanta Society in New York in 1895. Indeed, Vivekananda might be seen as the first effective proponent of Hinduism as a world religion. Upon returning to India in 1895 he founded the Ramakrishna Mission, a monastic order which differs from traditional Hindu orders in promoting education and social reform, and in helping the sick. The mission lays great importance on this aspect of its work which it regards as karma yoga, the yoga of action or good works, and there are colleges, high schools and hospitals run by the Ramakrishna Mission throughout India. The order disseminates Vivekananda's vision of Hindu modernism as Neo-Vedanta: that there is an essential unity of Hinduism underlying the diversity of its many forms. Whereas Christianity accepts only itself as the truth, claimed Vivekananda, Hinduism is pluralistic and accepts all religions as aspects of the one truth. This message had great popularity among India's emergent, English-educated, middle classes, along with Vivekananda's stress on Hinduism as a 'scientific' religion, something of which Indians should be proud rather than apologetic. While this view of Hinduism tends to override the differences within Hindu traditions and has been criticized as leading to a kind of woolly thinking very differs from the intellectual thoroughness of the theological traditions, it never the less provides a strong ideology to link into Indian nationalism on the one hand, and the construction of Hinduism as a world religion on the other. Vivekananda might be regarded as the first to clearly articulate the idea of Hinduism as a world religion, taking its place alongside Christianity, Islam, Judaism and Buddhism.

The Maharaja of Mysore asked Vivekananda to represent Hinduism at the World Parliament of Religions that was planned in Chicago in 1893 for the fourth centenary of Columbus' discovery of America. The Maharaja covered all expenses and provided him with names and addresses of Hindus in Chicago who were prepared to offer him lodging. Vivekananda, arriving a month ahead of time, had lost the slip with the addresses, and quite literally had to spend the first night on the streets. Well-to-do theosophists whom he met by chance gave him accommodation until he established contact with the Hindu community.

After his first speech at the Parliament he was hailed as the most important delegate. He pleaded with Americans not to send Christian missionaries, but teachers and technical experts to India. He told him that it was an insult to a hungry person to teach her metaphysics, and an affront to starving people to offer them religion. They try to save bodies from starvation if they were interested in saving souls. Vivekananda also reinterpreted Vedanta in a novel and exciting fashion. While all religions contain truth, Hinduism, in his opinion, will be the religion of the future, because it comprises all, possesses absolute tolerance, and has already reached its highest degree of perfection. Vivekananda stayed in America for more than three years giving lectures, organizing aid missions for India, and establishing Vedanta societies in order to alleviate the spiritual poverty of the West. His ideal, as he presented it, was a combination of Indian religion and American science and management skills.

After landing in Colombo on 15 January 1897, Vivekananda was triumphantly welcomed as a hero throughout India: he had given

Hindus new pride in their tradition. In order to have a headquarters for his mission he founded the first Advaita Astrama in Almora, in the Himalayana foothills. His 'practical Vedanta' was initially resisted by his fellow monks, who saw it as contrary to the purely spiritual teachings of Sri Ramakrishna. Vivekananda explained to them: 'See God in every man, every woman, every child. You cannot help them; you can only serve the One, who cares for them. Do it as a service to God. You must see God in the poor. The poor and the suffering exist for our salvation so that we can serve God, who appears in the guise of the beggar, the leper and the sinner'.

Visit to the West

Vivekananda's journey to America took him through China and Canada and he arrived at Chicago in July 1893. But to his disappointment he learnt that no one without credentials from a bona fide organisation would be accepted as a delegate. He came in contact with Professor John Henry Wright of Harvard University who invited him to speak at the university. On learning that Vivekananda lacked credential to speak at the Chicago Parliament, Wright is quoted as having said, "To ask for your credentials is like asking the sun to state its right to shine in the heavens." Wright wrote a letter to the Chairman-in-charge of delegates, "Here is a man who is more learned than all of our learned professors put together." On the Professor, Vivekananda himself writes "He urged upon me the necessity of going to the Parliament of Religions, which he thought would give an introduction to the nation."

Parliament of the World's Religions opened on 11 September 1893 at the Art Institute of Chicago as part of the World's Columbian Exposition. On this day Vivekananda gave his first brief address. He represented India and Hinduism. Though initially nervous, he bowed to Saraswati, the Hindu goddess of learning and began his speech with, "Sisters and brothers of America!". To these words he got a standing ovation from a crowd of seven thousand, which lasted for two minutes. When silence was restored he began his address. He greeted the youngest of the nations on behalf of "the most ancient order of monks in the world, the Vedic order of sannyasins, a religion which has taught the world both tolerance and universal acceptance." He thundered:

"Come up, O lions, and shake off the delusion that you are sheep;

you are souls immortal, spirits free, blest and eternal; ye are not matter, ye are not bodies; matter is your servant, not you the servant of matter."

He quoted two illustrative passages from the Bhagavad Gita—"As the different streams having their sources in different places all mingle their water in the sea, so, O Lord, the different paths which men take, through different tendencies, various though they appear, crooked or straight, all lead to Thee!" and "Whosoever comes to Me, through whatsoever form, I reach him; all men are struggling through paths that in the end lead to Me." Despite being a short speech, it voiced the spirit of the Parliament and its sense of universality.

Dr. Barrows, the president of the Parliament said, "India, the Mother of religions was represented by Swami Vivekananda, the Orange-monk who exercised the most wonderful influence over his auditors." He attracted widespread attention in the press, which dubbed him as the "Cyclonic monk from India". The New York paper wrote, "He is an orator by divine right, and his strong, intelligent face in its picturesque setting of yellow and orange was hardly less interesting than those earnest words, and the rich, rhythmical utterance he gave them." The New York Herald wrote, "Vivekananda is undoubtedly the greatest figure in the Parliament of Religions. After hearing him we feel how foolish it is to send missionaries to this learned nation." The American newspapers reported Vivekananda as "the greatest figure in the parliament of religions" and "the most popular and influential man in the parliament". The Boston Evening reported that Vivekananda was "a great favourite at the parliament...if he merely crosses the platform, he is applauded". He spoke several more times at the Parliament on topics related to Hinduism, Buddhism and harmony of religions. The parliament ended on 27 September 1893. All his speeches at the Parliament had the common theme of universality, and emphasised religious tolerance.

"I do not come", he said on one occasion in America, "to convert you to a new belief. I want you to keep your own belief; I want to make the Methodist a better Methodist; the Presbyterian a better Presbyterian; the Unitarian a better Unitarian. I want to teach you to live the truth, to reveal the light within your own soul."

Following the Parliament of Religions, Vivekananda spent nearly three years lecturing in various parts of eastern and central United

States, mostly in Chicago, Detroit, Boston, and New York. By the spring of 1895, his busy and tiring schedule led to poor health. He stopped lecturing tours, and started giving free and private classes on Vedanta and Yoga. Starting in June 1895, he conducted private lectures to a dozen of his disciples at the Thousand Island Park in New York for two months. Vivekananda considered this to be the happiest part of his first visit to America. He later founded the "Vedanta Society of New York".

During his first visit to the West, he travelled to England twice—in 1895 and 1896. His lectures were successful there. There in November 1895, he met Margaret Elizabeth Noble, an Irish lady, who would later become Sister Nivedita. During his second visit to England in May 1896, Vivekananda met Max Müller, a renowned Indologist from Oxford University who wrote Ramakrishna's first biography in the West. From England, he also visited other European countries. In Germany he met Paul Deussen, another famous Indologist. He received two academic offers, the chair of Eastern Philosophy at Harvard University and a similar position at Columbia University. He declined both, saying that as a wandering monk, he could not settle down to work of this kind.

His disciples—Marie Louise, a French woman, became Swami Abhayananda, and Mr. Leon Landsberg, became Swami Kripananda. He initiated several other followers into Brahmacharya. Vivekananda's ideas were admired by scholars such as William James, Josiah Royce, C. C. Everett, Dean of the Harvard School of Divinity, Robert G. Ingersoll, Nikola Tesla, Lord Kelvin, and Professor Hermann Ludwig Ferdinand von Helmholtz. Other personalities who were attracted by his talks were American poets Harriet Monroe and Ella Wheeler Wilcox; Dr. Lewis G. Janes, president of Brooklyn Ethical Association; Sara C. Bull, wife of Ole Bull, the Norwegian violinist; Sarah Bernhardt, the French actress and Madame Emma Calvé, the French opera singer.

From West, he also set his work back in India in motion. Vivekananda wrote several letters to India, giving advice and sending money to his followers and brother monks. His letters from the West in these days laid down the motive of his campaign for social service. He constantly tried to inspire his close disciples in India to do something significant. His letters to them contain some of his strongest words. In one such letter, he wrote to Swami Akhandananda, "Go from door to door amongst the poor and lower classes of the town of Khetri and teach them religion. Also, let them have oral lessons on geography and such other subjects. No good will come of sitting idle and having princely dishes, and saying "Ramakrishna, O Lord!"—unless you can do some good to the poor." Eventually in 1895, money sent by Vivekananda was used to start the periodical *Brahmavadin*, for the purpose of teaching the Vedanta. Later, Vivekananda's translation of first six chapters of *The Imitation of Christ* was published in Brahmavadin (1889). Vivekananda left for India on 16 December 1896 from England with his disciples, Captain and Mrs. Sevier, and J.J. Goodwin. On the way they visited France and Italy, and set sail for India from the Port of Naples on 30 December 1896. He was later followed to India by Sister Nivedita. Sister Nivedita devoted the rest of her life to the education of Indian women and the cause of India's independence.

Back in India (1897–1899)

The ship from Europe arrived in Colombo, Sri Lanka on 15 January 1897. Vivekananda received an ecstatic welcome. In Colombo, he gave what constitutes his first public speech in the East, India, the Holy Land. From there on, his journey to Calcutta was a triumphal progress. He travelled from Colombo to Pamban, Rameshwaram, Ramnad, Madurai, Kumbakonam and Madras delivering lectures. People and Rajas gave him enthusiastic reception. In the procession at Pamban, the Princes of Ramnad personally drew Vivekananda's carriage. On way to Madras, at several places where the train would not normally stop, the people squatted on the rails and allowed the train to pass only after hearing him. From Madras, he continued his journey to Calcutta and then to Almora. While in the West he talked of India's great spiritual heritage; on return to India he repeatedly addressed social issues—uplift of the population, getting rid of the caste system, promotion of science, industrialisation of the country, addressing the widespread poverty, and the end of the colonial rule. These lectures, published as "Lectures from Colombo to Almora", show his nationalistic fervour and spiritual ideology. His speeches had influence on the contemporaneous and subsequent Indian leaders such as Mahatma Gandhi, Bipin Chandra Pal, Balgangadhar Tilak and Netaji Subhas Chandra Bose.

Founding of the Ramakrishna Mission

On 1 May 1897 at Calcutta, Vivekananda founded the Ramakrishna Mission—the organ for social service. The ideals of the Ramakrishna Mission are based on Karma Yoga. Its governing body consists of the trustees of the Ramakrishna Math—the organ to carry out religious works. Both Ramakrishna Math and Ramakrishna Mission have their headquarters at Belur Math. He founded two other monasteries—one at Mayavati on the Himalayas, near Almora, called the Advaita Ashrama and another at Madras. Two journals were started, *Prabuddha Bharata* in English and *Udbhodan* in Bengali.

Vivekananda insisted that the social worker should never believe that she or he was actually improving the world, which is, after all, illusory. Service should be performed without attachment to the final results. In this manner, social service becomes karma yoga, the disciple of action, that ultimately brings spiritual benefits to the server, not to those being served.

Vivekananda had earlier inspired Jamsetji Tata to set up a research and educational institution when they had travelled together from Yokohama to Chicago on Vivekananda's first visit to the West in 1893. Now Vivekananda received a letter from Tata, requesting him to head the Research Institute of Science that Tata had set up. Vivekananda declined the offer saying that it conflicted with his spiritual interests.

Vivekananda visited western Punjab with the mission of establishing harmony between the Arya Samaj which stood for reinterpreted Hinduism and the Sanatanaists who stood for orthodox Hinduism. At Rawalpindi, he suggested methods for rooting out antagonism between Arya Samajists and Muslims. His visit to Lahore is memorable for his speeches and his association with Tirtha Ram Goswami, a professor of Mathematics, who later took monasticism as Swami Rama Tirtha and preached Vedanta in India and America. After brief visits to Delhi and Khetri, he returned to Calcutta in January 1896. He spent the next several months consolidating the work of the Math and training the disciples. He composed the arati song, *Khandana Bhava Bandhana* during the consecration of Ramakrishna's temple at a devotee's house.

Second visit to the West (1899–1902)

Vivekananda once again left for the West in June 1899 despite his declining health. He was accompanied by Sister Nivedita and Swami Turiyananda. He spent a short time in England, and went on to the United States. During this visit, he founded the Vedanta societies at San Francisco and New York. He also founded "Shanti Ashrama" (peace retreat) at California. He attended the Congress of Religions in Paris in 1900. The Paris addresses are memorable for the scholarly penetration evinced by Vivekananda regarding the worship of Linga and authenticity of the Gita. From Paris he went to Brittany, Vienna, Istanbul, Athens and Egypt. For the greater part of this period, he was the guest of the philosopher Jules Bois. He left Paris on 24 October 1900 and arrived at the Belur Math on 9 December 1900.

After spending a few days at Advaita Ashrama, Mayavati, he settled at Belur Math, guiding the work of Ramakrishna Mission and Math and the work in England and America. Thousands of visitors came to him during these years including the Maharaja of Gwalior and the leaders the Indian National Congress including Bal Gangadhar Tilak. In December 1901, he was invited to Japan to participate in the Congress of Religions; however his failing health made it impossible. He undertook pilgrimages to Bodhgaya and Varanasi towards his final days. Declining health and ailments such as asthma, diabetes and chronic insomnia restricted his activities. Three days before his death he pointed out the spot for his cremation—the one at which a temple in his memory stands today. He had remarked to several people that he would not live to be forty.

After his return to the Belur Math, Vivekananda said in the course of a conversation: 'I thought of having one centre at least from which the external worship of Sri Ramakrishna would be excluded. But I found that the Old Man had already established himself even there. Well! Well!' The above incident should not indicate any lack of respect in Vivekananda for Sri Ramakrishna or dualistic worship. During the last few years of his life he showed a passionate love for the Master. Following his return to the Belur Math he arranged, the birthday festival of Sri Ramakrishna and the worship of the Divine Mother, according to traditional rituals.

Vivekananda real nature was that of a lover of God, though he appeared outwardly as a philosopher. But in all his teachings, both in India and abroad, he had emphasized the non-dualistic philosophy. For Ultimate Reality, in the Hindu spiritual tradition, is nondual. Dualism is a stage on the way to non-dualism. Through non-dualism alone, in the opinion of him, can the different dualistic concepts of the Personal God be harmonized. Without the foundation of the non-dualistic Absolute, dualism breeds fanaticism, exclusiveness, and dangerous emotionalism. He saw both in India and abroad a caricature of dualism in the worship conducted in the temples, churches, and other places of worship.

In India he found that non-dualism had degenerated into mere dry intellectual speculation. And so he wanted to restore non-dualism to its pristine purity and glorious majesty. With that end in view he had established the Advaita Ashrama at Mayavati, overlooking the gorgeous eternal snow of the Himalayas, where the mind naturally soars to the contemplation of the Infinite, and there he had banned all vestiges of dualistic worship. In the future, he believed, all religions would receive a new orientation from the non-dualistic doctrine and spread goodwill among men.

On his way to Mayavati Vivekananda had heard the melancholy news of the passing away of the Raja of Khetri, his faithful disciple, who had borne the financial burden of his first trip to America. The Raja had undertaken the repairing of a high tower of the Emperor Akbar's tomb near Agra, and one day, while inspecting the work, had missed his footing, fallen several feet, and died. 'Thus' wrote he to Mary Hale, 'we sometimes come to grief on account of our zeal for antiquity. Take care, Mary, don't be too zealous about your piece of Indian antiquity.' (Referring to himself.) 'So you see', he wrote to Mary again, 'things are gloomy with me just now and my own health is wretched. Yet I am sure to bob up soon and am waiting for the next turn.'

Vivekananda left Mayavati on January 18, and travelled four days on slippery slopes, partly through snow, before reaching the railroad station. He arrived at the Belur Math on January 24. Vivekananda had been in his monastery for seven weeks when pressing invitations for a lecture trip began to pour in from East Bengal. His mother, furthermore, had expressed an earnest desire to visit the holy places situated in that part of India. On January 26 he wrote to Mrs. Ole Bull: 'I am going to take my mother on pilgrimage...This is the one great wish of a Hindu widow. I have brought only misery to my people all my life. I am trying to fulfil this one wish of hers.'

On March 18, in the company of a large party of his sannyasin disciples, he left for Dacca, the chief city of East Bengal, and arrived the next day. He was in poor health, suffering from both asthma and diabetes. During an asthmatic attack, when the pain was acute, he said half dreamily: 'What does it matter! I have given them enough for fifteen hundred years.' But he had hardly any rest. People besieged him day and night for instruction. In Dacca he delivered two public lectures and also visited the house of Nag Mahashay, where he was entertained by the saint's wife.

Next he proceeded to Chandranath, a holy place near Chittagong, and to sacred Kamakhya in Assam. While in Assam he spent several days at Shillong in order to recover his health, and there met Sir Henry Cotton, the chief Government official and a friend of the Indians in their national aspiration. The two exchanged many ideas, and at Sir Henry's request the Government physician looked after his health.

Vivekananda returned to the Belur Math in the second week of May. Concerning the impressions of his trip, he said that a certain part of Assam was endowed with incomparable natural beauty. The people of East Bengal were more sturdy, active, and resolute than those of West Bengal. But in religious views they were rather conservative and even fanatical. He had found that some of the gullible people believed in pseudo-incarnations, several of whom were living at that time in Dacca itself. He had exhorted the people to cultivate manliness and the faculty of reasoning. To a sentimental young man of Dacca he had said: 'My boy, take my advice; develop your muscles and brain by eating good food and by healthy exercise, and then you will be able to think for yourself. Without nourishing food your brain seems to have weakened a little.' On another occasion, in a public meeting, he had declared, referring to youth who had very little physical stamina, "You will be nearer to Heaven through football than through the study of the Gita."

The brother disciples and his own disciples were much concerned about his health, which was going from bad to worse. The damp climate of Bengal did not suit him at all; it aggravated his asthma, and further, he was very, very tired. He was earnestly requested to lead a quiet life, and to satisfy his friends he lived in the monastery for about seven months in retirement. They tried to entertain him with light talk. But he could not be dissuaded from giving instruction to his disciples whenever the occasion arose.

He loved his room on the second storey, in the southeast corner of the monastery building, to which he joyfully returned from his trips to the West or other parts of India. This large room with four windows and three doors served as both study and bedroom. In the corner to the right of the entrance door stood a mirror about five feet high, and near this, a rack with his ochre clothes. In the middle of the room was an iron bedstead with a spring mattress, which had been given to him by one of his Western disciples. But he seldom used it; for he preferred to sleep on a small couch placed by its side. A writing-table with letters, manuscripts, pen, ink, paper, and blotting-pad, a call-bell, some flowers in a metal vase, a photograph of the Master, a deer-skin which he used at the time of meditation, and a small table with a tea-set completed the furnishings.

Here he wrote, gave instruction to his disciples and brother monks, received friends, communed with God in meditation, and sometimes ate his meals. And it was in this room that he ultimately entered into the final ecstasy from which he never returned to ordinary consciousness. The room has been preserved as it was while he was in his physical body, everything in it being kept as on the last day of his life, the calendar on the wall reading July 4, 1902.

On 19 December, 1900, he wrote to an American disciple: 'Verily I am a bird of passage. Gay and busy Paris, grim old Constantinople, sparkling little Athens, and pyramidal Cairo are left behind, and here I am writing in my room on the Ganga, in the Math. It is so quiet and still! The broad river is dancing in the bright sunshine, only now and then an occasional cargo boat breaking the silence with the splashing of the waves. It is the cold season here, but the middle of the day is warm and bright every day. It is like the winter of southern California. Everything is green and gold, and the grass is like velvet, yet the air is cold and crisp and delightful.'

After the his return from East Bengal he lived a relaxed life in the monastery, surrounded by his pet animals: the dog Bagha, the she-goat Hansi, an antelope, a stork, several cows and sheep and ducks and geese, and a kid called Matru who was adorned with a collar of little bells, and with whom he ran and played like a child. The animals adored him, Matru, the little kid, who had been — so he pretended — a relation of his in a previous existence, slept in his room. When it died he grieved like a child and said to a disciple: 'How strange! Whomsoever I love dies early.' Before milking Hansi for his tea, he always asked her permission. Bagha who took part in the Hindu ceremonies, went to bathe in the Ganga with the devotees on sacred occasions, as for instance when the gongs and conchs announced the end of an eclipse. He was, in a sense, the leader of the group of animals at the Math. After his death he was given a burial in the grounds of the monastery.

Referring to his pet animals he wrote to an American disciple on 7, September, 1901: 'The rains have come down in right earnest, and it is a deluge — pouring, pouring, pouring, night and day. The river is rising, flooding the banks; the ponds and tanks have overflowed. I have just now returned from lending a hand in cutting a deep drain to take off the water from the Math grounds. The rainwater stands at places some feet deep. My huge stork is full of glee and so are the ducks and geese. My tame antelope fled from the Math and gave us some days of anxiety in finding him out. One of my ducks unfortunately died yesterday. She had been gasping for breath more than a week. One of my waggish old monks says, "Sir, it is no use living in the *Kaliyuga*, when ducks catch cold from damp and rain, and frogs sneeze!" One of the geese had her plumes falling off. Knowing no other method of treatment, I left her some minutes in a tub of water mixed with mild carbolic, so that it might either kill or heal — and she is all right now.'

Thus Vivekananda tried to lead a carefree life at the monastery, sometimes going about the grounds clad in his loin-cloth, sometimes supervising the cooking arrangements and himself preparing some delicacies for the inmates, and sometimes joining his disciples and brother monks in the singing of devotional music. At other times he imparted spiritual instruction to the visitors, or engaged in deep thought whenever his inner spirit was stirred up, occupied himself with serious study in his room, or explained to the members of the Math the intricate passages of the scriptures and unfolded to them his scheme of future work. Though his body was wearing away day by day, his mind was luminous. At times his eyes assumed a far-away look, showing how tired he was of the world. One day he said, 'For one thing we may be grateful: this life is not eternal.'

The illness did not show any sign of abatement, but that did not dampen his spirit to work. When urged to rest, he said to a disciple:

'My son, there is no rest for me. That which Sri Ramakrishna called "Kali" took possession of my body and soul. That makes me work and work and never lets me keep still or look to my personal comfort." Then he told the disciple how the Master, before his passing away, had transmitted his spiritual power to him.

During the later part of 1901 he observed all the religious festivals at the Math. The Divine Mother was worshipped in strict orthodox fashion during the Durgapuja, Lakshmipuja and Kalipuja. On the occasion of the Durgapuja the poor were given a sumptuous feast. Thus he demonstrated the efficacy of religious rituals in the development of the spiritual life. In February 1902 the birth anniversary of Sri Ramakrishna was celebrated at the Belur Math, and over thirty thousand devotees gathered for the occasion. But he was feverish. He was confined to his room by the swelling of his legs. From the windows he watched the dancing and the music of the devotees.

To the disciple who was attending him he said: 'He who has realized the Atman becomes a storehouse of great power. From him as the centre a spiritual force emanates, working within a certain radius; people who come within this circle become inspired with his ideas and are overwhelmed by them. Thus without much religious striving they derive benefit from the spiritual experience of an illumined person. This is called grace.' 'Blessed are those,' he continued, 'who have seen Sri Ramakrishna. All of you, too, will get his vision. When you have come here, you are very near to him. Nobody has been able to understand him who came on earth as Sri Ramakrishna. Even his own nearest devotees have no real clue to it. Only some have a little inkling of it. All will understand in time."

It is said that the spot immediately beneath a lamp is dark. And so it was that the orthodox people of the neighbouring villages hardly understood the ideas and ideals of the Belur Math. The monks there did not in all respects lead the life of orthodox sannyasins. Devotees from abroad frequented the monastery. In matters of food and dress the inmates were liberal. Thus they became the butt of criticism. The villagers invented scandals about them and the passengers on the boats passing along the Ganga would point out the monastery with an accusing finger. When Vivekananda heard all this he said: 'That is good. It is a law of nature. That is the way with all founders of religion. Without persecution superior ideas cannot penetrate into the heart of society.' But the criticism of the neighbours in time gave place to pride in having in their midst so many saintly souls.

Many distinguished Indians used to visit him at this time. With some of them he discussed the idea of founding a Vedic Institution for the promotion of the ancient Aryan culture and the knowledge of Sanskrit. This was one of the his favourite thoughts, on which he dwelt even on the last day of his life on earth.

Towards the end of 1901 two learned Buddhists from Japan came to the Belur Math to request him to attend a Congress of Religions that was being contemplated in Japan at that time. One of them was the famous artist and art critic Okakura, and the other Oda, the head priest of a Buddhist temple. Vivekananda became particularly fond of Okakura and said, 'We are two brothers who meet again, having come from the ends of the earth.' Though pressed by the visitors, he could not accept the invitation to go to Japan, partly because of his failing health and partly because he was sceptical that the Japanese would appreciate the monastic ideal of the non-dualistic Vedanta. In a letter to a Western lady written in June 1902, he made the following interesting observation about the connexion between the monastic ideal and fidelity in married life:

"In my opinion, a race must first cultivate a great respect for motherhood, through the sanctification and inviolability of marriage, before it can attain to the ideal of perfect chastity. The Roman Catholics and the Hindus, holding marriage sacred and inviolate, have produced great chaste men and women of immense power. To the Arab, marriage is a contract or a forceful possession, to be dissolved at will, and we do not find there the development of the idea of the virgin of the brahmacharin. Modern Buddhism — having fallen among races who had not yet come up to the evolution of marriage — has made a travesty of monasticism. So until there is developed in Japan a great and sacred ideal about marriage (apart from mutual attraction and love), I do not see how there can be great monks and nuns. As you have come to see that the glory of life is chastity, so my eyes also have been opened to the necessity of this great sanctification for the vast majority, in order that a few lifelong chaste powers may be produced." He used to say that absolute loyalty and devotion between husbands and wives for three successive generations find their expression in the birth of an ideal monk.

Okakura earnestly requested him to accompany him on a visit to Bodh Gaya, where Buddha had attained illumination. Taking advantage of several weeks' respite from his ailment, he accepted the invitation. He also desired to see Varanasi. The trip lasted through January and February 1902, and was a fitting end to all his wanderings. He arrived at Bodh Gaya on the morning of his last birthday and was received with genuine courtesy and hospitality by the orthodox Hindu monk in charge of the temple. This and the similar respect and affection shown by the priests in Varanasi proved the extent of his influence over men's hearts. It may be remembered that Bodh Gaya had been the first of the holy places he had visited during Sri Ramakrishna's lifetime. And some years later, when he was still an unknown monk, he had said farewell to Varanasi with the words: 'Till that day when I fall on society like a thunderbolt I shall visit this place no more.'

In Varanasi he was offered a sum of money by a Maharaja to establish a monastery there. He accepted the offer and, on his return to Calcutta, sent Shivananda to organize the work. Even before Vivekananda's visit to Varanasi, several young men, under his inspiration, had started a small organization for the purpose of providing destitute pilgrims with food, shelter, and medical aid. Delighted with their unselfish spirit, he said to them: "You have the true spirit, my boys, and you will always have my love and blessings! Go on bravely; never mind your poverty. Money will come. A great thing will grow out of it, surpassing your fondest hopes." He wrote the appeal which was published with the first report of the 'Ramakrishna Home of Service,' as the institution came to be called. In later years it became the premier institution of its kind started by the Ramakrishna Mission.

Vivekananda returned from Varanasi. But hardly had he arrived at Belur when his illness showed signs of aggravation in the damp air of Bengal. During the last year and a half of his life he was, off and on, under the strict supervision of his physicians. Diabetes took the form of dropsy. His feet swelled and certain parts of his body became hypersensitive. He could hardly close his eyes in sleep. A native physician made him follow a very strict regime: he had to avoid water and salt. For twenty-one days he did not allow a drop of water to pass through his throat. To a disciple he said: "The body is only a tool of the mind. What the mind dictates the body will have to obey. Now I do not even think of water. I do not miss it at all.... I see I can do anything."

Though his body was subjected to a devitalizing illness, his mind retained its usual vigour. During this period he was seen reading the newly published *Encyclopaedia Britannica*. One of his householder disciples remarked that it was difficult to master these twenty-five volumes in one life. But he had already finished ten volumes and was busy reading the eleventh. He told the disciple to ask him any question from the ten volumes he had read, and to the latter's utter amazement he not only displayed his knowledge of many technical subjects but even quoted the language of the book here and there. He explained to the disciple that there was nothing miraculous about it. A man who observed strict chastity in thought and action, he declared, could develop the retentive power of the mind and reproduce exactly what he had heard or read but once, even years before.

The regeneration of India was the ever recurring theme of his thought. Two of the projects dear to his heart were the establishment of a Vedic College and a Convent for women. The latter was to be started on the bank of the Ganga under the direction of the Holy Mother and was to be completely separated from the Belur Math. The teachers trained in the Convent were to take charge of the education of Indian women along national lines.

But Vivekananda's heart always went out in sympathy for the poor and neglected masses. During the later part of 1901 a number of Santhal labourers were engaged in leveling the grounds in the Math. They were poor and outside the pale of society. He felt an especial joy in talking to them, and listened to the accounts of their misery with great compassion. One day he arranged a feast for them and served them with delicacies that they had never before tasted. Then, when the meal was finished, he said to them: 'You are Narayanas. Today I have entertained the Lord Himself by feeding you."

He said to a disciple: 'I actually saw God in them. How guileless they are!' Afterwards he said, addressing the inmates of the Belur Math:

'See how simple-hearted these poor, illiterate people are! Will you be able to relieve their miseries to some extent at least? Otherwise of what use is our wearing the ochre robe of the sannyasin? To be able to sacrifice everything for the good of others is real monasticism.

Sometimes I think within myself: "What is the good of building monasteries and so forth? Why not sell them and distribute the money among the poor, indigent Narayanas? What homes should we care for, we who have made the tree our shelter? Alas! How can we have the heart to put a morsel into our mouths, when our countrymen have not enough wherewith to feed or clothe themselves?...Mother, shall there be no redress for them? One of the purposes of my going out to preach religion to the West, as you know, was to see if I could find any means of providing for the people of my country. Seeing their poverty and distress, I think sometimes: "Let us throw away all the paraphernalia of worship — blowing the conch and ringing the bell and waving the lights before the image....Let us throw away all pride of learning and study of the scriptures and all spiritual disciplines for the attainment of personal liberation. Let us go from village to village, devoting ourselves to the service of the poor. Let us, through the force of our character and spirituality and our austere living, convince the rich about their duties to the masses, and get money and the means wherewith to serve the poor and the distressed....Alas! Nobody in our country thinks for the low, the poor, the miserable! Those who are the backbone of the nation, whose labour produces food, those whose one day's absence from work raises a cry of general distress in the city — where is the man in our country who sympathizes with them, who shares in their joys and sorrows? Look how, for want of sympathy on the part of the Hindus, thousands of pariahs are becoming Christians in the Madras Presidency! Don't think that it is merely the pinch of hunger that drives them to embrace Christianity. It is simply because they do not get your sympathy. You are continually telling them: "Don't touch me." "Don't touch this or that!" Is here any fellow-feeling or sense of dharma left in the country? There is only "Don't-touchism" now! Kick out all such degrading usages! How I wish to abolish the barriers of "Don't-touchism" and go out and bring together one and all, crying: "Come, all ye that are poor and destitute, fallen and downtrodden! We are one in the name of Ramakrishna!" Unless they are elevated, the Great Mother India will never awake! What are we good for if we cannot provide facilities for their food and clothing? Alas, they are ignorant of the ways of the world and hence fail to eke out a living though labouring hard day and night for it. Gather all your forces together to remove the veil from their eyes. What I see clear as daylight is that the same Brahman, the same Sakti, is in them as in me! Only there is a difference in the degree of manifestation — that is all. Have you ever seen a country in the whole history of the world rise unless there was a uniform circulation of the national blood all over the body? Know for certain that not much can be done with that body one limb of which is paralysed, even though the other limbs are healthy."

One of the disciples pointed out the difficulty of establishing unity and harmony among the diverse sects in India. Vivekananda replied with irritation:

"Don't come here any more if you think any task too difficult. Through the grace of the Lord, everything becomes easy of achievement. Your duty is to serve the poor and the distressed without distinction of caste and creed. What business have you to consider the fruits of your action? Your duty is to go on working, and everything will set itself right in time, and work by itself. My method of work is to construct, and not to destroy that which is already existing....You are all intelligent boys and profess to be my disciples — tell me what you have done. Couldn't you give away one life for the sake of others? Let the reading of Vedanta and the practice of meditation and the like be left for the next life! Let this body go in the service of others — and then I shall know you have not come to me in vain!"

A little later he said:

'After so much tapasya, austerity, I have known that the highest truth is this: "He is present in all beings. These are all the manifested forms of Him. There is no other God to seek for! He alone is worshipping God, who serves all beings."'

In this exhortation is found Vivekananda's message in all its vividness. These words are addressed to India and the Western world alike. The West, too, has its pariahs. He who exploits another man, near or distant, offends God and will pay for it sooner or later. All men are sons of the same God, all bear within them the same God. He who wishes to serve must serve man — and in the first instance, man in the humblest, poorest, most degraded form. Only by breaking down the barriers between man and man can one usher in the kingdom of heaven on earth.

There were moments when Vivekananda felt gloomy. His body was wasting away, and only a few young men came forward to help him in his work. He wanted more of them who, fired with indomitable faith in God and in themselves, would renounce everything for the welfare of others. He used to say that with a dozen such people he could divert into a new channel the whole thought-current of the country. Disregarding his physical suffering, he constantly inspired his disciples to cultivate this new faith.

Thus we see him, one day, seated on a canvas cot under the mango tree in the courtyard of the monastery. Sannyasins and brahmacharins were busy doing their daily duties. One was sweeping the courtyard with a big broom. Swami Premananda, after his bath, was climbing the steps to the shrine. Suddenly Vivekananda's eyes became radiant. Shaking with emotion, he said to a disciple:

'Where will you go to seek Brahman? He is immanent in all beings. Here, here is the visible Brahman! Shame on those who, neglecting the visible Brahman, set their minds on other things! Here is the visible Brahman before you as tangible as a fruit in one's hand! Can't you see? Here — here — is Brahman!'

These words struck those around him with a kind of electric shock. For a quarter of an hour they remained glued to the spot, as if petrified. The broom in the hand of the sweeper stopped. Premananda fell into a trance. Everyone experienced an indescribable peace. At last Vivekananda said to Premananda, 'Now go to worship.'

The brother disciples tried to restrain the his activities, especially instruction to visitors and seekers. But he was unyielding. 'Look here!' he said to them one day. 'What good is this body? Let it go in helping others. Did not the Master preach until the very end? And shall I not do the same? I do not care a straw if the body goes. You cannot imagine how happy I am when I find earnest seekers after truth to talk to. In the work of waking up Atman in my fellow men I shall gladly die again and again!'

Till the very end he remained the great leader of the Math, guiding with a firm hand the details of its daily life, in spite of his own suffering. He insisted upon thorough cleanliness and examined the beds to see that they were aired and properly taken care of. He drew up a weekly time-table and saw that it was scrupulously observed. The classes on the Vedas and the Puranas were held daily, he himself conducting them when his health permitted. He discouraged too much ritualism in the chapel. He warned the monks against exaggerated sentimentalism and narrow sectarianism.

But the leader kept a stern watch on the practice of daily meditation on the part of the inmates of the monastery. The bell sounded at fixed hours for meals, study, discussion, and meditation. About three months before his death he made it a rule that at four o'clock in the morning a hand-bell should be rung from room to room to awaken the monks. Within half an hour all should be gathered in the chapel to meditate. But he was always before them. He got up at three and went to the chapel, where he sat facing the north, meditating motionless for more than two hours. No one was allowed to leave his seat before he set the example. As he got up, he chanted softly, 'Siva! Siva!' Bowing to the image of Sri Ramakrishna, he would go downstairs and pace the courtyard, singing a song about the Divine Mother or Siva. Naturally his presence in the chapel created an intense spiritual atmosphere. Swami Brahmananda said: 'Ah! One at once becomes absorbed if one sits for meditation in company with Naren! I do not feel this when I sit alone.'

Once, after an absence of several days on account of illness, he entered the chapel and found only two monks there. He became annoyed; in order to discipline the absentees he forbade them to eat their meals at the monastery. They had to go out and beg their food. He did not spare anyone, even a beloved brother disciple for whom he cherished the highest respect and who happened to be absent from the chapel that morning. Another day, he found a brother disciple, Swami Sivananda, in bed at the hour of meditation. He said to the latter 'Brother! I know you do not need meditation. You have already realized the highest goal through the grace of Sri Ramakrishna. But you should daily meditate with the youngsters in order to set an example to them.'

More and more Vivekananda was seen to free himself from all responsibilities, leaving the work to other hands. 'How often,' he said, 'does a man ruin his disciples by remaining always with them! When men are once trained, it is essential that their leader leave them, for without his absence they cannot develop themselves.' 'Plants,' he had said some time before, 'always remain small under a big tree.' Yet the near and dear ones thought that he would certainly live three or four years more. He refused to express any opinion on the question of the day. 'I can no more enter into outside affairs,' he said; 'I am already on the way.' On another occasion he said: 'You may be right; but I cannot enter any more into these matters. I am going down into death.'

But it was difficult for him to give up what had been dearer to him than his life: the work. On the last Sunday before the end he said to one of his disciples: 'You know the work is always my weak point. When I think that might come to an end, I am all undone.' He could easily withdraw from weakness and attachment, but the work still retained its power to move him.

Sri Ramakrishna and the Divine Mother preoccupied his mind. He acted as if he were the child of the Mother or the boy playing at the feet of Sri Ramakrishna at Dakshineswar. He said, 'A great tapasya and meditation has come upon me, and I am making ready for death.' His disciples and spiritual brothers were worried to see his contemplative mood. They remembered the words of Sri Ramakrishna that Naren, after his mission was completed, would merge for ever into samadhi, and that he would refuse to live in his physical body if he realized who he was. A brother monk asked him one day, quite casually, 'Do you know yet who you are?' The unexpected reply, 'Yes, I now know!' awed into silence everyone present. No further question was asked. All remembered the story of the great nirvikalpa samadhi of his youth, and how, when it was over, Sri Ramakrishna had said: 'Now the Mother has shown you everything. But this realization, like the jewel locked in a box, will be hidden away from you and kept in my custody. I will keep the key with me. Only after you have fulfilled your mission on this earth will the box be unlocked, and you will know everything as you have known now.' They also remembered that in the cave of Amarnath, in the summer of 1898, he had received the grace of Siva — not to die till he himself should will to do so. He was looking death in the face unafraid as it drew near.

Everything about him in these days was deliberate and significant, yet none could apprehend its true import. People were deceived by his outer cheerfulness. From the beginning of June he appeared to be regaining his health. One day, about a week before his death, he told a disciple bring him the Bengali almanac. He was seen several times on subsequent days studying the book intently, as if he was undecided about something he wanted to know. After the passing away, the brother monks and disciples realized that he had been debating about the day when he should throw away the mortal body. Ramakrishna, too, had consulted the almanac before his death. Three days before the mahasamadhi, Vivekananda pointed out to Swami Premananda a particular spot on the monastery grounds where he wished his body to be cremated.

On Wednesday Vivekananda fasted, following the orthodox rule: it was the eleventh day of the moon. Sister Nivedita came to the monastery to ask him some questions about her school; but he was not interested and referred her to some other Swamis. He insisted, however, on serving Nivedita the morning meal. To quote the Sister's words:

Each dish, as it was offered — boiled seeds of the jack-fruit, boiled potatoes, plain rice, and ice-cold milk — formed the subject of playful chat; and finally, to end the meal, he himself poured the water over her hands, and dried them with a towel.

'It is I who should do these things for you, Swamiji! Not you for me!' was the protest naturally offered. But his answer was startling in its solemnity — 'Jesus washed the feet of his disciples!' Something checked the answer, 'But that was the last time!' as it rose to the lips, and the words remained unuttered. This was well. For here also, the time had come.

There was nothing sad or grave about Vivekananda during these days. Efforts were made not to tire him. Conversations were kept as light as possible, touching only upon the pet animals that surrounded him, his garden experiments, books, and absent friends. But all the while one was conscious of a luminous presence of which his bodily form seemed only a shadow or symbol. The members of the monastery had never felt so strongly as now, before him, that they stood in the presence of an infinite light; yet none was prepared to see the end so soon, least of all on that Friday, July the Fourth, on which he appeared so much stronger and healthier than he had been for years.

On the supreme day, Friday, he rose very early. Going to the chapel, alone, he shut the windows and bolted the doors, contrary to his habit, and meditated for three hours. Descending the stairs of the shrine, he sang a beautiful song about Kali.

Then he said, almost in a whisper: 'If there were another Vivekananda, then he would have understood what this Vivekananda has done! And yet — how many Vivekanandas shall be born in time!'

He expressed the desire to worship Mother Kali at the Math the following day, and asked two of his disciples to procure all the necessary articles for the ceremony. Next he asked the disciple Suddhananda to read a passage from the Yajurveda with the commentary of a well-known expositor. The Swami said that he did not agree with the commentator and exhorted the disciple to give a new interpretation of the Vedic texts.

He partook of the noon meal with great relish, in company with the members of the Math, though usually, at that time, he ate alone in his room because of his illness. Immediately afterwards, full of life and humour, he gave lessons to the brahmacharins for three hours on Sanskrit grammar. In the afternoon he took a walk for about two miles with Swami Premananda and discussed his plan to start a Vedic College in the monastery.

'What will be the good of studying the Vedas?' Premananda asked.

'It will kill superstition,' Swami Vivekananda said.

On his return the Swami inquired very tenderly concerning every member of the monastery. Then he conversed for a long time with his companions on the rise and fall of nations. 'India is immortal,' he said, 'if she persists in her search for God. But if she goes in for politics and social conflict, she will die.'

At seven o'clock in the evening the bell rang for worship in the Math. The Swami went to his room and told the disciple who attended him that none was to come to him until called for. He spent an hour in meditation and telling his beads, then called the disciple and asked him to open all the windows and fan his head. He lay down quietly on his bed and the attendant thought that he was either sleeping or meditating. At the end of an hour his hands trembled a little and he breathed once very deeply. There was a silence for a minute or two, and again he breathed in the same manner. His eyes became fixed in the centre of his eyebrows, his face assumed a divine expression, and eternal silence fell. 'There was,' said a brother disciple of him, 'a little blood in his nostrils, about his mouth, and in his eyes.' According to the Yoga scriptures, the life-breath of an illumined yogi passes out through the opening on the top of the head, causing the blood to flow in the nostrils and the mouth. The great ecstasy took place at ten minutes past nine. Vivekananda passed away at the age of thirty-nine years, five months, and twenty-four days, thus fulfilling his own prophecy: 'I shall not live to be forty years old.' The brother disciples thought that he might have fallen into *samadhi*, and chanted the Master's name to bring back his consciousness. But he remained on his back motionless. Physicians were sent for and the body was thoroughly examined. In the doctor's opinion life was only suspended; artificial respiration was tried. At midnight, however, Vivekananda was pronounced dead, the cause, according to medical science, having been apoplexy or sudden failure of the heart. But the monks were convinced that their leader had voluntarily cast off his body in samadhi, as predicted by Sri Ramakrishna.

Vivekananda died at ten minutes past nine p.m. on 4 July 1902 while he was meditating.

In the morning people poured in from all quarters. Nivedita sat by the body and fanned it till it was brought down at 2 p.m. to the porch leading to the courtyard. It was covered with ochre robes and decorated with flowers. Incense was burnt and a religious service was performed with lights, conch-shells, and bells. The brother monks and disciples took their final leave and the procession started, moving slowly through the courtyard and across the lawn, till it reached the vilva tree near the spot where Vivekananda himself had desired his body to be cremated.

The funeral pyre was built and the body was consigned to the flames kindled with sandalwood. Across the Ganga, on the other bank, Ramakrishna had been cremated sixteen years before.

Nivedita began to weep like a child, rolling on the ground. Suddenly the wind blew into her lap a piece of the ochre robe from the pyre, and she received it as a blessing. It was dusk when the flames subsided. The sacred relics were gathered and the pyre was washed with the water of the Ganga. The place is now marked by a temple, the table of the altar standing on the very spot where his body rested in the flames.

Gloom and desolation fell upon the monastery. The monks prayed in the depths of their hearts: 'O Lord! Thy will be done!' But deep beneath their grief all felt that this was not the end. The words of the leader, uttered long before his death, rang in their ears:

'It may be that I shall find it good to get outside my body — to cast it off like a wornout garment. But I shall not cease to work. I shall inspire men everywhere, until the world shall know that it is one with God.'

And: 'May I be born again and again, and suffer thousands of miseries, so that I may worship the only God that exists, the only God I believe in, the sum total of all souls.'

For centuries to come people everywhere will be inspired by Swami Vivekananda's message: O man! first realize that you are one with Brahman — *aham Brahmasmi* — and then realize that the whole universe is verily the same Brahman — *sarvam khalvidam Brahma*.

On the day of his death he woke up very early in the morning, went to chapel and meditated for three hours, sang a song on Kali and then he whispered, "If there were another Vivekananda, then he would have understood what this Vivekananda has done!" He taught Shukla-Yajur-Veda to some pupils in the morning at Belur Math. He had a walk with Swami Premananda, a brother-disciple, and gave him instructions on the future of the Ramakrishna Math.

Vivekananda left a body of philosophical works. Only a handful of those were published during his lifetime. A notable theme in his works is different ways of worshiping suggested for varied types of individuals. Vivekananda observed that human could be classified into four categories—those who were in constant activity, or the worker; those who were driven by their inner urge, or the emotional; those who tended to analyse the working of their minds, or the mystical; and those who weighed everything with reason, or the rational. So he discussed four ways of worships—*Karma yoga* for the worker, *Bhakti yoga* for the emotional, *Raja yoga* for the mystical, and Jnana yoga for the rational. Majority of his published works were compiled from lectures given around the world. Vivekananda was a singer and a poet, and composed many songs and poems including his favourite Kali the Mother. He blended humour in his teachings; his language was lucid. His Bengali writings stand testimony to the fact that he believed that words—spoken or written—should be for making things easier to understand rather than show off the speaker or writer's knowledge.

Vivekananda believed a country's future depends on its people; his teachings focussed on this area. He wanted "to set in motion a machinery which will bring noblest ideas to the doorstep of even the poorest and the meanest." He believed that the essence of Hinduism was best expressed in the Vedanta philosophy, based on the interpretation of Adi Shankara. He summarised the Vedanta's teachings as follows:

Each soul is potentially divine, The goal is to manifest this Divinity within by controlling nature, external and internal, Do this either by work, or worship, or mental discipline, or philosophy—by one, or more, or all of these—and be free, This is the whole of religion. Doctrines, or dogmas, or rituals, or books, or temples, or forms, are but secondary.

2

Vivekananda's Chicago Address

It is pertirent to know that to commemorate the 400th anniversary of Columbus's expedition to America, the World's Columbian Exposition was held in Chicago in 1893. The primary purpose of the exposition was to demonstrate man's material progress in the nineteenth century. However, to give a comprehensive scope to the Fair, 20 congresses were formed, focusing on such issues as women's progress, the public press, medicine and surgery, commerce and finance, music, government and law reform, economic science, and religion. Of these congresses, the Parliament of Religions was by far the most widely promoted and highly acclaimed.

Vivekananda first heard about this Parliament of Religions in 1892, while he was travelling in Junagadh, Western India. Then, in Porbandar, Dewan Shankar Pandurang, who was impressed with his learning and personality, said to Vivekananda: "Swamiji, I am afraid you cannot do much in this country. Few will appreciate you here. You ought to go to the West where people will understand you and your worth. Surely you can throw a great light upon Western culture by preaching the *Sanatana Dharma*." This line of thought began to work imperceptibly on his mind.

In the early part of 1893, after visiting western and southern India, he arrived in Madras. G. S. Iyer, editor of The Hindu in Madras, wrote several articles on the Parliament of Religions and news of it spread all over India. Vivekananda revolutionary ideas, magnetic personality, and erudition very quickly attracted a group of people in Madras. They insisted that he go to Chicago and represent Hinduism at the Parliament of Religions. When an orthodox pandit of Pondicherry heard about this, he blurted out: '*Kadapi na! Kadapi na*! (Never! Never!). According to the Pandit, the Hindus were, not to go to the West, because it was considered the lard of mlechchhas (outcastes).

Sister Devamata (Miss Laura Glenn, an American devotee) recorded the following reminiscences of a professor in a leading college of Madras (most probably Alasinga Perumal):

"On the second day, I remember, he (Swamiji) talked of the East and West and he said: 'You (the Hindus) need more ruggedness and the West needs more gcntleness.' I asked, 'Why do you not go to the parliament of Religions in Chicago to represent Hinduism?' 'I have no objection to going,' he replied, 'if someone will send me.' One of us offered him some money (two rupees). It was the first time he had taken money and he laughed and said, 'I will give it to the first beggar I meet,' and actually he gave it to some poor beggars. When the first subscription for his journey came (two hundred and fifty rupees) he took it, went at once to the shops, and bought a cart and a number of toys for some children whom he loved very much."

On August 20, 1893, Vivekananda wrote from America to Alasinga, 'I have a call from Above.' This statement of Vivekananda is very significant, because it proves that he did not go to America to fulfill any personal ambition or out of pressure from his followers. In India he had desperately prayed for divine guidance—for a direct command. It had come to him in this way: As he lay half-asleep one night, the command did come, in a symbolic dream. He saw the figure of his Master, Sri Ramakrishna, walking from the seashore into the waters of the ocean, and beckoning him to follow. Peace and joy filled his whole being as he became fully awake; the order 'go' had been impressed on his mind, as it were. The vision convinced him. He knew it to be a divine command. His doubts and misgivings were dispelled.

Although Vivekananda was now certain of his duty, he still felt it necessary to have Holy Mother's permission and blessings. He wrote to Swami Saradananda: 'I have had a vision in which the Master is telling me to go to the West. My mind quite disturbed. Please tell Holy Mother everything and let us know her opinion.' Swami Saradananda went to Holy Mother and read his letter to her. Holy Mother did not give her opinion immediately, but asked Saradananda to wait. After couple of days, she told Saradananda, 'Please write to Narenth at he should go to the West.' Before giving her permission, Holy Mother half had a dream. She saw the Master walking over the ocean waves and asking Narendra to follow him. Vivekananda overjoyed when he received Holy Mother's approval and blessings.

After announcing his intention of going to the West, he told to his Madrasi followers:

"The time has come for the propagation of our faith. The time has come for the Hinduism of the rishis to become dynamic. Shall we stand by whilst alien hands attempt to destroy the fortress of our ancient faith? ... Shall we remain passive, or shall we become aggressive, as in days to fold, preaching unto the nations the glory of the *Dharma*? Shall we remain encased within the narrow confines of our social groups and our provincial consciousness, or shall we branch out into the thought worlds of other peoples, seeking to influence these for the benefit of India? In order to rise again, India must be strong and united, and focus all its living forces."

This inspiring speech created tremendous enthusiasm among his friends in Madras. They responded: 'It must be done, Swamiji, and you are the one man to do it. You will work wonders.' These young people then began to raise money, going from door to door. They wrote to the Raja of Ramnad, who had once offered 10,000 rupees for his passage money. Later, however, he refused to contribute, because he was afraid that he, a highly educated Bengali, might indulge in politics and cause him trouble. When the Raja later discovered that some high government officials were contributing money for Swamiji's passage, he also contributed 500 rupees.

The Madrasi devotees raised 4,000 rupees. They reserved a second class berth on the Pacific and Orient steamer Peninsular, and gave 179 pounds (Rupees 2,685) to him. Later, when Raja Ajit Singh of Khetri, one of his disciples, took charge of his arrangements, he asked his private secretary, Munshi Jagmohanlal, to change the ticket from second class to first class. Jagmohan then went to Bombay with Swamiji and bought silk robes, turbans, and other necessary items for him.

In spite of the American missionaries' best efforts for half a century to paint this sub-continent as dark as Africa, infiltration of Hindu thought into the States predates Chicago. The seeds of German and English romanticism fell on the Unitarian soil of New England.

'The metaphysics of Kant, the mysticism of Jacobi, the idealistic egoism of Fichte, the transcendentalism of Schliermacher—the new gospel of the renascent German spirit—these were the living water to the thirsty minds of New England. The Unitarians had pronounced human nature to be excellent, the Transcendenialists pronounced it to be divine. The secret voice of God was discovered in man's instinct. If man is indeed a child of God, let him live unto God. The dogmatic pessimism of New England Puritanism was discarded for a new faith and a new dream. Stripped of its idealistic philosophy, the master idea of Emerson is the divine self-sufficiency of the individual.

Emerson made references to Hindu religious texts in his journal beginning in 1830, and expressed belief in the Self, akin to the concept of Atman-Brahman, in a Harvard lecture (1838). While he seldom went deeper than extracts from Hindu texts, Thoreau, a neighbour of Emerson between 1837 and 1862, introduced the Bhagavad Gita to him. Thoreau had been initiated into Oriental wisdom by Bournouf's French translation of the Gita. He was also well acquainted with the researches of the Asiatic Society of Calcutta. This ardent Asiaticism found a motto – Ex Oriente Lux (Light from the East) and infected Emerson. Emerson's pome, 'Brahma', written in 1856, reached the high watermark of Vedantism n America. As for society and politics, Emerson bordered on utopian anarchism. The crass materialism of the Democrats and the whigs, the capitalists, as well as the planters, drove him to exasperation and tempered his optimism, though he scarcely admitted it.

Walt Whitman's *Leaves of Grass* published in 1855 and Edgar Allan Poe's 'Eureka', in Rolland's view, also expressed thoughts echoing those of the Upanishads. Whitman stressed the greatness of religion along with the greatness of love and democracy. The America was betraying Whitman's idealism. Identity with all forms of life at every instant, immediateness of realised Unity, and the certainty of Unity are some of the basic features of Whitman's religion. Emerson's faith in individual self-realization could easily be twisted, during a period of rising entrepreneurship, into a defence of a ruthless rat race. Is man to be fulfilled only in order to liberate himself from government, church, society, or is he to be fulfilled in order to help liberate others – women, slaves, immigrants and Red Indians? Inventions were to him man's power to impose will on history.

The Parliament of Religions

The Parliament opened on 11 September, 1893, befittingly, with a prayer. The solemnity and grandeur of the occasion must have overawed Vivekananda. No wonder he felt nervous, and when asked to speak in the forenoon, he declined several times. 'I was so nervous, and could not venture to speak in the morning,' he himself said, he spoke in the afternoon. He greeted the audience as 'Sisters arid brothers of America.' An unusual address, but the audience responded with cheering. People rose to their feet, shouted with joy, and threw hats and handkerchiefs into the air. They cheered and cheered. The President had difficulty in controlling them. When quiet prevailed, Vivekananda made a breathtaking speech. He did not praise Hinduism. He only praised the spirit of tolerance. Even 'tolerance' was not enough for him; he preferred 'acceptance'. Each religion must be accepted and given a place of honour. He quoted a Sanskrit verse which says: "As the different streams having their sources in different places all mingle their water in the sea, so, O Lord, the different paths which men take through different tendencies, various, though they appear, crooked or straight, all lead to Thee." He insisted that no religion has a monopoly on holiness. All religions have had their share of great saints, and this is proof of their equal validity.

This set the tone for the proceedings of the Parliament of Religions. If any delegate secretly hoped to prove the supremacy of his religion, he refrained from saying anything to that effect. The atmosphere completely changed. Peace and harmony were on everybody's lips. This was very aptly expressed by him in his concluding remarks when ha said, 'The Christian is not to become a Hindu or a Buddhist, nor a Hindu or a Buddhist to become a Christian.' 'Upon the banner of every religion will soon be written, in spite of resistance: "Help and not Fight," "Assimilation and not Destruction."

The impact of Vivekananda's speeches was electrifying. From obscurity he leaped into worldwide fame. In his official report, Dr. Barrows, President of the Parliament of Religions, characterized address as 'noble and sublime'. The Boston Evening Transcript said, 'Vivekananda's address before the Parliament was broad as the heaven above us, embracing the best in all religions, as the ultimate universal religion.' The press hailed him as a Prophet and a Seer. The New York Herald said: 'He is undoubtedly the greatest figure in the Parliament of Religions. After hearing him we feel how foolish it is to send missionaries to this learned nation'.

Merwin-Marie Snell, President of the Scientific Section of the Parliament wrote: 'Swami Vivekananda..., in fact, was beyond question the most popular and influential man in the Parliament....The people thronged about him wherever he went and hung with eagerness on his every word....The most rigid of orthodox Christians say of him, "He is indeed prince among men". Vivekananda was popular both inside the Parliament and outside. Many thought it a privilege to be able to touch him, shake hands with him, or merely speak lo him. It was not only his oratory that impressed the people; his life and character impressed them more. Some regarded him as another Christ or Buddha.

All this was pleasing to Vivekananda, but he had not gone to the West with personal -ambitions. His concern was for mankind as a whole, and for the Indian poor specially. Sometimes rich people invited him to stay with them, but he never enjoyed the comforts they provided. The miseries of the people back in India haunted him. He had at ore time seriously considered raising funds in America for his people. He, however, never tried it. He sensed that this would not work. He did not even ask his disciples for money for himself. A monk, according to him, should never have anything to do with money.

Swami Vivekananda earned the title '*The Cyclonic Hindu*', because he traveled through America like a cyclone; lecturing. His lecture engagements carried him far and wide. Sometimes he gave three or four lectures a day. He lectured in churches, public halls, universities, in private homes, and once at least in an open field. It was killing, but he never balked. He was an inspired soul and he felt he had no right to withhold the message he carried. 'I have a truth to teach, I, the child of God'.

But what was that Truth ? It was the Truth common to all religions—the Truth that 'each soul is potentially divine. The goal is to manifest this divinity within by controlling nature, external and internal.'

'Do this either by work, or worship, or psychic control, or philosophy—by one, or more, or all of these—and be free.

'This is the whole of religion. Doctrines, or dogmas, or rituals, or books, or temples, or forms, are but secondary details.'

The universal element in every religion is how can man be perfect? Every religion is universal, if the focus is on this universal element. He may have talked about history, philosophy, religion, literature, and science, but the gist of whatever he taught was Love.

This is not to say that he lived in an ivory tower. Man was his supreme concern, specially the oppressed, the poor, the backward. In his letter of 9 July 1897, to Mary Hale, he wrote, 'May I be born again and again, and suffer thousands of miseries so that I may worship the only God that exists, the only God I believe in, the sum .total of all souls; and above all, my God the wicked, my God the miserable, my God the poor of all races, of all species, is the special object of my worship.' He declared that 'Truth is my God, the universe my country.'

A century has passed since Swami Vivekananda delivered his historic address at the 'Parliament of Religions held in Chicago,' and though we remember the occasion with pride and honour for the uniqueness of "the event that a member of the subject race, could speak with his head high and a fearless heart those flaming words at such a congregation in a foreign land, yet in all these long years we have hardly cared to focus our attention on the import or significance of that unique address. It appears that whatever the great Swami preached later on in the brief span of his life of thirty-nine years, is contained in a seed in that address which flowed from his lips inspiringly at that hour before a gathering in which almost the entire world was represented through the spokesmen of its different religions.

The keynote of his historic address was sounded at the outset by the very way he addressed the august gathering as 'Sisters and Brothers of America." He was going to speak on the unity of all existence, and as it happened to-be a Parliament of Religions, he had to confine himself primarily to the unity of all religions. By this unique way of addressing the audience, he bound himself in an indissoluble tie of unity with all who had gathered there on the occasion, and thereby established a rapport with them immediately. It was a heart speaking to other hearts, and that is why his words had an electrifying effect and practically -mesmerized everyone.

Vivekananda delivered six addresses on the occasion, beginning from the 11th September, 1893, and ending on the 27th. The briefest were the first and the last, while the longest, the third one, was delivered on the 19th when he presented a paper on Hinduism, which he was supposed to represent at the Parliament. There, again, while quoting a famous utterance of the seers of India, he explained, as it were, why everyone is a sister and brother to him and in an ecstasy he. exclaimed: — 'Children of immortal bliss — what a sweet; what a hopeful name! Allow me to call you, brethren, by that swept name — heirs of immortal bliss.. ..Ye are the Children of God, the sharers of immortal bliss, holy and perfect beings; This unity lies in our divinity, and his primary and single mission in life was to awaken this divinity in man. So he immediately gave a soul-stirring call to all who had assembled there: 'Come up, O lions, and shake off the delusion that you are sheep; you are souls immortal, spirits free, blest and eternal....'

Thus, in this call Vivekananda indicated the two main principles of the Vedanta, viz. the immortal and eternal nature of the spirit and also the delusion which covers up this true nature. In other words, *Brahman*, or *Atman*, and *maya*, which were to become the main subjects of his exposition in all his subsequent lectures, became focussed in this luminous call. Strangely enough, he never mentioned the term Vedanta in any of his six addresses, except casually in his third lecture on Hinduism, while affirming the all-inclusive nature of the Hindu religion. He said that : the high spiritual flights of the Vedanta philosophy, of which the latest discoveries of science seem like echoes, to the low ideas of idolatry with its multifarious mythology, the agnosticism of the Buddhists, and the athcisin of the Jains, each and all have a place in the Hindu's religion.

It is clear from this statement of the Vivekananda that he placed the Vedanta philosophy at the top without ignoring what lies below, viz. the low ideas of idolatry with its multifarious mythology,' which are as much a part of the Vedas, of which he speaks again and again as the fountainhead of the Hindu religions. He affirmed: 'The Hindus have received their religion through revelation, the Vedas,' and there he goes on to enlighten his audience about the true nature of the Vedas: 'But by the Vedas no books are meant. They mean the accumulated treasury of spiritual laws discovered by different persons in different times.

This 'accumulated treasury of spiritual laws,' viz. the Vedas, therefore, contained in a broad and all-embracing sweep even "the agnosticism of the Buddhists and the atheism of the, Jains,' and possibly to prove Vivekananda chose to speak separately on Buddhism on the 26th September, before delivering his final address on the 27th: This is also an amazing event, how this representative of Hinduism could dare, to speak on Buddhism too, though it had its own spokesman at the Parliament. His claim to speak on Buddhism must have been challenged, as is clear from the opening sentence of his address on the 26th, 'I am not a Buddhist, as you have heard,' and again, some must have apprehended that he was insisting to speak on Buddhism just to criticize it, to which also he refers at the outset: 'You have just now heard that I am going to criticise Buddhism... Yet in spite of all this opposition and apprehension this self-appointed spokesman of Buddhism proved to the entire audience that the country which he was representing at the Parliament of Religion, viz. India, had not given birth to two separate religions called Hinduism and Buddhism, but it was a land of one religion only, the eternal religion, *Sanatana Dharma*, of absolute unity, which was in fact the religion of which other religions were only different expressions and manifestations.

Vivekananda had made himself one with the entire audience by the way he addressed them, so he again established his oneness with the other religion that had its birth in his homeland by boldly declaring: 'I am not a Buddhist, as you have heard, and yet I am.' He claimed to be a Buddhist though being a Hindu because he felt that "...Sakya Muni came not to 'destroy, but he was the fulfilment, the logical conclusion, the logical development of the religion of the Hindus.' He was even bold enough to affirm that in the case of Buddha, it was his own followers who did not realise the import of his teachings. The fault lay, according to him, not with the Buddha but with the Buddhists, who misinterpreted the teachings of the Master and thereby broke themselves away from the main stream of Hinduism which finally led to its "natural death in. India'.

Vivekananda unerringly pointed out the cause of this natural death of Buddhism, which was brought about by the very 'disciples of the Great Master.' It was two-fold: on the philosophic side the disciples of the Great Master dashed themselves against the eternal rocks of the Vedas and could not crush them, and on the other side they took away from the nation that eternal God' to which every one, man" or woman, clings so fondly.

In other words, the very source of all philosophies in India, viz. the Vedas, were denounced by the disciples of the Buddha in their zeal to uphold the words of their Master as superior to them all, and on the other hand, the existence of God was denied by them, which alone sustains the faith of the multitude in India. By these two acts, the Buddhists practically signed the death-warrant of Buddhism in India.

Being himself the very embodiment of the soul of India, Vivekananda knew that the source and foundation of all religions in India, as declared by Manu long ago, are the Vedas, and therefore no religion can be acceptable here wihich runs counter to the Vedas. There is nothing dogmatic in this affirmation of the supremacy of the Vedas, as is generally supposed, but it is, on the contrary, a denial or prohibition of all dogmatism that is sought to be conveyed through it. No exclusiveness, no dogmatic adherence to a particular personal view, is permitted, and however great may be a person or his realization, or it cannot stand apart from the accumulated treasury of spiritual laws discovered by different persons in different times, which the Vedas really are. It must conform to the Vedas or be confirmed by them. When it is thus included or incorporated in the main body of knowledge, the Vedas only then become acceptable in India. The Buddhists insisted on maintaining a separate identity of their own, adhering only to the words of their Master to the exclusion of all else. Here the person was counted supreme, whereas in the Vedas, significantly impersonal, is the principle. The Vedas, therefore, affirm the unity of all religious or spiritual experiences and do not accept or entertain any experience which is not in unison with this eternal storehouse of knowledge or experience.

While tracing the downfall of Buddhism in India, he beautifully pointed out the two aspects of Hinduism thus: 'The religion of the Hindus is divided into two parts : the ceremonial and the spiritual. The spiritual portion is specially studied by the monks. Here, again, he is referring to the two aspects of the Vedas, viz. the karmakanda and the jnanakanda. Through the former a person tries to fulfil all his desires by invoking divine powers with the help of ceremonies, while through the latter, one tries to check or restrain all desires by knowing their futility in the light of spiritual experience. The latter is pursued mainly by the monks, and the Buddha happened to be its most ardent protagonist, being himself a monk. Vivekananda acknowledged his most significant and unique contribution in this field: He was the first being in the world who brought missionarisng into practice — nay, he was the first to conceive the idea of proselytising. The sangha, or cohesive body of *bhiksus* or mendicants, was thus formed for the first time, and its only mission was to spread the message of renunciation and utter extinction or nirvana of the individual self or soul with all its craving.

The Buddhists, unfortunately, completely ignored the first part, the ceremonial aspect (the *karmakanda*) of the Vedas and even denounced it as useless, and in the process, denied the existence of God. In thus emphasizing only the spiritual aspect (the *jnanakanda*) and carrying it to the extreme of a zero, they lost touch with, the concrete world of the common man, to whom this pursuit of the abstract meant nothing but self- extinction. Vivekananda in his wonderful analysis of Buddhism, pointed out the indispensable necessity of a faith in God for the heart of man. He insisted that whatever may be the position of philosophy, whatever may be the position of metaphysics, so long as there is such a thing as death in the world, so long as there is such a thing as weakness in the human heart, so long as there is a cry going out of the heart of man in his very weakness, there hall be a faith in God.

Even Marx too has been forced to admit this. The pursuit of philosophy and metaphysics may suit a few heroic souls who are capable of climbing the dizzy heights without anything to hold on to, but for the weak human masses the only anchorage in the storm-tossed sea of life is a God. Buddhism took away this anchorage and could provide people with nothing in its place, which made Buddhism absolutely abstract barren and lifeless, leading to its natural death. Only much later, the image of the Buddha himself came to be worshipped as God to fill this vacuum and meet the demand of the human heart, while the Buddhists themselves were forced to leave the narrow or low and small path of Himayana they were pursuing so long and take the high or great road of Mahayana, in which the worship of the Buddha as well as other deities came to be introduced.

Thus, according to Vivekananda, Buddhism fell because of its exclusive pursuit of only one aspect of Hinduism, viz. the spiritual, to the complete neglect and denunciation of the ceremonial. Throughout his Chicago addresses, Vivekananda had only one purpose in view; the establishment of unity. He was always fighting against separation, and he had the boldness to declare that 'this separation between the Buddhists and the Brahmins is the cause of the downfall of India.' He had realized that "Hinduism cannot live without Buddhism, nor Buddhism without Hinduism. The one was the head and the other was the heart, of the same one universal religion, and so he pleaded, while concluding his address 'Let us then join the wonderful intellect .of the Brahmins with the heart, the noble soul, the wonderful humanising power of the Great Master."

Before putting up his own theory on the matter, Vivekananda warned that if anyone here hopes that this unity will come by the triumph of any one of the religions and the destruction of the others, then, it is an impossible hope." By this warning, he affirmed once again that unity can never be achieved' by exclusion or suppression of other viewpoints but only through inclusion and assimilation of all of them. The unique contribution of the Swami lies here, in the formulation of the principle, of unity, which deserves a very careful and in-depth study.

He said that '...each must assimilate the spirit of the others and yet preserve his individuality and grow according to his own law of growth.' He was thus hinting about an organic, ever-developing, growing unity and not a mechanical, static unity. He illustrated this unity beautifully through a very common example taken from nature:

"The seed is put in the ground, and earth and air and water are placed around it. Docs the seed become the earth, or the air, or the water? No. It becomes a plant, it develops after the law of its own growth, assimilates the air, the earth, and the water, converts them into plant substance, and grows into a plant. Similar is the case with religion."

In his addresses at the Parliament of Religions, Vivekananda preached in the name of Vedanta an integrated Vedanta and not the isolated Vedanta that Rammohan had previously carried to the West, which denounced the ceremonies and confined itself only to the spiritual. Vivekananda's Vedanta was all-inclusive and not exclusive at all. He noted that 'from the lowest fetishism to the highest absolutism every step is looked upon as '...so many attempts of the human soul to grasp and realise the Infinite, each determined by the conditions of its birth and association,' and therefore, 'each of these marks a stage of progress... Through a beautiful imagery, he visualizes this growing sense of unity thus: "...Every soul is a young eagle soaring higher and higher, gathering more and more strength, till it reaches the Glorious Sun."

Vivekananda offering an integrated view of unity proclaimed: "To the Hindu, man is not traveling from error to truth, but from truth to truth, from lower to higher truth. "

Truth, therefore, cannot be divided into degrees as such. This is also the standpoint of Sankara, who is an uncompromising Advaitist, who owns the truth only of the Absolute, or Brahman, and completely disowns the truth of the relative, i.e. the existent world, by calling it mithya, maya or unreal. Vivekananda never mentioned Vedanta by name in any of his Chicago addresses except once . while placing it at the very top of the Hindu's religion, but the unity" of which he was speaking over and over again in all his addresses and which seems to have been the main theme that he wanted to emphasize. It was totally based on the Advaita Vedanta of 'Sankara, and in putting up this theory of degrees of truth, he was not contradicting Sankara.

Vivekanand on Maya

The potion of maya is a point around which the philosophical thought in India has ever revolved. At some stage or other in his life, an Indian makes it a point to brush aside a frustrating experience a hopelessly incurable situation, even the day-to-day fact of existence, as perishable maya. With the passage of time and with the ever stable impact of the Upanisadic the word has acquired so popular and persuasive a usage that most often in the Indians' life and literature both poverty and richness, sickness and health, failure and success, danger and safety, death and life, are banished indiscriminately as merely diverse facets of maya.

Strictly philosophically, the word maya describes the spatio-temporal universe, which in relation to the self-luminous transcendence of Brahman or Being, is contingent and as empty as non-existence. The Vedas and the Upanisads show an utter lack of, control on the usage of this word, so much so that, as Ranade has studiously pointed out, in some contexts in the Vedic-Upanisadic literature it signifies untruth (*anrita*), in others uncertainty (*adhruva*), and in still others powers (*sakti*).' It is therefore reasonable to argue that at no period before Gaudapada's Vedanta was the theory of maya set so explicitly as to vindicate the thesis that from the point of view of the transcendental domain the practical universe, is a mirage.

For Sankara, the world is a shadow of the ontological reality; and whatever be its final destination, its emergence is a phenomenon tied to the naive part of one's existence. Sankara adhere to the Upaniadic suggestion of the maya notion in its true spirit, and unlike its fluctuating sense in the thinking of their predecessors, confer upon it a largely disciplined and unambiguous application.

The problem which the Upanisads posed Sankara happened to see with unusual philosophic profundity. It is to explain how the world of physical phenomena is a product of man's ignorance (*avidya*) and what exact motivation man can have for abandoning this world and for identifying himself with thereality beyond. By any evaluation, Sankara exhibits tremendous acumen while pointing out that from the sphere of the highest and the most immaculate consciousness a false, but spatiotemporally perceptible, worldliness has to follow inevitably. The intensity with which he sees this question, and the ingenuity with which he leaves a totally abstract solution to it speak for his intellectual flight combined with a sense of mission.

Sankara was a mystic, a determined monist and an absolutist, but not a dogmatist. His brilliance as the builder of a metaphysics out of irregular fragments of his predecessors thoughts has remained the unique treasure in Oriental thought. He condemns the supremacy of reason, expresses a theological, undertone in his argument, and yet exercises logic with the poignancy of a dialectician. Although he philosophizes with a feeling of having gripped the most fundamental problem human mind can ever think of he hardly succumbs to a sense of pride or complacence. The Commentary on the Brahma-Sutra, is an elaborate explication of the central thesis of the Upanisads. However, it can hardly be doubted that through Sankara comes perhaps the most comprehensive metaphysical thought in India; and so far as its influence on later philosophies is concerned, it cannot be equalled by any other that appeared on the Indian scene.

According to Sankara, Brahman is the unqualified (nirguna) and unconditioned reality. In its essence it is knowable as something beyond the logical categories, or beyond the categories of empirical experience, such as-space, time, causality, change, substance and relation. When in complete fusion with itself, the individual ego (atman, Brahman) would acquire the experience of absolute freedom and absolute fulfilment. But because of the influence of maya or the cosmic nescience, Brahman is manifest as God (Isvara), the human souls (*jivas*) and the phenomenal world (jagat), and leads to the advent of all sorts of tribulations. To belong to the world, therefore, is to remain bound by appearances and shadows. Sankara describes these as constituting a jagatprapanca or uvavaharikasatta (the worldly affairs). He reiterates the value of abandoning them when we are intent on realizing transcendental consciousness (atman or Brahman).

Although Brahman is originally trans-empirical and pure, it is conditioned by maya in some mysterious way and made to figure, in relation to the universe, as Isvara. It is to Isvara that the process of the universe must be attributed. He is in complete control of the fates of individual selves (jivas), which are what they are because of their body, sense organs, mind, intellect, and so on. Concealed within a jiva is the atman—that self-shining homogeneous spirit whose apprehension implies no limitations whatsoever. The question why and how Brahman or atman becomes Isvara or Jiva was can be embarrassing to Sankara, and for that matter, to any Vedantin. Yet he approaches the whole issue in such a manner that neither Brahman nor atman ultimately seems to retain its purity against the onslaught of maya. Maya in this sense has been aptly understood as sakti or power.

By themselves Brahman atman are beyond any conditioning forces, beyond names and forms, beyond empirical commitments, beyond concrete representations. But once under the sway of sakti, atman generates out of itself the entire panorama of world events and. literally subjects the pure consciousness to contingency, untruth, illusion and error.

Strictly speaking, the term "maya" does not describe anything real or existent. It is a hypothesis employed by Indian thinkers to account for the transition of .the absolute into the empirical. Although this hypothesis does violate Ockham's Razor by creating an additional requirement for its own explanation, it has come to be valued for its profound authority on Indians attitude towards the world. All men—victims as they are to the eternal vortex ofbirths and deaths and rebirths—are advised to imbibe a spirit of indifference and noninvolvement towards all that they experience during their contact' with the world. For all things and occurrences in the world are a false growth.

Thus for all practical purposes maya is this world and every past or possible world. It is a domain of antithetical situations, subject object distinctions, paradoxes and antinomies. Indeed, such a domain might not have sprung from the principle of absolute delight, absolute perfection, absolute truth, absolute transcendence and absolute freedom. The fact that it has come about all the same must lead us to believe that Brahman or atman must have veiled itself by means of the world. Why has it veiled itself? Because, the Vedantins state, it has just happened to influence itself by the; power of nonexistence, unreality, abhasa.

There can be two equally reasonable versions of the maya hypothesis. According to one which is strong and is reflected in the Madhyamika school of Buddhismin general and in Nagarjuna's thoughts in particular, the world results from ignorant veiling human consciousness. On account of ignorance eternal nothingness is perceived as the spatiotemporal universe. Therefore, taken in this sense, maya is generated by the naivete of the subject, bestows positivity on what is fundamentally empty and void, and produces a formidable illusion of existence. The Madhyamika Buddhism declares that Reality is sunya or cipher and that the phenomenal universe is a cruel deception.

Under the weak version, the reality of the external world is entirely dependent on man's consciousness, i.e. it has no subsistent being. The world is as it is perceived to be only from the mundane perspective of ours; it would not be so from a transcendental perspective. While we have every reason to believe that the strong version of maya would reckon the Buddhists' view regarding the world's reducibility to Nothingness, the weak version would apply to the restrained Vedanta view that the world exists but appears different from what it really is.

The mixed dimensions the maya hypothesis might take in practice are not controllable, although as a metaphysical conception maya can be an effective foundation for humanism. It is not likely to produce any unwanted consequence if it is prescribed as a principle for fashioning one's broad-minded, generous and tolerant view towards mankind and the world. A critical observer of the history of Indian consciousness would easily find out that the maya principle 'has frequently demonstrated remarkable power of suggesting to an entire community the virtue of sympathy and compassion towards all. Since life is basically an illusory spectacle where the victor and the vanquished, the gifted and the miserable, the high and the low are all children of the same eternal sport (*lila, krida*) of Brahman, it could be argued that the sole objective one may live to realize is the emancipation of all.

However, not seldom has the maya hypothesis been literally adhered to, with the result that even obnoxious things have been explained away as shadowy and therefore not deserving any concern from man. Coupled with the deterministic theory of karma, it has sometimes left Indian masses inactive, fatalistic, chronically oblivious of the solid circumstances of file, and to unpreparedly aspire after the otherworldly bliss at the cruel cost of indispensable material necessities. And much more strangely than its original expounders might have visualized, it has taught some to justify their behavior, however antisocial or selfish, under the pretext of world's nonbeing.

Nowhere else in the world has the impact of a metaphysical theory on the attitude of the common people been so great and so varied. It has made the mendicants and the derelicts to go about singing the virtues of poverty and self-denial, the diseased and the deformed to accept suffering without a whimper, the wealthy to give away fabulous donations, squadrons of unpaid social workers to serve and die for the people. And in a rather sinister way it has made exploiters and wrong-doers to disown responsibility for their acts, the power-thirsty to vie for superiority, the regressive to adhere to communalism and casteism, the opportunists to look at good and evil with unhealthy equanimity.

The greater of capacity of the maya-vada to prevent man from an indulgence in the worldly temptations and to trim them to suit a catholic outlook, the greater chance it will have not to be forgotten as an undesirable myth.

The maya hypothesis must have originally struck the Indian mind as a tool for counteracting the tedious complexities of the day-to-day living. Psychologically considered, it has the power to heal Indians of frustrations, failures, fears ennui, shocks, the lack of adjustment, defeats, and so on. Particularly in its strong sense, therefore, it can be and has proved to be a tranquillizing agent to people in all situations, and perennially has made them accept both life and death with a certain amount of neutrality and unconcernedness.

Even in India of our own times, instances of family priests, aging folks, village chiefs, popular Puranas (ancient mythological lores), temple singers, cinemas, theatre, literature, oft-repeated religious quotations, or mass preachers keeping the maya message ever alive in the ethos of the people are not rare. It appears that the doctrine of karma and the doctrine of maya are the main elements of a massive, through unorganized, philosophical education that have exercised tremendous teaching force on Indian consciousness at all times.

Surely the Upanisadic thinkers were too directly concerned with the physical environment to hold that it is all a mirage. They therefore did not explicitly stretch the maya concept to the point of annulling the factual experiences in toto. But on the other hand, they indicated the relative status of the universe against the absolute, pure and all-inclusive unity of Brahman. Thus Sankara describe the phenomenal world as *adhyasa* (illusion), *anirvacaniya* (indescribable), *avyakta* (potential), *brahma* (neurosis), *ajnana* (ignorance), *vivarta* (transformation), *nama-rupa* (name-form) —words more or less synonymous with maya—they reassert the Upanisadic thesis that the world is an appearance hut not a total unreality. By doing this, as a matter of fact, they water down the strong version of the maya hypothesis, i.e. the *Sunya-vada*, and concede some degree of existence to the world.

Had Sankara cancelled the perceptible presence of the universe altogether, he would not have aspired to construct a comprehensive theory of Brahman, in which everything including the illusoriness of the world is sought to be included as elements within a whole. Unfortunately, he has been misunderstood by many, and pushed into the rank of nihilists.

There is probably a reason why Sankara was misunderstood, and why his conception of the universe was interpreted negatively. It is comfortable for a community, brought up in a milieu pervaded by the theory of karma, to be taught that the phenomenal world is there, not put of any transcendental necessity, but only appears as an outcome of man's evil deeds of the previous lives. The world is an illusion, as if suspended to the original karma-free atma. The status of the world is therefore conditional, inasmuch as the worldliness functions merely in the life of unfreed and sub-transcendental souls. Thus although Sankara had no conscious intention to bind the law of karma and the notion of maya together, and consequently twist the epistemological character of the latter by the use of the ethical considerations involved in the former, his followers have found the illusion idea a consoling corollary from the karma doctrine. Moreover, the voidist view, spread far and wide by the Buddhists, was, psychologically speaking, more straightforward and ascetic, and as such, could not have failed to lead people's understanding of Sankara's maya-vada in the direction of extreme nihilism.

Sankara frequently condemns the emergence of the world by equating its falsity with that of optical illusions, such as mirage, silver in a shining shell, snake in a rope see in semidarkness, the double moon perceived by the pressed pupil of the eye. But all these metaphors must be recognized as implying that even illusions are objects of experience, possessing the power of generating mental states in us. Sankara's must not be taken too literally. They serve to elucidate the incomprehensible and immanent nature of the universe against the pure and transcendent nature of Brahman. Sankara puts forward the notable distinction between the practical and the philosophic standpoints, he clearly suggests that the experience of worldliness is conjoined with our natural existence, with our individuality. We are inseparable from this experience as long as we are bound by the results of karmas and the laws of the cosmos. It is to commonsense and to discursive intellect that the finite reality reveals itself. On the contrary, for the philosophical standpoint all the categories of empirical knowledge are a manifestation of ignorance, error and absurdity. Further, for this standpoint the entire domain of spatiotemporal and causal relations is a fanciful fabrication.

For Sankara and for all orthodox tendencies in Indian thought as for the Upanisads, the inauthenticity of our commonsense view of the universe can be established when by means of a concentrated and arduous endeavor, we heighten our trans-empirical approach and reach the supreme and transcendental Brahman. What hinders our direct access to the higher knowledge is our habituation to the lower knowledge in fact, inherently perfect individuals or atmans as we are, there is no reason why we should be reduced to a state of dislocation from our essential being and be made to live in the form of *jivas.*

Even when it is admitted that the Aarma-infected men must undergo, by the very logic of the law of karma, the experience of ignorance and thence the experience of the whole array of phenomena, it is not simple to understand to what category avidya belongs and how it operates towards contaminating the purity and transcendence of the atmans. A series of post-Sankara commentators and Vedantins seem to have reflected on this problem, and their arguments, although always hovering around Sankara's principal thesis, have presented several perspectives for its solution. A treatment of all these cannot be attempted in the present book. What would be pertinent, however, is some amount of reflection on some of the most ingenious of these perspectives.

Surely the Vedantins must have been bothered much by the question whether ignorance is the product of Brahman or whether it is an inherenj quality of the individual souls. It is obvious that since Brahman has nowhere been regarded as "defilable," it can hardly be the seat of ignorance. Again, if it is held that ignorance is inborn m individual soul, they would not be accepted as the expression of and potentially as pure as Brahman. Where then does ignorance originate from? A number of Vedantins are found to have faced this question squarely and evolved solutions for it. And whatever the type of the solution offered, a Vedantin is fully conscious of the fact that his approach to the question of the source of avidya or maya ought to adhere to the norms of intellectual consistency.

According to Suresvara! (A.D. 800), one of the most talented of Sankara's disciples, avidya should be called maya or a false experience because it is neither a property (*svabhava*) of Brahman nor is distinct from it, neither real nor unreal, but is indefinable ; and indescribable. He says that ignorance belongs to the jivas or souls, which are modes of the psychic and spatiotemporal living. It is on account of ignorance or ajnana that the pure selves fall into the ordeal of births and deaths and generate the awareness of the material world with feelings, desires, hopes, and so on. Although Suresvara sees no solution to the problem of what is prior to the soul under the influence of ajnana, he does argue that the soul and (he ajnana exist eternally, the former causing the latter and the latter conditioning the former again. Moreover, the very separation of jivas from Brahman has been brought about by the ignorance of jivas themselves.

But how do ignorant jivas emerge from Brahman? The answer is that *jivas* are internally self-contradictory entities, and perpetually under the grip of imagination. Out of this imagination they constitute the world—the maya. As long as maya dominates human souls there is no freedom to them; but as soon as *vidya* or knowledge dawns on them they become freed and enlightened.

In the Naiskarmya-siddhi, Suresvara defines avidya as the non-perception of the ultimate oneness of the Self, and freedom or enlightenment as the ultimate realization of this oneness. It is because ignorance has rested on Brahman that the latter has transformed itself into the subject-object relation and has generated the entire domain of world distinctions. One must say that the pure Self is ignorant in regard to itself and eventually produces the illusion of individual persons and empirical phenomena.

However, with the rise of real knowledge in the self, the self's consciousness of the objective universe with all its accompanying paraphernalia vanishes. Actually,' even when the self is under the duress of ignorance, its purity is only temporarily eclipsed. The essence of self is not basically disturbed by the agency' of *avidya*. For all Vedantins, the entire realm of empirical experience is a superimposition on pure consciousness. To reason that had there been no ignorance in us, there would have been no consciousness of the world is the same as to assert that had there been Brahman without any inconsistency within it, there would have been no maya at all. Accordingly the emancipation of the *jivas* is ultimately an emancipation of Brahman from its own 'artificial and absurd manifestations. Thus, the total world-being is the product of nescience or false illusion masking the self.

Padmapada (A.D. 820), the author of the famous *Pancapadika* and one of the direct pupils of Sapkara, remarks that avidya is an obstruction to the pure and self-contained reality of Brahman. As a result of various agencies such as karma, the impressions of past experiences (*purva-prjna-Samskara*) arid ignorance (*avidya*), pure consciousness appears as an individual personality and figures in different situations as a doer and a sufferer. Padmapada does not explicitly say whether jivas alone are the seats of ignorance. He holds that it is on account of ignorance exercising its control on the self-revealing nature of Brahman that individual consciousnesses emerge.

Avidya, being positive and somewhat of material origin, re-mains the cause of the world-appearance, which is itself material. The original self-luminous fit man or Brahman by coming under the activity of avidya becomes a perceiver and an enjoyer; of world events. And as the existential states of a person change, he as a phenomenal being is mare and more immersed in empirical consciousness, more and more aware of subject-object hiatus in experience. Therefore, once they come under the shadow of *maya*, the whole range of possibilities happens to characterize *jivas*. The only way of release from this situation is through the knowledge of the exact nature of Being.

Muni tells us that the ultimate cause of everything is Brahman, and that it is Brahman which through the mechanism of ignorance generates illusory consequences. He like Sankara, who was his master's master, argues that God (*Imam*), the souls (*jivas*) and the world (*jagat*) are the three-fold activity of Brahman under the shadow of ajnana. What then is the status of Brahman? Is Brahman also as illusory as maya, which is "held" by Brahman? *Sarvajnatma* suggests that we ought to draw a distinction between two facets of Brahman, namely, Brahman as the primordial ground (*adhisthana*) of everything, and Brahman as the support of ignorance. The latter facet of Brahman is but false. Therefore, the question of the integration of the avidya-supporting Brahman with Brahman in-itself, or with Brahman as the ontological principle does not arise.

Sarvajnatma thinks that ajnana or avidya has no real existence. Although it does misguide the soul and does create in it an awareness of the world, like butter in presence of heat it melts away the moment true knowledge of Brahman emerges in the soul. *Sarvajnatma* believes that Brahman's transcendence and purity are not altered or contaminated by ajnana. The products of ajnana are felt by us in all spheres of our contact with the world; but they cease to appear no sooner than we penetrate through and grasp the inner core of things, i.e. Brahman.

Such perspectives about the genesis and the abode of maya are numerous in the history of Indian thought. There have been Vedantins who reverentially followed their teachers and repeated almost verbatim what the previous thinkers had said. A combined feeling of piety, loyalty and imitativeness towards the spiritual superiors has been the unique feature of the attitude of Indian philosophers. The original truisms taught by the Upanisadic sages, therefore, that Brahman in all its ontological purity is ever the destination of human endeavor, and that the phenomenal world as an offshoot of nescience i an unwanted obstacle, have always been adhered to by the Vedantins of all times. The maya hypothesis, specifically in its weak version, has remained an inseparable part of the philosophical consciousness of the Indian people—the very essence of Indian life and thought.

As it was pointed out earlier, the concept of mayo, represents an exclusive metaphysical height attained by the Indian mind. Its basic aim is to show the absurdity and the grotesqueness of man's life in the world, vis-a-vis the perfect and all-inclusive domain of transcendental Being. Thus whatever their variation from the maya notion of the Advaita Vedanta, the post-Sankara Vedanta tendencies have consistently asserted that the world is the outcome of the inherent naivete of man, of man's confrontation with his own projected-subjectivity. They have interpreted the presence of the world from the standpoint of an extreme transcendental idealist, of a phenomenologist, and under the enchantment of Brahman, rejected the being of that which to commonsense always remains "natural" and indubitable. Their attempt has been to doubt the world, to hold it out of consciousness, to refuse to recognize it, to put out its very existence, on account of its supposed superimposition on man's pure ego-experience.

The *maya-vadins* cannot .place both Brahman and the universe on an equal footing. They cannot, like realists, propose a uniform valuation of the otherworldly and the worldly. They are determined to realize a region of experience, which, they are sure, is not only complete and absolutely given, but also, in contrast with the experience of worldliness, is totally positive and blissful. Even the bhedabheda-vadins, Ramanuja and the Vedantin triumvirate—Madhva, Nimbarka and Vallabha—can fit into maya-vada in its weak version, in spite of their disagreement with Sankara. Although they show no inclination to regard the world, as illusory, and notably like so many absolutists, firmly accept and account for the reality of the phenomenal world as a part and parcel of Brahman, they never suggest that man's consciousness of the world is not the outcome of his intellectual and moral imperfection. They do not digress from the fundamentally ethicoreligious assumption of the Upanisads.

The question whether a metaphysics free from the maya hypothesis has an edge over that: of the pro-Sankara Vedantins is not of direct relevance in the present context. It is enough to state that so far as their approach to the incidence of *maya* or *avidya* is considered, Ramanuja, Madhva, etc, have unanimously professed a kind of universal spiritualism which tries to harmonize the transcendental and the mundane within one and the same thing. The problem of the seat of *avidya* occurs, therefore, in the pro-Sankara Vedantins; it does not and need not occur in the latter's thinking.

For instance, whatever is empirically experienced is, according to the *bhedabheda-vadins*, beyond any incredibility. It construes an expression of Brahman. In order to explain it, they thought, we would require a method that presupposes its objective presence without at any time doubting it; Bhaskara and Yadavaprakasha condemned Sankara's *maya-vada* and furnished a moderate solution to the riddle of the Brahman-avidya connection by holding that the universe ought to be perceived as a transition of the Supreme Reality (Brahman) and not rejected as a dream or hallucination.

And Ramanuja is not a softer repudiator of the maya theory. When he evolves a monistic pluralism in which God (*Isvara*), the selves (*jivas*) and the material world are bound up together as a transformation of Brahman, his reluctance to posit the ultimately real as divorced from and independent of the world is clearly evident. It is significant, therefore, that the anti-*maya-vada* of these post-Sankarites with its intense theological bias did disturb the transcendentalist foundation of the Brahman-world relation, and introduced most successfully the notion of the divine absolute in the- predominantly world-negating Vedanta thought. And yet to the extent to which they like Sankara looked upon the world as a sphere man is helplessly condemned to, and aspired after !a way out of it, their perspective of the world remained but negative and life forsaking.

We take out personality to be our most intimate and deepest possession, our sovereign good. But it belongs to the object side, itself shaped by relative happenings, mutable and accidental, as compared with the self. We can think about it, calculate its interests, sacrifice them on occasions. It is a sort of psychological being that answers to our name, is reflected in the looking-glass (*namarupa*), a number in statistical tables. It is subject to pleasure and pain, expands when praised, contracts when criticized, admires itself, and is lost in. the masquerade. The Mundaka Upanisad makes a distinction between the two birds which dwell in the same tree, one eating the sweet fruit and the other looking on without eating. The former is the empirical self and the latter the transcendental self.

The phenomenal character of the empirical self and the world .answering to it is denoted by the word maya, which signifies the fragility of the universe. Maya does not mean that the empirical world with the selves in it is an illusion, for the whole effort of the cosmos is directed to and sustained by the one supreme self, which though distinct from everything is implicated in everything. The criticism that Hindu thought is pantheistic makes out that the supreme being, which is complete and impenetrable, is yet filled with things which live, breathe, and move each according to its nature. Nothing can be born, exist, or die in any degree, nothing can have time, place, form, or meaning, except on this universal background.

Maya is a term employed also to indicate the tendency to identify ourselves with our apparent selves and become exiled from our spiritual consciousness with its maximum of clarity and certainty. This tendency is the expression of the working of self-conscious reason. Intellectual activities are a derivation, a selection, and, so long as they are cut off from the truth which is their secret source, a deformation of true knowledge (*avidya*) which has its natural result in selfishness. The aim of all human living is self-definition. It is to isolate the substantial permanence which each finite life possesses deep down from the strife of empirical happenings. We can exceed the limits within which human consciousness normally functions. Man can abstract-from his body and flesh, from his feelings and desires, even from thoughts which rise like waves on the surface of his mind, and reach a pure awareness, the naked condition of his pure selfhood. By steady discipline he can be led back to the pure being, the subject that reflects, and reach that state of immediacy and unity in which all chaos disappears. When we break through the ring f smoke round the self, unwrap the sheaths which cover it, we achieve here and now in the flesh the destiny of our being.

We quake and shiver, bleed and moan with a longing gaze at it. We dare not even lift up our eyes. We are filled with a desire to escape from the world of discord and struggle. In this mood we represent the supreme as the sovereign personality encompassing this whole world, working through the cosmos and ourselves for the realization of the universal kingdom, if the personal concept is more prominent, the individual seeks his development in a humble, trustful submission to God. We may adopt the mode of bhakti or devotion, or the method of jnana or contemplation by which the self, set free from all that is not self, regains its pure dignity. The attainment of spiritual status when refracted in the logical universe appears as a revelation of grace.

Samkara brings out clearly the distinction between the absolute self, the divine person, and the human individual:

Therefore the unconditioned self, being beyond speech and undifferentiated and one, is designated as "not this, not this"; when it has the limiting adjuncts of the body and organs which are characterized by imperfect knowledge, desire, and work, it is called the empirical individual self; and when the self has the limitation of the creative power manifesting through eternal and unlimited knowledge, it is called the inner ruler and divine person. The same self, as by its nature transcendent, absolute, and pure, is called the; immutable and supreme self.

When we seek to grasp the reality super personal in itself, personal from the cosmic end, by conceptual methods, we must note that logically precise formula are at best provisional and incomplete. The definiteness and transparency of the symbols do not mean that the thing signified has been grasped completely. Those who have no contact with reality, no insight into truth, accept the relative symbol for the absolute truth. In their self-confident jugglery with symbol and definitions, they forget the thing itself. Only the background of reality can transform the empty sounds of words into significant expressions of truth.

The two familiar criticisms that for Hindu thought the world is an illusion (*maya*), that it is divine (pantheism) cancel each other and point out that the Hindu is aware of both the upward and the downward movements. The way to the knowledge of the divine has two sides, the negative and the positive. The negative takes us to the spiritual consciousness, the silent witness which dissolves all form and thought. At the 'Divine Darkness, 'the nameless, formless nothing'. But there is the way of affirmation by which the God-conscious man affirms that the great silent sea of infinity, in whose mysterious embrace the individual loses his name and form, is also the over-mastering, all-embracing life. Here is the refrain of the Chandogya Upanisad. 'This whole world has that being for itself. That is reality. That is the self. That art thou, O Svetaketu.' The self is the core of being, the inner thread by being strung on which the world with all its variety exists. It is the real of the real, satyasya satyam. The manifold universe is not an illusion; it is being, though of a lower order, subject to change, waxing and waning, growing and shrinking. 'He who dwells in the Earth, who is other than the Earth, whom the Earth does not know, whose body the Earth is, who controls the Earth from within, he is yourself, the inner controller, the Immortal.' This is said to be true of all things in the world, subjective and objective, which are the manifestations of the "unseen seer'. Even Samkara admits that 'This whole 'multiplicity of creatures existing under name and form in so far as it has the supreme Being itself for its essence is true; if regarded as self-dependent is untrue'. Everything everywhere is based on reality. For the Hindu thinkers, the objective world exists. It is not an illusion. It is real not in being ultimate, but in being a form, an expression of the ultimate. To regard the world as ultimately real is delusion (*moha*).

While the criticism regarding the illusory nature of the world suggests the super-personal restful character of the supreme, that of pantheism brings out its ceaseless self-expression or active creativity. It is not true to contend that the experience of the pure realm of being, timeless and perfect, breeds- in us contempt for the more familiar world of existence, which is unhappily full of imperfection. Reality and existence are not to be set against each other as metaphysical contraries. Nothing on earth is utterly perfect or utterly without perfection. Those who have the vision of perfection strive continually to increase the perfection and diminish the imperfection. Life is for ever striving for its fuller creative manifestation. For one who has the vision of the supreme, life, personality, and history become important. The life of God is the fullness of our life.

When man apprehends the supreme being, returns to the concrete, and controls his life in the light of its truth, he is a complete man. He reaches an almost inconceivable universality. All his powers which have been hitherto bound up with narrow pursuits are liberated for larger ends. The doctrine of maya tells us that we fall away from our authentic being if we are lost in the world of .empirical objects and loving.

When the Hindu thinkers ask us to free ourselves from maya, they are asking to shake off our bondage to the unreal values which are dominating us. They do not ask us to treat life as an illusion or be in-different to the world's welfare. They are asking us to escape from the illusion which holds us by the throat and makes us pursue physical satisfaction or corporate self-seeking as the highest end. It is the function of religion to reaffirm the intuitive loyalty to life and solidarity of human nature, to lift us out of the illusion of isolation and take us back to reality. The religious soul does not seek for release from suffering in the present life or a place in paradise in the next life'. His prayer, in the words of the Upanisad, is 'Lead me from the unreal to the real, lead me from darkness to light, lead me from death to immortality'. The resurrection is not the rise of the dead from their tombs but the passage from the death of self-absorption to the life of unselfish love, the transition from the darkness of selfish individualism to the light of universal spirit, from falsehood to truth, from the slavery of the world to the liberty of the eternal.

How can we rise above the present vision of the world with its anarchic individualism, its economic interpretations of history, and materialist views of life? This world of maya has thrown our consciousness out of focus. We must shift the focus of consciousness and see better and more. The way to growth lies through an increasing impersonality, through the unifying of the self with a greater than the self.

The mystery cults of Greece had for their central doctrine that man's soul is of divine origin and is akin to the spirit of God. The influence of these mystery cults on Socrates and Plato is unmistakable. When Jesus tells Nicodemus that until a man is begotten from above he cannot see or enter the Kingdom of God,1 when Paul declares that he that soweth to the flesh shall .of the flesh reap corruption; but he that soweth to the spirit shall of the. spirit reap everlasting life', they are implying that our natural life is mortal and it is invaded by sin and death, and that the life on spirit is immortal. St. John in the First Epistle says: 'the world passeth away, and the lust thereof but he that doeth the will of God abideth for ever. We are amphibious beings, according to Plotinus, We live on earth and in a world of spirit.

Although the view about the coexistence of the human and the divine in close intimacy and interpenetration may be true, does not Hindu thought declare that life is empty and unreal, and that it has no purpose of meaning? Schweitzer tells us that for the Upanishad the world of the senses is a magic play staged by the universal soul for itself. The individual soul is brought into this magic play under a spell. By reflection about itself it must become capable of seeing through the deception. Thereupon it gives up taking part in the play. It waits quietly and enjoys its identity with the universal soul until, at death, the magic play for it ceases to be.' 'Man cannot engage in ethical activity in a world with no meaning.' 'For any believer in the maya doctrine ethics can have only a quite relative importance. This account is be no means a fair representations of the position of the Upadisads. The long theistic tradition interprets the doctrine of the Upanisads in a way directly opposed to this account. Samkara adopts the doctrine .of may a, and it is doubtful whether Schweitzer's view is adequate to Samkara's thought. Religious experience, by its affirmation that the bask fact in the universe is spiritual, implies that the world of sound and sense is not final. All existence finds its source and support in a supreme in a supreme reality whose nature is spirit. The visible world is the symbol of a more real world. It is the reflection of a spiritual universe which gives to it its life and significance. What is the relation of absolute being to historical becoming, of eternity to time? Is succession, history, progress, real and sufficient in its own right, or does man's deep instinct for the unchanging point to an eternal perfection which alone gives the world meaning and worth? Is the inescapable flux all, or is there anything which abides? Religious consciousness bears testimony to the reality of something behind the visible, a haunting beyond, which of change is said to be unreal.

Gaudapada argues that 'whatever is non-existent at the beginning and in the end is non-existent in the middle also'. In other words, the things of the world are not eternal. The world is maya, i.e. passes away, but God is eternal. Change causality, activity are finite categories and the Eternal is lifted above them. God is not a mere means to explain the universe or improve human society.

Samkara, who is rightly credited with the systematic formulation of the doctrine of maya tells us that the highest reality is unchangeable, and therefore that changing existence such as human history has not ultimate reality. He warns us, however, against the temptation to regard what is not completely real as utterly illusory. The world has empirical being which is quite different from illusory existence. Human experience is neither ultimately real nor completely illusory. Simply because the world of experience is not the perfect form of reality, it does not follow that it is a delusion, without any significance. The world is not a phantom, though it is not real. Brahman is said to be the real of the real, satyasyasatyim. In all objective consciousness, we are in a sense aware of the real.

Similarly, all knowledge presupposes the knower who is constant, while the known is unsteady. When Plato tells us that we bring universal ideas with us from the world in which we lived before our birth, he is referring to the non-phenomenal, time-transcending power in us which belongs to a different world from the observed phenomena. The 'nous' which organizes the facts of experience and interprets them is not itself a fact of experience. It must have had its origin in and belong to another world. It beholds by virtue of its own nature eternal realities. This presence in us is an assurance that we are in touch with reality. Spirit is real being and the rest its limited activity. The spirit is pure existence, self-aware, timeless, spaceless, unconditioned, not dependent for its being on its sense of objects, rot dependent for its delight on the gross or subtle touches of outward things. It is not divided in the multitude of beings. Samsara's advaita or non-duality has for its central thesis the ion-difference between the individual self and Brahman. As for difference of multiplicity (*nanatva*), it is not real. Its self-discrepant character shows that it is only an appearance of the real. All schools of advaita are agreed on these two propositions. Differences arise when the nature of actuality of the manifold world as distinct from the reality is described. Samkara accepts the empirical reality of the world, which is negated only when perfect insight or insight or intuition of the oneness of all is attained. Until then it has empirical validity or pragmatic justification. There are advaitins who argue that the world of difference has not even empirical validity. Samakra, however, tells us that so long is we are in the world of maya and occupy a dualistic stand-point, the world is there, standing over against us, determining our perceptions and conduct.

Besides, the world we see and touch is not independent and self-sufficing. It carries no explanation of itself. It is a world reflecting the condition of our minds, a partial construction made from insufficient data under the stress of self conscious individuality with its cravings and desires. What is perceived and shaped into meaning depends on the powers of apprehension we employ and the interests we possess. Our passion-limited apprehension gives us the world of common sense. Matter is not primal. It is a thing made, not self-existent. It is not unreal but being as it forms itself to sense. It is not a baseless fiction but at the lowest a misrepresentation of truth; at the highest an imperfect representation or translation of the truth into a lower plane. Even as our knowledge implies the presence of a constant consciousness, the object of our knowledge implies the reality of pure being. Our conceptions of the universe answer to our degrees of consciousness. As our consciousness increases in its scope, we see more clearly. We now see partly as an animal and partly as a human being. Sometimes the world is viewed as one of self-satisfaction, at other times as an object of curiosity and contemplation.

It is not therefore mere waking dream. Maya is not solipsism. It does not say that suns and universes are the invention of the solitary mind. Samkara proclaims his opposition to *Vijnanavada* or mentalism. He argues that' waking experiences are distinct from dream-states, though neither can be regarded as real metaphysically. Our world of waking experience is net the ultimate reality, but neither is it a shadow show. We are surrounded by something other than ourselves, which cannot be reduced to states of our own consciousness. Though the world is always changing, it has a unity and a meaning. These are revealed by the reality present all through it. This reality lies not in the facts but in the principle which makes them into a whole. We are able to know that the world is imperfect, finite, and changing, because we have consciousness of the eternal and the perfect. It is by the light of this consciousness that we criticize ourselves or condemn the world. Even as the-human individual is a complex of the eternal and the temporal, the world which confronts him contains both. It is for Samkara a mixture of truth and illusion. It partakes of the characteristics of being and non-being (*sada-sadatmaka*). Although, therefore, it has a lower form of reality than pure spirit, it is not non-existent.

This brings us to the problem of the relation between the unchanging real and the changing world. Whatever the nature of the world may be, finite or infinite, it is contingent. The question remains, why does the world exist at all? To say that it is a mystery is perhaps true, but it can hardly be called an answer. No theory can be logically satisfactory since the question itself is not logically framed. It involves a confusion of standpoints. We are using temporal terms with reference to an order which is essentially non temporal. The Psalmist, tells us, 'God is in heaven, and thou upon earth; therefore let thy words be few.' When Augustine was asked, 'What was God doing, before He made heaven and earth?' he answered, 'Preparing hell for the over-curious.' Time was with creation, and so the question of 'before' has no meaning. As to how the primal reality in which the divine light shines everlastingly can yet be the source and fount of all empirical being, we can only say that it is a mystery, maya.

The explanation offered by Samkara admits that the universe is dependent on the Absolute, though not the Absolute on the universe. A distinction is made between manifestation or transformation and one-sided dependence. The illustrations used for explaining the latter type of dependence suggest the illusory theory of the world. The world is said to depend on the Absolute, even as die appearance of snake depends on the rope, or that of a mirage on shining sand particles, or that of silver on a conch-shall. The point of these illustrations is to affirm that the production and cessation of the appearances make no difference to the reality of which they are the reflections. In the case of transformation, the substance itself is changed. When the effect is destroyed, the cause also is destroyed.

So it is said that it does not itself become many but seems to have become many through maya. Aristotle tells us that the world defends on God, though God is completely unaware of and unaffected by it. The temporal yields a real apprehension of the eternal, though it does not contain or exhaust the eternal.

Jnana, or seeing through the veil of may a, is the spiritual destiny of man. It is something more than ethical goodness, though it cannot be achieved without it. The difference is that between perfection and progress, between eternal life and temporal development, between time suspended and time extended. One is an improvement of human nature, while the other is a reorientation of it. We cannot reach perfection by means of progress any more than we can reach the point where the clouds touch the horizon by running.

The old sage Yajnavalkya, in order to follow the way of salvation, gives up his possessions, leaving them to his two wives. But his wife Makreyi refuses these riches'of the world with the words, 'What are these to me if I am not thereby to gain life eternal?' All activity only helps that which is perishable; the seeker after perfection is not satisfied by it. A well-known Sanskrit verse asks: 'What if a man has all the wealth to realize his ends? What if he defeats his enemies; what if he helps his friends by gifts to them all? What if he continues to live endlessly in an embodied existence?' We can become perfect only by overcoming selfishness. The moral man battles with selfishness but works all the time under tie-illusion of egoism. The saint 'covers himself with the truth of the universal self.'

The view which regards the multiplicity as ultimate is deceptive (*mayo*), for it causes the desire to live separate and independent lives. When we are. under the influence of maya, we think we are completely separate entities, sharing little and mistaking individuality, which is one of the conditions of our life in space-time, for isolation and not wishing to lose the hard outlines of our separate existence. Maya keeps us busy with the world of succession and finitude. It causes a certain restlessness in our souls, fever in our-blood. It tempts us to accept, as real, bubbles which will be broken, cobwebs which will be swept away. This wearing of masks, this playing of roles, this marionette performance of ourselves, is .mistaken for truth. We forget that we are more closely allied in spirit than we suspect, that we share infinitely more than we realize. The Bhagavadgita tells us that 'the wise one is awake when it is night for all others and he looks upon that as night in which other living beings art awake'. The genuineness of one's awakening is directly proportionate to one's apprehension of truth. Wisdom liberates while ignorance binds, and the inner change is essential to perfection.

This self-finding or becoming one with the infinite, is 'a pure act of the spirit which has nothing to do with ethics'. Progress is represented as a growing out of ignorance into knowledge. This knowledge is not merely intellectual any more than ignorance is error. Ignorance and selfish desire are two phases of one phenomenon. Patanjali traces the karmas which bind us to the cycle of birth and death to ignorance (*avidya*), egoism, attachment, hatred, and self-love. These five are different expressions of the fundamental ignorance. Only when a man rises to dispassion and acts without selfish attachment is he really free. The ego is the knot of our continued state of ignorance, and so long as we live in the ego we do not share in the delight of the universal spirit. In order to know the truth we must cease to identify ourselves with the separate ego shut up in the walls of body, life, and mind. We must renounce the narrow horizon, the selfish interest, the unreal objective. This is an ethical process.

Truth can never be perceived except by those who are in love with goodness. Again, the delivery from the illusion is not achieved by means of carried out with poise and serenity. The man of wisdom is interested in promoting the welfare of all created beings according to the Bhagavadgtta.

Freedom, love, light, and power are not to be confused with dejected looks or depression of mind. Spirit without mind or spirit without body is not the aim of human perfection. Body and mind are the conditions or instruments of the life of spirit in man, valuable not for their own sake but because of the spirit in them. In the Maitri Upanisad the knower of the self is compared to a smokeless fire burning as it were with glow. The body becomes a transparency through which the spirit shines, a glass for its indwelling flame. The spiritual tendency does not move in the region of the abstract, but has its grip on the actual and embraces the complexity of thought arid the richness of life. Body and mind are the conditions and instruments of the life of spirit in man.

The dualism between body and spirit is not radical. Without maltreating the oody we can attain to the freedom of spirit. In a famous passage we are called upon to make body and the senses, speech and' thought worthy of the infinite spirit which dwells in them. 'May the earth, water, fire, air and ether that compose my body become purified; may sound, touch, vision, taste and' smell become purified . . . may my thought, speech, actions become purified . . . may my soul become purified so that I may become the effulgent spirit, free from-sullying passion and sin.' The distinctive feature of the Hindu view is that it does not look upon the development of mind, life, and body as the primary ends of life.

Mysticism has its fanatics who look upon the real as spiritual freedom and contrast it with the actual in its bond age, declaring .that birth is an error of thesoul and our chance of liberation lies in shaking off these shackles. The theory of maya has been interpreted in this negative sense so as to lend' support to the doctrine that man's life has no real meaning, that it is a mistake of the soul, an error that has inexplicably crept into being. Since the real is the supreme Brahman, the only thing to do is to get away from all existence, celestial or terrestrial. The illusion is real to itself and it binds us so long as we rest in it. Our true aim should be to get rid of the error and thus of life. *Moksa* or release is the extinction of the individual, his annulment in the Absolute. Since the world is an illusion, it is a waste of energy to spend labour and heroism in battling with its merely illusory events. Our duty consists in putting up uncomplainingly with its annoying-semblance of reality. By adopting an ethic of quietism and resignation we are enabled to enter in some measure into the peaceful being of the Absolute, which knows nothing of errors and illusions and is tirelessly at rest. If this view is accepted, the path of the universe becomes an aimless one.

Such exaggeration are to be met with in mysticism Eastern as well as Western. But Samkara has nothing in common with people who will not accept the- visible world any more than with those who will accept nothing else. Exclusive absorption in a super-historical goal often produces the feeling that all things 'temporal are so fragile and fleeting that they are hardly worth our serious attention.

The liberated individual works for the welfare of the world. The Bhagavadglta tells us, 'Man does not attain to the state of being without: work by undertaking no work, nor does he reach perfection by simply shunning the world.' It is improper for man to remain without sharing in the work of the world even when God consents to work for the universe. Besides, so long as man lives, he cannot remain even for an instant without activity. The sage is not egocentric in the sense of caring for his own soul, or altruistic in the sense of caring for others, or theocentric in the sense of wishing to enjoy God in the solitude of his soul. He is at the heart of the universe in which he himself and others live, move, and have their being. He is conscious of the wider destiny of the universe.

The great text That are Thou (*tat ruam asi*) is bound up with an ethic of active service. He writes: 'Easy as it would be to turn the doctrine of tat asi in an ethical direction, they nevertheless neglect to do it.' At the end of his Indian tour Dr. Paul Deussen said to a gathering at Bombay: 'The Gospels quite correctly establish as the highest law of morality, "Love your neighbour as yourselves." But why should I do so since by the order of nature I feel pain and pleasure only in myself, rot in my neighbour? The answer is not in the Bible . . . but it is in the Veda, in the great formula That art Thou which gives in three words the combined sum of' metaphysics and morals. You shall love your neighbour as yourselves because you are your neighbour.' In the words of the Bhagavadgita: 'He who knows himself in everything and everything in himself will not injure himself by himself.' Every person round me is myself at a different point of space and time and at a different grade of being. When one realizes that 'all beings are but the self one acts not selfishly but for all beings.

The followers of Samkara repudiate the Mimamsa view that works lead to salvation and argue that spiritual insight (*jnana*) is the only way to it. When the theory of 'put -a penny in the slot and pull out a pardon' became fashionable in Christianity, Luther held justification is by faith alone and not by works. Release is eternal, while pursuit of works is transient. The latter is helpful in hindering the hindrances to spiritual life. The conception of saintliness which is beyond good and evil is not an invitation to practise unethical conduct. Katha Upanisad declares that 'he who has not ceased from immoral conduct cannot obtain God through intelligence'. Immoral conduct and spiritual life are incompatible, since the eternal, is pure and free of all evil. That pure being can be apprehended only by those 'whose nature is purified'. God is both truth and virtue. 'Only when one's whole nature is purified are the bonds released which keep the soul from God.'

This contention is based upon' the conception of God as superior 'to the categories of the world. We cannot speak of Him as doing right and wrong. In its inmost being reality is neither good nor evil, neither moral nor immoral, just as it is neither high nor low, neither coloured nor colourless. These distinctions belong not to reality as such but to the human world which is a part of this cosmic process, which is itself a phase in which being is alienated from itself. Not that the distinctions of good and evil are arbitrary or conventional; they are certainly reasonable and natural, and they express absolute truths of the moral order, but they are fundamentally the categories of this world. They are symbolic, not images or shadows. The symbolism is not artificial, accidental, or false. It tells us about the ultimate reality, but darkly, reflected as it were in the mirror of the world. As good and evil belong to this world, and as the real is beyond good and evil, the problem for man is to pass from symbols to reality. When he succeeds in his attempt he is beyond good and evil. In the life of spirit, all symbolism is overcome.

Asceticism is associated with all religions and represents a basic need of human nature. It is the outgrowth of the demand that the highest religion requires the surrender of the individual claim and identification with the universal life. The essential quality of asceticism is the denial of the individual desires, which is a part of religious life. Ascesis is training, and a religious man is in training all his life. Ascetic practices are adopted for different reasons. Some take to them in order that they may escape from the corruption of society, which makes life in the world almost intolerable to gentle spirits. Others are' prompted by the desire to achieve invulnerability. Still others hope that the mystic vision which they wish to enjoy may sometimes be induced by physical buffetings. The wish to harden the will against the temptation of the senses is also among the motives of asceticism.

For the sake of self-knowledge, some enter monasteries and hermitages not because they are afraid of life or are cowardly, but in order that they may train themselves for the work of: the world and approach it with in inextinguishable hope, a vision of divine purpose at work, which a deeper peace in the acceptance of sorrow and a beauty of holiness.

The opposite of outward action is not inaction but inward action. Buddha went to a rich farmer of Benares and asked alms of him. He said to Buddha, 'I having ploughed and sowed eat; you, on the other hand, purpose to eat without ploughing and sowing.' Buddha replied that he was engaged in an even more important tillage of the spirit. 'Faith is the seed, penance the rain, understanding my yoke and plough, modesty the pole of the plough, mind the i.e, thoughfulness my ploughshare and goad.... Exertion is my beast of burden carrying me without turning back to the place, where, having gone, one does not grieve. ... So this ploughing is ploughed; it bears the fruit of immortality.' What is called passivity is not inertia. The Hindu emphasis on inner life seems to many leaders of our generation, apostles of success and efficiency, a sheer waste of time. We are asked to get out and do something. The man who bakes bread or builds a house is said to be doing something useful, while he who paints pictures or composes music is doing something selfish. A variation of this astonishing doctrine animates the work of social uplifters. The royal road to the Golden Age is the road of economic reform or military conquest or armed revolution or the dictatorship of the proletariat: all these method insist on social machinery and letariat : all these methods insist on social machinery and organization. Humanity is plunged to the depths in external things, class and nation, State and society. Man is treated as a part of the objective world and is not permitted to remain himself, have his own inner being. The emphasis on negative virtues such as gentleness and love, passivism and lack of aggressiveness, which makes one surrender one's rights rather than fight for them, appears to those engaged in the busy life of politics and sport to be weakness and cowardice. But like all Eastern religions Christianity also preaches a gospel of renunciation, of passivity, of withdrawal from the traffic of external things. The Cross signifies that progress is achieved not by those who fight for it but by those who suffer for it. It appealed to the Western mind in the turbulent times of the Roman Empire, when life was insecure and injustice rife.

The perfection of a human being differs from that of an instrument or a machine. We may judge the latter by its capacity to produce certain goods which are external to it, by its speed and efficiency in its productivity. We are not right in judging human civilization by the same standards of energy and efficiency.

The great teachers are united in thinking that the soul of man is more precious than the immensity of the world and its growth is effected in moments of leisure and meditation.

It is a one-sided view of contemplation that makes it exclusive of moral 'activity. Inner perfection and outer conduct are two sides of one life. Contemplation and action, the yoga of Krsna and the *dhanus* of Arjuna are two movements merged in one act.

In spite of our strong dislike of monasticism, it is well to remember that the Christian monks took the leading part rebuilding European civilization after the barbarian hordes had almost destroyed it. The lamp of knowledge was kept burning in the Dark Ages in the monasteries by the teachers and scholars who sought the deep places of truth and counted all else as dross. The life and work of Dr. Schweitzer are themselves an example of disciplined asceticism at a time when both purpose and discipline are lacking in the world. India, however, is full of mendicant ascetics who wander from one part of that vast continent o the other, leaving the world around to its fate. But these are not the true representatives of the genius of India who, with a perception of the unity of thing move at ease in he world of spirit and the world of sense.

The semblance of truth which this view of the world negating character of Hinduism has is due to the impression that Hindu culture has not resulted in a strong and successful organization of life such as Europe shows to us. Because India has blundered in life and failed to make the best of the her material resources, she is said to be a nation of unpractical dreamers, world-shunning ascetics, patient and docile, inept and inefficient. Because the West has recently made marvelous progress in science and technology, social reform and political advancement, Christian religion, which is professed in the West, is said to be world-affirming in character. Any such sharp contrast confuses different questions. What is civilized life? Is the great Western civilization the only measure and standard by which we judge human achievement? Vedanta can heal the scars of history. The idea of human equality contained in the Upanishads can be a template for all inter-religious movements.

Hinduism, which has a billion followers around the world, is the oldest, continuing religion dating back to several millennia B.C. During this long period it has produced a rich and vast corpus of scriptures that cover almost all aspects of human life. Among these the most significant are the Upanishads, those glorious dialogues which represent the foundation of all later schools of Indian philosophy collectively they are the basis of the Vedanta, as they come at the chronological end of the Vedas and also represent the high watermark, not only of Hindu but of world philosophy. The basic features of the Vedanta give us a holistic philosophy of life and death, cutting across all barriers between human beings. This is particularly important today when all sorts of regressive concepts are propagated in the name of Hinduism.

The basic concept is that of all-pervasive Brahman — *'Ishavasyamidam Sarvam Yatkincha Jagatyam Jagat'*: Whatever had, does or will exist and wherever it exists, whether it is moving or not, is permeated by the same divine power and force. The Upanishadic view is that in the ultimate analysis all is a manifestation of the divine. Indeed there can be no manifestation without the divinity behind it, and this in a way parallels the realisation of modern science. In the post-Einsteinian situation there is now the realisation that whatever exists is really the same energy appearing as a particle or as a wave. The unified field theory, which the scientists have been desperately seeking, has its spiritual counterpart in the concept of the all-pervasive Brahman of the Upanishads.

The second basic concept is that this Brahman resides within each individual's consciousness, in the *Atman*. The *Atman*, as it were, is the reflection of this all-pervasive Brahman in individual consciousness; but the *Atman* is not ultimately separate from the Brahman. The concept of 'Ishwarah'—the Lord residing within the heart of each individual — is the second great insight of the Upanishads, and all the four yogas — *Jnana, Bhakti, Karma* and *Raja*— are directed towards bringing about the union between the *Atman* and the Brahman.

Flowing from this is another important Vedantic concept, which is that all human beings are in the final analysis members of a single, extended family. The Upanishads have a beautiful word for the human race — *Amritasya Putrah'*, children of immortality — because we all carry within our consciousness the light and the power of the Brahman. For those of the greater consciousness, the entire world is a family, *Vasudhaiva Kutumbakam*.

A fourth major philosophical concept of the Upanishads is the essential unity of all religions — *'Ekam Sadviprah Bahudha Vadanti'* as the Rig Veda has it; the Truth is one, the Wise call it by many names. All creeds and religious formulations arise in different times and areas, but if they have a true aspiration, they reach the same goal.

A fifth Vedantic concept is the welfare of all beings — *'Bahujana Sukhaya Bahujana Hitaya Cha'*, The Vedanta seeks the welfare of all creation, not only of human beings but also of what we call the lower creatures. In our arrogance and ignorance we have destroyed the environments of this planet. We have polluted the oceans, made the air unbreathable, desecrated nature and decimated wildlife. Thousands of species have become extinct because of our hubris as human beings; and thousands more are on the verge of extinction. But the Vedantic seers knew that man was not something apart from nature, that human consciousness grew out of the entirety of the world situation, and therefore they had compassion for all living beings. That is why the Vedanta constantly exhorts us that while we are working for our own salvation we must also shun the path of violence and of hatred. We must seek to develop both elements of our psyche, the inner and the outer, the quietist and the activist.

While working out our own destiny we also have social responsibility, and as long as we are embodied we have to continue to work for the welfare of all beings and of the planet itself.

These five concepts of the Vedantas — the all-pervasive Brahman the *Atman*, which resides in all beings; the four-fold Yoga, which seeks to unite them; the concept of the human race as members of an extended family regardless of all differences; the idea that all religions are essentially different paths to the same goal; and the concept that we must work for the welfare of society and of all beings—taken together provide a comprehensive world view which can greatly help humanity in the process of globalisation upon which it has embarked, and enable us to overcome the many psychological, economic and political problems that we face.

The last century, despite its extraordinary scientific and technological achievements, has been one of the most lethal in human history. Two World Wars and dozens of inter-regional and intra-regional conflicts have left millions dead and tens of millions uprooted from their homes. A disturbing feature is the revival of religious fanaticism that poses a major threat to humanity in the 21st century. It is, therefore important to re-discover and re-articulate the foundational principles of the many religions that flourish on planet earth. In my view the Vedanta represents the fundamental principles of Hinduism, and, I make bold to say, can provide a template for the inter-religious movements around the world.

Vivekananda contends that man's free agency is not of the mind, for that is bound. There is no freedom there. Man is not mind, he is soul. The soul is ever free, boundless, and eternal. Herein is man's freedom, in the soul. The soul is a ways free, but the mind identifying itself with its own ephemeral waves, loses sight of the soul and becomes lost in the maze of time space, and causation—*Maya*. This is the cause of our bondage. We are always identifying ourselves with the mind, and the mind's meant changes.

That which differentiates one thing from another is time, space, and causation. The differentiation is in the form, not in the substance. He further says that one may destroy the form and it disappears for ever; but the substance remains the same. You can never destroy the substance. Evolution is in nature, not in the soul — evolution of nature, manifestation of the soul.

Vivekananda says that maya is not illusion as it is popularly interpreted. *Maya* is Real, yet it is not real. It is real in that the Real is behind it and gives it its appearance of Reality. That which is real in *Maya* is the Reality in and through *Maya*. Yet the Reality is never seen; and hence that which is seen is unreal, and it has no real independent existence of itself, but is dependent upon the Real for its existence. *Maya* then is a paradox — real, yet not real, an illusion, yet not an illusion. He who knows the Real sees in *Maya* not illusion, but reality. He who knows not the Real sees in *Maya* illusion and thinks it real. We are bound to earth by desire and also to God, heaven, and the angels. A slave is a slave whether to man, to God, or to angels.

Vivekananda argues that the idea of heaven must pass away. The idea of heaven after death where the good live a life of eternal happiness is a vain dream, without a particle of meaning or sense in it. Wherever there is happiness there must follow unhappiness sometime. Wherever there is pleasure there must be pain. This is absolutely certain, every action has its reaction somehow. The idea of freedom is the only true idea of salvation—freedom from everything, the senses, whether of pleasure or pain, from good as well as evil.

More than this even, we must be free from death; and to be free from death, we must be free from life. Life is but a dream of death. Where there is life, there will be death; so get away from life if you would be rid of death. We are ever free if we would only believe it, only have faith enough. We are the soul, free and eternal, ever free, ever blessed. Everything in time, space, and causation is bound. The soul is beyond all time, all space, all causation. That which is bound is nature, not the soul. Time, space, and causation we call *Maya*.

When one sees a mirage for the first time, he mistakes it for a reality, and after vainly trying to quench his thirst in it, learns that it is a mirage. But whenever he sees such a phenomenon in future, in spite of the apparent reality, the idea that he sees a mirage always presents itself to him. So is the world of *Maya* to a *Jivanmukta*.

What is Spencer's unknowable? It is our *Maya*. Western philosophers are afraid of the unknowable, but our philosophers have taken a big jump into the unknown, and they have conquered. He gets across *Maya* who gives up all attachment, serves the great ones, lives alone, cuts the bondages of this world, goes beyond the qualities of nature, and depends upon the Lord for even his living.

He who gives up the fruits of work, he who gives up all work and the dualism of joy and misery, who gives up even the scriptures, gets that unbroken love for God; The Vedas are divided into two portions, the *Jnana-kanda* (knowledge-portion) and the *Karma-kânda* (ritual-portion). The ceremonies and the fruits of the *Karma-kanda* are confined within the limits of the world of *Mâyâ*, and therefore they have been undergoing and will undergo transformation according to the law of change which operates through time, space, and personality. Social laws and customs likewise, being based on this Karma-kanda, have been changing and will continue to change hereafter. Minor social usages also will be recognised and accepted when they are compatible with the spirit of the true scriptures and the conduct and example of holy sages. But blind allegiance only to usages such as are repugnant to the spirit of the *Shastras* and the conduct of holy sages has been one of the main causes of the downfall of the Aryan race.

It is the *Jnana-kanda* or the Vedanta only that has for all time commanded recognition for leading men across *Maya* and bestowing salvation on them through the practice of Yoga, *Bhakti*, *Jnana*, or selfless work; and as its validity and authority remain unaffected by any limitations of time, place or persons, it is the only exponent of the universal and eternal religion for all mankind.

The progress of the world means more enjoyment and more misery too. 'This mixture of life and death, good and evil, knowledge and ignorance is what is called *Máyá*—or the universal phenomenon. One may go on for eternity inside this net, seeking for happiness—one finds much good, and much evil too. To have good and no evil is childish nonsense. Two ways are left open—one by giving up all desire to take up the world as it is and bear the pangs and pains in the hope of a crumb of happiness now and then. The other, to give up the search for pleasure, knowing it to be pain in another form, and seek for truth—and those that dare try for truth succeed in finding that truth 'as ever present—present in themselves. Then we also discover how the same truth is manifesting itself both in our relative error and knowledge—we find also that the same truth is bliss which again is manifesting itself as good and evil, and with it also we find real existence which is manifesting itself as both death and life.

Thus we realise that all these phenomena are but the reflections, bifurcated or manifolded, of the one existence, truth-bliss-unity—our real Self and the reality of everything else. Then and then only is it possible to do good without evil, for such a soul has known and got the control of the material of which both good and evil are manufactured, and he alone can manifest one or the other as he likes, and we know he manifests only good. This is the *Jivan-mukta*—the living free—the goal of Vedanta as of all other philosophies. -

Vivekananda insists that all reasoning and arguing is within the limit of the realm of Maya; it lies within the categories of space, time, and causation. But He is beyond these categories. We speak of His law, still He is beyond all law. He creates, or becomes, all that we speak of as laws of nature, and yet He is outside of them all. He on whom His grace descends, in a moment goes beyond all law. For this reason there is no condition in grace. It is as His play or sport. And this creation of the universe is —It is the pure delight of sport. Is it not possible for Him who creates and destroys the universe as if in play to grant salvation by grace to the greatest sinner? But then it is just His pleasure, His play, to get somebody through the practice of spiritual discipline and somebody else without it.

Vivekananda declares : "I am not a fool to believe anything and everything without direct proof. And coming into this realm of *Mahâmâyâ*, oh, the many magic mysteries I have come across alongside this bigger magic conjuration of a universe! *Mâyâ*, it is all *Maya*! Goodness! What rubbish we have been talking so long this day! By thinking constantly of ghosts, men become ghosts themselves, while whoever repeats day and night, knowingly or unknowingly," "I am the eternal, pure. free, self-illumined *Atman*", verily becomes the knower of Brahman.

Vivekananda has warned that "Don't allow all that worthless nonsense to occupy your mind. Always discriminate between the real and the unreal, and devote yourself heart and soul to the attempt to realise the *Atman*. There is nothing higher than this knowledge of the Atman; all else is Maya, mere jugglery. The *Atman* is the one unchangeable Truth. This I have come to understand, and that is why I try to bring it home to you all. "One Brahman there is without a second, There is nothing manifold in existence".

Vivekananda argues that all reasoning and arguing is within the limit of the realm of *Maya*; it lies within the categories of space, time, and causation. But He is beyond these categories. We speak of His law, still He is beyond all law. He creates, or becomes, all that we speak of as laws of nature, and yet He is outside of them all. He on whom His grace descends, in a moment goes beyond all law. For this reason there is no condition in grace. It is as His play or sport. And this creation of the universe is like His play. It is the pure delight of sport. Is it not possible for Him who creates and destroys the universe as if in play to grant salvation by grace to the greatest sinner? But then it is just His pleasure, His play, to get somebody through the practice of spiritual discipline and somebody else without it.

This is borne out once again by the way Vivekananda explained the doctrine of maya, without mentioning it by name, when he tried to answer the question: 'Why should the free, perfect, and pure being be thus under the thralldom of matter... ? In other words, why and how is this unity impaired, or how does the "free, perfect and pure being1 come under the bondage of imperfection and impurity? This is the question of all questions and in answering it, Vedanta puts up the theory of maya, which has baffled many and has confounded even the highest intellectuals even up to the present day. But it was left to the genius of Vivekananda to grasp it in its true implications entirely: *Maya* is only another name for what is indeterminable or inexplicable and is thus only a statement of fact. Without mentioning the word maya, he, in his Chicago address, boldly explains and upholds the theory that the Hindu is sincere. He does not want to take shelter under sophistry. He is brave enough to face the question in a manly fashion; and his answer is: 'I do not know. I do not know how the perfect being, the soul, came to think of itself as imperfect, as joined to and conditioned by matter.' But the fact is a fact for all that. It is a fact in everybody's consciousness that one thinks of oneself as the body.

For Advait Vedant this delusion is a fact and also, at the same time, to take the resolve to 'shake off the delusion'. First of all, he reminded people again and again that 'maya is not a theory, it is simply a statement of facts about the universe as it exists....' Secondly, he refuted the .ordinary' interpretation of maya is not illusion by affirming again and again, that '*maya* is not illusion as it is popularly interpreted', that it is 'erroneously explained as illusion' and that 'the translation of the word is neither happy nor correct.' And then he went on to explain the true nature and significance of maya by stating that '*Maya* is neither existence nor non-existence' and also by rightly indicating what it is: 'This mixture of life and death, good and evil, knowledge and ignorance is what is called *Maya*.'

Vivekananda clear grasp of this most baffling concept by following Sankara throughout in his exposition of Advaita Vedanta. Yet, modern Indian thinkers and intellectual giants such as Sri Aurobindo, Rabindranath, and others, have raised their chorus of vehement protest against Sankara, especially denouncing his mayavada, which, to them, does not explain anything but rather explains away all phenomenon as false.

Among the intellectual interpreters of Hinduism, Sankara towers like an unreachable giant above his fellows. As a philosopher, as a metaphysician, as a powerful logician and victorious disputant his greatness can hardly be measured. For a hundred years and more he has stood in the heavens of Indian thought, his head far away in the altitudes of Advaita, his feet firmly planted on the lifeless remnants of crushed systems and broken philosophies, the wreckage of his logical conquests, his mouth like Trishira's swallowing up the world, annihilating it in the white flame of the Vedant, his shadow covering our intellects and stunting the efforts of all who have dared to think originally and dispute his conclusions.

Vivekananda ventured throughout to differ from the King of commentators—almost even to ignore this great and invincible disputant. When the great Vivekananda, potent seedsower of the future, in answer to the objection of the Pundits, 'But Shankara does not say that' replied simply but finally, 'No, but I, Vivekananda, say it,' he pronounced the decree of liberation not only for himself but for all of us from the yoke, the golden but heavy yoke, of the mighty. For this was Vivekananda's mission to smite away alt obstacles, however great and venerable, and open the path to the resurgence of Indian originality and the direct confrontation of the soul of men with the living truth. He was our deliverer not only from ignorance and weakness, but from the systems of knowledge that would limit us and impose a premature finality.

We have presented this long quotation from the luminous pen of Sri Aurobindo in order to assess if Vivekananda really broke away from the system of knowledge propounded by Sankara by freeing himself from 'the golden and heavy yoke of the mighty Dravidian' that had been holding the entire Indian thought, in thraldom for centuries. In other words, did Vivekananda preach a neo-Vedanta, as is generally supposed and attributed to him now, which is distinct and divergent from the Advaita Vedanta of Sarikara? The answer to this question has again to be found in the conception of unity which Vivekananda put forth in all his later lectures and of which he laid the seed, as we have seen, in the Chicago address.

In his Chicago address, Vivekananda could have easily quoted from the Vedas themselves, of which he speaks so much again and again in his later addresses, to support and confirm his conception of unity. There is no dearth of such statements in the Vedas, such as *'Ekam sad vipra bahudha vadanti* or *'Ekam va idam vibabhuva sarvam,* which affirm this unity. But he instead chose to quote a verse from the famous hymn on Siva by Puspadanta, which itself indicates that he was speaking of a flowing or growing unity in which each religion has an existence of its own, like the different streams or rivers. Though in their essence the rivers contain and are made up of the same one water, they, ultimately merge in the ocean, losing their names and forms. Through this most apt illustration, he wanted to convey the three stages of this unity, which was to be his favourite theme later on in all his subsequent lectures.

In the first stage, there is a distinct division or separation between the river and the ocean, yet .there is a strong pull of the one towards the other, which makes the river flow unconsciously and spontaneously towards the ocean. If there had not been an underlying unity between the two, this attraction for each other would never have been there. There is thus a dim perception of-this unity even in duality and a movement towards it. In the second stage, as the river moves further on and nears the ocean, it feels that it is organically related to the other because there is an interaction between the two. The perception of unity thus gets clearer and deeper. And finally, in the third stage, there is a complete fusion between the two, and the river cannot be distinguished separately from the ocean any more. Here the unity is at its highest and best, though this utter and absolute unity is beyond the grasp or comprehension of the human intellect or mind.

It was possible only for such a rare soul as Vivekananda to integrate these three stages, or levels of unity, and herein lies his most original contribution to human thought in general and to Vedanta in particular. We have already observed how through the quotation of a verse by Puspadanta in which the imagery of the river and the ocean has been used to illustrate this unity. Unfortunately, he did not live long enough to fulfil his life's one great ambition of writing on the three aspects of Vedanta, viz. dualism, qualified monism, and absolute monism, as steps or stages towards the same one unity. The world was thereby deprived of a priceless treasure which would have been his magnum opus as a gospel of unity.

However, he has touched upon this favourite theme of his in many of his later lectures. For instance, in his lecture on 'Steps of Hindu Philosophic Thought,' Vivekananda first speaks of 'dualism, pure and simple' and then moves to "the higher Vedantic philosophy' which comes next, by which he means qualified monism: 'The second holds that there are God, soul, and nature, and soul and nature form the body of God, and, therefore, these three form one unit.' He also very clearly sets forth the distinction between the' two steps thus: "In dualism, the universe is conceived as a large machine set going by God, while in qualified monism, it. is conceived as an organism, interpenetrated by the Divine Self." "The last are the non-dualists' and he presents their view so lucidly as is rarely to be found anywhere else. According to them, It is impossible to divide infinity and as a consequence, 'How can there be many? It is the one Infinity. So the non-dualists say: "This universe does not exist at all; it is all illusion. The whole of this universe, these Devas, gods, angels, and all the other beings born and dying, all this infinite number of souls coming up and going down, are all dreams. At the same time, the non-dualists remind us that a dream cannot be without a reality and that reality is the one Infinite Existence.' After elaborating this last view, he concludes: 'And this is called Advaita, the non-dualistic Vedanta philosophy.'

About this ultimate or final unity, the view of Vivekananda is in total agreement with that of Sankara, though he may not have agreed with Sankara in other matters and often criticized him. We have already observed how in his exposition of mayavada, he was so faithful to Sankara and had not a word of censure or criticism anywhere against this mayavada, in whose 'white flame', all else has been annihilated. Sri Aurobindo, who seems to have derived all his inspiration for synthesis of yoga, or integral idealism, from

Vivekananda, did not see eye to eye with Sankara in his exposition of mayavada and has, therefore, indulged in vehement criticism of Sankara in all his writings. By his wonderful genius and unique realization, Sri Aurobindo has undoubtedly made an original contribution in the field of philosophy through his concept of integralism. But in the process of achieving this synthesis, Sri Aurobindo seems to have dwarfed this highest ideal of unity and diluted the supreme concept of the Absolute as an un differentiated unity in his anxiety to preserve the existence of the world.

On the contrary, Vivekananda upholds this mayavada in order to achieve this highest unity because he knows that 'there is absolutely no other explanation of Advaitavada except *Mayavada*. He is also aware that "in reality there is one, but in maya it is appearing as many and 'when one goes beyond this maya, then only the Oneness is realised.... By his total acceptance of Sankara's mayavada and strict adherence to it, he wants to emphasize that this unity or oneness of all existence is always there as an eternal fact and only its apprehension or awareness remains veiled due to some inexplicable phenomenon called maya. That is why, he reminded his audience at the Parliament of Religions that already they are the 'Children of God, the sharers of immortal bliss, holy and perfect beings' and the only thing they have to do is to 'shake off the delusion.'

There is thus no becoming here but only an awakening to an an eternal fact of being. Our being or existence is always one and it only appears as many due to our delusion. In all his lectures on Vedanta, he again and again affirms that 'the reality of all these is the Absolute; through maya it is seen to be diverse and reminds us that 'You are already that, only the intervention of a non-intelligent mind is hiding that knowledge. Therefore, according to him, 'he who knows the Real sees in *maya* not illusion but reality,' On the contrary, 'He who knows not the Real sees in *maya* illusion and thinks it real.' This is exactly the view of Sankara, who does not deny the reality of worldly actions and modifications but only points out that they are real or true only when looked upon from the standpoint of the Real. Divorced from that Real if they are cognized as distinct or separate, they are all unreal or false.

Thus the unity as the keynote of Vivekananda Chicago addresses from the beginning to the end, is a fundamental fact, the truth or reality of which is ever self-evident or established in itself. As such, reality or truth cannot have any degrees in itself as it is entirely one undivided absolute existence beyond all relativity. But the apprehension or cognition of this reality or unity has certain degrees or stages, depending on the refinement of the mind that apprehends it. When he speaks of 'man travelling from lower to higher truth,' he is simply referring to the degrees of awareness of this one indivisible truth and not to any degrees in the reality or truth itself.

Vivekananda's distinct contribution is Vedanta. It is not that he created Vedanta, he recreated it. Vedanta had always been known, but not known in the form he preached it. It had been known only among a certain class of scholars who enjoyed studying and debating its propositions. That it had or could have any bearing on life never seemed to occur to those scholars. They pursued their daily life as if Vedanta meant nothing to them. They were caste-ridden, and an individual was important or not important, depending upon the caste he belonged to. Religion was rituals, which they performed with great care, never questioning what purpose they served. They were intelligent, also scholarly, but they were more concerned with the crust than with the essence. They turned away from the freedom Vedanta offered; they preferred to stay in the sects. Vivekananda had preached Vedanta in the West—perhaps he was the first to do so. He had watched with joy the response it evoked. The people in the West had grown sick of the narrow creeds their church leaders preached. The people in India were equally sick of the stereotyped belief and practices handed down to them as religion. Vedanta brought them fresh air for which they were gasping. It rejuvenated them, giving them a new view of life.

We may therefore conclude that Vivekananda had seized the truth .of this unity in its entirety by strictly following and adhering to the line of Advaita Vedanta. By ascending to the rare and topmost height of utter and absolute unity, he could 'place the different, levels of relative unity in their proper places and integrate them. In him, therefore, we find the fulfilment of that transcendent realization of the truth of all truths, of which Advaita Vedanta has been the custodian through all ages and which has been so much misunderstood and misinterpreted due to the lack of comprehension of its essential nature. This truth of all truths is the ultimate secret of the Upanisads, the hidden name which denotes the supreme reality, or Brahman. It does not abrogate the truth of all existence and never cancels, denies, or annuls the reality of the world and the individual. It only affirms that they are all apparently real while Brahman is truly real.

Vivekananda was well aware that all people cannot take up this Advaita philosophy; it is hard. He also explained why it is so hard: 'First of all, it is very hard to understand it intellectually. It requires the sharpest of intellects, a bold understanding. Secondly, it does not suit the vast majority of people. Therefore, he delineated the three steps to reach this highest unity of absolute Advaita, but he never compromised with any other view to accommodate the truth of worldly existence by lowering down the supreme truth of all truths. Vivekananda was thus not a neo-Vedantist, preaching a Vedanta of his own as distinct from the traditional Advaita Vedanta of Sankara, but a total and complete Vedantist whose three eyes were wide open. Sankara Bharati, an illumined soul and a profound thinker and interpreter of the Advaita school in modern times, brings out the uniqueness of the vision of the true Vedantist. It notes that there are some in whom the inner vision alone is predominant, in others both the outer and the inner and again, in some others the divine vision dominates but the Vedantists have all the three eyes wide open because they plunge in that placid and luminous lake, of Advaita or non-duality without ignoring or disregarding the inner and outer existences of mind and matter.

This is the true, wide vision of unity which Swami Vivekananda wanted to present to the world in his Chicago addresses where there is no need to shut or turn one's eyes away from anything because everywhere there is the same One manifesting itself in so many forms and under so many garbs and coverings. The only thing necessary is to remove the veil of delusion, or maya, for which he gave a fervent call to all mankind. He knew that the doctrine of maya is not meant to teach the futility of all things but it has its utility in affirming that the unity is always there unimpaired, the multiplicity being only apparent and ephemeral, created by the unity itself for its own play. In his poem, 'A Song I Sing to Thee,' he unfolds the true nature and purpose of maya:

I play with My own maya,
My power Divine.
The One, 1 become the many, to behold
My own form.

The dawning of this sense of unity is the only panacea for all the ills of the world, which is today torn by division, discord, and dissension. Vivekananda presented Vedanta in a simple and lucid language, devoid of technicalities, yet; in a form entirely rational and, above all, springing from the depths of his personal realization. His luminous personality speaks through every word of his. As he himself put it: The abstract Advaita must become living—poetic—in everyday life; out of the hopelessly intricate mythology must come concrete moral forms; and out of bewildering Yogism must come the most scientific and practical psychology. One of the most attractive features of his teachings is that they are so universal in their content, applicable to men and women of whatever religion they may belong to, following whatever.

In her introduction to the Complete Works of Swami Vivekananda, Sister Nivedita says:

"For ages to come, the Hindu man who .would verify, the Hindu mother who would teach her, children, what was the faith of their ancestors will turn to the pages of these books for assurance and light long after, the English language has disappeared from India, the gift that has here been' made, through that language, to the world, will remain and bear its fruit in East and West alike.... The truths he preaches would have been as true, had he never been born. Nay more, they would have been equally authentic. The difference would have lain in their difficulty of access, in their want of modern clearness and incisiveness of statement, and in their loss of mutual coherence and unity. Had he not lived, texts that today will be the bread of life to thousands might have remained the obscure disputes of scholars. He taught with authority, and not as one of the Pundits. For he himself had plunged to the depths of the realization which he preached, and he came back, like Ramanuja, only to tell its secrets to the pariah, the outcast, and the foreigner."

The religious climate in the West is already undergoing a slow change. There is less claim of a monopoly of truth or of the superiority of one religion over another. Vivekananda's teachings may have a significant bearing on this change.

In his concluding address at the Parliament in Chicago, Vivekananda declared :

It (the Parliament of Religions) has proved to the world that holiness, purity and charity are not the exclusive possessions of any church in the world, and that every system has produced men and women of the most exalted character ... upon the banner of every religion will soon be written, in spite of resistance: 'Help and not Fight,' 'Assimilation and not Destruction,' 'Harmony and ' Peace and not Dissension.'

Swami Vivekananda's Chicago address was a proclamation of India's perennial philosophy, but what motivated it was the response of a modern Indian to the challenge of the Wes In one way it can be interpreted simply as the legacy of Sri Ramakrishna, the Great Master. In another, it could be seen as the reinterpretation of this legacy by his most percipient and articulate disciple to suit the needs of the new age. Often described as the counterattack of the East, it actually implied a warm invitation to the West to provide the money and the technology for modernising India in exchange for her spiritual values that the West needed so much to cure herself of the canker of materialism. Vivekananda's sojourn in the West was a two-way mission. The bridge he was to build would help both to meet and mingle and learn from each other:

On 11 September, 1893, the very first day of the Parliament of Religions, he thanked the august assembly 'in the name of the most ancient order of monks in the world' and 'in the name of the mother of religions'. The Parliament was being held to discover a way out of the murky atmosphere of sectarianism, bigotry and fanaticism, which 'filled the earth with violence, drenched it often with human blood, destroyed civilisation and sent whole nations to despair'. While America was breaking down 'barriers of this little world of ours', India could help with her message of universal toleration, nay, universal acceptance. This message was contained in her great scripture —the Vedanta, and it had been recently propounded, in simple folk language, by Sri Ramakrishna. Through his various religious experiments and experiences, Sri Ramakrishna had become a one-man Parliament of Religions himself.

Chicago had been anticipated at Dakshineswar. Vivekananda had seen it with his own eyes, heard it with his own ears and felt it with all his heart as early as 1881, when, as Naren Datta, still in the midst of a university education, he had been steeped in Mil!, Spencer, Huxley and Comte. Mill created in him disbelief in an omnipotent and benevolent creator. Hume asserted that nothing could be discovered by reasoning on metaphysical objects, self was only a collection of fleeting perceptions and even cause and effect were not connected by logical necessity. Comte's religion of humanity failed to explain the problem of evil in man and nature. Darwin left creation to evolve without a creator.

Naren was introduced to Shelly's impersonal world-love, pure monism, Hegel's dialectic of the absolute idea and the French revolutionary thought. Nothing gave him peace, neither pure reason nor platonic transcendentalism. The Brahmo Samaj failed to quench his emotional thirst for a mystic experience. In this dark night of the soul Sri Ramakrishna came to him like an angel and spoke with the voice of a mother. He was 'a phenomenon', who dared to assert that he had seen God, that religion might be sensed in an infinitely more intense manner than the world of matter. The rustic priest, who was no prince like Rama, or superman like Krisna, or intellectual like the Buddha, could expound the highest secrets of the Vedanta in a homespun and humorous prose. How could he? Why did he experiment with all modes of sadhana, when any one was good enough for saints? Why, again, after repeated samadhi (direct realisation), would he choose to pass his days near a crowded city like Calcutta, and enjoy teaching worldly men to renounce their craze for kama and kanchnnu (lust and greed), to fill their emptiness with love of God? He was no "dry sannyasin' either, with a glum face and an all-knowing air. He communed with God through songs, dance and ecstasy and held his disciples together with limitless affection but in iron control. Above all shone his daily life, 'broad as the sky, deep as the ocean, strong as adamant, pure as crystal.' He was the embodiment' of all systems, and yet their rigour was mellowed by a compassion for his fellow-men whom he considered to be inherently divine but unable to realise their divinity due to the veil of *maya* or *avidya*. For six long years Naren fought the Master, trying to keep his individualist freedom of judgement. Little by little, however, his resistance crumbled—at a song, a touch, an ecstasy and an overwhelming love till he found peace in surrender.

A great man may have disappeared from our sight, but history records the story of his life his; struggles and achievements, his message, and his influence on humanity. Vivekananda lived only 39 years, but referring to mankind, he said, 'I have given them enough for fifteen hundred years.' Sri Ramakrishna knew that Vivekananda would carry the message of eternal religion, so he transferred his power to him and wrote on a piece of paper, "Narendra (Vivekananda) will teach others. Later on, when the disciples were going through hardships at the Baranagore Math, Vivekananda told his brother monks, 'You will see, our names will be recorded in history."

In 1976, during the bicentennial celebration of American Independence, the : Smithsonian Institute of Washington, D. C. arranged an exhibition depicting 31 foreigners who had contributed to American culture, heritage, and history: Swami Vivekananda was the only Indian in that exhibition. The best thing about Vivekananda was that he did not try to build a religion or a sect around Sri Ramakrishna.

You keep separate (he wrote his brother disciple on 14 April 1896) from such attempts. Neither encourage nor discourage. The masses will always have the person; the higher ones, the principle. We want both. But principles are universal, not persons. Therefore stick to the principles he taught, and let people think whatever they like of his person.

Secondly, those principles, based on Advaita, were couched in obscure terminology and made even more confusing by commentaries written'from conflicting philosophical standpoints. The original ecstasy of direct realisation was gone when Sankara took it to the hills and forests. Following up hints from Ramakrishna, more illuminating than any commentary, Vivekananda himself made an in-depth study of the Vedanta. It is interesting to note the metamorphosis the Vedanta had gone through between the time Rammohun published his Vedanta grantha in 1815 and Vivekananda gave his discourses in the West. Vivekananda's lucid expositions overwhelmed even the great German Orientalist, Deussen. Who wrote the Vivekananda made the abstract "Vedanta poetic, living, a matter for strengthening everyday life.

There is no doubt of his impact on the extremists and the revolutionaries, though he himself kept aloof from politics and advised Nivedita to do the same. The monks of his Mission heard another call—*atmano moksanham jagaddhitaya ca*—Not for your salvation only but for the good of al! mankind. The monks were given another kind of battle to fight. 'Kill therefore with the sword of wisdom the doubt born of ignorance that lies in thy heart. Be one in self-harmony, in yoga, and arise, great warrior, arise.' Work for the good of mankind would help to burn the bondage of work itself.

His interpretations of Hindu texts (the Vedanta and the Gita) do not run counter even to the findings of very modern science, viz., quantum mechanics, relativity and the chaos theory. Indian philosophy holds that though thought takes place in time, vision can transcend it. Vision is bound up with a space of a higher dimension, and is therefore timeless. As Vivekananda said, 'Time, space, and causation are like the glass through which the absolute is seen timeless. As Vivekananda said, 'Time, space, and causation are like the glass through which the Absolute, is seen ... In the Absolute there is neither time, space, nor causation.' The reality of the atomic physicist, like the reality of the Eastern mystic, transcends the nartrow framework of causality and apposite concepts. De Broglie, be both particle and wave at the same time. Bohr said this in his 'principle of complementarily', which proposed that whether light or electrons were waves or moving particles depended entirely on the specific properties which were being investigated; the subject under study had dual characteristics, and whether it conformed to those we know as wavelike properties or to those we know as particles depended solely on how we studied it. Heisenberg further made the suggestion that a satisfactory picture of the physical world consisted in a description not of events but of their probabilities. This was his famous 'uncertainty principle'.

Quantum physics now appeared to be governed by statistical laws and not by any causal mechanisms—hidden or otherwise. The Objective world, the immutable laws independent of observers, were all gone. In Max Born's words, 'As in life, the audience and workers were the same persons, the experimentalist designed the apparatus which determined the essential features of the observations.' The objectively existing situation of classical physics has ceased to exist.

But are not force and matter, particles and waves, motion and rest, existence and non-existence, all dualities, being transcended in modern physics to affirm the Vedantic concept of Advaita? Do not indeterminacy, statistics of probabilities, the observations being controlled by the observer indicate the play of maya? In fact, Oppenheimers words seem to echo the world of the Upanisads describing Brahman;

It moves. It moves not.
It is far, and It is near.
It is within all this
And It is outside of all this.

The response was deafening applause. It appeared that the whole audience had been patiently awaiting this message of religious harmony. A Jewish intellectual remarked to the present writer, years later, that after hearing Vivekananda he realized for the first time that his own religion, Judaism, was true, and that the Swami had addressed his words on behalf of not only his religion, but all religions of the world. Whereas every one of the other delegates had spoken for his own ideal or his own sect, the Swami had spoken about God, who, as the ultimate goal of all faiths, is their inmost essence. And he had learnt that truth at the feet of Sri Ramakrishna, who had taught incessantly, from his direct experience, that all religions are but so many paths to reach the same goal. The Swami gave utterance to the yearning of the modern world to break down the barriers of caste, colour, and creed and to fuse all people into one humanity.

Not a word of condemnation for any faith, however crude or irrational, fell from his lips. He did not believe that this religion or that religion was true in this or that respect; to him all religions were equally effective paths to lead their respective devotees, with diverse tastes and temperaments, to the same goal of perfection. Years before, young Narendra had condemned before his Master, in his neophyte zeal, a questionable sect that indulged in immoral practices in the name of religion, and Ramakrishna had mildly rebuked him, saying: 'Why should you criticize those people? Their way, too, ultimately leads to God. There are many doors to enter a mansion. The scavenger comes in by the back door. You need not use it.'

How prophetic were the master's words that his Naren would one day shake the world! Mrs. S.K. Blodgett, who later became the Swami's hostess in Los Angeles, said about her impressions of the Parliament: 'I was at the Parliament of Religions in Chicago in 1893. When that young man got up and said, "Sisters and Brothers of America," seven thousand people rose to their feet as a tribute to something they knew not what. When it was over I saw scores of women walking over the benches to get near him, and I said to my self, "Well, my lad, if you can resist that onslaught you are indeed a God!"'

How did America impress Swami Vivekananda during his second visit to the West? What impressions did he carry to India of the state of things in the New World? During his first visit he had been enthusiastic about almost everything he saw — the power, the organization, the material prosperity, the democracy, and the spirit of freedom and justice. But now he was greatly disillusioned. In America's enormous combinations and ferocious struggle for supremacy he discovered the power of Mammon. He saw that the commercial spirit was composed, for the most part, of greed, selfishness, and a struggle for privilege and power. He was disgusted with the ruthlessness of wealthy business men, swallowing up the small tradespeople by means of large combinations. That was indeed tyranny. He could admire an organization; 'but what beauty is there among a pack of wolves?' he said to a disciple. He also noticed, in all their nakedness, the social vices and the arrogance of race, religion, and colour. America, he confided to Miss MacLeod, would not be the instrument to harmonize East and West. During his trip through Eastern Europe, from Paris to Constantinople, he smelt war. He felt the stench of it rising on all sides. 'Europe,' he remarked, 'is a vast military camp.' But the tragedy of the West had not been altogether unperceived by him even during his first visit. As early as 1895 he said to Sister Christine: 'Europe is on the edge of a volcano. If the fire is not extinguished by a flood of spirituality, it will erupt.'

One cannot but be amazed at the Swami's prophetic intuition as expressed through the following remarks made to Christine in 1896: 'The next upheaval will come from Russia or China. I cannot see clearly which, but it will be either the one or the other.' He further said: 'The world is in the third epoch, under the domination of the *vaisya*. The fourth epoch will be under that of the *sudra*.'

But his path was not always strewn with rose petals. Vivekananda was an outspoken man. Whenever he found in American society signs of brutality, inhumanity, pettiness, arrogance, and ignorance concerning cultures other than its own, he mercilessly criticized them. Often small-minded people asked him irritating questions about India, based upon malicious and erroneous reports, and he fell upon them like athunderbolt. 'But woe to the man,' wrote the Iowa State Register, 'who undertook to combat the monk on his own ground, and that was where they all tried it who tried it at all. His replies came like flashes of lightning and the venturesome questioner was sure to be impaled on the Indian's shining intellectual lance....Vivekananda and his cause found a place in the hearts of all true Christians.' Many Christian ministers became his warm friends and invited him to speak in their churches.

Swami Vivekananda was especially bitter about false Christianity and the religious hypocrisy of many Christian leaders. In a lecture given in Detroit he came out in one of his angriest moods, and declared in the course of his speech:

You train and educate and clothe and pay men to do what? — to come over to my country and curse and abuse all my forefathers, my religion, my everything. They walk near a temple and say, 'You idolaters, you will go to hell.' But the Hindu is mild; he smiles and passes on, saying, 'Let the fools talk.' And then you who train men to abuse and criticize, if I just touch you with the least bit of criticism, but with the kindest purpose, you shrink and cry: 'Do not touch us! We are Americans; we criticize, curse, and abuse all the heathens of the world, but do not touch us, we are sensitive plants.' And whenever you missionaries criticize us, let them remember this: If all India stands up and takes all the mud that lies at the bottom of the Indian Ocean and throws it up against the Western countries, it will not be doing an infinitesimal part of what you are doing to us.

Continuing, the Swami said that the military conquests of the Western nations and the activities of the Christian missionaries, strangely enough, often proceeded side by side. Most people were converted for worldly reasons. But the Swami warned:

Such things tumble down; they are built upon sand; they cannot remain long. Everything that has selfishness for its basis, competition for its right hand, and enjoyment as its goal, must die sooner or later. If you want to live, go back to Christ. You are not Christians. No, as a nation you are not. Go back to Christ. Go back to him who had nowhere to lay his head. Yours is a religion preached in the name of luxury. What an irony of fate! Reverse this if you want to live; reverse this. You cannot serve God and Mammon at the same time. All this prosperity — all this from Christ? Christ would have denied all such heresies. If you can join these two, this wonderful prosperity with the ideal of Christ, it is well; but if you cannot, better go back to him and give up these vain pursuits. Better be ready to live in rags with Christ than to live in palaces without him.

On one occasion he was asked to speak in Boston on Ramakrishna, a subject dear to his heart. When he looked at the audience — the artificial and worldly crowd of people — and contrasted it with his Master's purity and renunciation, he practically dropped the subject and mercilessly inveighed against the materialistic culture of the West. The audience was resentful and many left the meeting in an angry mood. But Vivekananda, too, had his lesson. On returning home he recalled what he had said, and wept. His Master had never uttered a word of condemnation against anybody, even the most wicked person; yet he, while talking about Ramakrishna, had criticized these good-hearted people who were eager to learn about the Master. He felt that he was too unworthy of Sri Ramakrishna to discuss him or even to write about him.

Swami Vivekananda's outspoken words aroused the bitter enmity of a large section of the Christian missionaries and their American patrons, and also of Christian fanatics. Filled with rancour and hatred, these began to vilify him both openly and in private. They tried to injure his reputation by writing false stories traducing his character. Some of the Indian delegates to the Parliament, jealous of his popularity and fame, joined in the vilification. Missionaries working in India and some of the Hindu organizations started an infamous campaign against his work. The Theosophists were particularly vindictive. They declared that he was violating the laws of monastic life in America by eating forbidden food and breaking caste laws.

His friends and disciples in India were frightened and sent him cuttings from Indian papers containing these malicious reports. One article stated that one of his American hostesses had had to dismiss a servant girl on account of his presence in the house. But the lady published a vehement denial and said that he was an honoured guest in her home and would always be treated with affection and respect. Vivekananda wrote to his timorous devotees in India concerning a particular American paper that had criticized him, telling them that it was generally known in America as the 'blue-nosed Presbyterian paper', that no educated American took it seriously, and that, following the well-known Yankee trick, it had tried to gain notoriety by attacking a man lionized by society. He assured them that the American people as a whole, and many enlightened Christian clergymen, were among his admiring friends, and he asked them not to send him any more of such newspaper trash—with articles from his vilifiers. He told them, furthermore, that he had never deviated from the two basic vows of the monastic life, namely, chastity and poverty, and that as regards other things, he was trying to adjust himself to the customs of the people among whom he lived.

To the accusation from some orthodox Hindus that he was eating forbidden food at the table of infidels, he retorted:

"Do you mean to say I am born to live and die as one of those caste-ridden, superstitious, merciless, hypocritical, atheistic cowards that you only find among the educated Hindus? I hate cowardice. I will have nothing to do with cowards. I belong to the world as much as to India, no humbug about that. What country has a special claim on me? Am I a nation's slave? ...I see a greater power than man or God or Devil at my back. I require nobody's help. I have been all my life helping others."

To another Indian devotee he wrote in similar vein:

"I am surprised that you take the missionaries' nonsense so seriously....If the people of India want me to keep strictly to my Hindu diet, please tell them to send me a cook and money enough to keep him....On the other hand, if the missionaries tell you that I have ever broken the two great vows of the sannyasin — chastity and poverty — tell them that they are big liars. As for me, mind you, I stand at nobody's dictation, and no chauvinism about me....I hate cowardice; I will have nothing to do with cowards or political nonsense. I do not believe in any politics. God and truth are the only politics in the world; everything else is trash."

Swami Vivekananda remained unperturbed by opposition. His lectures, intensely religious and philosophical, were attended everywhere by eminent people. Many came to him for private instruction. His aim was to preach the eternal truths of religion and to help sincere people in moulding their spiritual life. Very soon his dauntless spirit, innate purity, lofty idealism, spiritual personality, and spotless character attracted to him a band of sincere and loyal American disciples, whom he began to train as future Vedanta workers in America.

It must be said to the credit of America that she was not altogether unprepared to receive the message of Vivekananda. Certain spiritual ideas, which were congenial for the reception of the Vedantic ideals presented by him, had already begun to ferment underneath the robust, picturesque, gay, and dynamic surface of American life. Freedom, equality, and justice had always been the cherished treasures of American hearts. To these principles, which the Americans applied in politics and society for the material and ethical welfare of men, Swami Vivekananda gave a spiritual basis and interpretation.

Religion had played an important part from the very beginning of American Colonial history. The pilgrims who crossed the Atlantic in the 'Mayflower' and landed on the barren cost of Cape Cod in November 1620, were English people who had first left England and gone to Holland for freedom of worship. Later they were joined by other dissenters who could not submit to the restrictions placed upon their religious beliefs by the English rulers of the time. These were the forbears of the sturdy, religiousminded New Englanders who, two centuries later, became the leaders of the intellectual and spiritual culture of America. Swami Vivekananda found among their descendants many of his loyal and enthusiastic followers.

Both the Holy Bible and the philosophy of Locke influenced the Bill of Rights and the American Constitution. Leaders imbued with the Christian ideal of the Fatherhood of God and the brotherhood of men, penned the second paragraph of the Declaration of Independence, which clearly set forth its political philosophy, namely, the equality of men before God, the state, and society. Thomas Paine, one of the high priests of the American Revolution, was an uncompromising foe of tyranny, and an upholder of human freedom. The same passion for equality, freedom, justice, enduring peace, and righteousness was later to permeate the utterances of the great Lincoln.

The political structure of America shows the sagacity and lofty idealism of her statesmen, who built up the country after the War of Independence. The original thirteen colonies, which had wrested freedom from England, gradually became the United States of America. The architects of the American Government might have created, following the imperialistic pattern of England, an American Empire, with the original thirteen states as a sort of mother country and the rest as her colonies. But instead, the newly acquired territories received complete equality of status. It may also be mentioned that, with the exception of the Mexican War of 1845, America has never started a war.

Within a hundred years of her gaining independence, America showed unprecedented material prosperity. The country's vast hidden wealth was tapped by European immigrants, who brought with them not only the flavour of an older civilization, but technical skill, indomitable courage, and the spirit of adventure. Scientists and technologists flooded the country with new inventions. Steamboats, a network of railroads, and various mechanical appliances aided in the creation of new wealth. Towns grew into cities. As big business concerns expanded, workmen and mechanics formed protective organizations. Ambition stirred everywhere, and men's very manners changed with the new haste and energy that swept them on.

Material prosperity was accompanied by a new awakening of men's minds and consciousness. Jails were converted into penitentiary systems, based upon humanitarian principles, and anti-slavery societies were inaugurated. During the five years between 1850 and 1855 were published some of the greatest books in American literature, hardly surpassed in imaginative vitality. Democracy was in full swing and it was the people's day everywhere. The crude frontier days were fast disappearing.

The Transcendentalist Movement, of which Emerson was the leader, with Thoreau and Alcott as his associates, brought spiritual India into the swift current of American life. The old and new continents had not been altogether strangers. Columbus had set out to find the short route to India, known far and wide for her fabulous wealth, and had stumbled upon America instead. The chests of tea of the Boston Tea Party, which set off the War of Independence, had come from India. Moreover, the victory of the English over the French in the eighteenth-century colonial wars in India contributed to the success of the American colonists in their struggle for freedom begun in 1775. And finally, Commodore Perry in 1853 made it possible for American merchant ships to trade with the Far East and thus visit Indian coastal towns on their long journeys.

The development of Emerson's innate idealism had been aided by the philosophy of Greece, the ethics of China, the poetry of the

Sufis, and the mysticism of India. Emerson, a keen student of the Bhagavad Gita, was familiar with the Upanishadic doctrines and published translations of religious and philosophical tracts from the Oriental languages. His beautiful poem 'Brahma' and his essay 'The Over-Soul' show clearly his indebtedness to Hindu spiritual thought. But Emerson's spirit, pre-eminently ethical and intellectual, could not grasp the highest flights of Hindu mysticism; it accepted only what was in harmony with a somewhat shallow optimism. Emerson's writings later influenced the New Thought movement and Mary Baker Eddy's Christian Science.

Thoreau, Emerson's neighbour for twenty-five years, read and discussed with him in great detail the Hindu religious classics. Thoreau wrote: 'I bathe my intellect in the stupendous and cosmogonal philosophy of the Upanishads and the Bhagavad Gita, in comparison with which our modern world and literature seem puny and trivial.' He wanted to write a joint Bible, gathering material from the Asiatic scriptures, and took for his motto Ex Oriente Lux. Alcott was genuine friend of Indian culture. He was instrumental in bringing out the American edition of Sir Edwin Arnold's *The Light of Asia*, and this made the life and teachings of Buddha accessible, for the first time, to American readers. The Transcendental Club, founded in Concord, near Boston, reached its height by 1840. The American Oriental Society was formed in 1842, with aims similar to those of the European Oriental societies.

Walt Whitman (1819-1892), a contemporary of the Concord philosophers, seems to have come very near to Vedantic idealism. There is no reliable evidence to show that Whitman was directly influenced by Hindu thought. He is reputed to have denied it himself. A great religious individualist, he was free from all church conventions and creeds. To him, religion consisted entirely of inner illumination, 'the secret silent ecstasy.' It is not known if he practised any definite religious disciplines; most probably he did not. Yet Swami Vivekananda once called Whitman 'the sannyasin of America.' *Leaves of Grass*, which Swami Vivekananda read, breathes the spirit of identity with all forms of life, and Whitman's 'Song of the Open Road' is full of the sentiments that were nearest to the heart of Vivekananda. Here, for example, are three stanzas: "spiritual heritage. In the midst of her struggle for existence she had preserved her spiritual sensitivity. But in the wake of the Civil War the desire to posses 'bigger and better things' cast its spell everywhere. Big utilities and corporations came into existence; the spiritual and romantic glow of the frontier days degenerated into the sordidness of competitive materialistic life, while the unceasing flow of crude immigrants from Europe made difficult the stabilization of American culture."

Emerson was disillusioned by the aftermath of the Civil War. He had hoped 'that in the peace after such a war, a great expansion would follow in the mind of the country, grand views in every direction — true freedom in politics, in religion, in social science, in thought. But the energy of the nation seems to have expended itself in the war.'

Walt Whitman was even more caustic. He wrote bitterly:

"Society in the States is cramped, crude, superstitious, and rotten.... Never was there, perhaps, more hollowness of heart than at present, and here in the United States. Genuine belief seems to have left us....; The great cities reek with respectable, as much as non-respectable, robbery and scoundrelism. In fashionable life, flippancy, tepid amours, weak infidelism, small aims, or no aims at all, only to kill time.... I say that our New World Democracy, however great a success in uplifting the masses out of their sloughs in materialistic development, and in a certain highly deceptive superficial popular intellectuality, is so far an almost complete failure in its social aspects. In vain do we march with unprecedented strides to empire so colossal, outvying the antique, beyond Alexander's, beyond the proudest sway of Rome. In vain we annexed Texas, California, Alaska, and reach north for Canada or south for Cuba. It is as if we were somehow being endowed with a vast and thoroughly appointed body, and left with little or no soul."

But the material prosperity or the triumph of science could not destroy the innate idealism of the American mind. It remained hidden like embers under ashes. Thoughtful Americans longed for a philosophy which, without going counter to the scientific method, would show the way to a larger vision of life, harmonizing the diverse claims of science, the humanities, and mystical experience. Now the time was ripe for the fulfilment of Thoreau's dream of the marriage of East and West, a real synthesis of science and religion. And to bring this about, no worthier person could have been found than Swami Vivekananda of India. This accounts for the spontaneous welcome received by this representative of Hinduism, who brought to America an ancient and yet dynamic philosophy of life.

Vivekananda and the Vedant

Once an individual attains this superconscious stage, the imperatives of the 'practical normative code are no longer applicable; he has been able to reach this state, in fact, by scrupulously following the moral and ethical code designated as desirable. As the Absolute, however, the individual is neither bound by social mores nor ordinary moral and ethical codes. The Bhagavadgita's recommendation of performing actions without a thought about their consequence, even if performing karma might mean fratricidal violence and socially sanctioned murder, is accepted without a challenge. Vivekananda's rhetorical claim of his brand of absolute oneness being the soul of Vedanta had to be grounded in arguments that were more substantial; they had to be intelligible as 'India's religion' and also fulfill the test of universality.

The primacy of the Vedanta for Vivekananda was not negotiable. It was also his notion of the Vedanta that had to take precedence over all other historically valid interpretations of the Upanishadic legacy that constituted the Vedanta corpus. The Vedantic seers had seen the truth. It was not a relative truth but one that had existed from time immemorial and one that would continue to exist in times to come. For Vivekananda, these were not merely truths that the sages had stumbled upon which they had not understood as was in the case of Prophet Muhammad. These truths were religious laws as well as the grand truths of spirituality. Their status as eternal truths and laws rested on the absence of their not having either a beginning or an end. More so, their supremacy was further enforced because of their independence from texts and prophets.

The sublimity of the law propounded by Ramayana or Bharata does not depend upon the truth of any personality like Rama or Krishna, and one can even hold that such personages never lived, and at the same time take these writings as high authorities in respect of the grand ideas which they place before mankind. Our philosophy does not depend upon any personality for its truth. Thus Krishna did not teach anything new or original to the world, nor does Ramayana profess anything which is not contain in the Scriptures. It is to be noted that Christianity cannot staid without Christ, Islam without Mohammed, and Buddhism without Buddha, but Hinduism stands independent of any man....

Calling it the impersonal nature of truth, Vivekananda goes on to argue that the 'Vedanta is the rationale of all religions,' and, therefore, for instance, Christians could never understand the New Testament without understanding the Vedanta. Understanding and acknowledging Vedanta was what made any religion worthy of name. Failing to do so rendered them to the status of mere superstitions. Establishing the superiority of the Vedanta and proclaiming its universal authenticity as the only true, eternal and tenable moral law was for Vivekananda only a first step. The debunking of the prophetic and revelatory traditions had to be taken to its logical conclusion.

Vivekananda no longer wanted prophets selected by society or by chance, Neither did he believe in prophets being anointed through acts of will or claims of superior intelligence. Instead, the truths of the Vedas and the Upanishads had to be realized and disseminated in society. This could be done only by training people to become prophets. He proposes that to become religious was the act of becoming a prophet and no one could be called religious till he or she turned into a prophet. To study religion was to train people into becoming prophets; he proposes that schools and colleges ought to be training grounds for manufacturing prophets. In his characteristic hyperbole, he proposes the universalizing and democratizing of the prophetic tradition: 'The whole universe must become prophets; and until a man becomes a prophet, religion is a mockery and a by-word unto him. We must see religion, feel it, realise it in a thousand times more intense.

For an unsuspecting moment, it might seem that Vivekananda seems to be proposing a return to the mystic intensity of Ramakrishna's faith in proposing a religion that is based on seeing, feeling and realizing God. But this is not remotely the case. For him, religion is a scientifically demonstrable entity. To be religious and to know religion is to use one's reason. Those who believe through non-rational ways are worthy of being compared to beasts. Mystical flights, ecstatic love, talking to Kali and hearing her talk back was just an individual attribute of being peculiar and having this special gift by chance. In the modern world, Vivekananda concludes, no one ought to believe in anything that is left to chance and not mediated through modern scientific rationality. The peculiar and the particular were characteristic features of Dualism: they ignored the principle. Religion for Vivekananda was destruction of peculiarity.

Having chipped away at the claims of the Dualists as well as those following the prophetic-revelatory traditions, Vivekananda introduces into the argument a note that seems to contradict all that he seems to have argued till this moment. It is, in fact, a celebration of a plurality of stints, religions scriptures and prophets in the world. But this plurality on close examination is welcome only in the order to apply to it the scientific method. At no point does Vivekananda ask questions regarding the correctness or viability of the scientific method, Nor does his entrenched belief in it go beyond demonstrable verification of things through what he called reasoning, which for him consisted of starting from the particular and moving towards a principle. The sense in which he uses reason is, however, purely instrumental; it helps him debunk everything else other than the Vedanta and his interpretation of Advaita Vedanta. He is conscious that he could argue for seeming plurality in the world of religious symbols and forms while simultaneously reducing these to insignificance by arguing in favour of the Vedantic idea of a unity that permeates and circumscribes the universe: Take for instance this passage: 'The Mohammedans want to have the whole world Mohammedan; the Christians, Christian; the Buddhist; Buddhist; but the Vedanta says: "Let each person in the world be separates if you will; the one principles the unity will be behind"

It is only when humans have name, form and histories that the question of any moral and ethical engagement with each other arises. Vivekananda pushes the idea of oneness as the core of Vedanta in order to forestall a debate regarding ethical questions; after all, the abstraction called the immortal soul as contrasted to the perishable body in the Bhagavadgita was a response to Arjuna's ethical dilemma. Vivekananda takes the but is just a single continuum There is no diversity or plurality but everything is myself. If I am of the tree one tree dies, the idea of the tree continues because every tree is part. of the whole called universe. Therefore, there is one mind, one body, one soul that really exist. Universal oneness and not central thought conveyed by the Upanishads. Having stated his view of the Vedanta, Vivekananda gives short shrift to the question of human action and its consequences: 'I am the same as any other man, as any animal - good, bad, anything.' Having recommended transformation of all humans into prophets, he now wants every living being metamorphosed into the divine: 'You are all Gods. One God is not sufficient. You are all Gods, says the Vedanta.' While ethical dilemmas are hardly the stuff of prophets and gods, the question of action and its consequences is also neatly relegated to the recesses of the inner realm, The Vedanta, after all, teaches that to discover truth but is within oneself.

The God of the Vedanta, Vivekananda emphasizes, is an impersonal principle and not a person. There is no Personal God, but 'You and I, the cat, rat, devil, and ghost, all these are Its persons — all are Personal Gods'. The human body is the temple inside which resides this 'Lord of souls and the King of kings.' The Hindus, laments Vivekananda, are wedded to the idea of God as the king of the earth rather than the king of souls. Vedanta reason cannot flourish in India. The concept of all living beings as prophets and gods he elaborates, is a democratic idea that can flourish only in America. Hindus, on the other hand, were busy building temples and seeking the truth elsewhere.

"We do not see that, so we make stone images of Him and build temples over them. Vedanta has been in India always but India is full of these temples but also caves containing carved images. 'The fool, dwelling on the bank of the Ganga, digs a well for water!' Such are we! Living in the midst of God - we must go and make images. We project Him in the form of the image, while all the time He exists in the temple of our body. We are lunatics, and this is the great delusion."

Vivekananda takes recourse here to a reading of the Mahabharata and the character of Krishna in it. The question of action and its consequences is dexterously sidestepped: 'Krishna shows the way how to do this, — by being non-attached: do everything but do not get identified with anything. You are the soul, the pure, the free, all the time; you are the Witness. Our misery comes, not from work, but by getting attached to something. The Hindus, he explains, had discovered the concept of the Atman or the universal soul. It was this discovery that was the basis of ethics for the Hindus.

Though all religions have taught ethical precepts, such as, 'Do not kill, do not injure; love thy neighbour as yourself,' etc., yet none of these has given the reason. Why should I not injure my neighbour? To this question there was no satisfactory or conclusive answer forthcoming, until it was evolved by the metaphysical speculations of the Hindus who could not rest satisfied with mere dogmas.

Here Vivekananda dismisses Christian ethics as dogma. Next, the question of injuring one's neighbour, assuming that the injury is physical1 is resolved through the metaphysical speculations as they evolved among the Hindus.

For the Hindus this *Atman* is absolute and all-pervading, therefore infinite. There cannot be two infinities, for they would limit each other and would also become finite. Also each individual soul is a part and parcel of that Universal Soul, which is infinite. Therefore in injuring his neighbours the individual actually injures himself. This is the basic metaphysical truth underlying all ethical codes.

Vivekananda's refusal to grant any legitimacy to the world of appearances, and the body as one such tangible object among many, is what a perceptive modern commentator has called 'the refusal of the body as a site of any experience, any tragedy, any remorse, and above all, any politics. The emphasis, as we have seen on the superconscious state was to transcend the body, which could be a site of contestation, argument, and, religions the superconscious state is identical. Hindus, Christians, Mohammedans, Buddhists, and even those of no creed, all have the very same experience when they transcend the body. Injury to the neighbour is, then, not a real injury, but only something that is part of metaphysical speculation. All that it serves is the claim that the truth of the universal Atman enables the Hindus to understand the religious truth of all religions, from the lowest to the highest.

In establishing the sovereign authority of Vedanta, Vivekananda posits three stages in the spiritual growth of every individual. These three stages correspond to the evolution of all other faiths. The Vedanta, he argues, contains these these three stages. It is a process of evolution, Dualism Vishishtadvaita or qualified monism and Advaita or absolute monism. Vedanta had to be applied according to needs, locale and nationality, but it was also important to remember that there was no difference, whatsoever, between the idea of religion and Vedanta. The only religion in the universe was Vedanta and Vedanta was the only religion worthy of the name. In a passage that presumptuous, but also historically and philosophically inaccurate, Vivekananda dismisses Jainism and Buddhism as mere clones of Vedanta.

Much of Vivekananda's mystique rests on his perceived liberality with respect to other faiths. Vivekananda notes that religions might differ in word, ritual, doctrine and emphasis but all faiths are ultimately paths to the same God. In many of his public speeches explicitly seeks to convey that his message was one of peace and a united religion and not of antagonism. Having studied comparative religions, he finds all faiths to have had the same foundations as his own faith. There were differences, only in the realm of the non-essential elements within faiths. Going a step further, he wants a plurality of faiths in the world to suit a variety of contexts. In a world that is infected constantly with religious strife and the violence such words and thoughts can be seductively reassuring. Vivekananda is talking about the desirability of different faiths:

"I dot deprecate the existence of sects in the world. There would be Gods twenty million or more, for the more there are, there will be a greater field for selection. What I do object trying to fit one religion to every case. Though all religions are essentially the same, they must have the varieties of form produced by dissimilar circumstances among different nations."

This sounds perfectly reasonable. He calls them 'sects' and religions. But the overall tone and tenor is one of remarkable pluralism. Now read the last line of the quote: 'We must each have our own individual religion, individual so far as the externals of it go.' The plurality of faiths, then, is limited to the externals. Remove the externals and what wil emerge is a universal faith. The Vedantic ideal of Oneness and the Universal Soul would ultimately prevail.

When a plea for a single universal faith is announced, Vivekananda abandons even the 'We must each have our own individual religion' rhetoric with alacrity: 'There never was my religion or yours, my national religion or your national religion; there never existed many religions, there is only the one, One Infinite Religion existed all through eternity and will ever exist, and this Religion is expressing itself in various countries, in various ways.' What, then, about the argument that promised to accommodate even twenty million or more sects in the world. It ends with the following sentence: "Therefore we must respect all religions and we must try to accept them all as far as we can. The respect for other religions was, therefore, conditional. It depended on so far as the externals of it go' and 'as far as we can'.

The refrain of not judging others and not being contemptuous towards other faiths occurs regularly within the Vivekananda corpus. Vivekananda argues that Nature always represents unity in variety, that '... through all these variations of the phenomenal runs the Infinite, the Unchangeable, the Absolute Unity'. What was true of Nature is also true for humans: '... the microcosm is but a miniature repetition of the macrocosm.' This is the reason, affirms Vivekananda, why no man's faith ought to be disturbed. While this too sounds utterly reasonable, it also is part of the same trajectory where other faiths are limited and inadequate.

Having pronounced his version of the Vedanta as the only religion in the world, Vivekananda wants every 'narrow, limited, fighting ideas of religion' to be eliminated. Sects, tribes and nations have their own ideas of religion and of God and this caused them to quarrel over claims to superiority. Such ideas of a Personal God were the scourge brought about by Dualism, which was another name for superstition. To move the future, this deadweight of the past had to be abandoned. The influence of German philosophy is starkly visible here, as is in the rest of his philosophical edifice. There is a marked influence of nineteenth-century German philosophical tradition on—the structure as well as content of his thought Hence, echoing Hegel, but more so Schopenhauer's principle of the sufficient reason of becoming, Vivekananda proceeds to define a religion that must leave behind all specificity.

Religion is not in doctrines, in dogmas, nor in intellectual argumentation; it is being and becoming; it is realisation. We hear so many talking about God and the soul, and all the mysteries of the universe, but if you take them one by one, and ask them, 'Have you realised God? Have you seen your Soul?' how many can say they have. And yet they are all fighting with one another!

Denying intellectual argumentation is ironical because during the years he had known his young pupil, Ramakrishna despaired of Vivekananda' s relentless discussion and debate on matters that, for the Master, could only he resolved through sincere longing and ecstatic love.

In order to explain his conception of universal religion, Vivekananda proposes yet another fourfold classification of humans. The man is the worker, the emotional man is the lover of the sublime and the beautiful, the mystic is one whose mind wants to analyse its own self, and finally the philosopher who weighs everything with the use of his intellect. Any religion attempting to claim universality ought to satisfy all these natures. Having arrived at this classification, Vivekananda claims that the plan of the universe exhibits unity in variety. What is this ultimate unity? It is God, he says. But the reality and existence of this ultimate unity do not mean that differences have to be obliterated. Neither does it mean that one be believed by all mankind; just as all face cannot be the same, so can there be no single set of doctrines that are shared by all humanity. Variation, he elaborates, is a natural necessity just as unity is equally a natural necessity. Translated in theological terms, this merely means that 'truth may be expressed in a hundred that each of these ways is true as far as it goes.' Put differently, while a thousand ways of expressing truth could be allowed, truth itself was what the Vedantic seers had propounded in the pages of the Upanishads. The religious pluralism attributed to Vivekananda is only in name: it is, in fact, the space he creates for others to acknowledge the truth designated by him as ultimate and universal. He argues that religion is Vedanta and Vedanta is religion. Hence, after arguing that there can be no single set of doctrines in the world, he offers a Vedanta-inspired definition of religion that neutralizes the concession granted to differences in favour of unity. The 'hundred thousand ways' of expressing truth are merely ways by which inadequate notions of religion attempt to approximate to the idea of the Vedantic truth.

In the primitive category of mythologies, he elaborates, the emphasis is usually on portraying their heroes as strong and gigantic. After this stage has been crossed, the higher mythologies have great moral men as their heroes, men whose actual strength lies in becoming moral and pure. 'The final stage in the development of religions is even lower than creation of myths. He calls it the invention of symbolism. This manifests in the form of rituals and ceremonials. It is an expression of the lowest minds where symbolism works as the 'kindergarten of religion'. Religions that rely excessively on myths and symbols discover that 'all that is left to them is but an empty shell, a contentless frame of words and sophistry'. In his relentless and systematic demolition of all other faiths and sects, Vivekananda now adds another element. He wonders if the methods of modern science can at all be applied to the science of religion, and, unsurprisingly, answers in the affirmative: 'Not only will it be made scientific — as scientific, at least, as any of the conclusions of physics or chemistry but will have greater strength, because physics or chemistry has no internal mandate to vouch for its truth, which religion has."

With the dazzling brilliance and perfection with which Vivekananda endows his version of the Vedic religion, clearly no other faith, sect, prophet or doctrine could remotely stand and be counted in comparison. The only sliver of hope now rested in seeking refuge in science. Having mentioned the possibility of applying methods of modern science to the science of religion, would Vivekananda relent and allow other faiths and sects to at least appropriate the methods of science and become scientific.

Characteristically, Vivekananda begins with an imaginary conversation between a Christian and a Muslim, both claiming the inherent superiority of their respective faiths. It quickly moves to the question of conversion in Islam, invoking well-known stereotypes as the use of force, and the killing of infidels if conversion was resisted. At the conclusion of this conversation, Vivekananda lays the blame for this conflict on the Christian and Islamic preoccupation with sacred books, a conflict that the sacred books themselves cannot resolve. He then moves to elaborate the operative part of his argument: there ought to be an outside agency, something higher than all conflict. He claims demands something that is higher than the claims of every set of individual inspirations, an external agency that would arbiter between 'inspiration and inspiration'. Scientific reason, he concludes, was to be that external agency to arbiter between rival claims made by different faiths. Scientific reason has this edge because—firstly, 'the particular is explained by the general, the general by the more general, until we come to the universal'. But this was not enough. A second way of looking at the principles of reason was to seek the explanation of a thing from the inside and not the outside. In one word, what is meant by science', he explains, 'is that the explanations of things are in their own nature, and that no external beings or existences are the universe'. For Vivekananda, the idea that the explanation of everything comes from inside the thing itself tallies with the modern law of evolution as well, Evolution is nothing but a thing reproducing its own nature', that the effect is nothing but the cause in another form, that all the potentialities of the effect were present in the cause, that the whole of creation is but an evolution and not a creation'. Having established the two principles upon which scientific reason was to arbiter between claims of superiority put forth by various sects and religions, Vivekananda finds only one religion fulfilling the requirements of these principles.

Modern science, then, proves the Vedantic ideal of unity and oneness. The Brahman, the God of the Vedanta, is everything. There is nothing external to him. The only religion that can stand the test of modern reasoning is the Advaita Vedanta. All other faiths and sects entertain the idea of a Personal God, which is not a true generalization; the real absolute God is impersonal: 'The Self is the essence of this universe, the essence of all souls: He is the essence of your own life, nay, "Thou art That". You are one with this universe. He who says he is different from others, even by a hair's breadth, immediately becomes miserable.' The Impersonal God is, therefore, not a relative God.

Despite emphatic assertions about not disturbing anyone's faith, Vivekananda rarely saw anything worthwhile in other religions. He was skeptical of the Islamic idea of universal brotherhood, a concept whose operation he saw as one that was inextricably linked to the actual fact of being a Muslim. If an individual did not conform to Islam, not only would be remain outside the pale of universal brotherhood, but 'he will more likely have his throat cut'. The same conditions applied to being accepted as part of the Christian idea of universal brotherhood, and any deviation from the prescribed path could send an individual 'to that place where he will be eternally barbecued'. Islam and Christianity were, after all, primitive religions where there was first the idea of the universe created by a 'certain Being'. Only much later did they develop an equally primitive idea of the soul encased in the body which was not the same as the body but distinct from it. The Christians also entertained ideas and doctrines like the world coming into existence because Adam ate an apple for escaping the wrath of an angry God, or even founding the basis of faith on the death of one man, in this instance, Jesus Christ.

So Vivekananda, asserted there can be only one religion. The moment one names another religion with its own truth, it ceases to be a religion and becomes a sect. A religion has to be eternal, not the creation of a historically identifiable individual and unattached to any sacred book. Only the Vedas could ever satisfy all the three parameters.

More than damning other faiths and making them seem incomplete and inadequate, Vivekananda still had the task of fabricating 'our religion', 'India's religion', a faith that would happily resonate with the plan of establishing a European society in India. As religion, this entry had to permeate every aspect of human life, invade all arenas of thought, and, above all, be increasingly practical. Vivekananda wanted Vedanta to be 'intensely practical'. Any proposed model of religion had to have Rajas driving individuals and nations towards sattva and hence, be imbued with the kind of energy and activity exemplified by the ancient Greeks, the modern Europeans and the kshatriyas in India. For Vivekananda, the tenets of such a faith could only come from such people who were actively involved in the world, the ruling monarchs from among the kshatriyas, and not from those who gave up the world to retire into the forest to contemplate. Practical Vedanta, as Vivekananda chose to call this 'new' religion.

3

Deconstruction of Hinduism

Vivekananda represents the high tide of a Hindu revival, both in popular perception and serious national discourse. Expectedly, in the Vishwa Hindu Prishad's 1993 celebration of the centenary of the Chicago Congress of Religions where Vivekananda made his debut, they claimed the Patriot- Prophet as one of their own. Many scholars' study of the Hindu revival confirms this received perception, even if they recognises the complexity and nuances of Vivekananda's mission. The Hindu revival, a phenomenon I would prefer to as the Hindu reaction, was at best peripheral and for the most part antagonistic to Vivekananda concerns. His role and his personality were misinterpreted in his own time for identifiable reasons.

There are three distinct, though necessarily interrelated features in Vivekananda's religious concerns. First, his personal quest was defined early in life as a quest for ultimate realisation. He sought its fulfilment as a disciple of the saint Ramakrishna.

The second component of his religious concern was articulated during his first visit to the USA and Europe. It consisted in an exposition of the highest spiritual truths attained in the Indian religious tradition, but the ultimate truth underlying all religious beliefs. He also did his best to counter the mischievous propaganda which had long presented Hindu faith and practice as forms of extreme barbarism. The rapturous reception he received in India as a hero of militant Hinduism derives primarily from this two-fold agenda for his actions abroad. But the way his role abroad was interpreted in India had more to do with the cultural insecurity of middle-class Hindus in his day than with what he actually sought to achieve. And the stereotyping of Vivekananda as a militant Hindu has persisted for ideological sectarian reasons.

His agenda for national revival in which the Ramakrishna Order of monks and nuns were to play a central role is the third component of his religious world view. The monistic doctrine of Vedanta was to be the inspiration of this activity; but the virtues he preached for the benefit of Indians was not particularly Hindu, and in fact not particularly religious in any accepted sense of the term. There is, however, a self-consciously Hindu orientation in this agenda but only up to a point. His agenda for national regeneration was unique for his time and that explains much of the contemporary as well as later misinterpretations of his objectives. His personal faith, a belief in Advaita, non-duality without any qualification, is summed up in a letter to one of his American devotees:

"He who is eternal, without limits, omnipresent and all-knowing is not an individual person, but only a consciousness. You, I and everyone else are but manifestations of that consciousness. Finally everyone must become his image in full. ..and then in reality everything will become one. Religion is nothing but this. The obsolete and lifeless rituals and notions regarding godhood are but ancient superstitions."

Vivekananda also accepted without qualification the doctrine of maya. 'This world which you behold he told his disciple Sarat Chakravarti, does not exist. Everything is an act of imagination. Advaita, or non-duality as projected in Vedanta, is certainly a central theme in the Brahmnical tradition. But in the perceptions of Vivekananda and his guru it transcended the limits of any particular religious or cultural tradition. The distinction between castes, religions and races ceased to have any meaning for the enlightened. The plea is not for syncretism but a recognition of the fundamental unity of all religions. Its cultural antecedents were the doctrines of the medieval saints and the Upanishadic dictum, *ekarn sat-vipra bahudha vadanti* ('the truth is one, only the sages state it in many different ways').

There is an aspect of Vivekananda's personal faith which certainly belongs to the Hindu tradition, but which he firmly refused to project beyond the immediate circle of his fellow believers. He was under some pressure to declare this faith as the foundation of the Order credo. There is little reason to doubt that he more than shared this faith. It was he who composed the mantra for the worship of Ramakrishna in the monastery. The rules he laid down for the members of the order contained the following instruction:

"Teach them that one may bow to all other deities, but we worship only Ramakrishna... The other deities have become old and obsolete. We have a new India now, a new deity, a new faith, a new Veda."

He wrote to his fellow disciple, Swami Sivananda, in his characteristic irreverent slang, do not have the least doubt that Ramakrishna is the father of God himself... We do not know if Krishna was ever born or not, Buddha and Chaitanya now appear to be hackneyed. Ramakrishna Paramhansa is the latest and most perfect.... Can anyone else be compared to him? But he was averse to forcing this belief down people throats, partly because he did not want to establish another sect. Besides, he explained, he understood him very little. I consider him so great that I am afraid to say anything about him, lest I demean him by painting him in my own light. In the Indian tradition, every incarnation has a particular purpose. The reason for the advent of Ramakrishna according to Vivekananda was to end sectarianism in all its forms and hence the disciple could not risk founding one more sect in the name of the master. The belief in incarnations combined with the faith that Ramakrishna was born to end all sectarianism locates Vivekananda in a curious relationship to the Hindu tradition.

Yet there was an element of ambivalence here. Vivekananda celebrated the ritual worship of Durga, Kali and Lakshmi in the monastery he set up, and would have sacrificed animals but for Sarada Devi's refusal to allow it. The orthodox pundits who came to the monastery went back satisfied that the monks of the order were true Hindus. These rituals were of course unacceptable not only to non - Hindus, but to Hindu sects like the Vaishnavas.

Vivekananda's image as the champion of militant Hinduism derives above all from his mission in the USA and Europe. But one needs to emphasise here that he certainly did not go to the USA primarily with the object of propagating Hinduism. The purpose of his visit is stated quite explicitly in a letter to Mary Hale : 'In fact I came here with the object of quietly raising some funds; but I have been caught in a trap, and now I shall not left in peace." Shortly before his death he again told his disciple Sarat Chakravarti that one major object of his Western mission was to find some way of providing for the poor in India. It is not quite clear how he proposed to set about achieving this end. We have somewhat imprecise references to his twofold expectation he might help secure Western technology for India's Industrial development and the Americans would help with funds to set up a monastery in India which would be the centre of a programme for ameliorating the condition of the masses.

Arguably, that plan had very little to do with the propagation of Hinduism in any accepted sense of the term, despite the fact that he stood forth as the representative of the Hindu religion at the Chicago Congress. What he actually said in different sessions of that Congress needs to be analysed carefully. His famous speech at the inaugural session emphasised his pride in belonging to a religious tradition which taught people to accept all religious opinions as true: do not merely tolerate all religions, but accept them all to be true. He concluded his speech with the expression of a robust faith that sectarian conflicts which had drenched this earth with human blood would now come to an end. The speech on 19 November, 1893 addressed the metaphysical and philosophical foundations of Hindu practice. But its central emphasis was on a spiritual or rather mystical ideal: does not consist in any effort to believe in any creed or dogma; its prime object is the realisation of the transcendent, to merge in the ideal...

The Hinduism he preached in the West during the years which followed was also primarily an exposition of Vedantic metaphysics. Beside, he also lectured and wrote on the fourfold path to realisation: karma, (action without attachment), bhakti, (the path of devotion), jnana, (knowledge) and raja-yoga, (the techniques of a mystical regime) expounded in Patanjali Yogasütra. The Vedic and Puranic Karmakand, ritualistic duties so central to Hindu practice and beliefs, is totally absent from these expositions.

In a letter written to a fellow disciple in December 1895, he explained the nature of his mission in the West:

"I am not writing any book on Hinduism at the moment.... Every religion is an expression, a language to express the same truth, and we must speak to each in his own language.... We will see about Hinduism at some point later. Our main concern is his (i.e. Ramakrishna religion. Let the Hindus call it Hindu religion let others similarly name it (what they like).... Does our master belong only to India? India's degeneration is the result of such narrow attitudes. Any beneficial outcome is impossible unless these are destroyed."

There is no scope for misreading this statement, he was in the West to preach the universal spiritual truth embodied in the life of his guru. The Hindus might call it Hinduism and others by other names, but his concern was to break down all such barriers. The same idea is made even more explicit in a letter to Mrs. Bull:

"My master used to tell us that Hindu, Christian etc. are different names of the same truth. They are barriers to fraternal feelings between human beings. We must first try to break these down.... Even the best among us behave like monsters under their evil influence. Now we have to work hard to break these down and we will surely succeed."

In his farewell speech at the Congress of Religions he stated unequivocally what he did not want:

"Much has been said here about the common ground for unity among religions.... But if anyone here hopes that such unity will be achieved by the triumph of one of the many religions now current and the destruction of others, I tell him, yours is a false hope. Do I wish that the Christians should become Hindus? God forbid. Do I wish that any Hindu or Buddhist should become Christian? God forbid."

Vivekananda had praised West, not so much for its material achievement as for the immense energy which informed it. He conceptualised it in terms of rajas or virtues one associated with the Kshatriyas, and saw in it a moral quality of great merit. He also perceived a fundamental difference between the dominant value systems of India and Europe. "Celibacy and purity, he concluded, meant very different things in the two cultures. The Western equivalents of these terms were virtue and courage. The ultimate human aspiration in India was moksa, liberation; in the West, it was a virtuous life on earth. The West, inspired by the quality of rajas, had reached the ultimate limits of worldly enjoyment and was now hungry for something else. Science having undermined their faith, Christianity could no longer satisfy that hunger. India, which had nothing else left to compare with the West, still had an immense spiritual heritage. India still had an immense advantage and could forever be a teacher to the West. This would be like a repetition of an old history, Greece conquering Rome." In return, India could learn from Europe and America-the worldly knowledge she needed so badly. A brotherhood of man would emerge on the basis of this fair exchange.

Such aspirations and ideals were counterbalanced by a cultural propaganda which had nationalistic overtones. The vocabulary and concerns of that propaganda had a clearly Hindu orientation, the sort of thing which might even warm and please the protagonist of Hindu Right. However, one needs to consider this propaganda in its proper context. It is necessary to remember his mercurial temper and his tendency to lash out against whatever he considered unacceptable. This trait in his personality undermined much of his popularity in India and also alienated quite a few friends and devotees in the West, including some persons very close to him. Besides, he went to the USA equipped with a fair experience of missionary propaganda against Hindu belief and practice. He encountered the same in its most blatant form in America taking the tiger in its own den. Besides, while some of his best friends were indeed Christian missionaries.

He had to deal with questions in the USA as to whether Hindu mothers actually threw their babies to crocodiles, as described in missionary tracts on India. He replied that this was indeed so, but he personally had been rejected by discriminating crocodiles because as an infant he was much too fat. In a more serious vein he combated all statements regarding the condition of Indian women projected by the Ramabai Circle, even though at home he was often a virulent critic of the same practices. The reason for this, as he explained to Sister Nivedita, was that only a fool would wash his dirty linen in public. Incidentally, it should be noted that in a letter to the lady editor of *Bharati* he expressed his great admiration for Ramabai and what she had achieved for India in the West. Evidently, his motive in countering her accounts of Indian womanhood in the USA was inspired by nationalism rather than Hindu chauvinism. He was speaking to different audiences under different contexts. Otherwise his admiration for a Hindu widow who had converted to Christianity cannot be explained. He was however an uncompromising opponent of all religious conversion and was convinced that nearly all conversions to Christianity in India were based on the exploitation of Indian poverty. And he made no bones about stating this belief of his in particularly strong language. A further element of Hinduness in his propaganda was the belief that Christianity owed its origin to Hindu and Buddhist influences. But here probably the element of nationalism which also had pan-Asian dimensions was more important than any Hindu chauvinism. One has only to recall in this context his proud account of Islam contribution to modem European civilisation and his comparison of Christianity's historic record with that of Islam, tilted very much in favour of the latter.

Vivekananda's Indian agenda, more than his personal faith and his mission abroad, does up to a point provide evidence in support of the thesis which projects him as a hero of neo-Hinduism, albeit a reformist one. His chief handiwork back home, the Ramakrishna Mission, did have in practice a strong Hindu orientation, both in its ideological pronouncements and in the sections of the population it actually served. Vivekananda's self-conscious and persistent efforts to counterbalance this bias however needs to be emphasised. In a letter dated 1897, he states specifically that from the very beginning the Mission did not discriminate between the different communities of India in their programme of service. His plans for national reconstruction gave a priority to the Hindus, but did not exclude others. In his view the decline of India was the end result of its culture of discrimination, its long tradition of contempt for others. That decline began the day the contemptuous epithet, 'mleccha' was invented. To reverse that process, it was first necessary to raise the entire Hindu community from its fallen state and then revitalise the whole of mankind.

Paradise has been lost, Paradise must be gained. The process of regeneration for the Hindus had to proceed step by step. First, the divisions within each caste had to be abolished, then all castes had to be given the sacred thread until every Hindu had attained the status of Brahmins. All Hindus were brothers.' Despite the revolutionary implication of such a programme as spelt out by Vivekananda that the Brahmin and the Chandal must be placed on an equal footing it does sound like an agenda for Hindu communal solidarity.

Such an interpretation of his objectives are however countered by other features of the same programme. The Ramakrishna Mission under his leadership dedicated itself to task initiated by Ramakrishna of establishing a close relationship among the followers of all religions in the knowledge that all religious beliefs in this world were but the varied expressions of the same eternal truth. He declared that the reason for the advent of Ramakrishna was the destruction of communal barriers, '*sampraday-bihinata*'.

The monastery, guided by the spirit of Ramakrishna, was to be the centre for the union of all faiths, sarvadharma-samanvay. The Mission's mouthpiece, the *Brahmavadin*, was to contain translations of religious texts in Arabic and Persian as the basis for an enquiry into the fundamental truth underlying all scriptures. He explained his understanding of the advent of Ramakrishna in the following words:

"The *Satyayuga*, the age of truth, dawned the day he was born. All divisiveness ended from that day.... He was the one who would resolve all conflicts, distinctions between Hindus and Muslims, Christians and Hindus, all these disappeared. Those sectarian conflicts belong to another age; in this age of truth everything is submerged in the flood of his love."

The point of radical departure in Vivekananda's Indian mission was his emphasis on the masses, the deprived and the underprivileged people of the country. Service to the poor, in the belief that in serving them one served God, does have antecedents in the Hindu tradition. And other Indian reformers like Ranade had organised volunteer groups to offer help to those most in need. But Vivekananda understanding of the Indian problem differed from theirs, because he attributed to the underprivileged in India a centrality in the life and history of the country in a way which has no precedents. In course of his travels in India as a parivrajaka, a mendicant, he discovered Indian poverty and developed a passionate empathy with the Indian masses. He had not found God in his travels but had learned to love human beings. He could not see God in temples but he saw him in huts and cottages of the poor. One boasted of one's ancestors who had written a few philosophical texts and constructed a few temples, but remained oblivious of the poor on whose labour the whole structure of civilization was raised. It was his firm belief that the future belonged to the masses and the only worthwhile task before the educated middle classes in India was to make them aware of their power, especially through education.

Some have dismissed such statements as little but rhetoric and that Vivekananda had no worthwhile plans for the exploited social groups. He certainly was no Mao-Tse Tung and had no plans for a social revolution. He functioned as pragmatist inspired by a certain idealism and it is in these terms that one must assess his programme of action. He wanted the Mission named after his guru to develop as a band of dedicated ascetics, both men and women, whose primary task would be to attend to the physical needs of the poor and bring to them the benefits of modem education. Education of the masses, eradication of illiteracy, was of primary importance.

He had no faith in any religion that was unconcerned with the physical misery of human beings and was contemptuous of bhadralok politics which paid no attention to such things as mass illiteracy. A few thousand graduates, he argued, could not be the basis of a nation. India had become a land of the dead. Educating the masses was the only way to revive it. Once they were aware of the world around them and their own power they would know what to do. People of his own class would have no further function in Indian life. It is difficult to read into this agenda any message for Hindu revival or Hindu chauvinism.

Of course the programme he chalked out for the Mission had less mundane concerns as well. The dedicated missionaries were to preach the message of Vedanta and try to realise its ideals in their own lives. Detailed instructions were laid down as to what to avoid lokachara, or popular practices, and bamachara, the extreme form of Tantricism. A knowledge of the Yogas was also to be propagated. In all this the non-denominational spirituality of the doctrines was to be emphasised.

Such an agenda was of course within the Hindu tradition and could well be construed as one form of contribution to Hindu nation-building. Yet, any careful reading of Vivekananda's words and writings leaves one with a very firm impression that the centre point of his Indian agenda was an effort to create mass consciousness as empowerment. Hindu revivalism was inconsistent with such an objective. The regeneration of the Indian people, with the masses installed in the position of primacy which they had always been denied, rather than the revival of Hinduism.

Interestingly while he decided to write on philosophical themes, his spirituality was not for the weak nor possible on a hungry stomach. Indian veins must throb with this-worldly virtues, with rajas, before the country could absorb the heroic message of non-duality. His aim, he explained, was a Western-type society in India, with a powerful material civilisation, but inspired by Vedanta. Some claim he hoped to establish institutions for technical education to improve the agriculture, commerce and industry of India. The export of Indian industrial products would then be promoted abroad and Indians would be encouraged to consume home products only.

Elsewhere he stated that he wanted the future Indians to have strong Muslim bodies and Vedantic souls. Incidentally, he was among the earliest nationalist thinkers to claim the Indo-Islamic past as part of the Indian heritage. His disciple, Sister Nivedia records his intense pride in the Mughal era and his admiration for the Mughal policy of taking Hindu brides so that the rulers of India had Muslim fathers and Hindu mothers. No Hindu revivalist of his day could have imagired shared or acepted this particular enthusiasm.

It is important to remember that Hindu orthodoxy found him and his ways unacceptable. They questioned this non-Brahmin youth right to be an ordained monk. They considered his journey across the black waters a violation of taboo and they suspected that he had not observed ritual taboos about food when he was abroad and of course they were right. His answer to such criticism was unequivocal:

"When was I an orthodox Puranic Hindu? I have read carefully into our scriptures and find that spirituality and religion are not for the *Sudras*. Even if he observes the taboos about food etc. and journeys abroad, he does not acquire any merit. It is all wasted effort. I am a Sudra and as mleccha should I bother about all that?"

He described the Hindu orthodoxy of his days as a religion of 'touchism' where virtue had finally found a shelter in the purity of cooking pots. He blasted as 'crushed by the wheels of caste divisions, superstitious, without an iota of charity, hypocritical, atheistic cowards'.

He castigated what he described as the mindless imbecilities of popular Hinduism in equally strong language:

"Today there are bells [for the worship], to-morrow there will be trumpets in addition. Whether the bell should be rung on the right side or the left, whether the sandal paste mark should be placed on the forehead or some other part of the anatomy; people who spend their days and nights in such thoughts are truly wretched. And we are the wretched of the earth and are kicked around because our intelligence goes no further."

The lines which follow have a peculiar relevance to the contemporary strategies of Hindu chauvinism:

"Ten million rupees are spent to open and close the temple doors at Kashi and Brindaban. Now the deity is changing his attire, now he is having his meal, or maybe he is providing pinda for all the ancestors of the stupid bastards and all the time the living god perishes for the want of food, for want of education. A mortal sickness is abroad in our land. The entire country is one vast lunatic asylum."

His prescription for the country's material and spiritual well-being in this context was simple and direct: "away the bells and the rest of the rubbish into the river Ganges, and worship the incarnate God in man, worship all that are born as human beings."

Amiya Sen in his monograph on Hindu revivalism has discussed at length the massive campaign against the Age of Consent Bill. He identifies it correctly as the high watermark of the Hindu reaction. Vivekananda described that agitation as a matter for shame. Let us quote his words because there is no other way one can convey adequately the vehemence of his feelings on the subject:

"I deeply despise the custom of child marriage. Our people are paying for this grievous sin. I shall be an object of contempt to my own self if I support this monstrous practice directly or indirectly I must kick hard with all my might at the inhuman custom known as child marriage."

His diatribe concludes with a swipe at the mindless ritualism of the Hindu tradition. What could one expect of a culture, he wrote, in which the best minds have been debating for over two millenia whether to eat with the right hand or the left. He lashed out at those who blamed the Muslims for the purdah system.

It is difficult for the protagonists of the Rama temple controversy or their intellectual ancestors, to imagine that. Vivekananda did not spare even the great Vedantin, Adi Sankaracharya for his lack of generosity in denying to non-Brahmins the right to supreme knowledge, and his cruelty in forcing his defeated Buddhist opponents to immolate themselves. There was an unbridgeable chasm between his sensibilities and those which inspired the Hindu reaction in his time. Vivekananda was not just a reformer who wanted to rid Hinduism of some of its blemishes. He had a deep feeling of revulsion for many of the fundamentals of the Brahminical tradition. His concern was only with an inheritance of high spirituality which, he believed, was realised in its ultimate perfection in the life of his guru. And he read in that life also a message of universalism. He sought to base a movement on that message, a movement which would revive India and do so by helping the masses achieve their rightful place in the life of the country.

This role which he gradually defined for himself has been transformed in popular narrative into one of leadership of a Hindu revival. The Ramakrishna-Vivekananda movement, we are told, stemmed the tide of reform and helped restore people's confidence in the popular Hindu tradition, earlier shaken by Western as well as reformist criticism. We interrogate this thesis for a number of reasons. Vivekananda certainly had little sympathy for what he called '*bhadralok*' inspired reform. In fact, he had open contempt for the social class from which he came. It derived partly from the fact that he saw them as blood-suckers totally indifferent to the masses. There were many meetings organised by the bhadralok, but he had not come across even one for the masses. He was of the belief that criticism without sympathy, which he saw as the hall-mark of bhadralok attempts at reform, was of little use. All that one could hope to do was to create a consciousness through service, example and propaganda and leave it to people to work out their own destiny. The psychological insecurity of middle class Bengalis inspired much of the enthusiasm for Vivekananda who was believed to have achieved great victories for Hinduism abroad. His deep concern, for the masses made little or no impact on his middle class followers. At best, they could respond to his call to serve, but his passionate plea for efforts which would restore the masses to their rightful position in Indian society went unheeded. Little was done by anyone for mass education.

Vivekananda had a two-fold agenda which he had time to pursue for less than a decade: to preach an universalist spiritual faith based on the life of his master which he saw as the ultimate realisation of the Vedantic truth, and secondly, to create a mass consciousness through service and education. The seed fell on very infertile ground. He was hailed in his own time as a hero of Hinduism who had conquered the West. Today understandably the VHP more so the Hindu Right has the audacity to claim him as their own. It is difficult to imagine him as the ideological ancestor of who incite the ignorant to destroy other people places of worship in a revanchist spirit.

Vivekananda, argued that modern Europe, the proud inheritors of the mantle of ancient Greece, had come in the form of the English. Their presence in India was nectar as well as poison. English laws in India were dismantling customs and traditions, At this juncture, Vivekananda makes two very significant observations. Firstly, he questions the desirability of some of the old customs in India being swept away by English rule, European technology and English laws after all worth preserving. Secondly, he firmly believes that 'the power of stemming this tide is not in Hindu society'. This powerlessness was a direct result of an excessive obsession with absolute purity of mind or the *sattva guna*. While *sattva* was not only desirable but the highest form of knowledge, it demanded a level of renunciation impossible among the masses. *Sattva* and its glorification had led people to mask their laziness, stupidity and inactivity behind the so-called quest for transcendence and ultimate knowledge. The result was not an excess of sattva, but the country has sunk in 'the ocean of Tamas or dark of ignorance'.

What we should have is, what we have not, perhaps what our forefathers even had not; — that which the Yavanas had; that, impelled by the life-vibration, is issuing forth from the great dynamo of Europe, the electric flow of that tremendous power, vivifying the whole world. We want that energy, that love of independence, that spirit of self-reliance, that immovable fortitude, that dexterity in action, that bond of unity of purpose, that thirst for improvement, we want that expansive vision infinitely projected forward; and - that intense spirit of activity (Rajas) which will flow through our every vein, from head to foot.

The enterprise, energy, vitality and love of independence of the Greeks had to be emulated. The ancient Greeks embodied rajas and it was rajas that ought to lead the way towards attaining *sattva*. In a subtle, but significant inversion, Vivekananda argues thata man had to pass through a stage of possessing rajas in order to eventually aspire for the perfect sattvica state. *Bhoga* or enjoyment had to come before yoga. *Sambhog* has to come before Samadhi. It is action with desire that leads to action without desire.

Vivekananda does create the usual binaries of the, sattva-less West and the rajas-less India, arguing that nations that do not have *sattva* perish and ones that have sattva are immortal. He also speaks of the judicious synthesis between the rajas of the West and the sattva of India. But the inevitability of importing the rajas as represented by ancient Greece and its heirs and inheritors was clear and categorical. Even English rule, which was described as a mixture of nectar and poison, was, after all, a great good for this very reason:

He praises the English Conquest. England, the whole of Europe, has to thank Greece for its civilization. It is Greece that speaks through everything in Europe. Every building, every piece of furniture has the impress of Greece upon it; European science and art are nothing but Grecian. To-day the ancient Greek is meeting the ancient Hindu on the soil of India.

The blueprint was clear: ancient Greece and ancient India were the epitome of civilization. While modern Europe had inherited the mantle of ancient Greece, modern India had woefully failed to follow suit. Modern India's redemption lay in emulating ancient Greece, alive in modern Europe, and creating in India a European society with India's religion. Incorporating the West within a blueprint for future India was not sufficient. Vivekananda had to convincingly articulate his celebration of ancient Greece and the continuity of its legacy in modern Europe in a language that was religious and recognizably 'Hindu'. The first step in this direction he takes is to identify and create a distinction between the core ideas in India and in the West: he called these the driving force and the operative impulses. In the case of India, he argues, the overwhelming desire is for mukti or liberation from the bondage of the world. But the West quests after dharma: this is used in the sense of the Mimamsakas. *Dharma* is that which makes man seek for happiness in this world or the next. *Dharma* is established on work: *Dharma* is impelling man day and night to run after and work for happiness.' To build an argument Vivekananda turns to myths in order to push forward his blueprint. At other times, he may have called myths in the Puranas grotesque, esoteric unhistorical, but their momentary usefulness in order to legitimize the need for absorbing the rajasic West in India was beyond doubt and dispute. He presents the story of the Devas and the Asuras. "The Devas have faith in their soul, in God, and in the after-life, while the Asuras give importance to this life, and devote themselves to enjoying this world and trying to have bodily comforts in every possible way. The Asuras seems to be, more like men and far more manly than the Devas; the Devas are inferior, without doubt, to the Asuras, in many respects. Now, to understand the East and the We, we cannot do better than interpret the Hindus as the sons of the Devas and the Westerners as the sons of the Asuras."

Vivekananda's analysis of the state of Hindu India, its people and their degradation was always lyrical, though his prescription to rectify this was always direct and uncomplicated. He argued that in our country, it is as if the blood has become congealed in the heart, so that it cannot circulate in the veins - as if paralysis has overtaken the body and it has become languid. Therefore it is first to make people active by developing their Rajas, and thus make them fit for the struggle for existence. With the help of Western science dig the earth and produce food stuffs — not by means of servitude of others but by their own exertions aided by Western science. "Throw aside your scriptures in the Ganga and teach the people first the means of procuring their food and clothing, and then you will find time to read to them the scriptures. If their material wants are not removed by the rousing of intense activity, none will listen to words of spirituality".

In his espousal of Western science as a means of removing servitude and poverty, Vivekananda is far removed from any serious critique of the flip side of modern science and technology. He does sometimes refer to the vicious cycle of desire and greed in the West, but unequivocally approved the activity, enterprise and the West's power to 'make the five elements play like puppets in their hands. But the same Vivekananda who after Ramakrishna's death was preaching the futility of worldliness and exhorting everyone else to give up women and gold.

As a nationalist, Vivekananda implicates the lack of attention to material civilization as the reason for all calamities and all misfortune for the Hindus. Though conquest by Muslims is listed as one such calamity, it offered an opportunity to conquering Muslims to teach the Hindus to wear tailor-made clothes. Vivekananda had one single model to measure material wealth and poverty, and that was America and Europe of his time.

Religion, as it had existed in his day, was the reason for hunger, poverty and a lack of material well-being. He calls it the tyranny of the sages, of the spiritual, of the wise and of the intellectual — a tyranny, he suggests, more powerful than the tyranny of the ignorant. These categories of men had forced their fellow human beings into accepting a view that rejected the goods of life and the importance of making money. Also, excess of religion and no sense of political power had led to India's slavery and poverty. The sudden interpolation of political power as an element in a discussion on material civilization was part of the same glorious rajas story, something that the ancient Greeks had gifted to the world and something that the liberation-loving Hindus did not have, Vivekananda asserted.

The story, then, was one of excess and shortage: excess of sattva and of religion and lack of rajas and of material well-being. A first step in order to rectify this imbalance, urges Vivekananda, was to make all vain gods disappear, only to be replaced by another god. He calls this god, the Virat. The metaphor '*Virat*' taken from Krishna's revelation of his all- encompassing form, mentioned as the *Vishvarupa* in the eleventh chapter of the Bhagavadgita. It is also called the *viratrupa*, implying Krishna's vast and imposing form in which the entire universe could reside and manifest. He urges that all Indians purify their hearts by worshipping the *Virat*. Who, or, what is the *Virat*? He insists:

"This is the only God that is awake, our own race, everywhere His hands, everywhere His feet, everywhere His ears, He covers everything. All other Gods are sleeping. What vain Gods shall we go after and yet cannot worship the God that we see all round us, the Virat. These are all our Gods, — men and animals, and the first Gods we have to worship, instead of being jealous of each other and fighting each other."

At his rhetorical best, he often failed to notice the contradictions generated by his own evocative utterances. He could, therefore, speak of the laziness, inertia and inactivity of a vast majority of Hindus, and, simultaneously speak of the people 'of our race' as the only god that was awake and worthy of worship. The abstract idea of the Hindu masses had to be worshipped; because the Virat is constituted by 'our own race'.

Except as an emotive and rhetoric hypebole, Vivekananda had little faith in the multitude of Indian masses, whether seen in purely racial terms, or conceived as the sum total of all people in India. The real custodians of religion and philosophy, perceived in their purest form, are the cultured, and it is learning and intellect that keep the intellectual and social capital of a community safe. Slavery over the centuries had accustomed Indians to covet power only to produce more slaves and not share one's liberty; freedom for the slave always translates into keeping some other people subjugated. Neither did the people of India have any sense of the principles of self-government. Historically, whether under Hindu, Buddhist or Mughal rule, they were ruled by a godlike paternalistic king and did little for the common good or for self-defence. The Buddhist period, the ascendency of the Rajputs and the eventual rise of the Mughal power had one thing in common: the decline of the priestly caste and that of the spiritual brilliance of the brahmins. Vivekananda had an idealized view of the priestly caste and of the brahmins and always held them as an ideal indispensable for India. All his diatribes against brahmins that are often quoted to argue that he was against the varna system are far off the mark in understanding his views on the subject. In fact, the converse is true: Vivekananda believed that the revival of the priestly power in India and the revival of India were inextricably linked.

As a votary of the spiritual brilliance of the brahmins, Vivekananda strongly resented brahmins expousing more popular forms of religion, whether *Bhakti* or Tantra. For him all non-Vedic and non-Vedantic forms of belief were to be condemned as dualism and branded as undesirable superstitions and rituals. Attributing intensions of wanting to control the masses, he linked popular and ritualistic forms of brahminical practices to one form or the other of predatory exploitation. The proliferation sects that preferred bhakti as the ideal way to reach God, or saw in Tantra a way of understanding the mysteries of life and the universe, also regularly rejected the straitjacket of Hindus social order based on caste and its fourfold division. In ignoring popular manifestations of heterodox Hindu sects, and in idealizing caste as well as the brahmins, Vivekananda brought together the existence of spiritual power among certain individuals with the priestly functions of the brahmins. But what is more fraught and highly contentious in this instance is the unequivocal location of spirituality within the ambit of the priestly caste. Here is an example of Vivekananda creating a double caricature. Paraphrase his ideas:

"The Prophet Mahomet himself was dead against the priestly class in any shape, and tried his best for the total destruction of this power by formulating rules and injunctions to that effect. Under the Mussalman rule, the king himself was the supreme priest; he was the chief guide in religious matters; and, when he became the emperor, he cherished the hope of being the paramount leader in all matters, over the whole Mussalman world. To the Mussalman the Jew or the Christian is not an object of extreme detestation; they are, at the worst, men of little faith. But not so the Hindu. According to him the Hindu is idolatrous, the hateful Kafir; hence, in this life he deserved to be butchered; and in the next, eternal hell is in store for him. The utmost the Muslim kings could do as a favour to the priestly class, the spiritual guides of these Kafirs, — was to allow them to somehow pass their life silently and wait for the last moment. This was again considered too much kindness! If the religious ardour of any king was a little more uncommon, they would immediately follow arrangements for a great Yajna, by way of Kafir-slaughter."

Vivekananda regrets that after the waning of Mughal power, the Sikhs and the Marathas too did little to revive priestly power. The Brahmins, then, were the spiritual mentors of the Hindus. They were also the real custodians of learning and intellect. Having thus argued, Vivekananda goes a step further. He condemns all sectarian religions for believing in the essential equality of all human beings. Not only is the proposition of equality of all humans untenable, it is also unscientific; differences in mind are greater than differences in bodies. People who preach doctrines that suggest descent on earth and the eventual equality of all humans are nothing more than sincere fanatics; he believed that fanatics among human beings are also the most sincere. Vivekananda squarely condemns any advocacy for the desirability of equality as just another millenarian idea; he does admit that equality could be a great motivation towards encouraging humans to put in greater effort and work in anticipation of a better tomorrow. Christianity grew, he argues, on the basis of the fascination of this fanaticism, and that is what made it so attractive to the Greek and the Roman slaves. Modern ideas of liberty, equality and fraternity also were modem versions of the same millenarian aspiration and reflected the same fanaticism. True equality has never been and never can be on earth, he emphasizes, and contrasts it with one of Hinduism's fundamental doctrines which believes that all men are different, only constituting a unity in variety. The Aryan idea of caste embodied this notion of unity in variety.

If equality was a millenarian dream, was there an alternative in Vivekananda's view that was more desirable? Since the words 'liberty' and 'freedom' appear in the Vivekananda corpus often, it is surprising that he rejects its modern variant. The precise reason for which he rejects the modern idea of liberty is its conjunction with equality and fraternity. Instead, the political liberty of the Greeks for him was worthy of emulation: in Vivekananda's reading of the political liberty of the Greeks, which he erroneously identifies with social liberty, greater emphasis lay on protecting the nation, patriotism and primacy of the country. Vivekananda believes that inequality is necessary for creation itself, that all the formative forces of nature manifest themselves through struggle, competition and conflict. Equally, he believed that limiting inequality also entails a struggle. If Hindus believed in humans being different and unequal, the question that needed an urgent answer was whether India had the appetite for conflict, struggle and competition to create as well as limit inequality.

Vivekananda's analysis of nineteenth-century Indian life is familiar and quoted often, It speaks of the lack of mental activity, lifelessness among people, and absence of hope; its people lack will, enthusiasm, and are incapable even of expressing emotions. In the fashion of European writers on India in the eighteenth and the nineteenth centuries, the early lndologist and orientalists contributed to a picture of India as despotic, stagnant and benighted. They all found Hinduism as it existed in the eighteenth and nineteenth centuries inadequate and degrading. Positing a Hindu Golden Age they tried to find justification for a Hinduism that in their view was monotheistic, equalitarian and non-idolatrous. The attitude of the Indologists and orientalists finds its most comprehensive articulation in Hegel's writings on what he called the religion of the Indians: "But what lions and oxen could not do, men themselves have done; the Indians and Egyptians, for example, had in animals their consciousness of the divine. Moreover they have had this consciousness in the sun, the stars, and ultimately in something still more trifling in the most grotesque and deplorable products of an eccentric and ill-started imagination."

Even the tremendous logical capacity of the Hindus had over a period of time degenerated into just an excess of logic without being accompanied by action, an effect that was felt in every sphere, from art to the sciences and even music. Vivekananda calls India of his time the "Kurukshetra (battle-field) of malady and misery, the huge cremation-ground, strewn with the dead bones of lost hope, activity, joy and courage...' This is what, he says, is visible to the European traveller visiting India. Though this dismal picture of India is presented from the perspective of the European traveller, it is as much Vivekananda's own view as it is of any outsider. For him, what compounds the malady and misery is the indifference of the yogin, 'sitting in august silence... absorbed in deep communion with the Spirit.

Vivekananda's representation of Hinduism at the World's Parliament of Religions attempted to demonstrate the universal principles of Hinduism itself. In a sense, it was an attempt to take his master's maxim of '*yata mat tata* path' further. His dramatic first presentation 'Sisters and Brothers of America' brought 'a peal of applause that lasted for several minutes'. Even in his first address at the parliament he presented himself in terms of a bearer of spritual tradition – a tradition large enough to accept the whole world and subsume individual religious identities:

"I thank you in the name of the mother of religions; and I thank you in the name of millions and millions of Hindu people of all classes and sects.... I am proud to belong to a religion which has taught the world both tolerance and universal toleration, but we accept all religions as true."

Thus Vivekananda established three essential features of Hinduism at the very beginning: its ancient origins, its vast following and its universal toleration. In his long presentation on Hinduism on 19 September 1893, he developed these ideas with a special emphasis on the universalism of Hinduism. According to Vivekananda, Hinduism essentially required a pedagogy of the spirit which could move from perfection to everlasting perfection. He carefully developed this point to illustrate the superiority of Hinduism over Christianity and other religions. Thus he argueds that Hindu believes that he is a spirit, the sword cannot pierce the fire cannot burn – whom the water cannot melt – who the air cannot dry'.

"The soul will go on evolving or reverting back from birth to birth and death to death. But there is another question: Is man a tiny boat in a tempest, raised one moment on the foamy crest of a billow and dashed down into a yawning chasm the next... .a powerless, helpless wreck in an ever-raging, ever-rushing uncompromising current of cause and effect."

He went on to illustrate the fundamental difference in approach between Christianity and Hinduism. Far from being tied mechanically to the of causation, the Hindus perceived themselves as of bliss. In this, Vivekananda pointed out, lay the triumph of Hinduism: "me to call you brethren, by that sweet name of immortal bliss, holy and perfect beings. Ye divinities on earth – sinners!"

It is a sin to call a man so; it is a standing libel on human nature'.

Vivekananda's delineation of the characteristics of Hinduism had the Christian insistence on Original Sin as an important subtext. The Hindu, in Vivekananda's construction, was able to move from perfection to higher perfection because Hinduism admitted of man's perfectibility. He attempted to demonstrate at the Parliament that Hinduism treated human nature with greater dignity than did Christianity, which assumed that man was essentially sinful and debased, and could only be redeemed by Divine grace. His speeches at the Parliament presened a startling contrast to his speeches in India, where he bitterly criticised Hindu ritual practices as degrading women and humiliating man higher nature. Having established Hinduism as superior to Christianity in this respect, Vivekananda declared that because of its unique balanced approach to human nature, Hinduism could claim to be a universal faith that did not need to proselytise. Hinduism was thus presented as a universal faith of which the world was in need. Vivekananda's comparison of Hinduism with Christianity and with Islam, Buddhism and Jainism in other speeches erased the difference these belief systems might have and fitted them into a structure of comprehension that was essentially Hindu.

While scholarly attention has often focused on the contributions of missionary thought to such 'neo-Hindu' articulations, very little attention has been given to the impact of such articulations on missionaries themselves. Following Vivekananda repeated pronouncements on the universal and tolerant nature of Hinduism at the Parliament of Religions and throughout his stay in America, missionary discourse in India was forced to face a different evangelizing strategy by the turn of the century. 'The present religious outlook of India' on the fourteenth day of the Parliament, Slater pronounced with some alarm that the present traditional phase in

India was marked by the awakening of India from the 'sleep of ages', brought about by influence Slater saw in this the first stirrings of an imminent nationalist movement. Movement, said Slater, was "far more popular, because more really Indian, and has been bitterly opposed to Christianity. The danger lay precisely in contemporary statements on Hinduism that presented it as a universal religion: for Slater warned, are now reading Christianity into Hinduism. This was a problem for the missionaries. The most difficult aspect of this new, contending discourse was its elusive, non-proselytising tolerance, its readiness to claim even Jesus Christ as one of the its avatars.

Within early nationalism Vivekananda was one of the most articulate voices. His construction of Hinduism in universalist idioms gave the emerging nationalist discourse much of its force and direction. However, there were certain specific themes that became very important by the last decade of the nineteenth century. The identity that was being formulated by the English-educated middle class through religion was entangled in a complex way with notions of womanhood. At the Chicago Parliament too, questions of identity were closely tied up with notions of gender.

Vivekananda role in this particular celebration of Western manliness offshoot of material progress and prosperity- to question this notion of manhood and emphasise the need for a different kind of strength – that of the spirit. He specially focused on the West's 'false' worship of Shakti, a depraved understanding of its true nature. Writing to Swami Shivananda in 1894, he emphasised this lack of understanding in the West of the spiritual significance of Shakti that was essentialized in the Indian worship of the Mother:

"What do I find in America and Europe? worship of Shakti, the worship of Power. Yet they worship her ignorantly through self-gratification. Imagine then what a lot of good they will achieve who will worship her in all purity, in a *Sattvika* Spirit, looking upon Her as their Mother."

Just as Vivekananda perceived the West's religiosity as being seriously flawed, so was the excessive emphasis on masculinity. Only Hinduism's 'true' understanding of Shakti – the female principle – could set the balance right. This glorification of the female principle was also extended to represent the Hindu woman as the glorious signifier of spiritual strength. In India, the repeated nationalist stress on the glory of Hindu womanhood was partly an attempt to refute missionary misconstructions, and partly a compensatory image challenging the colonial allegation that Bengali men lacked masculinity. The image of the Hindu woman had therefore become a significant cultural marker.

After Indian delegate Mazoomdar's impassioned plea on behalf of the child-widow, it is a trifle surprising to note Vivekananda's apparent lack of interest in the issue when he spoke on the ninth day of the Parliament. Vivekananda's construction of Hindu womanhood operated within certain codes that had been standardized by the nineteenth-century Bengali middle-class patriarchy. However, the constraints that operated on these codes in a foreign country are of particular interest here. The conflicts Vivekananda had with the Ramabai circle in Boston and Brooklyn that originated just before the Parliament, provide some important insights into this mechanism of constraint.

In a letter to his disciple Alasinga written from Breezy Meadows, Metcalfe, Massachusetts, dated 20 August 1893, Vivekananda mentioned an invitation speak at a Ramabai's center. Although there seem to be no existing reports of this subsequent developments in the Brooklyn Ramabai Circle reveal that Vivekananda's idealistic depiction of child-widows in India came in for severe criticism. A later lecture entitled of Indian Womanhood delivered on 20 January 1895, reveals some of the possible causes of the controversy. Vivekananda silence about the fate of the child-widow in India aroused the fury of the Ramabai Circle in Brooklyn.

According to Marie Louise Burke, who has compiled American newspaper reports during Vivekananda's visit to America, the missionary propaganda in of 'savagery' and 'superstitions' as constituting the Hindu way of life must have confronted Vivekananda in the 1890s in America. Vivekananda's silence is indicative of a power-laden encounter demonstrating how knowledge becomes a contested site. The contest here was between two avowedly 'authetnic' self-representations. At one end of the spectrum stood Ramabai with her understanding, as a widow herself of the position of the widowed woman in Hindu society, while at the other stood Vivekananda with his idealised representation that denied Ramabai any legitimacy. Indeed, Vivekananda construed Ramabai's activities as ultimately strengthening the hands of the missionaries, and his silence and his contrary assertions form an essential part of his validation of a Hindu identity.

While Vivekananda was extremely critical of traditional Hindu social practices such as child-marriage, he was reluctant to admit any of these customs before his American audiences. Although he did not do so in his speeches before the Parliament, he consistently glorified motherhood as a marker for Hindu womanhood in his other lectures in America. In so doing he diverted attention away from the Hindu family apparatus of patriarchy used to consolidate male power. By describing it as being a woman arena of control, he constructed the Hindu woman as a powerful matriarch at the head of the household. Therefore, according to Vivekananda the whole force of womanhood is concentrated in motherhood.' In addition, Vivekananda strategy was very similar to the manner in which the emerging discourse of Hindu nationalism in India represented the ideal in preference to the real in its claims for cultural superiority. Women were thus mythologised into glorious mother-figures, the bearers of a distinguishing tradition.

The emergence of an indigenous self-descriptive discourse about Hinduism in India involved an active interaction with official, Orientalist and missionary discourses. The construction of a nationalist Hindu identity absorbed modes of presentation that included Western forms of abstraction. Hinduism thus was presented in a system of thought that would appear comprehensible to its Western critics. These attempts at self-representation, both in India and in the West, came primarily from English-educated middle-class men, though women who shared the platform with them also shared the same class background. The prevailing discourse about a Hindu identity was therefore constructed by specific circumstances in a space that was colonially defined. The presentations at the World Parliament of Religions reconstructed Hinduism in certain ways which duplicated debates in India.

4

Idea of Religious Pluralism

Indianness is marked by the principle and sentient of pluralism. It has been neatly expressed in the well-known quotes of India's oldest book, rgveda, *Ekam Sat, vipra bahudha vadanti* (that which is, is one; sages describe it in manifold ways). It reflects the great sense of inter-religious and intercultural understanding. It also cultivated an attitude of hospitality to diverse people and religions in which religious pluralism operated. Another ancient Sanskrit saying, (which is also reflected in other proverbial expressions in other languages of India), gives us an idea of the acceptance .of the working out of unification *patitam toyam yatha gacchati sagaram: sarva devanamaskrarah kesavam pratigacchati* (Just as water falling from the sky goes to the sea, so the salutations offered to various gods reach God alone.)

In a pluralistic philosophy of religion, there is a place for various sects and cults as one finds in the religious heritage of India. India has also facilitated in the enrichment of various religious and cultural ideas by its long association with the peoples of Central Asia. The relation with China through the ages has also been mutually beneficial. It is accepted by Indian Christian tradition that there is a strong possibility that St. Thomas, the disciple of Christ, was welcomed to preach Christianity in the southern coastal states of India. Later Syrian Christians who came as traders were welcomed to merge with the St. Thomas Christians, instituting the Syrian Christian churches in Kerala. Hindu rulers gave them land and extended special privileges to these Christians, early Jewish settlement and the Synagogue, tracing its foundation to the pie-Christian era, also found hospitality in Kochi, Kerala. The Zoroastrians, who fled from persecution by the Muslim Arabs, also sought and found refuge in India. They made India their home and became a part of the Indian cultural milieu and attributed to the prosperity of India. The arrival of Muslims in different stages also influenced the Indian thought and culture. Indian religious pluralism has endeavored to establish religious harmony. The goal was to absorb all that is good from all religions and appropriate those as India own. However, whenever religious fundamentalism raised its ugly head from various religious quarters, religious harmony had been jeopardised. All the same, the dynamic of religious pluralism seems to re-establish itself from time to time leading again to harmony.

The practice of morality is conceived as having different dimensions, Hindu ethical heritage of social ethics, psychological ethics, and transcendental ethics has been carried over in some way or the other for a total ethical reality in India. It implies the observation of the rules and regulations that preserve harmony among various groups and various stages in life at the social level. The psychological ethics has its focus on the inner self and its purification as an ethical activity. At the level of transcendental ethics, the individual is challenged to grow further and rise above good and evil and be a liberated and fully divine person rather than one bound by rules and regulations alone.

The meaning and connotation of secularism has special significance in the context of India. Secularism in the Indian context is the supportive acceptance and understanding of the Indian society as a heterogeneous society. Harmony has to be established among the religious and sub-cultural heterogeneity. It means the acceptance of the principle of coexistence-spirit of the heritage of Indian civilization. During the latter part of the twentieth century, the Indian mantra of secularism got popularly expressed in sarvadharma samabhava—acceptance of the peaceful coexistence of all religions by rendering equal respect to all religions).

Several leading thinkers of modern India contributed to the revival of this concept. Raja Rammohan Roy, who is acknowledged as the first representative of the new national spirit of the religious and social awakening of modern India, promoted the unity of Godhead which means also the brotherhood of all humans. God is not divided and all humans are brothers and sisters. He published his (1820) hoping that such a code of religion and morality is so admirably calculated to elevate men to high ideas and liberal notions of God.

Another Brahmo leader, Keshub Sen conducted an exercise of spiritual pilgrimage and migration providing time for study, meditation, communion and the realization of the spirit of the selected prophets and saints of all the religions of the world. On specified days, the Indian pilgrim reads Moses, Socrates, Sakyamuni, the Rishis, Jesus Christ, Mohammed, Chaitanya. One of the goals was to help the pilgrim to have the experience of bringing together of all the saints and prophets of the world by going through their life sketches, life and teachings. It encouraged the seekers to understand that spirituality transcends caste, color and creed, thus leading all people to a family and consequently promoting religious harmony. Ramakrishna promoted the ideal of a mystic experience among people all of religions reporting his personal experience of spiritual encounter with goddess Kali, Jesus Christ and Mohammed. He experienced a common ground of essence of spirituality through the spiritual exercise. He noted:

"There is only one God, but endless are his aspects and endless his names. Call him by any name and worship him in any aspect that please you, you are sure to see him."

An echo of the was heard in the most well known speech of Swami Vivekananda when he declared his faith in his address in the final session of the Parliament of Religions, Chicago, on September 27, 1893 in the spirit of assimilation of spiritual truth of each other:

"Do I wish that the Christian would become Hindu? God forbid

Do I wish that the Hindu or Buddhist would become Christian?

God Forbid. ...The Christian is not to become a Hindu or a Buddhist. Nor a Hindu or a Buddhist to become a Christian. But each must assimilate the spirit of the others and yet preserve his individuality and grow according his own law of growth."

Mahatma Gandhi, the apostle of nonviolence, Satya and Ahisma visualized a spiritual basis for secularism He believed that all humans are children of God and therefore, should be considered as equal. The Gandhian spirit of secularism can be better understood in his own words: it is not a religion of the prison house. It has room for the least God' creation. He believes in the absolutes oneness of God. Though we may have many bodies, we have but one soul. The rays of the sun are many through refraction, but they have the same source. Sarvepalli Radhakrishnan promoted a spirit of cooperation in the pursuit of common peaceful goals in an international fellowship of all religions. He advocates that followers of different religions should focus on matters of agreement rather than differences and disagreements His hope was that a time would come when a gradual assimilation of religions of the world will emerge into a world faith, a universal religion ruled by spirituality and peace. Such a heritage of perceptions of Indian secularism without abandoning religion and spirituality denotes a noble aspect of absorbing Indian thought constructively. It is a challenging task for every Indian to translate into practical terms.

The nature of Indian spirituality defies definition. At its best it may be conceived as darsana, a vision of truth and ultimate state of spirituality. The transforming presence of divinity is dormant in every human. Spirituality is the outcome of the awakening of the divine potential in the human. The promotion of spirituality for India is an inter-religious project. Indian spirituality cannot be conceived as an exclusive reality but is an integrated vision of any body from any religious organization with an accomplished experience of the vision. It is highly respected, admired and sought after.

Indian spirituality disregards the borders of religious organizations based on caste, creed or racial affiliation once the spiritual accomplishment has been realized with a deep spiritual behavioral pattern in action. The efforts of fundamentalist forces from any religion to limit spirituality to a specific pattern are not accepted as the integrated vision of Truth and its dynamics of spirituality. The spirit of Indian spirituality affirms that there is a common ground in all true spiritual experience though the particularity of the experience at the level of ordinary human perception restricted by a particular religious practice, may differ in its format. Thus, it acknowledges a diversity of symbols, myths, scriptures and traditions, which could be instrumental in experiencing the integrated vision of Truth. The focus is on the depth and universality of spirituality and not on the particularity propagated by organized religions.

In India, religious identity gets in terms of cultural identity which covers customs, etiquette and manners, in reinforcing individual and social relations. Since what is called Indian culture is a product of several centuries, the reality of Indian culture is a composite culture. Though the particularity differs regionally, and according to the long drawn traditions of universality of cultural values runs through and binds all together like Indian hospitality respect for the elders, spiritually accomplished gurus, upholding the good values of the ancestors, etc. While there may be disagreement among Indians on the particularity of the culture, the universal cultural values transcend the particularity. Since the rich Indian cultural heritage is referred to as Hindu, certain segments of the contemporary political force gained a dominant place to relapse into the old ways in the name of cultural nationalism. Cultural nationalism assumed the identity of Hindutva, a misrepresentation of the true nature of Indian culture. Indian composite culture formed by numerous contributions from diverse sources and is still being enriched by diverse elements making it as a contribution of all. It will be a matter of hubris to assign it to any particular group as its custodial monopoly is unjustified for her identity. Looking at religious identity from such a narrow aspect also cannot be justified as Indian. Thus religious identity in terms of cultural identity has to go beyond the narrow domains to make it truly Indian. It is understood that followers of all religions nurtured on the Indian soil have contributed to the Indian culture over the contries of their existence here in India.

In the context of Indian history and politics the word 'Hindutva' is of recent origin and currency. It is now being used rather freely and carelessly, in India and abroad, to describe a particular trend which is clearly more related to politics and the power struggle than to religious behaviour and the beliefs of the people. This has been the result of an unfortunate and unhappy mixing of the political power-game with religion. The use of religious sentiment and symbols in politics is not a new trend in India. Not only traditions, beliefs and symbols but the names and faces of great historical personalities have been freely used in political arguments and battles with which, ironically, such men had very little connection, if any.

In this ongoing search for new recruitment and more powerful weapons, Vivekananda's name has figured most prominently. He finds himself in the middle of a tug-of-war between the forces of Hindu fundamentalism and secularism. Vivekananda, in his introductory paragraph to *Essentials of Hinduism*, wrote:

"The word Hindu, by which it is the fashion nowadays to style ourselves, has lost all its meaning, for this word merely meant those who lived on the other side of the river Indus (in Sanskrit Sindhu). The name was murdered into Hindu by the ancient Persians, and all people living on the other side of the river Sindhu were called by them Hindus. During the Mohammedan rule we took up the word ourselves. There may not be any harm in using the word, of course, but it has lost its significance."

The word 'Hindu', Vivekananda pointed out, thus covered the people of all religions living on the other side of the river Sindhu, who included the Hindus, Muhammadans, Chritians, Jains and people of other faiths. To him, the word Vaidika or Vedantist was much better than the word 'Hindu'. For in one way or another, all the present religions of India can be traced back to the ideas of the Upanishads. Some of the philosophies have been converted to symbols of household worship.

Vivekananda was fully aware of that problem and he later put forward his own ideas for reconciling it. But these was no over-sensitivity to the word Hindu or Hinduism in Vivekananda.

The essentials or the fundamentals of the religion which Vivekananda propagated, call it Hinduism or Vedanta need to be identified before one can analyse how they compare with the Hindu fundamentalism or Hindutva of today. The principles of Vedanta are the essential foundations of religion, for all are built upon the eternal principles that are in man and nature. Ideas about the soul, going to heaven, and so on, can never change. Hindus must believe in creative energy, which is working all around us, day and night...if that stops for a second, the whole thing falls to the ground. The idea that came and created the world, and since that time has been sleeping is not true. The creative power which is behind all manifestations is Brahman. He is eternal, eternally pure, eternally aware, the almighty, the all-knowing, all-merciful, the omnipresent. He creates the Universe. Vivekananda also includes the law of karma as an essential foundation of the Hindu religion. Another cardinal point is belief in the soul. The knowledge of God can only come through the heart, the human soul. The most important knowledge to have is that the soul is present in all living creatures. The differences are only in manifestation. The concept of brotherhood of a man, of universal life, is founded on the existence of the soul. The earth is the *karma bhumi*. Liberation from the cycle of birth and death, even life in heaven, is the ultimate object. It is mukti that is worth having. This is only possible through knowledge and that knowledge can only come through love, by the worship of God, by loving all beings as the temples of god. Man is travelling from 'truth to truth, from lower to higher truth'. All religions, the lowest fetishism to the highest absolutism', mean so many attempts of the human soul to grasp and realise the Infinite. God understands human failings and becomes man to do good to humanity.

It is important to note that caste, images, rituals, place and form of worship, dogmas or doctrines had no place in Vivekananda's concept of the theoretical and philosophical foundations of Hinduism. Yet time and again he stressed that 'India's theme is religion', and warned that if Indians succeeded in their attempt to throw off their religion, the vitality of India's national life would become extinct. This necessitates a closer scrutiny of what he meant by religion's inseparable link with national life. Today's concept of Hindutva rings the same bell. There was no ambiguity in his mind. Three things, he stressed, make a man as well as a nation great. These are: conviction of the powers of goodness; absence of jealousy and suspicion; helping all those who are trying to be and do good. All stain of jealously must be removed. Be broad, try to amalgamate and universalize. The only real necessities for achieving greatness and true spirituality are love, sincerity and patience. Above all, 'if you cannot worship your brother man, the manifested God, how can you worship a God who is unmanifested? You may build a temple in which to worship God, and that may be good, but a better one, a much higher one, already exists, the human body'. The real dharma was doing good to others. 'Injuring others is sin, Loving others is virtue, hating others is sin'.

What was the place of a disbeliever, an atheist, in Vivekananda's concept of religion and of its role in the building up of India? The number of people going to the church in Western countries is declining rapidly. The picture in India, among the educated youth in particular, is not very different. Even though a majority would not be conscientious and committed atheists, they would be indifferent to the existence or otherwise of a God or of gods and goddesses. In a country which is rapidly going through a period of scientific and technological change, economic difficulty, unemployment and lack of the basic needs of life, philosophical issues and polemics have little relevance to actual life. This is not merely an urban phenomenon in India. The difference been an urban and rural life is becoming less distinct. What appeal can there to a generation that is sceptical about God and religion? In some places in India today one is not required to state to which faith one belongs. In fact, atheism for Vivekananda, is not a problem. An atheist is more welcome than a believer if he only has faith in two other fundamentals. One is faith in himself. Vivekananda explained, 'The old religions said that he was an atheist who did not believe in God. The new religion says that he is the atheist who does not believe in himself. But it is not selfish faith. It means faith in all Second essential requirement is that of character. There is no question of rejecting any one atheist, pantheist, monist, polytheist, agnostic; the only condition of being a disciple is modeling a character at once the broadest and the most intense.

He explained:

"The idea that one man is born superior to another has no meaning in the Vedanta; that between two nations, one is superior and the other inferior has no meaning whatsoever. Put them in the same circumstances and see whether the same intelligence comes out or not."

There was no question of establishing the supremacy of one faith over another. Even toleration was not enough, for 'so called toleration is often blasphemy'. Instead, all religions should be accepted as true: this is what he had learnt from the life and teachings of Sri Ramakrishna. Thus he could proclaim:

"I shall go to the mosque of the Mohammedan; I shall enter the Christian church and kneel before the crucifix. I shall enter the Buddhistic temple, where I shall take refuge in Buddha and in his law. I shall go into the forest and sit down in meditation with the Hindu, who is trying to see the light which enlightens the heart of everyone."

How sincere was Vivekananda when he made such statements? Were these mere emotional outbursts, a naive expression of his universalism or, even worse, a mere polemic weapon, mere rhetorical claptrap? The answer is to be looked for in his own life, the relations between what he professed and actually practiced. The first and the most important will be an examination of his attitude to Islam and Muslims. In the context of modern India this should be an acid test for anyone spirit of toleration, not to speak of a readiness for acceptance and assimilation. For a Hindu monk and religious leader of the late nineteenth century it must be the most difficult to come through, especially in the eyes of a secularist.

Vivekananda's attitude to Islam, Muslim rulers in India and his personal contacts with all classes of Muslims in India may deserve to be the subject of independent study. Presumably, because of his own liberal family environment, Western education, association with the Brahmo Samaj and, last but not least, the all-pervasive example and influence of his guru Sri Ramakrishna, Vivekananda had inherited and imbibed a catholic and liberal attitude to all religions, prophets and saints. He had once been severely rebuked by Ramakrishna for denigrating the rites and practices of one sect. The latter told young Narendranath that to every house there was a back door for cleaning the lavatories. But one should look for the front door to gain access to a house. Vivekananda never forgot this lesson The next and, perhaps, the most significant part of his training and realisation in this aspect of life was the experience he gained as parivrajaka, a wandering monk. No proper understanding of Vivekananda is possible without studying in detail the events of his life as a parivrajaka. Those wandering years with only a staff and a satchel throughout the country transformed Narendranath Datta into Swami Vivekananda. Ramakrishna had foreseen and predicted it. Once, a few miles from Almora, he was almost on the verge of death because he had been without food for many hours. He had fainted on the roadside opposite a Muslim cemetery. But his life was saved by the keeper of the cemetery, a fakir named Zulfikar Ali, who offered him a cucumber to eat, Vivekananda often recounted the story with gratitude and acknowledged that the fakir had saved his life. In February 1891, in Alwar, he had an intimate discussion on religion with a Maulavi who taught Urdu and Persian in a local high school. Of the Koran, Vivekananda said, is one thing very remarkable about eleven hundred years ago. It retains its pristine purity and is free from interpolations'. He was well acquainted with the Islamic scriptures and had made the Koran intellectual and spiritual possession. This came as a big surprise to many Muslims. Coming to know of his presence many other Muslims came to meet and talk to him. There were also people from other Hindu sects. They had wonderful stimulating discussions on religions along with singing of Urdu songs, *Kirtans* and *bhajans*. The Moulavi invited Vivekananda for a meal at his residence with much diffidence and he doubted whether a Hindu monk would agree to take food in a Muslim home. But Vivekananda accepted the invitation with great pleasure. Hereafter many other Muslims invited him to their homes. There were many other similar occasions.

Vivekananda had also lived in Muslim homes. At Mount Abu he was living in an abandoned cave which had become inhabitable with the coming of heavy rains. A Muslim lawyer invited him to stay in his home promising that he would make separate arrangements for his food. Vivekananda accepted the generous invitation but turned down the proposal of making separate arrangements for him. The private secretary of the Raja of Khetri was astounded to find this out. Bewildered, he asked Vivekananda how, being a Hindu monk, he could do it. Raja said, is it that you are living with a Muslim? Your food may then be touched by him. Vivekananda flared up and answered back, 'I am above all your social conventions. I can dine even with a Bhangi. I am not afraid of you people and your society. You know nothing of God and the scriptures.' While traversing through Indian villages, watching the life of the village folk and their simple religious life and beliefs, Vivekananda realized the inherent unity of the Indian people. In his eyes the piety of the Hindus on the banks of the river Ganga, and the piety of the Mussalman kneeling in prayer at the appointed hours, were equally Indian and of equal worth. This was the core of his attitude to the relationship between the two religions and the two communities. It sounds unbelievable even today given his image as a protagonist of Hindu revivalism, that he could, after returning to India from the West, worship in Kashmir the little daughter of his Muslim boatman as the symbol of the Divine Mother.

Vivekananda's religious pluralism is to be found in a private letter that he wrote some years later to a brother monk in India who was in charge of an orphanage of the Ramakrishna order. A Muslim orphan boy had been given shelter in the orphanage and brother monk was seeking the advice of Vivekananda on what to do with that boy. Vivekananda wrote back that he was happy that the Muslim orphan had been taken in. He advised that he must be looked after and brought up well. But it must be made sure that he grew up as a Muslim and there was no interference with his religion.

Vivekananda believed in free will and freedom of choice. Even in choosing one own religion he was in favour of exercising choice.

Within one family there could be members of different faiths. A Muslim father could have a Christian wife and a Buddhist son if each one so desired. As in all other spheres of life there could be unity in diversity in religious beliefs within the same family. This attitude to freedom of choice in religious matters would be considered too radical and revolutionary in any modern society anywhere in the world. He admired Rammohan Ray for his foresight and breadth of vision. One of Rammohan's pioneering messages, according to Vivekananda, was the former's acceptance of the Hindu and the Muslim on an equal footing. Vivekananda's quest was for the underlying unity of all the diversities of customs and traditions of India. He found the differences between the Muslim and Hindu worlds as more apparent than real. To him the Muslims were a race as generous and humane, and at heart as Indian, as the Hindus. There was affinity between Sufism and Advaita Vedanta. To him Hindus and Muslims were Indians first. The distinction between them by reason of their different beliefs was subordinate to their identity as fellow countrymen. Vivekananda knew this from his personal experience. It was not a fancy dream. He had received a warm welcome, sincere appreciation and respect from Muslims even before he became a national hero after his triumphant visit to the West. He was given a reception in Hyderabad in February 1893 when he was practically a young unknown Hindu monk. Many of the notable Muslim personalities of Hyderabad met him and received him with warmth and respect.

In Ambala he made it a point to visit the Hindu Muslim School because, to him, it was symbolic of the spirit of unity between the two great Indian communities. This was one of his cherished dreams. In his well-known letter to Sarfaraz Hussain, Vivekananda wrote that from the Advaitic point of view one can look upon all religions and sects with love. He expressed his deep conviction that the help of practical Islam, theories of Vedantism, however fine and wonderful they may be, are entirely valueless to the vast mass of mankind. For our own motherland a junction of the two great systems, Hinduism and Islam-Vedanta brain and Islam body the only hope he wished to see a world where there would be the Vedas, nor the Bible, nor the Koran and this was to be done by harmonising the Vedas, the Bible and the Koran. This was a utopian thought, a dream that has not shown any sign of realisation in the last hundred years. But can he be the fountainhead of Hindu supremacy and militant aggressive Hinduism?

The political environment of the era when Vivekananda was expressing his views should be reckoned with. Separatist and communal politics had already shown clear indications of growing into a major factor in national life. Both the Wahhabi and the Faraizi movements, seeking to remove the depression of the Muslims and purify Islam in Bengal, had a very strong communal character which, in the course of time, helped the growth of separatism among the Muslims. Ameer Ali had turned down Surendranath Banerjee's invitation by the Muslims to join the Indian National Congress. He made it clear that the Muslims needed a political association of their own. The National Mahomedan Association (1878) had raised demands for preferential treatment for the Muslims. Muslim communal sentiment had been accentuated in East Bengal by the prevailing land system and the oppression and exploitation of the peasantry by the zamindars, most of whom were Hindus. The Muhammadan Anglo-Oriental College in Aligarh had been founded in 1877 and the fear of Hindu dominance had been planted by Sir Syed Ahmad Khan.

On the other side was the growing Hindu overtone of the national movement. It was largely a legacy of the Hindu Mela and an inevitable result of the very nature and character of the Bengal Renaissance or the Indian Awakening. Historical forces had combined to give political developments this character. Hindu nationalism had become a powerful appealing concept by the end of the century. The vision of 'a Hindu *Rastra*, which would unite under one political whole of the Hindu people, united already by communities of traditions and scriptures' had become a 'grand idea'. Bipin Chandra Pal had noticed it like many others. Shivaji in many parts of the country, and Ranjit Singh, particularly in Punjab, had become models of patriotism and heroism. Bal Gangadhar Tilak was speaking of 'the feeling of Hindutva' as the 'common factor in Indian society'. Even a Brahmo leader like Bipin Chandra concluded that Hinduism was 'the original stock and staple of Indian life'.

Vivekananda was fully aware of all the current developments and trends, not only in India but in other parts of the world. His knowledge, perception and capacity to analyse forces of history and directional trends were phenomenal. It is, indeed, a mystery how he could have such an outlook and view of Hindu-Muslim relations and the future of India as he had. Interestingly, Tilak and

Vivekananda had mutual admiration; they had met, discussed many issues and exchanged views. Tilak wrote in the *Kesari* (8 July 1902) after Vivekananda death that Vivekananda was a person of the stature of Sankaracharya, and recalled his great contributions to the establishment of the 'glory of Hinduism' in the world. But there was not ever any implicit reference to Vivekananda's support or enthusiasm for Hindutva or a Hindu *Rastra* as the common factor of Indian life.

We know from sister Nivedita, who was in Vivekananda's party when he visited northern India, that he admired the grandeur and greatness o the Mughal emperors. He was never tired to speaking of their greatness whenever reviewing the history of India. The historic cities of Delhi and Agra fascinated him. She wrote, 'He spoke on Shah Jahan... with a burst of enthusiasm.' Vivekananda was enthusiastic about Shah Jahan because the latter had a feeling for and discrimination of beauty that were unparalleled in history. Vivekananda was struck by a manuscript illuminated by Shah Jahan which he considered one of the art treasures of India. Nivedita also wrote, 'Oftener still, it was Akbar of whom he would tell, almost with tears in his voice and a passion easier to understand, beside that undomed tomb, open to sun and wind, the grave of Secundra at Agra."

Vivekananda's views on Muslim conquest and rule in India and the conversion of large numbers of Hindus to Islam are intriguing and, apparently, paradoxical. It has been a strong common belief among the Hindus that large-scale conversion to Islam was forcibly effected by the sword and threat of the Muslim power. This was the most widely accepted view in the last century when Vivekananda was speaking on a future India of Islamic body and Vedantic brain. He had the courage not only to challenge that belief, but call it the 'height of madness' to think that 'it was all the work of sword and fire'. Far more important causes were, he argued, the desire of the neglected, oppressed, so-called lower classes of Hindus to free themselves from the clutches and ruthless exploitation of the zamindars and the priests. It was the curse of untouchability, 'Don't touchism' and denial of human rights and dignity to the lower classes that caused large-scale conversions. A religion that allowed this to happen was not a religion – it was 'the devil's dance'. A country in which this could happen was 'hell'. He did not stop even there, and went on to say, 'The Muhmmadan conquest of India came as a salvation to the downtrodden, to the poor. That is why one-fifth of our people have become Muhammadans.'

It would be totally wrong to conclude from his observations cited above that Vivekananda as euophoric about the Muslim rulers and he was an uncritical admirer of Muslim rule in India. There are instances of his condemnation of many aspects of Muslim rule, and also his dislike for certain features of their religion. Vivekananda hated Muslim rule and had vehemently condemned the Islamic religion for shedding blood, committing acts of cruelty for propagating the faith, and, even, encouraging the killing of the unbelievers. Vivekananda was very critical of the Christian missionaries, who had never dared to criticize the Muslims so fiercely and fearlessly as they had the Hindus and the Hindu religion. This is further evidence of Vivekananda's anti-Muslim bias which was a major plank of his revivalist movement. But the most important point that cannot be overlooked is that Vivekananda was no less sharp and candid in criticizing other relgion as well, including his own. He was a great admirer, in many sense almost a devotee of Jesus. During his trip to Europe he worshiped the Virgin Mary by placing a flower at the feet of her statue. To him she was the Divine Mother. He said, 'Had I lived in Palestine in the days of Jesus of Nazareth, I would have washed his feet, not with my tears but with my heart's blood'. The Buddha, to him, was a great preacher of equality, a man with a heart that was overflowing with love. He said, 'The Buddha is not a person; he is a realization... I worship him.' Yet, he was very critical about certain aspects of Christianity and Buddhism. Time and again he said very frankly what he believed to be wrong. Mincing of words or insincere pleasantries and, especially, appeasement of any person, order or belief did not fit in with his character and personality. Many times this caused unpleasantness and embarrassment. But he did not care. One may point out contradictions in his different observations and assessment. That is a common feature of all great thinkers and original minds. But one has to take into consideration the situation, time, environment and the personality of man. Through all this the man in his totality emerges. Isolated quotations taken out of context are often misleading and scandalous.

A main feature of the new incarnation of Hindutva is the effort to install a national model and ideal for all Indians irrespective of their religious faith. This is something new in the long history of India and the Hindu religion. Even though they have been subjected to much ill-natured ridicule, sarcasm and abuse the Hindus have been quite happy with their millions of gods and goddesses. They have enjoyed a wide choice among these deities with their numerous forms, shapes and attributes. Among the major ones, whether Krishna, Rama, Siva or Vishnu, no one had ever enjoyed an absolute spell and devotion from all Hindus living in the country. For that matter, from the Vedic period on, .one can ignore all of them, even God Himself, and still contrive to be in the Hindu fold. This has been a cherished privilege of a Hindu which one would very much like to retain at any price. Vivekananda always stressed this feature of Hinduism. Rama, Krishna, Buddha, Sankaracharya, Ramanuja, Nanak, Chaitanya and all other gods, prophets and saints, were viewed by him as incarnations and messengers of God, constituting the nation's spiritual life. But there was no trace of dogmatism, not even any implicit effort to impose any one of them as the model on the Hindus, not to speak of people of other religions.

More recently, current Hindutva ideologies have been firmly rooted in the concept of Hindu nationality as an exclusive bond of 'blood' and race, history. This is an alarming trend for India as a nation. These are complex and crucial issues warranting careful examination. But it is pertinent to remember what Vivekananda thought about 'purity of blood' and the Hindus as a 'race'. We Indians are, in spite of our various castes, and in spite of the modern custom of marriage restricted within the sub-division of a caste, a mixed raced in every sense of the term. Vincent Smith has described India as an 'ethnological museum' and Vivekananda had the identical view of the colourful national fabric of India though, he strongly believed the history of India had to be written by Indians themselves. The distorted image of India given by Western historians hard to be reconstructed. Vivekananda described what he saw in his grand vision of the emergence of India :

"Well here are the Persians, the Greek, the Yucchi, the Hun, the Chin, the Scythian and many more, melted and fused, the Jews, the Arabs, Mongols, down to the Vikings, the lords of the German forests. An ocean of humanity, composed of these race-waves, seething, boiling, struggling, constantly changing form rising to the surface, and spreading and swallowing little ones, again subsiding – this is the history of India."

What was his feeling about himself, his own race and country? When the ship, carrying him back to India after his first visit to America and Europe, was nearing Port Said, Vivekananda wrote in a letter (3 January, 1897): 'From Suez begins Asia. Once again Asia. What am I? Asiatic, European, or American? I feel a curious medley of personalities in me.' We know from Sister Nivedita how scornful he was in his repudiation of the pseudo-ethnology of privileged races. Vivekananda told Nivedita, 'If I am grateful to my white-skinned Aryan ancestors, I am far more so to my yellow-skinned Mongolian ancestors, and most of all to the black-skinned negroids.' He was very proud of his physiognomy, especially of his 'Mongolian jaw', regarding it as a sign of 'bulldog tenacity of purpose'. Referring to this particular racial characteristic, considered to be behind every Aryan people, he said, 'Don't you see? The tartar is the wine of the race! He gives energy and power to every blood.'

Vivekananda himself had to face virulent opposition and criticism of Hindu orthodoxy. Being a Sudra he had no right to be a sanyasin; he had not been given the monastic name Vivekananda by his guru; a sannyasin could never cross the ocean, mix with Mlecchas, and socialize with them; take forbidden and socially contaminated food; smoke cigars and be fond of betel-nuts – the list of gross violations and sins committed by him was, indeed, formidable. The word 'fundamentalism' was not in vogue in those days. Otherwise, he could have been ostracized and heavily censored on charges of floating the fundamentals of Hindu religion. Many well-known members of the Hindu elite of Calcutta, even some Brahmo leaders, lent their support to the orthodox criticism of Vivekananda. Such a man, far from being a legitimate spokesman of Hinduism, was really an imposter, a charlatan. Those who did not go that far, still felt that he had violated the basic rules of Hinduism. Gooroodas Benerjee, a judge of the Calcutta High Court and an eminent educationalist, refused to be the chairman of the Reception Committee that was formed to welcome and felicitate Vivekananda when he returned to Calcutta from the West in 1897. Listening to the reasons of his refusal to be the chairman of the committee, Vivekananda infuriatedly told Gooroodas Banerjee, who has blamed him for going to the country of the Mlechhas, being a puritan Brahmin he has served under and worked with the Mlechhas throughout his life. The Shastras have prescribed hell-fire for such sins'. Even trhe person who chaired the reception meeting in Calcutta, Raja Pearymohun Mukhopadhyaya addressed Vivekananda as 'Brother' instead of 'Swami', as he still had doubts as to whether a Kayastha could become a genuine sanyasin. The various campaign against Vivekananda by orthodox people and groups and his detractors was carried out vigorously in America as well.

Vivekananda was unquestionably proud of his religion, his country, its culture and heritage. Religion to him was the central and perennial theme of India. To him religion was string running through the pearls binding them together His mission was to see a regenerated reawakened strong and Vibrant India: an India that would be self-confident and fearless, approaching the Western world on a footing of equality. She should build up a relationship of reciprocity and must not only be on the receiving side. Vivekananda's attitude to the West and the East-West relationship has to be seen in the light of his challenge to the long-standing 'subject-domination' concept. The Hindus, constituting the vast majority of the population, had a crucial role and responsibility in rebuilding India. But there was no question of any special privilege for them, excluding other faiths and communities. The most important thing was to be an Indian, to love India.

The Hindu community was perceived as weak, divided, sunk in controversy and thus unable to defend itself from more aggressive religions. Each group offered solution the problems of the present, but by opposing forms of action. Reformers, such as called for radical changes within Hindu religious practices in order to cleanse Hinduism of all accumulated errors. From the orthodox perspective, these reformers in attempting to purify Hinduism had achieved nothing and instead became part of the overall problem.

Vivekananda believed that the rituals, beliefs, sacred texts, and social structure of contemporary Hinduism were correct, proper, and even divinely inspired. Their authority lay in the ancient scriptures, the Vedas, Sruti, Smriti, the Puranas and Laws of Manu. These texts were not to be challenged by human reasoning, foreign religious doctrine or concepts of Western science. The revival of Hinduism and Hindus lay in inculcating respect for the ancient texts, for Brahmins, and the system of social structure with all its implications. Acceptance of the Varna system and all it meant, even untouchability, was deemed necessary and good for the moral condition of Hindus. Progress would be made by a return to belief in sacred authority and the practice of all religious acts, such as respect for the holy Ganga, Brahmin priests, idol worship, pilgrimages, and proper diet. Together they comprised *Sanatan Dharma*, the Eternal Religion, adherence to which would restore Hinduism to its proper place as the leader and teacher of all religions. True, each of these Hindu leaders had his own particular points of emphasis, but all shared the basic supposition as to what was wrong in Hinduism and what should be done to make it right again.

Other religions, particularly Islam and Christianity, were declared enemies, their doctrines and practices untrue, at times cruel, and above all, through conversion a threat to the Hindu community. At times competition took the form of violence, at other times missionaries challenged the beliefs and customs of Hinduism by presenting their alternative systems of belief and conduct. In addition Hindu youth faced an English education that taught both the language and culture from another civilisation, thus directly and indirectly supporting the campaigns of Christian missionaries. At times Vivekananda condemned both Islam and Christianity, specifically the activities of Christian missionaries in India and the United States. In his writing and speeches, however, he primarily championed Vedantic Hinduism.

Vivekananda's achievement marked him as different from all other religious leaders, for he also brought a new dimension to Hinduism by transforming the traditional Hindu institutions of the Hindu ascetic and monastery into vehicles of social service. He established the Ramakrishna Math and Mission that provided religious training and housing for Hindu ascetics. It also became a base for the management of social welfare institutions, which conducted forms of medical service and emergency relief. In so doing Vivekananda added to Hinduism a social gospel, whereby the tradition of Hindu monks followed a doctrine of action, karma yoga, that stressed action within the world rather than attempting to retreat from it, thus offering to both monks and laity a new path to the traditional goal of release from the cycle of rebirth.

Vivekananda is remembered today as a highly successful spokesman for Hinduism in North America and Europe and as an exponent of religious tolerance. He was also a defender of orthodox Hinduism.

It is clear that Vivekananda cannot he placed in a single category, for he was both complex and, at times, contradictory. A full understanding of Vivekananda requires of historians and students of religion that they explore the totality of his writings and speeches as well as other available historical sources.

A significant tenet in Vivekananda's teachingis – his belief in the unity of existence and the essential unity of all religions. It is his contention that God permeates all that exists from stone and plants to human beings and higher forms beings. The difference between one form of life or existence and another is a difference of degree rather than of kind. In the same way he upholds the concept of universal religion, but not in the sence of a single set of rituals, or a single mythology, or a single philosophy for the whole of mankind, rather,as he explains, in the sence of univarsal truth, asepcts of which every particular, historical religian proclaims according to its own insights. Each religion has to be regarded as one pearl on pearl on a string of pearls, and since they compalement one another it has to be acknowledged that no single form of religion will do for everyone. So it would seem that Vivekananda sees beauty as well as human necessity in variety and diversity: 'just as we have recognised unity by our very nature, so we must also recognice variation truth may be expressed in a hundred thousand ways.

This is an expession of the idealist phiosophy. It reflects the Platonic view that Forms or Ideas or Universal exist in themselves; that they are timeless, real, unchanging, ideal, perfect, transcendental substance; that particulars reflect universals or participate in forms or essnce; and that particulars also are inadequate, imperfect manifestations of form or essences or univesals. Like many idealists before and after him, Vivekananda upholds the essentialist position that religion is one in essence but diverse in manifestion, hence the need for toleration and the cultivation of an atttude that would deter us form looking for defects in religions other than our own. The existence of so many different religions in the world is, in his view, a divine dispensation, and since they are all basically good and in essence the same, they they should be allowed to increase in number until every man has 'a religion unto himself! It is clear that as an essntialist he is predisposed to accept the concept of universal truth, but this does not undermine his position as a pluralist nor adaversely affect his attitude to particular religions. On the contrary, since all religions are in essence one it would seem to him to be eminently desirable that diverse manifestations of this essence should be enouraged to multiply.

Vivekananda shares with Radhakrishnan and other idealists his belief in the basic oneness of existence and the essntial unity of religions. What Radhakrishan refers to as the religion of the spirit is in point of fact akin to Vivekananda's concept of universal religion. Both thinkers acknowledge that each particular religion follows its own path to the realisation of the goal of union with the divine. In the same way Radhakrishan's essentially spiricual interpretaion of the universe which enables him to see the cosmic process as a movement with an inherent teleogy and goal where all forms of life are expressions of the Divine Spirit, is at one with Vivekananda's belife that there is no discontinuity between animals life and human or spiritual forms of life, and that all forms of existence are manifestations or expressions of the spirit of God.

It is the Vedantic philosophical tradition that inspires Viveknanda. He explicitly acknowledges his indebtedness to it and it is implicit in all that he writes. The Vedantic docctrine of the divinity of man was one aspect of the message he proclaimed at the World Parliament of Religions in Chicago in 1893 and it was the same message that permeated his subsequent writings:

"One principle it (Vedanta) lays down and that is to be found in every religion in the world that man is divine, which we see around us is the out come of the consciousness of the divine. Everything that is strong, and good, and powerful in human nature is the outcome of that divint, all being alike divine.

The Vedantic natoin of Brahman as chitananad is echoed in Vivekananda's insistence that God is pure spirit, the soul, the Reality in us, the heart,the One through whom we know, see, think and exist: He is the essence of our Self. He is the essence of this ego, this I, and we cannot know anything excepting through that I. Therefore you have to know everything in and through the Brahman'. This corresponds to what Sankara has to say about knowing the self in the self alone through the self (atmani, atmanam, atmana), or experiencing the Brahman-atman identity in the depth of the atman. Vivekananda, claims that the impersonal God in Being itself, the only reality, all else being manifested by the power of maya. Gandhi was acquainted with the thought of Vivekananda. Both distinguished between personal and impesonal concepts of God, for examples, and both had significant things to say about the relation between Truth and God. For Vivekananda, however, as for Gandhi, it is the impersonal concept of god that has the greater appeal since the impersonal concept is infinite while the personal concept is limited. God is beyond the limited when we conceive of him as impersonal Being, but he is limited when we conceive of him in personal terms. But the similarity between Gandhi and Vivekananda goes even further than the distinction between personal and impersonal concept of God. Gandhi points to personifications of the ultimate indication of man's desire for symbols. In the same way Vivekananda, after the fashion of Adavaita, refers to forms and images as external symbols manifasting man's endeavour to apprehend the absolute or the eternal:

The Hindus have discovered that the absolute can only be thought of, or stated, through the relative, and the images, crosses, and crescents are simply so many symbols so many pages to hang the spiritual ideas on. It is not that this help is nesscessary for every one, but those that do not need it have no right to say that is it wrong. Both recognise the need for symbols represeatations of the ulatimate and both acknowledge that they are necessary in the spiritual life of some people. Both agree that image worship simply illustrates man's need for symbols and ought not to be construred as idol worship and both would express perference for the impersonal concept of God as Being itself (*sat*) or (*satya*). Yet both would agree that there is nothing basically wrong in conceiviving God in personalised terms. Radhakrishan makes a similar point when he distinguishes between the Supreme as abosolute spirit and the Supreme as personal God: It is a difference between God as He is and God as he seems to us. Personality is a symbol and if we ignore its symbolic character it shuts us out from the truth'

Vivekananda's expresseds prefcrence for the impersonal concept of God as the fundamental ground or basic for any understanding of the personal concept of God meant that the type or religion that had the greatest appeal for him was that which propounded impersonal rather the personal concept of the absolute. He was well aware that certain historical religions laid claim to universality, but he doubted whether it was possible for any historical religion to make such a cliam which presumalby included Adavaita Vadanta.

That is, he is suggesting that it was possible for any historical religion to be equated with a particular, historical reiglion with its own brand of philosophies, rituals and mythologies. Yet in the same way as he professes preference for impersonal concepts of God, so he expresses preference for impersonal concepts of the absolute. This prompts him to claim that Dvaita (dualism) is on a lower level of undestanding than qualified non dualism (visistadvaita) and perfcet Advaite (non-dualism):

Now as society exists at the present time, all these three stages are necessary; the one does not deny the other , one is simply the fulfilment of the other. The Adaitist or the qualifited Advaitist does not say that dualism is wrong; it is a right view, but a lower one. It is on the truth; therefore let everyone work out his own vision of this universe, according to his own ideas. Vivekananda expresses himself more forcibly when he criticises those religions that are based on historical data such as the historicity of a person,because if the historicity of personal is disproved the whole fabric of the religion concerned is uudermined. This criticism would not apply to Advaita Vadanta, he claims, since it does not depend on the life and teachaing of an historical person but is based rather on principles that are common to all religions.

Vivekananda's comments on this subject, which are prefectly in accord with the philosophical idealism that he supports and expounds, have elicited much criticism. He has been accused of adopting an exculusivist attitude to Advaita Vedanta and presenting it as the highest stage of religious awareness open to man in contrast to those dualistic forms of religion.

"That the whole world were Advaitists tomorrow, not only in theory, but in realisation. But if that cannot be, let us do next best thing; let us take the ignorant by the hand, lead them always a step just as they can go, and know that every step in all religious growth in India has been progressive."

This reference to the 'next best thing' may be an indication that Vivakananda regarded dualistic forms of religion as inferior to the monistic or the non-dualistic forms and that, in his view, dualism would need to be transcended and culminate in non-dualiam if the stage of perfection is to be attained or relised. The question is whether he equates non-perfection to be attained or realised. The question is whether he equates non-dualism with Advaita Vadanta as a particular, historical religion or rather as a principle that outght to determine our understanding of ulimate reality and the abolute. His critics world accuse him of the former and ipso facto guilty of sectarianism. There can be no doubt, however, that he accepted the validity of all religions and not just Advaita Vadanta. He claimed, for exmple, that he accpted the validity of Islam, Christianity and that he would be able to 'worship God with every one of them' But it is equally clear that all dualistic forms of religion are, in his view, valid only on the lower level of truth and that attainment of perfection is not possible.

There is a storng case for maintainting thatVivekananda's view of Adaita is not sectarian in the sense that he puts forward Advaita Vedanta as the most acceptable particular historical religion available, but rather that he regards non-duslism as a principle that ought to determine our attitude to the nature of ultimate reality. This would be totally in accord with philosophical idealistic view he upholds and expounds in his writings. He applauds the variety of religions traditions that exists and claims that Vadanta has nothing to say against any one of them: whether you are a Christian, or a Buddhist, a Jew, or a Hindu, whatever mythology you believe, whethert you owe allegiance to the propher of Nazareth, or of Meecca, or of india, or of anywhare else, whether you youself are a prophet it has nothing to say. It only preaches the principle which is the background of every realigion and of which all the prophets and saints and seers are illustrations and manifestations.

It is Vevekananda's convicition that man has religion in soul and that the aim of all religions is to realise God in the soul. That is the one universal religion:

"The greatest name man ever gave to God is Truth. Truth is the realisation; therefore seek it within the soul. Get away from all books and forms and let your soul see its Self....Religion is one, therefore, give his message; but not find defects in other religions. You must come out form all form if you world see the Light."

The essentialist view of religion which Vivekananda, like Rahhakrishnan, exemplifies is characteristic of an idealist phiosophical outlook. It may well be that Hegel as an absolute idealist was one of the formost thinkaers to regard religion as a self-subsisting essence, or a transcendental entity, underlying all particular historical manifestations. But it was Schleiermacher, the theologion of romanticium, the school that owed its origin to protest againts the tyranny of rationalism. Both were preceded by Plato, of course, with his theory of Forms and Ideas which insisted on the existence of praticulars. It argued that religion was not simply a theological system or a set of theories, doctrines, principle or ideals, or even an analysis of the nature of an incomprehensible being, but somethhing that had to do with man's soul. To discover what religion really is, he maintains one has to turn away from what is usually called religion. The primordial form of religion is the 'soul dissolved in the immediate feeling of the Infinite and the Eternal'

For Schleiermacher the starting point of religion is man. It originates in the soul's response and surrrnder to the Universe, the one, the whole, the Godhead, the Infinite. True religoin is the 'sense and taste for the Infinite. It cannot be equated with its outward form, though according to Schleiemacher it has to be acknowledged that its primordial essence does find expression in the form of earthly religion Each historical religoin is a distinct thought impure form of religion in its manifestation of the essnce of religion. It is interesting to note that this view is reflected in the teaching of Kirekegaard for whom limited outward expression of goodness succeed in conveying the meaning of absolute goodness . The impure form of historical religions means that, for Schleiermacher as for other idealists, it is not possible to nominate a particular historical religion as the perfect embodial of the essences of religion. This is not to say of course that essences or universals do not exits in themselves; they do according to Plato, because they are perfect.

It will be seen that Vivekananda from an idealistic standpoint propounnds an essentialist view of religion not dissimilar to that of Schleiemacher. He lays stress on the realisation of God in the soul in the same way as Scheiermacher refers to looking within at the pious soul. Both are wary of outward forms yet both see the need for diversity and multiplicity. The universal religion of Vivekananda is not far removed from the primordial essence of religion found in the writinges of Schliermachar. For both, religion is one in essence and diverse in manifestation, and both regard the transcendental unity of religion as a necessay prerequisite for the existence of histocal religion through which the essence of religion is manifested. As Radhakrishna correctly pointed out, 'The world has bled and suffered from the discase of dogmatism, of conformity', a sentiment echoed in Tillich's writings and focefullly expressed by Vivekananda when he referred to truth being expressed 'in a hundred thousand ways, and that each of these ways is true as far as it goes'.

The essentialist approach as exemplified by Vivekananda is in stark contrast to the reativist approch. His mature position is that all religion are culturally determined. For him the principle of development is so fundamental that we have to acknowledge the same kind of development in religious, ethical and philosahical ideas as we find in the spheres of legislation and economics. All religions contain an element of truth and although they move in the direction of unity they manifest individual differences which are likely to remain.

Vivekananda Inclusivist or Pluralist?

Many scholars have made attempts to assess the teachings of Vivekananda on the harmony of religions, through an analysis of whether he represented the school of pluralism or the school of inclusivism in the theology of religions. One may clearly identify that Vivekananda was never an exclusivist, but he may not have said anything substantial along the lines of pluralistic inclusivism either.

In the World Parliament of Religions, Chicago, 1893, Vivekananda called for religious unity by each religion assimilating the spirit of the other arid yet preserving its own identity. In his works we notice the thesis that the differences between religions are of expression and degree and not of substance. We can know through a study of religions that the essence of all of them is the same. He also said that she different religions will have to make concessions for achieving harmony; the more sacrifice a religion undertakes for the sake of harmony, the more it advances in truth. Vivekananda thought that the teaching to harmonise everything was first given by Sri Krisna in the Bhagavad Gita. He was also of the opinion that we have to harmonise the four yogas of work, devotion, control of the mind, and knowledge, and that the life of Sri Ramakrishna was such a harmony. According to him the history of India points to religious harmony and tolerance. He cited the examples of Emperor Asoka of the third century B.C., and of the Jews, Christians, and Parsees who were given shelter in India. Hinduism taught the world both tolerance and universal acceptance, and this teaching, he claimed, represents the kernel of all forms of religions.

According to Vivekananda the central teaching of his Master was openness to all religions, they being so many paths leading to the same goal, and the ideas that he preached were only attempts to echo the ideas of his Master. If God is the centre, religions represent the different radii converging to the same centre. Through various conditions and circumstances all are finally reaching the same goal. He was of the view that Hinduism recognises the right of each person to have his own Ista or chosen way. Our journey is not from error to truth, but from lower truth to higher truth. In our journey to the sun the photographs taken may differ widely, but they all are of the same sun. It was Vivekananda's contention that Truth is to be found not in subtraction but in addition. What is needed is universality, mutual acceptance of religions, which goes beyond the idea of just mutual toleration. If one religion is true, all the others must be true. Each religion has the same saving power as the other.

Vivekananda also made a distinction between religion and sectarian creed. According to him Religion embraces all religions, whereas the sectarian view is a 'frog-in- the- well' attitude of exclusivism. In the Parliament of Religions itself he had pleaded to have a wider outlook for each religion, to overcome the 'frog-in- the-well' attitude. All the sectarian religious quarrels, in the view of Vivekananda, are like the quarrels between blind persons regarding the shape of an elephant. This analogy is used not only in Hinduism, but also in Jainism and Buddhism. Sri Ramakrishna has also said that the dogmatists are like the blind people who examined an elephant.

In the World Parliament of Religions itself Vivekananda exhorted humanity to evolve a universal religion which would be a sum total of all religions, and yet have infinite space for development, and which would aid humanity to realise its own true divine nature. In his works Vivekananda explains that the ideal of a universal religion involves the recognition of the natural necessity of variation. What is practically possible is to 'maintain unity in variety'. We experience God according to our capabilities; God is the water filling our different mental vessels.

In teaching the harmony of all religions, Vivekananda can thus be considered as a follower of the school of pluralism. The pluralist standpoint holds that other religions are equally the paths to the one God. Pluralism also believes that he ultimate reality upon which the faith of all believers is focussed in every religion is the same, though interpretations of its essential nature may vary. . According to this school of the theology of religions, truth-claims are of a complementary nature and not of a conflicting nature.

Vivekananda also can be considered to be a true disciple and successor of Sri Ramakrishna on this matter, because Sri Ramakrishna had the firm conviction that in religious matters there are different paths:; leading to the same goal. In order to explain this important point he used the analogies of 'reaching the roof through different ways'; 'coming to Dakshineswar through different ways' and 'reaching the reservoir of Immortality through different means'. People worship God according to their tastes and temperaments, and this is like different children eating different dishes cooked by their mothers as per each one's taste. Also, for him all religions addressing the same Reality in different ways were like children addressing the same father differently. Ramakrishna repeatedly pointed out that those who quarrel over doctrines about God are like the blind people who examined the elephant or those who quarrelled about the colour of the chameleon.

We may note in this context that for pluralism, the best example from Indian religions is that of the Syadvada of Jainism. The Syadvada teaches that all predications are true only in reference to the standpoint occupied and the aspect of the object considered. All our judgements are relative because we can know only some aspect of reality. We quarrel and disagree because we forget this. Syadvada gives inspiration to its followers to respect the views of people of other living faiths and ideologies; other's views are also equally true from their respective standpoints, and these can be correlated well with our own views. Thus Jainism contributes epistemologically to the harmony of religions in India. Vivekananda has not spoken about Syadvada, but it is our submission that Syadvada strengthens the pluralist position of Vivekananda.

While we analyse the teachings of Vivekananda, it should be further noted that from the year 1895 he started projecting Advaita Vedanta as the harmoniser of all religions. Vedanta manifests the common ground between all religions—i.e., the one Atman runs through all this seeming variety. All are variations of the One Atman. Advaita considers all the different religions to be true manifestations of the same truth at different stages. If we seek out the reality in religions, that would be the Advaita Vedantic affirmation of the One Absolute. Advaita arrives at this not by denouncing the other ideas of God, but by seeking out the reality in them. It is the sum total of ail religions and includes all degrees of religious development. The different Vedantic schools of Dvaita, Visistadvaita, and Advaita are not contradictory; they all necessitate and fulfil each other; one is a stepping-stone to the other until the goal, which is Advaita, is reached.

Through the Advaita Vedantic understanding that each idea of God is but a stage in the religious journey, tolerance and acceptance of all different religions become natural and spontaneous for a Hindu. This fact Vivekananda demonstrated through the following expositions : For him the most significant message of Islam is equality, and so the Vedantic theory of equality in the one Atman is in reality put into practice by Islam. Therefore the future India should have a Vedantic brain and an Islamic body: Buddha, according to him, fulfilled Hinduism by proclaiming the truth hidden in the Vedas—that in the spiritual realm there is no caste distinction. He also had much appreciation for the Brahmo Samaj's social reforms, but not for its religious teachings. Similarly, he could perceive the religions of Christ and Vedanta to be identical, while rejecting the misrepresentations of Jesus by later Christianity.

When we compare the teachings of Vivekananda with those of his Master, Sri Ramakrishna, we notice that the proposal for a synthesis of all religions under Vedanta in terms of the idea that all religious experiences are a progression from Dvaita to Visistadvaita to Advaita is a new discovery by Vivekananda. What we find in Sri Ramakrishna is the synthesis of the Absolute and the Relative, the formless God and God with forms. Both were equally true and significant to him. He preferred God with forms and devotion as the easiest means to reach Him/Her. But Advaita became the supreme point of reference to synthesise all other points of view in Vivekananda.

There are no religions that are superior or inferior in Sri Ramakrishna's view. He gave equal respect for all paths. He belonged fully to the school of pluralism. Whereas we see Vivekananda oscillating between the schools of pluralism and inclusivism. There may be people who would point out that to the extent he considered Advaita as the highest standpoint in religion and tried to bring in other standpoints under its umbrella as lower stages of religious evolution, he was an inclusivist. The inclusivist approach affirms the salvific presence of God in other religions while still maintaining that one's own religious faith is the definitive and authoritative revelation of God. Inclusivism accepts the divine presence in other faiths, but rejects them as not being sufficient for liberation apart from one's own faith. All the truth in other religions belongs ultimately to one's own faith, which is the fulfillment of all of them. Thus inclusivism is both an acceptance and a rejection of the other faiths. But it should be noted that there are many statements in Vivekananda's writings, where he stresses his Master's, standpoint of all paths leading to the same goal. And so he may be considered equally to be a pluralist. The greatness of Vivekananda lies in the fact that he could expound his teachings in terms of the schools of inclusivism and pluralism a hundred years ago, during the last part of the nineteenth century.

Vivekananda was also a pioneer in the reinterpretation of Hinduism as what is now popularly known as neo-Vedanta. In his interpretation he was trying to synthesise the various schools of Hinduism as well as the various religious standpoints under Advaita Vedanta. After him, many scholars and saints have proceeded in the path pointed out by him—S. Radhakrishnan, to mention an internationally famous name. Also, Vivekananda in his thought synthesised spirituality with social action, and the Ramakrishna Mission today stands for this synthesis. We have already seen that he was for the synthesis of the different margas—karma, bhakti, yoga and jnana. Moreover, he wanted to see a synthesis of the different strata of society in order to overcome the barriers of the caste system. In him, secularism and communitarianism blend together to eliminate communalism. He was secular in the sense of holding and pleading for equality and the equal opportunity for all religions. He was communitarian because his cry was 'Arise! awake! and stop not until the goal is reached'.

Religion has played havoc in the world. In the name of religion horrendous deeds have been done. For the sake of religion men have earnestly affirmed and contradicted almost every idea and form of conduct. In the long history of religion appear chastity and prostitution, feasting and fasting, intoxication and prohibition, dancing and sobriety, human sacrifice and saving of life, orphanages and hospitals, superstition and education, poverty and wealthy endowments, prayer wheels and silent worship, gods and demons, one God and many gods, attempts to escape and to reform the world.

Vivekananda noted: "I accept all religions that were in the past, and worship with them all; I worship God with every one of them.... Is God's book finished? Or is it still a continuous revelation going on? It is a marvellous book—these spiritual revelations of the world. The Bible, the Vedas, the Koran, and all other sacred books are but so many pages, and an infinite number of pages remain yet to be unfolded.... We stand in the present, but open ourselves to the infinite future. We take in all that has been in the past, enjoy the light of the present, and open every window of the heart for all that will come in the future. Salutation to all the prophets of the past, to all the great ones of the present, and to all that arc to come in the future!"

Vivekananda wanted religion to be the supreme force in India, as he knew only too well that religion was the only language of India. And he knew what he meant by 'language*. 'Language is not merely a means of communication but a vehicle for expressing the emotions of your sorrow, love or hate.' He was a many-sided spiritual individual who could surely comprehend that India could not survive without religion.

Vivekananda knew that the evolving mankind needed a religion, and that that religion had not yet come into existence. Religion for him was realization, so his all-out effort was to raise the religio-moral standard of our people. He made it very clear that man was potentially divine, and man could become God. He said, 'Every religion is only evolving a God out of the material man, and the same God is the inspirer of all of them.'

More than hundred years ago Vivekananda took his position on the question of the human condition at the World Parliament of Religions at Chicago: "You are children of immortal bliss—amrtsya putrah. Try to manifest it. You are not children of sin, children of weakness, children of dull, dead matter. You are spirits free, eternal, and pure; matter is your servant, and not you the servant of matter."

Vivekananda wanted us to understand the meaning of spiritual growth and the meaning of the evolution of man beyond the organic dimension. It is psycho-social evolution and not mere organic evolution which would save mankind, he declared most emphatically. He argued that we have the best of physical equipment, this cerebral system. We do not need any new organ or organs; but we need to learn to use this unique cerebral organ of our system efficiently.

What Vivekananda wanted was that the new outlook demand of us more attention to 'modern science'. It is a question of either or: either human greatness or the reverse. He was convinced that 'the deepest problem of the modern world is to find a vision at once challenging and genuine'. He believed that the vision of a world to which God allowed real freedom to create itself was existing. It includes science and beyond. We live in a world where all sorts of tragedies occur, where much seems meaningless and cruel. Yet the very openness and unpredicability of nature, which allows these things to happen, provides freedom, human development, and ultimately human love. Gradually humankind begins to see a purpose even in what seems like senseless waste and tragedy. 'The world is in the making, history matters.' The freedom given us is to be used — and used not just for ourselves, but so that the whole universe can 'enter upon the liberty and splendour of the children of immortality,'

So, Vivekananda wanted that religion which 'tunes human actions to a view of the cosmic order onto the plane of human existence. In religious belief and practice a people's style of life, the design for living, is rendered intellectually reasonable; it is shown to represent a way of life ideally adapted to the world "as. it 'really', 'fundamentally,' 'ultimately' is.' Vivekananda upheld a style of life, or better, say an Indian view of life. 'Indian view' stands for the way of life which cultivates the age-old dictum: 'variety in unity.' At the Parliament of Religions he explained the convergence theme very eloquently: "From the high spiritual flights of the Vedanta philosophy, of which the latest discoveries of science seem like echoes, to the low ideas of idolatry with its multifarious mythology, the agnosticism of the Buddhists, and the atheism of the Jains, each and all have a place in the Hindu's religion." In the same lecture elsewhere he comes to the central point:

"The Hindu religion does not consist in struggles and attempts to believe a certain doctrine or dogma, but in realising — not in believing, but in being and becoming. Thus the whole object of their system is by constant struggle to become perfect, to become divine, to reach Cod and see God, and this reaching God, seeing God, becoming perfect even as the Father in Heaven is perfect, constitutes the religion of the Hindus."

Vivekananda's attitude towards Hinduism and Islam has to be viewed in the light of the above discussion. Trying to understand Islam, he often referred to the essence of Indian culture. One simple incident will illustrate his humanistic approach to the question of Hinduism and Islam. He was once asked by one of his fellow monks if he should admit Muslim boys to their ashram school. His answer was to this effect:

"You must admit Mohammedan boys too, but never tamper with their religion. The only thing you will have to do is to make separate arrangements for their food, etc., and teach them so that they may be moral, manly, and devoted to doing good to others. This indeed is religion."

Shelve your intricate philosophical speculations for the present. 'Unity in variety is the plan of the universe,' says Vivekananda. His argument:

"We are all men, and yet we are all distinct from one another. As a part of humanity 1 am one with you, and as Mr. So-and-so I am different from you. As a man you are separate from the woman; as a human being you are one with the woman. As a man you are separate from the animal, but as living beings man, woman, animal and plant are all one; and as existence, you are one with the whole universe..,. In Him we are all one. At the same time, in manifestation, these differences must always remain."

This explains why India abhors conformity: every person has a place in the sun. That's why he substantiates his contention with the following words: 'Take man where he stands, and from there give him a lift,' He beautifully preplaing.

"If it be true that God is the centre of all religions, and that each of us is moving towards Him along one of these radii, then it is certain that all of us must reach that centre. And at the centre, where all the radii meet, all- our differences will cease; but until we reach there, differences there must be."

Vivekananda never believed in half-truth. Therefore he wanted Hindus and Muslims both to remain in their own folds but exhorted them to go beyond the closed-door world. And he himself was a 'gradualist'. Never did he wish away reality, asking for too much in a night. He knew the Indian mind as much as he could understand the frailty of human life. So his warning was: change is all right, but it must be 'in the-limited.'

Vivekananda believed in the world because he believed in man, because he believed in Sri Ramakrishna. One must understand that he was making an act of faith which cannot be taken off from life. The notion that knowledge proceeds from a series of acts of faith—faith in spirit, in God, in man—is a crucial part of his thought. Otherwise we shall misinterpret the status of his humanist philosophy. The temptation is to make faith say what only man can say. It is important to stress his understanding of different levels of consciousness. It is this understanding which integrates reason and religion without making either say what can only be said by the other. Likewise Islam meets Hinduism, and Hinduism meets Islam. And these meetings have added enough magnificence and resilience to India's composite culture to fight the virus of hatred and animosity.

Vivekananda met many men and women in his life. And immediately he absorbed certain things which enabled him to form vitally important ideas about a religious community he did not belong to. One or two such incidents will suffice. In the Kashmir valley he came across a Kashmiri woman whose farm he visited and had begged for water, which she had at once given him. And before leaving her" he asked her, what Mother, is your religion? Thank God, Sir, by the mercy of the Lord, I am a *Mussalman*.' This episode Sister Nivedita noted in her *Notes of Some Wanderings with Vivekananda* with utmost care and affection. This particular incident left an indelible impression on the Vivekananda's mind. This self-respect and sense of pride for one's own religion is what everybody should cultivate, he affirmed. Again in Nainital a *Mussalman* had said to him. "Vivekananda, if in aftertimes some claim you as an Avatar, remember that 1, a Mohammedan, am the first.'

These tales tell another significant thing. What made these simple folk so straightforward? The religion itself. But, why? The answer may be given by another question asked by Vivekananda. 'How could Mohammedanism have lived, had there been nothing good in its teaching? There is much good.-Mohammed was the Prophet of equality, of the brotherhood of man, the brotherhood of all *Mussulmans*.' Elsewhere in the lectures he elaborated this point:

"Mohammed by his life showed that amongst Mohammedans there should be perfect equality and brotherhood. There was no question of race, caste, creed, colour, or sex. The Sultan of Turkey may buy a Negro from 'the mart of Africa and bring him in chains to Turkey, but should he become a Mohammedan and have sufficient merit and abilities, he might even marry the daughter of the Sultan."

This social conscience of Islam moved Vivekananda tremendously. However, all these are but the beginning of a realization: Islamic monotheism and Advaitism are but one single expression of spiritual realisation of Islam: 'The greatness of God in the life of men.' 'Taking God for God was the only heart and nerve of Mohammed's sense of avocation as the Koran embodies and fulfils it. Thus a Mussalman bends all his resources to reaffirm and, enforce this undivided worship. The most vital thing in Islam is unity of Godhead and worship. 'Islam lives in the conviction that human life is constituted, totally and essentially by Godward accountability. God's will and worship are the terms of reference of human existence.' Vivekananda absorbed all this very carefully. In this connexion the letter he wrote to Mohammed Sajfaraz Hussain of Nainital from Almora on 10th June 1898, is a footnote to the concept of inter-religious dialogue. I quote the letter in full:

"My dear Friend,

I appreciate your letter very much and am extremely happy to learn that the Lord is silently preparing wonderful things for our motherland. Whether we call it Vedantism or any ism, the truth is that Advaitism is the last word of religion and thought and the only position from which one can look upon all religions and seets with love. I believe it is the religion of the future of enlightened humanity. The Hindus may get the credit of arriving at it earlier than other races, they being an older race than cither Hebrew or the Arab; yet practical Advaitissn, which looks upon and behaves to all mankind as one's own soul, was never developed among the Hindus.

On the other hand, my experience is that if ever any religion approached to this equality in an appreciable manner, it is Islam and Islam alone.

Therefore, I am firmly persuaded that without the help of practical Islam, theories of Vedantism, however fine and wonderful they may be, are entirely valueless to the vast mass of mankind. We want to lead mankind to the place where there is neither the Vedas, nor the

Bible, and the Koran; yet this has to be done by harmonizing the Vedas, the Bible, and the Koran. Mankind ought to be taught that religions are but the varied expression of the Religion, which is Oneness, so that each may choose the path that suits him best.

For our own motherland a junction of the two great systems, Hinduism and Islam—Vedanta brain and Islam body-is the only, hope. I see in my mind's eye the future perfect India rising out of this chaos and strife, glorious and invincible, with Vedanta brain and Islam body. Ever praying that the Lord may make of you a great instrument for the help of mankind, and especially of our poor, poor motherland."

Vivekananda, even a century ago, envisaged mutual understanding. What appealed to Vivekananda most was the social dynamism of Islam. He appreciated the fact that the Prophet Muhammad gave a broader, clear vigorous political and social ideal to the Arabian people. Muhammad rejected all claims to work miracles, and he despised grandeur, and lived on principle of an extremely frugal life. All this immensely moved Vivekananda.

Thus true fulfilment of Vivekananda hopes and desires in this direction can only be attained by mutual study and appreciation of each other's religious literature and commentaries, cultural exchange, and social interaction. Not the *Masjid*, not the *Mandir*, but a forum for unity and harmony of he mankind can only save the world from the scourge of communal frenzy. Let us not get too emotionally involved but look at things in the light of Vivekananda's admonition that religion should be based on reason, not on sentiment. separation and division.

Many scholars have argued that Vivekananda's attempt to synthesise other religious experiences under Advaita would amount to the standpoint of inchisivism. If Advaita is standing for the potential divinity and the consequent equality of all, Advaita in principle is not discriminating between religious experiences or people. Advaita is equally for the Dalit's as well as the upper caste people. It is the same *Atman* that is in everyone, pervading, unifying, and illuminating.' In that, there is no caste, no untouchability; we are all one. We can all arise and work for the benefit of one another. If Vivekananda's adherence to Advaita pointed to this practical Vedanta, it would be a contradiction to say that he discriminated between people in terms of their religious convictions, wanting people to discard their religious convictions and progress towards Advaita. Advaita stands for the opposite, for the equality of all, and so, making Advaita a criterion for religious synthesis does not make one the adherent of inclusivism. Moreover, we should note that Vivekananda never rejected other faiths as not being sufficient for liberation apart from Advaita. Also, he never claimed that all the truth in other religions ultimately belongs to Advaita. Hence he cannot be called an inclusivist in the strict sense of the term.

In each religion there will be a universal principle in terms of which one can perceive other religions in a positive light, e.g., Advaita in Hinduism, Syadvada in Jainism, and Jesus in Christianity. This universal aspect of religious experience need not be static: 'it is dynamic, gradually manifesting new insights .and new meanings in the light of religious experiences from sister religions. And this intercommunication of religions is possible through pluralistic inclusivism, which is a viable school of theology of religions, specially in the Indian context. Pluralistic inclusivism inspires people of all living faiths to accomplish a dynamic growth from the standpoint of 'relational distinctiveness' to that of 'relational convergence' which is the need of the hour in dialogical theology.

Pluralistic inclusivism inspires each religious faith to be pluralistically inclusive—i.e., on the one hand each living faith is to become truly pluralistic by other faiths contributing to its conceptual content, and on the other hand inclusivism is to transform its meaning to witness the fulfilment of one's own faith in and through the contributions of other living faiths. In pluralistic inclusivism the insights regarding Jesus grow with the help of other religious experiences and teachings, for example, Advaita. Advaita Vedanta gives new meanings to Jesus. If Advaita Vedanta can give new meanings to Jesus, other religious experiences and concepts like Syadvada also can give new meanings to Indian Christian thought. The giving and taking is mutual; Advaita and Syadvada also receive new meanings and insights through Jesus and other universal religious principles, and thus all religions can possibly progress to relational convergence. Now the point is, such, significant religions principles which grow in insights by receiving meanings from other religious concepts and experiences cannot project inclusivism, but only the opposite of it—i.e., Advaita cannot project inclusivism, but only the opposite of it. Because, if in inclusivism other religious concepts are seen as undergoing gradual change through our own particular religious concept alone, here in pluralistic inclusivism our religious concept is getting enriched in meaning with the help of insights received from other religious conceptions and experiences. Advaita, Syadvada, Jesus, etc., which constitute universal religious principles, get enriched in meaning with the help of insights received from other religious conceptions and experiences. Vivekananda has not explicitly said so, but his overall teaching of the harmony of religions can in effect ratify such an approach to affect the relational convergence of religions.

Advaita stands for Oneness, cutting across all distinctions, barriers, and separations. Such a universal principle as Advaita cannot project its own distinction and superiority over other religious principles. Advaita, Syadvada, Jesus, etc., become what they are in true spirit through the sacrifice of their distinction and superiority and hence there is no quarrel between them; the quarrel is between the pseudo-followers of these universal principles, and it is not right lo picture Vivekananda as a pseudo-follower of Advaita.

We should also bear in mind the religious context in which Vivekananda expounded his teachings. The exclusivist of Christianity, with its intolerant altitude to other religions, specially Hinduism, was the dominant school of the day, and it was such conservative missionary- oriented Western which was confronted. Naturally he had to counter such a Christianity for self- survival. The Christian missionaries, he found, were attacking Hinduism, and they were arrogant and exclusive. The defect of religions like Christianity, according to him, was . that they have one set of rules for all people, whereas Hinduism is suited to all grades of religious aspiration and progress. What the Hindus wanted was the liberty to worship their deities; they could sacrifice everything else, but not religious freedom. Vivekananda carried out his counter-attack of Christianity gloriously because even while attacking Western Christianity he had all the respect in the world for Jesus and his teachings. He pointed out that between the religion of Jesus and Advaita Vedanta there is no difference. It is the later Western Christianity which has distorted the wonderful life and teachings of Jesus.

Vivekananda could understand Jesus only from within his own Advaita Vedantic background. But then we should understand that hermeneutically that is the only possibility; because our background and being contribute to the very content of our knowledge. Christians should gratefully acknowledge that they have been enriched by Vivekananda's Christological interpretations. Some aspects of the meanings of Jesus which had not been brought to light so far, could see light through the expositions of Vivekananda as well as the later neo-Vedantins who followed the line of thought inaugurated by him.

For Vivekananda, Jesus was an Advaitin because his supreme teaching was I and my Father are One.' Christ shows us the way to become perfect, he shows us our true nature, which is divine; he shows us that the Kingdom of God is within us. The difference between Christ and an ordinary human being is only a difference in the degree of manifestation of divinity. Jesus was one of the many incarnations. Christianity considers a human being to be a sinner, and it has the theory of atonement through the sacrifice of Jesus on the Cross. But the highest teaching of Jesus was on potential divinity, and the attempt to fit him in the Jewish idea of the Fall and the consequent sacrificial atonement was really unfortunate. According to Vivekananda, the West distorted the religion of the renunciation and realization of Jesus into a 'shop-keeping religion' of luxury and intolerant superstitious doctrines. What is needed today is to retain the essentials of Christianity, which are the teachings of Jesus, specially the Sermon on the Mount.

Coming back to the point of the attack on Hinduism by Christian missionaries and Vivekananda's counter-attack, it should be noted that he did not condemn Christianity altogether, because he was all for the harmony of religions. For him the journey is not from error to truth, but from truth to truth. H e could accommodate Christianity in his scheme of religious thought as a particular stage of truth which has to grow to its culmination, which is Christ or Advaita. If some Christians condemned Hinduism as error, Vivekananda was magnanimous enough not to follow their suit and condemn Christianity as error. Vivekananda had to come but with an inclusivist approach of accommodating Christianity under Advaita because the missionary exponents of Christianity were exclusivists. If the Christians had been pluralistic there is no doubt that Vivekananda also would have been a pluralistic. And so we will not be doing justice to Vivekananda if we categorise his theology of religions as inclusivism. Vivekananda was supremely a pluralist, drawing inspiration from his Master Sri Ramakrishna, and he was only sometimes forced to become an inclusivist in the context of his counter-attack on Christian Missionary exclusivism.

Inclusivist Hinduism and Vivekananda

The Frenchman Francois Bernier, who visited India between 1656 and 1668, wrote of the pluralism of Hinduism and tolerance of the Hindus. However, the conceptual framework for the inclusive model of Hinduism was laid at the end of the nineteenth century by the eminent Oxford Sanskritist Monier-Williams (1819-99). In his influential book, Religious Thought and Life in India, Monier-Williams writes, 'It (Hinduism) claims to the one religion of humanity, of human nature, of the entire world. It cares not to oppose the progress of any other system. For it has no difficulty in including all other religions within its all-embracing arms and ever-widening fold'. He describes the Hindu religion as one based on the idea of universal receptivity which has 'first with and then, so to speak, swallowed, digested, and assimilated something from all creeds', In a more recent reformulation, the German Indologist Paul Hacker, argued that the inclusivism (inklusivismus) associated with Hinduism is often confused with tolerance. According to Hacker, inclusivism 'consists in claiming for, and thus including in, one's own religion what really belongs to an alien sect'. He points out that 'it would perhaps be more, accurate to speak of inclusivism in many cases where we are inclined to see Hindu tolerance'. Hacker singles out Vivekananda and Radhakrishnan as the most notable practitioners of this method of inclusivism'. Both Vivekananda and Radhakrishnan were also leading proponents of Advaita Vedanta. Though Hackers additional assertion that there was inclusivism rather than tolerance in Indian tradition has been contested, his claim about the displacement of tolerance by inclusivism is useful in discussing the thoughts of Vivekananda and Radhakrishnan.

Perhaps the most powerful articulation of the inclusivist model of Hinduism was Vivekananda's now legendary address at the Parliament of Religions in Chicago in 1893 where he declared: 'I am proud to belong to a religion which has taught the world both tolerance and universal acceptance. We believe not only in universal toleration but we accept all religions as true'. This theme of the tolerance and universality of Hinduism, specifically Vedantic Hinduism, 0uld find pride of place in several of Vivekananda's speeches. At another lecture in America, Vivekananda clearly outlined his idea of an inclusivist Hinduism:

Ours, as I have said, is the universal religion. It is inclusive enough it is broad enough to include all ideals. All the ideals of religion that already exist in the world can be immediately' included, and we can patiently wait for all the ideals that are to come in the future to be taken in the same fashion, embraced in the infinite arms of the religion of the Vedanta.

Thus, the infinite capacity o accommodate differences and dissent becomes the principal feature of Hinduism.

Sect after sect arose in India and seemed to shake the religion of the Vedas to its very foundations, but like the waters of the seashore in a tremendous earthquake it receded only for a while, only to return in all-absorbing flood, a thousand times more vigorous and when the tumult of the rush was over, these sects were all sucked in, absorbed, and assimilated into, the immense body of the mother Faith.

According to Vivekananda, the Hindu religion was founded on the Vedas which 'are a series of books which, to our minds, contain the essence of all religion'. Mote importantly he believed that only Vedanta could be the basis of a universal religion.

Our claim is that the Vedanta only can be the universal religions that it is already the existing universal religion in the world, because it reaches principles and not persons. No religion built upon a person can be taken up as a type by all the races of mankind... Now, the Vedantic religion does not require any such personal authority. Its sanction is the eternal nature of man, its ethics are based upon the eternal spiritual solidarity of man, already existing, already attained and not to be attained.

Despite his professed openness to other religions, Vivekananda believed in the superiority of Hinduism. At a speech in Madras, he said, Outs is the religion of which Buddhism with all its greatness is as rebel child, and of which Christianity is a very patchy imitation'. Harking back to the theme that Vedantic religion represented eternal truths, Vivekananda emphasized that only Hinduism had the potential of being a universal religion:

You hear claims made by every religion as being the universal religion of the world. Let me tell you in the first place that perhaps there never will be such a thing, but if there is a religion which can lay claim to be that, it is only our religion and no other, because every other religion depends on some person... But the truths of our religion, although we have persons by the score, do not depend upon.

For Vivekananda, the Vedas were also the fundamental unifying force among Hindus belonging to different sects. Addressing a gathering in Lahore in 1897 Vivekananda spoke on 'The Common Bases of Hinduism'.

Perhaps all who are here will agree on the First point that we believe the Vedas to be the eternal teachings of the secrets of religion. We all believe that this holy literature is without beginning and without end, coeval with nature, which is without beginning and without end; and that all our religious differences, all our religious struggles must end when we stand in the presence of that holy book; we are all agreed that this is the last court of appeal in all our spiritual differences.

In keeping with his belief in a higher religion, Vivekananda castigated, as Tapan Raychaudhuri puts it, the 'mindless imbecilities of popular Hinduism'. To quote once again from Vivekananda's speech in Madras,

The fact is that we have many superstitions, many bad spots and sores on our body—these have to be excised, cut off, and destroyed—but these do not destroy our religion, our national life, our spirituality. Every principle of religion is safe, and the sooner these black spots are purged away, the better the principles will shine, the more gloriously.

Many of Vivekananda's ideas on Hinduism, especially its capacity to assimilate, its unique role as a universal religion and the centrality of the Vedas, would be distilled by Radhakrishnan to define Hinduism as a 'way of life' rather than, religion. Radhakrishnan has written how, as a young student, he was profoundly affected by Vivekananda and his mentor Ramakrishna Paramahansa, In the Upton lectures at Oxford in 1926, Radhakrishnan famously described Hinduism as 'Hinduism is more a way of life than a form of thought. While it gives absolute liberty in the world of thought it enjoins a strict code of practice. The theist and the atheist, the skeptic and the agnostic may all be Hindus if they accept the Hindu system of culture and life' (emphasis added).

Radhakrishnan goes on to compare Hinduism to a 'fellowship' by saying, 'Hinduism is not a sect but a fellowship of all who accept the law of right and earnestly seek for the truth'.

Radhakrishnan links the very difficulty of defining Hinduism, or finding common characteristics, to its ability to assimilate and absorb external influences: 'The ease with which Hinduism has steadily absorbed the customs and ideas of peoples with whom it has come into contact is as great as the difficulty we feel in finding common features binding together its different forms'. This is what anthropologist N.K. Bose called the 'Hindu mode of absorption'. This assimilative quality of Hinduism, according to Radhakrishnan, has enabled it to withstand the onslaught of different people and ideas that have poured into India since the earliest times.

Though peoples of different races and cultures have been pouring into India from the dawn of history, Hinduism has been able to maintain its supremacy, and even the proselytizing creeds backed by political power have not been able to coerce the large majority of Indians to their views.

Thus Hinduism has 'come to be a tapestry of the most variegated tissues and almost endless diversity of hues.'

For Radhakrishnan, like Vivekananda, the Vedas and Vedanta remained the spiritual core of Hinduism through its entire history of development. Though Hinduism has continued to develop and grow through the ages, it is 'not to be dismissed as a mere flow and strife of opinions, for it represents a steady growth of insight, since every form of Hinduism and every stage of growth is related to the common background of the Vedanta'. He writes that 'those parts of the new faith which are not conformity to the Vedic Canon tend to be subordinated and gradually dropd'. Again, like Vivekananda, Radhakrishnan believed that in spite of the surface differences there was a fundamental unity among Hindus, The inchoate nature of Hinduism does not deter Radhakrishnan from asserting, 'In spite of the fact that Hinduism has no common creed and its worship no fixed form, it has bound together multitudinous sects and devotions into a common scheme'.

5

Interrogating Modernity

The nineteenth century intellectual climate of Indian society witnessed the advent of modern Western ideas of material progress. Without dogmatically rejecting these ideas, Vivekananda qualified, formulated, distinguished and contrasted the West from India. This thus provided an updated framework that facilitated the classification of scattered perceptions of the West and India, modernity and tradition etc. Vivekananda's writings comprised of celebration of India's spiritual past; admission of India's poverty and its material backwardness; emphasis on the modern West's material success – its science-technology, industry, its notion of progress; acceptance of the material progress of the West – not in terms of its limitation but in positive terms; and the need to use the models of modernity to eliminate India's backwardness and in exchange give India's spirituality to the West This in fact, is the Orientalistic framework which equated the West with materialism and the East with spiritualism.

Vivekananda consistently equated India with spiritualism and the West with materialism. And throughout his writings and speeches Vivekananda's reading of Indian society contained two basic features. These were glorification of India's spiritualism, particularly its past, and especially the Advaita Vedanta and his critique of some aspects of Indian Society.

Celebration of India's Past

In Vivekananda's work we generally find his admiration of India. These are India's religious pluralism, tolerance towards other religions, and Vedanta meeting the tests of modern scientific reasoning.

Regarding India's spiritual pluralism he says: 'From the high spiritual flights of the Vedanta philosophy...to the low ideas of idolatry with its multifarious mythology, the agnosticism of the Buddhists, and the atheism of the Jains, each and all have a place in the Hindu's religion'. Regarding the Hindus' tolerance of other foreign religions he says, "India"...sheltered the persecuted and the refugees of all religions and nations of the earth. I am proud to tell you that we have gathered in our bosom the purest remnant of the Israelites, who came to Southern India and took refuge with us in the very year in which their holy temple was shattered to pieces by Roman tyranny. I am proud to belong to the religion which has sheltered and is still fostering the remnant of the grand Zoroastrian nation."

Vivekananda's attitude towards other religions is very ambivalent. He at times shows intolerance towards other religions and at other times displays tolerance towards them. It may perhaps be said that he was not against other religions as much as he was fond of Hinduism or Advaita Vedanta. All these unique cultural characteristics seem to be internal to India's past. There is, however, another important external test that the Vedanta excels: it meets the present-day test of modern scientific reasoning. Vivekananda says:

"The Vedas teach us that creation is without beginning or end. Science is said to have proved that the sum total of cosmic energy is always the same."

And,

"...the religion of the Vedanta can satisfy the demands of the scientific world, by referring it to the highest generalisations and to the law of evolution. That the explanation of a thing comes from within itself is still more completely satisfied by Vedanta."

Here it is interesting to observe that rather than the intrinsic features of scientific elements in Advaita, it is his endorsement and even covetous fascination for modern science, though with significant reservations. that seems to have forced Vivekananda to make an ex post facto recognition and identification of similar aspects in the Indian tradition, such as the capacity for 'highest generalizations and to the law of evolution', and recognition of reality as 'finer' and not the 'gross' form which is simply appearance.

Critique of Indian Society

Along with admiration of India's past, Vivekananda presents problems infecting Indian society. These are basically the poverty of the Indian masses, weakness of the Hindu race and the superstitions in Indian society. He identifies that an important thing that is at the root of all evils in India is the condition of the poor. He holds Hindu priests, foreign rulers, and the Hindu aristocracy responsible for the condition of the poor. According to him, both the priest power and foreign conquest have trodden the poor down for centuries. Finally, the poor of India have forgotten that they are human beings. And the chief cause of India's ruin has been monopolizing the whole education by dint of pride and royal authority, among a handful of men. He appeals that if 'we are to rise again, we shall have to do it in the same way, i.e. by spreading education among the masses'. Further, he maintains that the aristocratic ancestors in India trod the common masses underfoot till they became helpless, and they nearly forgot that they were human beings. In addition, he writes, they were made to believe that they are born as slaves.

The second important defect that Vivekananda identifies in Indian society is a cultural one. There is too much of "...inactivity, too much of weakness, too much of hypnotism..." in the Hindu race. This is responsible for the Hindus losing faith in themselves. This made the foreign invasion of India possible. He notes, 'Materialism, or Mohammedanism, or Christianity, or any other ism in the world could never have succeeded but that you allowed them'. And this is because we 'have lost faith in ourselves'.

The third important defect of Indian society is its superstitions. He says: "Superstitions have to be weeded out even on this soil, and thrown aside, so that they may die for ever. These are the causes of the degradation of the race and will lead to softening of the brain".

It is interesting to note that the problems of Indian society that Vivekananda directed out are by no means meagre. Seriously attending to these would call for major structural changes in the Hindu society. While holding the excessive spiritualism of Hindus responsible for the poverty of the masses, and the passiveness of Hindus, which resulted in their subjugation, he compliments the Muslims and the West for destroying the system of exclusive privilege enforced by Hindus and providing an occasion for the salvation of the poor. He says: "...to the Mohammedan Rule we owe that great blessing, the destruction of exclusive privileges.... The Mohammedan conquest of India came as a salvation to the downtrodden, to the poor'. Regarding the West, 'Materialism has come to the rescue of India in a certain sense by throwing open the doors of life to everyone, by destroying the exclusive privileges of caste."

And to overcome die submissiveness and passiveness of the Hindu race—to acquire vigour, strength in the nerves, iron muscles and nerves of steel,—there occurs two suggestions simultaneously in Vivekananda's work, one of them is internal and the other external: He suggests the need to give up mysticism and de-hypnotize the Hindu race, to move on the line laid down by the sages and shake off their inertia, preach the Advaita aspect of the Vedanta to rouse the hearts of men, to show them the glory of their souls. He also employs another source to overcome India's material backwardness. That is the need to learn from the West their material progress. Attributing Hindus' ignorance of material civilization as the reason for they being conquered by Muslims, he says:

"Material civilization is necessary to create work for the poor. Bread! Bread! I do not believe in a God, who cannot give me bread here, giving me eternal bliss in heaven! Pooh! India is to be raised, the poor are to be fed, education is to be spread, and the evil of priestcraft is to be removed.... More bread, more opportunity for everybody."

Sounding more emphatic in offering this latter solution he says that we talk foolishly against material civilization. The grapes are sour. And even taking this foolishness for granted, he retorts how many spiritual people are there in India. He further questions, 'In all India there are, say, a hundred thousand really spiritual men and women. Now, for the spiritualization of these, must three hundred millions be sunk in savagery and starvation?' Further, he says:

"when the Oriental wants to learn about machine-making, he should sit at the feet of the Occidental and learn from him. When the Occident wants to learn about the spirit, about God, about the soul, about the meaning and the mystery of this universe, he must sit at the feet of the Orient to learn."

Vivekananda accepted Sankara's philosophy with modifications, the chief of them being *Daridra Narayana Seva* which is a mixture of Buddhist compassion and modern philanthropy. Regarding the importance and necessity of the West to overcome the problems of

India, Sri Aurobindo like Vivekananda, says that we are to have what the West can give us, because what the West can give us is just the thing and the only thing that will rescue us from our present appalling condition of intellectual and moral decay, but we are not to take it haphazard, and in a lump; rather we shall find it expedient to select the very best that is thought and known in Europe, and to import even that with the changes and reservations which our diverse conditions may be found to dictate. Otherwise, instead of a simply ameliorating influence, we shall have chaos annexed to chaos, the vices and calamities of the West superimposed on the vices and calamities of the East.

It is only with the period of European influence, the circumstances and tendencies powerful enough to enforce the beginnings of a new age of radical and effective revaluation of ideas and things have come into existence. The characteristic power of these influences has been throughout – rationalistic, utilitarian and individualistic. It has compelled the national mind to view everything from a new, searching and critical standpoint, and even those who seek to preserve the present or restore the past are obliged unconsciously or halt-consciously to justify their endeavour from the novel point of view and by its appropriate standards of reasoning.... What it did not do from within, has come on it as a necessity from without and this externality has carried with it an immense advantage as well as great dangers.

We find there are two different streams in the thought Vivekananda — the celebration of India's spiritual glory and the acceptance of its material backwardness.

In a most contemplative mood he asks shall India die? Then from the world all spirituality will be extinct...all sweet-souled sympathy for religion will be extinct, all ideality will be extinct; and in its place will reign the duality of lust and luxury as the male and female deities, with money as its priest, fraud, force, and competition its ceremonies, and human soul its sacrifice.

Vivekananda while equating the West with materialism admits continuity within Western thought, from the Greek to the modern West. He says: "The one side, the Greek side, which is represented by modern Europe, insisted upon the knowledge of man.' Further elucidating the underlying continuity between the classical and the contemporary in the West which is effecting change in India, he says the British idea of expansion and progress is forcing us up, and let us remember "That the civilization of the West has been drawn from the foundation of the Greeks, and that the great idea of Greek civilization is that of expression. In India we think—but unfortunately sometimes we think so deeply that there is no power left for expression... Without expression, how can we live? The backbone of Western civilization is—expansion and expression. This side of the work of the Anglo-Saxon race, to which I draw your attention, is calculated to rouse our nation once more to express itself, and it is inciting it to bring out its hidden treasures before the world by using the means of communication provided by the same mighty race."

Vivekananda subscribes to the orientalist categorization that was actually used by colonial scholarship to justify colonialism in India. Having made the demarcation between India and the West, and unwittingly getting trapped in the orientalistic narratives and the colonial project, Vivekananda oscillates between two possibilities. These differences are arranged on a hierarchy where Indian spiritualism reins supreme and Western materialism given a secondary status. Vivekananda strongly believes that India should retain its spirituality and reject the Western materialism outright. However, there is in Vivekananda a recommendation for an exchange between Indian spiritualism and Western materialism. This is not to discount Vivekananda's critique of Western materialism. He warns that "the whole of Western civilization will crumble to pieces in the next fifty years if there is no spiritual foundation". No nation can be said to have become civilized only because it has succeeded in increasing the comforts of material life by bringing into use lots of machinery and things of that sort. The present-day civilization of the West is multiplying day by day only the wants and distresses of men. On the other hand, the ancient Indian civilization, by showing people the way to spiritual advancement, doubtless succeeded, if not in removing once for all, at least in lessening, in a great measure, the material needs of men. He again asserts that from the Orient came the voice which once told the world that if a man possesses everything that is under the sun and does not possess spirituality it is of no use.

The broad feature of his recommendation is that the exchange between Western materialism and Indian spiritualism is mutually beneficial. He admits that "Too early religious advancement of the Hindus and that superfineness in everything which made them cling to alternatives, have reduced them to what they are. The Hindus has to learn a little bit of materialism from the West and teach them a little bit of spirituality'. He says:

"just as the too active Western mind would profit by an admixture of Eastern introspection and the meditative habit, so the Eastern would benefit by a somewhat greater activity and energy."

Vivekananda specifies the elements to be exchanged. India should learn from the West her arts and her sciences... the sciences of physical nature, while on the other hand the West has to come to India to learn and assimilate religion and spiritual knowledge'. This exchange is desirable and without such an exchange each of the civilizations would remain incomplete. He complains that to '...care only for spiritual liberty and not for social liberty is a defect but the opposite is a still greater defect. Liberty of both soul and body is to be striven for. "When each assimilates the other, the ideal would be achieved. 'I would say, the combination of the Greek mind represented by the external European energy added to the Hindu spirituality would be an ideal society for India".

As a true nationalist and patriot he declares that India has given to antiquity the earliest scientific physicians, and according to Sir William Hunter, she has even contributed to modern medical science by the discovery of various chemical' and by teaching you how to reform misshapen ears and noses. Even more it has done in mathematics, for algebra, geometry, astronomy, and the triumph of modern science — mixed mathematics — were all invented in India, just so much as the ten numerals, the very cornerstone of ail present civilization, were discovered in India, and are in reality, Sanskrit words. And now, what has the world given to India in return for all that? Nothing but nullification.. .and curse and contempt.... But India is not afraid. It does not beg for mercy at the hands of any nation. Our only fault is that we cannot fight to conquer, but we trust in the eternity of truth."

Vivekananda offers a critique of the backwardness of India. He asserts that ninety nine percent of us made up of entirely foreign ideas and elements. This has to be thrown out if we want rise in the scale of nations. If we want to rise, we must also remember that we have many things to learn from the West... We Hindus must believe that we are the teachers of the World." He urges Indians to go out to England and America, not as beggars but as teachers of religion. The law of exchange must be applied to the best of our power. If we have to learn from them the ways and methods of making ourselves happy in this life, why, in return, should we not give them the methods and ways that would make them happy for all eternity?

Emphasizing on practicality as the important requirement Vivekananda says that the need of the people of India is not more religion, but, 'practicality'. In this context it is relevant to recall that he, like a true liberal, places liberty as the first condition of growth. He says, 'Just as man must have liberty to think and speak, so he must have liberty in food, dress, and marriage, and in every other thing, so long as he does not injure others'. Here he echoes the ideas of J.S. Mill.

Further, regarding the Indians' capacity to adopt European values he warns Indians not to copy the West blirdly. He argues that with us, the prominent idea is *Mukti;* with the Westeners, it is *Dharma.* What we desire is *Mukti;* what they want is *Dharma...* However, the central fact is that the fall of our country, is due to the utter want of this *Dharma.* If the whole nation practices and follows the path of *moksha,* that is well and good but is that possible? Without enjoyment, renunciation can never come; first enjoy and then you can renounce. Otherwise, if the whole nation, all of a sudden, takes up *Sanyasa,* it does not gain what it desires, but it loses what it had into the bargain—the bird in the hand is fled, nor is that in the bush caught.

Further reinforcing this difference he says: "The Greeks sought political liberty. The Hindus have always sought spiritual liberty. Both are one-sided. The Indian cares not enough for national protection or patriotism, he will defend only his religion; while with the Greeks and in Europe...the country comes first."

Vivekananda very confidently declares that by preaching the profound secrets of the Vedanta religion in the Western world, we shall attract the sympathy and regard of these mighty nations, maintaining for ever the position of their teacher in spiritual matters, and they will remain our teachers in all material concerns. The day when, surrendering the spiritual into their hands, our countrymen would sit at the feet of the West to learn religion, that day indeed the nationality of this fallen nation will be dead and gone for good. Nothing will come of crying day and night before them... When there will grow a link of sympathy and reward between both nations by this give-and-take intercourse, there will then be no need for these noisy cries.

In endorsing the possibility and the desirability of exchange between India and the West, Vivekananda is quick to set the terms of exchange First, the exchange must be on equal terms. He says that we have been clamouring here for getting political rights and many other such things. Very well. Rights and privileges and other things can only come through friendship, and friendship can only be expected between two equals. When one of the parties is a beggar, what friendship can there be? It is all very well to speak so, out I say that without mutual co-operation we can never make ourselves strong men.

Second, the exchange must be internally necessitated not externally thrust or imposed. He insights that it must always be we who build up a new India as an effect and continuation of her past, assimilating helpful foreign ideas wherever they may be found. Never can it be imposed; growth must proceed from within. All that England can do is to help India to work out her own salvation.

Finally the exchange should not be excessive. He says that we must learn many things from the West but there are fears as well... The spell of imitating the West is getting such a strong hold upon us that what is good or what is bad is no longer decided by reason, judgment, discrimination or reference to the Shastras.

But at some places he sounds as if the exchange between India and the West is inevitable. He notes that as Western ideas of organization and external civilization are penetrating and pouring into our country, whether we will have them or not, so Indian spirituality and philosophy are deluging the lands of the West. None can resist it, and no more can we resist some sort of material civilization from the West. A little of it perhaps, is good for us, and a little spiritualization is good for the West: thus the balance will be preserved.

The Gandhian defence of the pre-modern as well as his critique of modernity, and Vivekananda's limited fascination for modernity can become an important starting point to analyse this tension that would help us understand better the dynamics of contemporary Indian society. While Gandhi largely maintained his critique of modernity, Vivekananda, though not an ardent and consistent admirer of the West's modernity, was fascinated by it in the earlier part of his life, though later he denounced his admiration for the modern West. At the age of thirty-five, four years before his death, Vivekananda confessed that his patriorism and zeal as a nationalist reformer were wrong. He declared, "All my patriotism is gone". This fascination with Western modernity reflects one of the dominant trends in contemporary India. While this was a transitory phenomenon in Vivekananda, it remains dominant in contemporary Indian society. Vivekananda may have given up his predilection for the West but contemporary Indian society stubbornly and seductively clings to it. In contrast, Gandhi seemed to radically disagree with Vivekananda on this specific issue. These two, namely, Gandhi's disenchantment with the modern West and Vivekananda's fascination for the same, arc used here not as views expressed by them as authors but tendencies revealing larger and fast-changing socio-political contexts.

Tapan Raychaudhuri evokes the common ground between Vivekananda and Gandhi. He says that there is something very Gandhian in Vivekananda's rejection of western values. Like Gandhi, too, he is not particularly excited by the varied spectacle of western civilization.

One could agree with this statement only when one thinks of the later part of Vivekananda's life. Gandhi and Vivekananda held diametrically opposite views on the Western civilisation and the Gandhian project cannot be seen as a mere carrying forward of the politics Vivekananda. Ashis Nandy, clearly highlights the difference between Vivekananda and Gandhi. But we shall not discounting many areas of commonality between these two thinkers. For instance, Gandhi seems to have derived from Vivekananda that Truth and God are invariant.

Vivekananda anticipated Gandhi in two respects one of which surely is the attack on untouchability and human oppression in the name of caste and the other, the idea of voluntary movements and restoring the dignity of human labour. Though Sri Aurobindo finds artistic qualities in Bankim which leads him to hoist Bankim over other illustrious contemporaries, this artistic realm is nevertheless perceived largely as an elitist domain, that prevents Bankim's programme from taking the shape of a political programme. The characteristic form of nationalist thought at its moment of departure, leads inevitably to an elitism of the intelligentsia, rooted in the vision of a radical regeneration of national culture. In Bankim's time, the heyday of colonial rule, this vision could not find any viable political means to actualize itself. Instead, it became a dream: a Utopian political community in which the nation was the Mother, once resplendent in wealth and beauty, now in tatters. The limitation of the literary domain was not a problem with Vivekananda, as he operated with ease and success in the political domain and was also fairly successful outside Bengal since language was not a barrier for him as it was for Bankim. He operated outside Bengal both at the national and the international level and within the political sphere. By carrying within him a sense of his own psychological inviolacy, coupled with a stubborn will that held to the self-chosen course in the face of all outer obstacles, Vivekananda could project his vision with a passionate conviction capable of striking such a responsive chord in his audience that action on a large scale and resistance to the status quo (political and cultural) became possible.

Pointing out the contribution of Vivekananda in comparative terms vis-a-vis his predecessor like Ramakrishna and Rammohun Roy, we could argue that: neither Rammohun Roy nor Ramakrishna Paramahamsa developed a social philosophy proper in the sense of systematically philosophizing on social problems. This was achieved by Vivekananda, who rightly can be named the first among Indian philosophers for whom social philosophy constituted an integral part of his philosophic system. He was the first who connected his new interpretation of the Advaita Vedanta with the development of a social philosophy that corresponded to the requirements of a modern society.

Although Vivekananda's identification with resurgent Hinduism is in one sense more passionate than that of Bankim, educated Muslim public opinion was less hostile to Vivekananda than it eventually became in relation to the author of *Rajsingha* and *Anandamath*. Evidently it was Bankim who situated the Muslim as the historical/political adversary of the Hindu. It was the sheer power of grandiosity of the Mughal administration in India that impressed Vivekananda more than the preceding four hundred years of Indo-Islamic rule. Bankim on the other hand, as creator of a healthy Bengali provincialism, was prone to be more critical of the Mughals who brought the province under imperial control than of the Turk-Pathan rulers who helped Bengal retain her political autonomy.

But there are two important similarities between Bankim and Vivekananda. Bankin's acceptance of Western superiority is, however, a central theme in the discussion that follows. It has been suggested that he sought to compensate for the resulting sense of inferiority by identifying one value where India, in his view superior, namely, her spiritual heritage. Such a view, promoted among others by the Theosophists and Vivekananda in their very different ways, did become a part of the intellectual vocabulary in the late nineteenth century India. The secular objective of dharma was never very far from Bankim's mind. In looking upon religion and its reform as the road to patriotic ends he is in tune with one powerful school of thought of his days. Dayananda, Keshab Sen and later Vivekananda are all parts of this same tradition.

It is also quite likely that Vivekananda was somewhat influenced by Bankim's own writings of the earlier years which not only ridiculed the more irrational components of Hinduism but also tended to measure religion by standards of reason and utility. Interestingly enough, the mature Vivekananda may also have inherited from Bankim, the Hindu counter-aggression vis-a-vis muscular Christianity.

Vivekananda's Critic of Utilitarianism

It is precisely on this issue of Utilitarianism that Vivekananda's romance with modernity faces its tragic elements. He has offered a powerful critique of Utilitarianism the foundation of modern civilization. that one sees substantial differences between Vivekananda and Rammohun Roy. Vivekananda is not only against traditional medieval notions about man but also against the West European bourgeois conceptions of man. In this context he sharply criticizes hedonism and utilitarianism. And this very criticism, and the arguments used by Vivekananda initiate a distinctive tradition in the history of Indian philosophy of modern and contemporary period—with various modifications, this criticism would be reiterated later by Tilak, Aurobindo Ghosh, Tagore, Gandhi.

First of all, Vivekananda finds hedonistic 'going after pleasure' as humiliating for the dignity of man as the ascetic 'going after pain': "We are whipped, and when we begin to weep, nature gives us a dollar; again we are whipped, and when we weep, nature gives us a piece of ginger-bread, and we begin to. laugh again".

Turning pleasures into the main aim of man's life leads, in Vivekananda's view, to a blind alley. After the chain of enjoyments coining one after the other there inevitably comes saturation, and then the quest for fresh, more exquisite enjoyments and still more sharply expressed satisfaction etc. 'Superoriginal' methods of 'satisfying the nerves' are invented, these become the fashion, and people, like a herd of sheep, go after this fashionable illusion and find more and more disappointments. This criticism resulting from Vivekananda's impressions gained at the time of his travels in the countries of the West, undoubtedly testifies to the keen sense of observation of the thinker, who caught in infancy certain tendencies which appeared in full measure far later, in the twentieth century.

Vivekananda himself, however, believes that neither pleasure nor pain con serve as the highest principle, determining a man's conduct. What is important from his point of view is the process of formation of human character, of attainment of maturity by man and the capacity to discover and use the possibilities latent in him: 'Pleasure is not the goal of man... after a time man finds that both pleasure and pain are great teachers, and that he learns as much from evil as from good."

Similar is the criticism made of utilitarianism. When people make the attainment of profit the highest aim of their life irrespective of where this profit lies – in money, fame, power – the insatiable thirst makes them not live but pursue untiringly the uncapturable phantom of happiness, Vivekananda ironically expounds the credo of 'ordinary utilitarianists' as a corroboration of the fact that 'it is necessary to live to eat, and not to eat to live'. The most exquisite utilitarianism from his viewpoint is like the vital orientation of the members of a Muslim sect whose goal, from very childhood, is having for themselves a luxurious grave, which is safely reached by the end of the life.

Utilitarianism, in Vivekananda's view, does not simply place the cart before the horse and subordinate the process of life to something external in relation to it or having at best a secondary significance. It tries to reduce the highest manifestation of life to the lowest, and concern for all ethical ideals even the noblest manifestation of human spirit, aesthetic values, aspirations for truth to the same invariable calculation of profits and losses, a sober and prosaic calculation: 'In these days we have to measure everything by utility—by how many pounds, shillings, and pence it represents'.

By reducing morality, art, philosophy etc. to various spheres of operation of the principle of utility, the utilitarians are not in a position, from Vivekananda's viewpoint, to explain satisfactorily what belongs to these spheres. Thus, the utilitarians have not been able to establish the main ethical principle proclaimed by them ('maximum good for maximum number of persons'): 'You will find people saying nowadays that they have utilitarian grounds as the basis of morality. What is this basis ? Procuring the greatest amount of happiness to the greatest number. Why should I do this ? Why should I not produce the greatest unhappiness to the greatest number if that serves my purpose?' The utilitarians, by presenting people as egoistic, associated only by ties of mutual benefit of beings—'social atoms', deprive them, from Vivekananda's viewpoint, precisely of what is characteristic of man. A man differs from an animal not by his capacity to calculate profits, but by that of self-sacrifice, finding most lucid expression in extreme moral situations when there can be no question of direct or even indirect profit for any individual—just as an individual: 'the more a man is capable of sacrificing himself for the sake of others, the greater he is, while the most prominent in the animal world is that animal which is capable of killing the maximum number of other animals'. In his criticism of utilitarianism Vivckananda is in many ways right. The attempt to reduce all multiplicity of human relation to a relation of profit leads the representatives of utilitarianism to truly caricature conclusions. In the words of Marx, 'under the mask of his interest, the discerning bourgeois will always place some third thing between himself and his vital activity—a manner raised to truly classical form by Bcntham, for whom a nose must be of some interest before it decides to smell'.

Absolutizing some tendencies appearing in the life of bourgeois society, and applying these to all times as manifestations of some invariable 'human nature', the utilitarians act as apologists of the contemporary social reality. Interestingly, the relationship of utilitarianism to bourgeois reality is civilised by Vivekananda: 'At best, therefore, utilitarian theories can only work under present social conditions. Beyond that they have no value'. But he just defines this relationship; nothing more. He cannot explain it satisfactorily. In the ultimate end he explains both the 'adaptability' of utilitarian structures to 'present social conditions' as well as the 'complaisance' of the present: society in regard to these structures, by proceeding from spiritual and not material premises. The reason is the dominance of materialistic ideas. In the given case Vivekananda. follows the footsteps of his predecessors Ramakrishna and Dayananda. Like them, he tries to associate the failure of illusions of enlightenment in the eighteenth century with the spiritual unfoundedness of materialism and atheism. Like them again, he sees in religion the panacea for the misfortunes of capitalism.

The principles of utilitarianism and hedonism woven firmly .into the system of bourgeois morality rooted in the West, and partly influencing the outlook of Vivekananda's countrymen, were sharply, criticized by him. Vivekananda was quite familiar with the principles of utilitarian ethics and, in particular, with the ideas of J.S. Mill, whose works had attracted him as early as his college days. Later, becoming the famous religious preceptor, Vivekananda arrived at the deep conviction that 'enlightened egoism' could not be considered the basis of morality. From Vivekananda's point of view, the utilitarian and hedonistic principles are immanently inherent in modern Western morality, for these are conditioned by the pursuit of pleasure as the main aim of life which the peoples of the West are guided by. It is to be noted that Vivekananda frequently employs moral concepts while appraising any nation. Thus, he believed that every nation had its own character. And in this context his description of the so-called 'English character' is not without interest. 'In the English character, the "give and take" policy, the business principle of the trader, is principally inherent.'—wrote Vivekananda. "The Englishman humbly submits to the king and to the privileges of the nobility. . .but if the king wants money, the Englishman says: All right, but first let me understand why it is needed, what good it will bring; next, I must have my say in the matter of how it is to be spent, and then I shall part with it." The determining feature of 'Indian character', according to Vivekananda, is, however spirituality. 'The Hindu says,' he wrote, 'that political and social independence are well and good, but the real thing is spiritual independence—mukti. This is our national purpose.'

Thus, asserting that every nation has a national character and its own national purpose, and that 'the manners and customs of a nation must be judged from the standpoint of that purpose', Vivekananda draws the following conclusion: "The Westerners should be seen through their eyes; to see them through our eyes, and for them to see us with theirs—both of these are mistakes. The purpose of our life is quite the opposite of theirs. Our goal of life is *moksha*. The purpose of life in the West is *bhoga*, enjoyment."

Considering that the moral principles of the West are the opposite of, and incompatible with, the religious-moral requirements set for the man in India, Vivekananda not only stresses the distinctiveness of the latter but also strives to show their uniqueness. Although Vivekananda himself emphasizes the fact that in judging any manner of life one should proceed by taking into account the 'moral character' of the nation itself, keeping in mind its 'own moral purpose', his criticism nevertheless of utilitarian and hedonistic principles of the West is, on the whole, from Vedantic positions which manifest his ideas of national uniqueness, peculiar of him as a nationalist.

The Westerners, in Vivekananda's view, give priority to enjoyments and pleasures, which also serve them as very vital stimuli. This inevitably leads to development and predominance of egoistic tendencies, and to the fact that egoism and individualism become the practice of the Western mode of life. 'The vain ideas of individualism',—Vivekananda wrote,— 'to which man clings when he is trying to find... pleasure through the senses, have to be given up—say the laws of ethics.' 'You must,' — Vivekananda stresses, — 'put yourself last, and others before you. The senses say, "myself first," ethics says, "I must hold myself last"

Despite the traditional reference that all troubles have their source in the human body, Vivekananda in these judgements rightly criticizes utilitarianists for their lack of concern for the lofty spiritual aspirations of man. Observing at the time of his foreign travels an unrestrained egoistic pursuit of profit, possessive "individualism", receiving legal sanction in bourgeois society, Vivekananda rightly points to the spiritual poverty of the peoples concentrating all their attention on material needs and becoming, in the ultimate count, slaves of their desires. These desires inevitably devour the man; there is no end to them; a man can never fully satisfy his desires, 'The utilitarians say, "Don't talk of God and hereafter; we don't know anything of these things,"' — he wrote. 'As long as you are a slave of nature,' Vivekananda objects, 'how can you be free ?'

Vivekananda does not adopt the utilitarian criteria of usefulness, which are the yardsticks for measuring all manifestations of vital activity of man in the world surrounding him. 'In these days', he observes, 'we have to measure everything by utility — by how many pounds, shillings, and pence it represents.' It is to be noted that here Vivekananda rises in his judgements to the point of statement of definite dependence of utilitarian principles of morality on capitalist reality. Vivekananda wrote: '...the basis of utility is too narrow. All the current social forms and methods are derived from society as it exists, but what right has the utilitarian to assume that society is eternal ? . . . At best, therefore, utilitarian theories can only work under present social conditions. Beyond that they have no value."

The ethical views of Vivekananda objectively contain the admission that in the conditions of the bourgeois reality in the form in which he observed it in the West, love of man, equality and other sublime requirements cannot be achieved. The real principle of these requirements can only be high 'spirituality' which he identifies with Indian spirituality. The latter played a great role in his nationalistic Utopia, in the building up of a factually bourgeois society, shorn of those contradictions which it actually had.

The base of this spirituality, for Vivekananda was in the religious-moral principles of Vedanta, whose morality he had considered eternal and unchangeable, adaptable for all peoples, at all times, in any society. 'A morality, an ethical code, derived from religion and spirituality', wrote Vivekananda, 'has the whole of infinite man for its scope...and as it applies to the individual and his eternal relations, it must necessarily apply to the whole of society, in whatever condition it may be at any given time.'

The criticism of utilitarian principles which Vivekananda on the whole made from Vedantic positions, was dictated, however, not so much by the thinker's desire to demonstrate the superiority of the religious-moral principles of Vedanta, as by a patriot's concern for the destiny of his homeland, of his countrymen amongst whom the utilitarian moods had partly made their way. The moral indignation which Vivekananda expressed with regard to contemporary bourgeois norms of morality was extremely significant. His criticism of capitalism, as also the critical speeches of many other radical nationalists of the late nineteenth century, played a progressive role, for it helped in the growth of national liberation aspirations, and was the symptom of growing democratic upsurge in India and expressed it in its own way.

Vivekananda was attracted by the sober and practical attitude of the West to vital problems and situations, by the ability to set concrete tasks and fulfil them. In other words, the dynamism of the Western mode of life taken outside the extremes of utilitarianism and hedonism represented to Vivekananda the point at which it was necessary to turn his attention to his country men. And, in this context, the interpretation of Aesop's Fable given by Vivekananda in his lecture in 1896 is extremely significant. 'You all remember',—he said,—' how in *Aesop's Fables* a fine stag is looking at his form reflected in a lake and is saying to his young one, "How powerful I am, look at my splendid head, look at my limbs, how strong and muscular they are; and how swiftly I can run." In the meantime he hears the barking of dogs in the distance, and immediately takes to his heels, and after he has run several miles, he comes back panting. The young one says, "You just told me how strong you were, how was it that when the dogs barked, you ran away ?" "Yes, my son; but when the dogs bark all my confidence vanishes." Such is the case with us;'—concludes Vivekananda,—"we think highly of humanity, we feel ourselves strong and valiant, we make grand resolves; but when the "dogs" of trial and temptation bark, we are like the stag in the fable.'

It should be noted that despite his criticism of utilitarian morality, Vivekananda's attitude to it was ambivalent. He accepted some positive aspects of utilitarianism at a lower stage of moral development. 'I do not deny', he wrote, 'that men, on simply utilitarian grounds, can be very good and moral. There have been many great men in this world perfectly sound, moral, and good, simply on utilitarian grounds. But the world-movers, men whose spirit works in hundreds and in thousands, whose life ignites others with a spiritual fire—such men, we always find, have that spiritual background." Thus, emphasizing the obvious superiority of moral-religious principles of Vedanta over the utilitarian ethics of the West, Vivekananda nonetheless does not rule out the positive significance of some of these principles.

6

Interpreting the Bhagavadgita

One of the heroes of the Mahabharata, Arjuna, is persuaded by Krishna to fight in the war in state of his reluctance and hesitation. It is a paradigmatic case in which to promote the performance of dharma. Arjuna is a ksatriya, a member of the class of warriors. To abandon his duty by not fighting in the battle to come, even though his reluctance is prompted by his concern that he would kill his relatives if he fought, is a violation of dharma, Krishna argues. Though Arjuna's own argument in Gita chapter one was also an attempt to preserve the class structure with its duties, Krishna argues that he must fight because that is his class-duty. Twice the Gita declares that it is better to do one's own dharma poorly than to do another's well.

Beyond the commentaries and essays of the intellectual elite, it is difficult to determine how popular the Gita has been. Many scholars believe it had little popularity. The earliest illustrated manuscripts of the Gita available are from the 18th century, and earlier artistic representations fare rare. While the Krishna of the very popular Bhagavata Purana and scenes from the rest of the Mahabharata are to be found regularly, only two illustrations of the Krishna of the Gita are known: one in the 14th century at a temple at Pushpagiri in Andhra Pradesh and another in the late 12th century.

The Bhagavadgita clearly assumes a place of importance in the India of the nineteenth and twentieth centuries, among its elite religious thinkers. One modern Hindu defined this place as follows: "For the Hindu it is now the one book of books. The Gita is as fresh as ever and just as to the Christian is the Bible the Gita is to the Hindu." It played a part in Indian nationalism, in the rise of a 'Hindu' consciousness and the definition of a 'Hinduism', and in the growing interest in oriental studies. At the same time, it drew the attention of the West, beginning with its first translation into English by Charles Wilkins 200 years ago.

Within India, however, the modern period was a time of great ideological, political, and sociological upheaval. Foreign domination of Indian soil moved from the last vestiges of Moghul rule to the British raj, with Queen Victoria proclaimed Empress of India and suzerain over the Indian Princely States in 1876. Various opinions about the type of education to be offered to colonial India culminated in 1835 in the acceptance of the British educational system over the study of Indian subjects.

Indians were also exposed to the criticisms of 'Hinduism,' which was now being treated as a reified entity, by Western critics, particularly teachers and missionaries. Gandhi's characterization in his autobiography is representative of the feeling of many: "In those days Christian missionaries used to stand in a corner near the high school and hold forth, pouring abuse on Hindus and their gods. I could not endure this."

The modern Indian interpreters took the presuppositions behind these criticism to heart. Hinduism, they felt, was not essentially guilty as charged. Yet, the assumptions behind the charges were ones that, in many cases, these modern interpreters shared. Thus, they did not respond to them indifferently as people from worldviews which were traditional to India and other than those of the critics might have. Instead they defended their positions in their critics' terms, since the criticisms were rooted in ideals they also accepted. As such, criticisms that Hinduism is fatalistic, passive, lacking in concern for social ethics, otherworldly, idolotrous, etc., found a hearing in these thinkers, based on their 19th and 20th century backgrounds as well as their own ancient culture.

The answer of the divine teacher Lord Krishna to the first flood of Arjuna's passionate self-questioning, his shrinking from slaughter, his sense of sorrow and sin, his grieving for an empty and desolate life, his forecast of evil results of an evil deed, is a strongly-worded rebuke. All this, it is replied, is confusion of mind and delusion, a weakness of the heart, an unmanliness, a fall from the virility of the fighter and the hero. Not this was fitting in the son of Pandu, not thus should the champion of a righteous cause abandon it in the hour of crisis and peril or suffer the sudden amazement of his heart and senses, the clouding of his reason and the downfall of his will to betray him into the casting away of his divine weapons and the refusal of his God-given work. This is not the way cherished and followed by the Aryan man; this mood came not from heaven nor can it lead to heaven, and on earth it is the forfeiting of the glory that waits upon strength and heroism and noble works. Let him remove this weak and self-indulgent pity, let him rise and smite his enemies!

The answer of a hero to a hero, but not that which we should expect from a divine teacher from whom we demand rather that he shall encourage always gentleness and saintliness and self-abnegation and the recoil from worldly aims and cessation from the ways of he world? The Gita expressly says that Arjuna has thus lapsed into unheroic weakness, "his eyes full and distressed with tears, his heart overcome by depression and discouragement," because he is invaded by pity. Is this not then a divine weakness? Is not pity a divine emotion which should not thus be discouraged with harsh rebuke? Or are we in face of a mere gospel of war and heroic action, a Nietzschean creed of power and high-browed strength, of Hebraic or old Teutonic hardness which holds pity to be a weakness. But the teahing of the Gita springs from an Indian creed and to the Indian mind compassion has always figured as one of the largest elements of the divine nature. Lord Krishna himself enumerating in a later chapter the qualities of the godlike nature in man places among them compassion to creatures, gentleness, freedom from wrath and from the desire to slay and do hurt, no less than fearlessness and high spirit and energy. Harshness and hardness and fierceness and a satisfaction in slaying enemies and amassing wealth and unjust enjoyments are Asuric qualities; they come from the violent titanic nature which denies the Divine in the world and the Divine in man and worships desire only as its deity. It is not then from any .such standpoint that the weakness of Arjuna merits rebuke.

"Whence has come to thee this dejection, this stain and darkness of the soul in the hour of difficulty and peril?" asks Krishna to Arjuna. The question points to the real nature of Arjuna's deviation from his heroic qualities. There is a divine compassion which descends to us from on high and for the man whose nature does not possess it, is not cast in its mould, to pretend to be the superior man, the master-man or the superman is a folly and an insolence, for he alone is the superman who most manifests the highest nature of the Godhead in humanity.. This compassion observes with an eye of love and wisdom the strength and weakness of man, his virtues and sins, his joy and suffering, his knowledge and his ignorance, his wisdom and his folly, his aspiration and his failure and it enters into it all to help and to heal. In the saint and philanthropist it may cast itself into the mould of a plenitude of love or charity; in the thinker, and hero it assumes the largeness and the force of a helpful wisdom and strength. It is this compassion in the Aryan fighter, the soul of his chivalry, which will not break the bruised reed, but helps and protects the weak and the oppressed and the wounded and the fallen. But it is also the divine compassion that smites down the strong tyrant and the confident oppressor, not in wrath and with hatred, — for these are not the high divine qualities, the wrath of God against the sinner, God's hatred of the wicked are the fables of half- enlightened creeds, as much a fable as the eternal torture of the Hells they have invented, but, as the old Indian spirituality clearly saw, with as much love and compassion for the strong Titan erring by his strength and slain for his sins as for the sufferer and the oppressed who have to be saved from his violence and injustice.

But such is not the compassion which actuates Arjuna in the rejection of his work and mission. That is not compassion but an impotence full of a weak self-pity, a recoil from the mental suffering which his act must entail on himself,— "I see not what shall rust from me the sorrow that dries up the senses", — and of all things self-pity is among the most ignoble and un-Aryan of moods. Its pity for others is also a form of self-indulgence; it is physical shrinking of the nerves from the act of slaughter, the egoistic emotional shrinking of the heart from the destruction of the Dhritarashtrians because they are "one's own people" and without them life will be empty. This pity is a weakness of the mind and senses, — a weakness which may well be beneficial to men of a lower grade of development, who have to be weak because otherwise they will be. hard and cruel; for they have to cure the harsher by the gentler forms of sensational egoism, they have to call in Tamas? the debile principle, to help Sattwa, the principle of light, in quelling the strength and excess of their rajasic passions. But this way is not for the developed Aryan man who has to grow not by weakness, but by an ascension from strength to strength. Arjuna is the divine man, the master-man in the making and as such he has been chosen by the gods. He has a work given to him, he has God beside him in his chariot, he has the heavenly bow Gandiva in his hand, he has the champions of unrighteousness, the opponents of the divine leading of the world in his front. Nor is right to determine what he shall do or not do according to his emotions and his passions, or to shrink from a necessary destruction by the claim of his egoistic heart and reason, or to decline his work because it will bring sorrow and emptiness to his life or because its earthly result has no value to him in the absence of the thousands who must perish. All that is a weak falling from his higher nature. He has to see only the work that must be done, *kartavyam karma*, to hear only the divine command breathed through his warrior nature, to feel only for the world and the destiny of mankind calling to him as its God's agent to assist its march and clear its path of the dark armies that beset it.

Arjuna in his reply to Krishna admits the rebuke even while he strives against and refuses the command. He is aware of his weakness and yet accepts subjection to it. It is poorness of spirit, he owns, that has smitten away from him his true heroic nature; his whole consciousness is bewildered in its view of right and wrong and he accepts the divine friend as his teacher; but the emotional and intellectual props on which he had supported his sense of righteousness have been entirely cast down and he cannot accept a command which seems to appeal only to his old standpoint and gives him no new basis for action. He attempts still to justify his refusal of the work and puts forward in its support the claim of his nervous and sensational being which shrinks from the slaughter with its sequel of blood-stained enjoyments, the claim of his heart which recoils from the sorrow and emptiness of life that will follow his act, the claim of his customary moral notions which are appalled by the necessity of slaying his Gurus, Bhishma and Drona, the claim of his reason which sees no good but only evil results of the terrible and violent work assigned to him. He is resolved that on the old basis of thought and motive he will not fight and he awaits in silence the answer to objections that seem to him unanswerable. It is these claims of Arjuna's egoistic being that Krishna sets out first to destroy in order to make place for the higher law which shall transcend all egoistic motives of action.

The answer of the teacher proceeds upon two different lines, first, a brief reply founded upon the highest ideas of the general Aryan culture in which Arjuna has been educated, secondly, another and larger founded on a more intimate knowledge, opening into deeper truths of our being, which is the real starting- point of the teaching of the Gita. This first answer relies on the philosophic and moral conceptions of the Vedantic philosophy and the social idea of duty and honour which formed the ethical basis of Aryan society. Arjuna has sought to justify his refusal on ethical and rational grounds, but he has merely cloaked by words of apparent rationality the revolt of his ignorant and unchastened emotions. He has spoken of the physical life and the death of the body as if these were the primary realities; but they have no such essential value to the sage and the thinker. The sorrow for the bodily death of his friends and kindred is a grief to which wisdom and the true knowledge of life lend no sanction. The enlightened man does not mourn either for the living or the dead, for he knows that suffering and death are merely incidents in the history of the soul. The soul, not the body, is the reality. All these men for whose approaching death he mourns, have lived before, they will live again in the human body; for as the soul passes physically through childhood and youth and age, so it passes on to the changing of the body. The calm and wise mind, the thinker who looks upon life steadily and does not allow himself to be disturbed and blinded by his sensations and emotions, is not deceived by material appearances; he does not allow the clamour of his blood and his nerves and his heart to cloud his judgment or to contradict his knowledge. He looks beyond the apparent facts of the life of the body and senses to the real fact of his being and rises beyond the emotional and physical desires of the ignorant nature to the true and only aim of the human existence.

There is no such thing as death, for it is the body that dies and the body is not the man. That which really is, cannot go out of existence, though it may change the forms through which it appears, just as that which is non-existent cannot come into being. The soul is and cannot cease to be. This opposition of is and is not, this balance of being and becoming which is the mind's view of existence, finds its end in the realisation of the soul as the one imperishable self by whom all this universe has been extended. Finite bodies have an end, but that which possesses and uses the body is infinite, illimitable, eternal, indestructible. It casts away old and takes up new bodies as a man changes worn-out garment for new; and what is there -in this to grieve at and recoil and shrink? This is not born, nor does it die, nor is it a thing that comes into being once and passing away will never come into being again. It is unborn, ancient, sempiternal; it is not slain with the slaying of the body: Who can slay the immortal soul? Weapons cannot cleave it, nor the fire burn, nor do the waters drench it, nor the wind dry. Eternally' stable, immobile, all-pervading, it is for ever, and forever. Not manifested like the body, but greater than all manifestation, not to be analysed by the thought, but greater than all mind, not capable of change and modification like the life and its organs and their objects, but beyond the changes of mind and life and body, it is yet the Reality which all these strive to figure.

The Gita is a much-adored and much-interpreted 'Song Celestial'. It has lent itself to several readings to defend or contest various views on life, morality and metaphysics, to the sectarian claims, to universal truths. In the eighteenth century when modern Hinduism was 'discovered' it nearly achieved the status of the Bible. Not surprisingly it became an unfailing source of nationalist imagination and sustenance. The nationalist engagement with the Gita was both emotional and intellectual, since nationalism expressed itself, as a response, product of engagement with colonialism. Locating the source of nationalism in the Gita was a. way of rejecting the Western claim that nationalist impulse and ideology were its exclusive gift. It also meant sanctifying a modernist project with the words of God, and with the ethico-moral prescriptions excavated from the Gita. It was a way of nationalizing the Bhagavadgita. In fact, the nationalist dialogue with the Gita went beyond the sectarian universals. It sought out the various socio-political projects for the country, and people seeking freedom and change. That the Gita was able to provide such variety of answers to different interrogators is as much a measure of the variety of questions with which they went to the Gita as the conditions and compulsions that spawned the questions. Such dialogic possibilities have given the Gita an aura of a timeless text. The Gita presents the various styles and moods in which such nationalist dialogues were held in the nineteenth and twentieth centuries, producing different hues of ideological sanctions.

Drawing on religious texts—and in the process nationalizing them—is not an unfamiliar practice in the construction of nationalism. It more than fulfils the need for constructing a history and owning it. It transcends the mundane, daring to touch the spiritual and the divine. It explores and vindicates the ethico-moral realms of aspirations and achievements, traces the contours of social relations, and even looks for assuring, if hazy, political blue-prints. Invoking religious texts or harnessing them to the nation's cause confers on the project a halo of sanctity that conspires to make nationalism more than just a mundane scheme.

No religious text has been as frequently invoked or as passionately deployed by Indian nationalists as the Bhagavadgita. It was not that there were no other parallel texts at hand; India had obviously produced an abundant literature at different times such as the Srutis, Smritis, Puranas, political tracts like the *Arthasastra*, *Darshanas*, and even rich Sanskrit writings. Certain social reformers had even suggested the Vedas and Upanishads with their stress on monotheism and universalism as the basis of a renewed India. But no other text has attracted the heed of the nationalists as the Gita did. In fact, nationalists of different stripes, including exponents of modern Hinduism, critical modernists, ethical and spiritual nationalists, seem to agree that they could all draw sustenance and seek vindication from the Gita. After all, Lord Krishna did not address his words to Arjuna alone. Besides, the Bhagavadgita claims to be the quintessence of all the Upanishads, of the best and the noblest of all Indian thoughts. The greatest of the acharyas, including Sankara, Ramanuja, and Madhva, had interpreted or invested meanings into it. However, these credentials alone did not make the Gita the religious text par excellence of the Hindus. The context of colonialism and the making of colonial knowledge provide a clue to the new status which the Bhagavadgita acquired in the eighteenth century.

The European interface with India triggered off a passion to explore its religion and culture, producing sometimes overlapping and at other times conflicting results. Some did so out of personal or academic curiosity and others as part of the larger project of colonialism. Religion, particularly of others, can be both a matter of curiosity and of ready judgement. The European notion of religion with which they explored and evaluated other religions, was rooted in the making and practice of Semitic religions. Central to it are the notions of the Revelation, the Prophet, and the Book. Looking for these constituents, they found them in what the native informants told them as to what the sources of their religion were. The native informants were the brahmins—a small, literate monopoly class in the country, who thus became the sole spokepersons of religion. Brahminical religion became the Hindu religion, and Brahminical texts became the official Hindu texts. Of them Krishna and his Song Celestial seemed to meet the Semitic notion of a revealed religion. Here was an incarnation, a saviour, who not only fulfilled the purpose of his earthly descent but bequeathed to posterity His Song Celestial to guide it. He revealed Himself through His Words. He seemed to fit into the Semitic pattern the Europeans knew of Krishna became to Hinduism what Jesus was to Christianity, and the Bhagavadgita the Hindu Bible. The Orientalists and Sanskritists hastened to translate it into English, the first one being that of Charles Wilkins in 1785. It was to showcase the glory of Sanskrit and the loftiness of the Hindu thought although, as Thomas Trautmann shows, some of them like Sir William Jones could not help but link the Hindu thought with the Mosaic tradition. The Bhagavadgita won ecstatic plaudits from European Romantics like Schopenhauer, which was good advertisement for the Orientalists.

However, for strategic reasons the Christian missionaries preferred to latch on to their own constructed image of the 'Hindu Prophet' Krishna to compare him with their own Son of God. In their writings and preachings and in their roadside harangues they revelled in projecting Krishna as a cad, a prankster, a philanderer, a trickster, and a wily politician. His life had nothing gracious or divine about it and everything of an impostor. He could not be remotely compared with the noble Jesus who lived and died for the salvation of the human race. The missionaries could reject such things in Hinduism as polytheism, karma, rebirth, and so on, but these debates would not make much sense to their target groups. As a propaganda strategy they thought the best way to go about it was to show that people had been hitherto misled by a false prophet. How could an impostor like Krishna gift mankind anything remotely true and divine? Other gods in the Hindu pantheon too came in for their share of derision and repudiation, but Krishna remained the favourite punching bag. They also made fun of and poured scorn over, the fabulous chronology and geography of the Puranas—their outrageous time-spans, their seas of milk and honey, their jostling gods who could outdo even the worst sinners in their immoral pranks and foolish escapades, and who habitually fought with the demons and were as habitually beaten by them. The utilitarians like James Mill had distanced themselves from both the Orientalists and the Evangelical groups although they too, like the latter, did not have much to say in favour of Hindu religion or the scriptures that revealed it. Mill felt that they were responsible for the creation of despotism in thought and practice which had been the bane of India for centuries, and which was the duty of Britain to eradicate through education and legislations. Many of the debates around the religion and culture of India took place in the pages of Asiatic Researches and later Indian Antiquary. They fulfilled the intellectual urges of the colonial rulers as much as they allowed immense space for intellectual resolutions of their wish-fulfillment.

Thus, in the eighteenth century, we see both the Orientalist and missionary discourses nudging the Bhagavadgita and its author to the centrestage of attention and engagement. The Bhagavadgita became the text for Hinduism and Krishna the Prophet. India did not see it as a reductionist exercise but as a context to respond to. If nationalism is a response to the various colonial demands and challenges, the nationalist preference for the Bhagavadgita as the site for constructing their thoughts and schemes should not come as a surprise. It became a destination and sometimes a defence, of both the Prophet and his words. The Bhagavadgita became the reference point of Hindu wisdom, its timelessness and its perennial court of appeal. It became something of a symbol of Hindu conscience. The Orientalist applause and the missionary denigration had both projected it as the scripture par excellence. The reformers who wanted the society to change, slowly or in a hurry, appealed to it. So did die-hard conservatives. Raja Rammohun Roy had use for it in his campaigns for the abolition of sati his opponents too swore by Lord Krishna's words. Even Ambedkar, who repudiated nationalist status to the Gita on the ground that it offered a cogent defence of the brahminical point of view and hence constituted the central text of the counter-revolution against Buddhism, had used it in his nationalist discourse based on Buddhism. Everyone seemed to seek endorsement from the Gita. It seemed to speak, rising above partisanship, parochialism, and sectarianism, the universal language of wisdom. Krishna seemed to be with everyone who sought

Him, as He was with everyone of the adoring gopis in Brindavan. He did not even mind the occasional anger among His devotees!

There was a plethora of nationalist discourse based on the Gita by Bankimchandra Chatterjee, Balgangadhar Tilak, Swami Vivekananda, Aurobindo Ghosh, Mohandas Karamchand Gandhi, Vinoba Bhave, and B.R. Ambedkar. However, this is not to suggest that their views were identical on the Gita. Their temperament and nationalist agenda differed. The contexts of their projects differed too. If Tilak went to the Gita in a quiet mood of critical introspection and vindication of his political activism, Aurobindo sought to suffuse its spirituality into a nationalist project. Vivekananda's thoughts on the subject are dispersed but not any less intense, and they have to be gleaned from his lectures and writings often addressed to the Western audience. Vinoba's views on the Gita too were expressed in his lectures. Gandhi did nor write an exegesis on the Bhagavadgita but it was his constant companion and intimate counsel. Bankim was more analytical on the subject and more combative, which is indicative of his response to the missionary aggressions and provocations. He needed to prove the historicity of Krishna to match the historical presence of Jesus in the armoury of the missionaries. The contexts in which these persons dialogued with Gita influenced their views, and they go into their analyses. Together they reveal the myriad hues and moods that constituted Indian nationalism. In fact, the nationalist dialogues with the Bhagavadgita show that the text was frequently and compulsively contextualized and in the process, constituted. The study also unfolds the several national questions eager to find endorsement from the Gita, which was really their way of seeking the nation's approval. Dialogue with the Bhagavadgita was indeed a dialogue with the Self in the context of the Universal Self, which the nation stood for. They belonged to the rare moments when nationalism was sliding into spiritual realms. These moments could be fleeting and yet real.

Apparently Ambedkar's views on the Gita do not seem to fit into the conventional nationalist framework and project. He had rejected the brahminical hegemony in India and all those scriptural texts that sustained it. His critical engagement with the text and authority of Bhagavadgita was designed to question and reject the social inequities and injustice which it legitimized or sanctioned. His notion of nationalism went beyond the immediacy of anti-colonial struggles.

The liberating potential or efficacy of nationalism could be tested only if it could uplift millions of the downtrodden in India and give them freedom and justice. Nationalism is not a stagnant category; it is engaged in constant review of itself to renew itself. Spiritualism, political activism, pacifism, and even revolutionary extremism could be located in, and retrieved from, the Gita no doubt, but it could also be subjected to a critical interrogation. Instead of looking at it as the timeless words of God, it can be seen as a hegemonic text that ordered and sanctioned hierarchies, subordination, and exploitation in society. Marxist scholars like Kosambi had found in Gita the reflections of feudal ideology and the society that produced it. Ambedkar's dialogue was that of a person whose nationalism was rooted in a critical appraisal of Hindu society with a view to changing it. In rejecting the conventional affirmative evaluation of the Bhagavadgita, Ambedkar gives a critical dimension to its understanding.

Vivekananda can be described as utilitarian in his approach to the Gita, employing it to reinforce his message both to the West and within India. Yet this is not a casual functionalism. He wrote no commentaries or translations, and his only systematic treatises on the Gita are contained in three addresses in California in 1895 and one in Bengal about three years later. Nevertheless, his eight volumes of *Collected Works* are replete with references to it. Lectures, formal addresses, interviews, even his personal correspondence are laced with quotations from the Gita. If his method be deemed utilitarian, then any assessment of its worth must depend on the value we give to his objectives, and scholastically, our judgment as to whether his references to the Gita derive from a superficial or deeper understanding of its content.

The attitude of a young rampant Vedantist-cum Hegelian-cum revolutionary like Vivekananda towards the cult of religious ectasy and Kali-worship may be easily imagined; and the spectacle of a born iconoclast and free-thinker like him, a creative and dominating intelligence, a tamer of souls himself caught in the meshes of an uncouth, supernatural mysticism, was a riddle which his earlier philosophy of the pure reason could scarcely when at the time."

Vivekananda was receiving a thoroughly Western education at Scottish Presbyterian College in Calcutta, founded by Alexander Duff, when he began to be acquainted with Hinduism though

Ramakrishna. Alternating with a superficial skepticism, the mind of the young Naren was also engaged in a religious quest of some depth, as might be inferred from the question which he asked Ramakrishna on his first visit. It was a crash question, one which he had asked of other reputed sages: "Sir, have you seen God?" Instead of the usual evasions or qualified responses, Ramakrishna's was amazingly direct: "Yes, my son, I have seen God, just as I see you before me, only much more intensely". A powerful dynamic surfaced in subsequent encounters between the two, each recognizing an intense spiritual magnetism, but each giving time for testing. Naren soon discovered that Ramakrishna possessed a great intellect underneath the emotional nature that initially seemed so overpowering. "Outwardly he was all Bhakta but inwardly all Jnanin. I am the exact opposite". The combination of paths of which the Gita speaks seems to have been experienced personally by the young Vivekananda, as his relationship with Ramakrishna unfolded.

Although bereft by Ramakrishna's death in 1886, the group of monastic disciples began to pledge themselves to a common life that would give each the range to explore his own spiritual path. Naren, who had become, in effect, their recognized leader, was tempted by the reclusive life of the hermetic monk, sealed from the world in the vastnesses of the Himalayas. But word came to him that his sister, back in Calcutta, has taken her life, and so he returned, apparently to re-define his vocational goal. He was not to leave the monastic calling, but to make it responsive to human need.

After visiting renowned centers of pilgrimage, he turned to an intensive, probing look at modern India. His long and patient tour to the north of India, then down its western side, culminated in 1893 in his first out-of-the-body experience, which occurred at the tip of the sub-continent's Cape Comorin peninsula on a rock some two hundred yards out subsequently to be known as Vivekananda Rock, to which he swam through shark-infested waters. In this moment of geographical and psychological outsideness, looking back on Bharat Mata, Mother India, a sense of mission began to focus for him. He returned to Madras, rather than Bengal, where some friends helped him to sharpen that focus. A Parliament of Religions, with delegates from the world's nations and faiths, was gathering later that year in Chicago, as part of the Columbian Exposition. No matter that India's delegates had been determined some two years earlier. In recognition of Naren's natural gifts, and because of some economic gifts from the Maharajah of Kheri, it was that Naren, who now took the name of Vivekananda, should go to Chicago as India's best ambassador.

Vivekananda arrival in Chicago, a month early, allowed him to indulge in the various exhibits and attractions of the fair. Intoxicated by its circus atmosphere, and by his vastly intensified initial exposure to the West, Vivekananda soon found that his money was being rapidly depleted. A fortuitous trip to Boston, and the acquaintance and hospitality of some well-positioned friends there, assisted him greatly. Sanskrit Professor J.H. Wright invited him to speak at Harvard, and on learning of his not having credentials to speak at the Parliament, is quoted as having said, "To ask for your credentials is like asking the sun to state its right to shine in the heavens." Wright then addressed a letter to the chairman in charge of delegates, saying, again extravagantly, "Here is a man who is more learned than all of our learned professors put together". Armed with this letter, but with no formal presentation, Vivekananda nevertheless rose late in the first day's proceedings and gave his first brief address, which began with his striking words, "Sisters and Brothers of America!" It seemed to strike an authentic keynote, and responding to his ringing words and regal bearing the press reports that the audience rose to applaud for several minutes before he could continue.

He had a message for the West, distilled from the ancient wisdom of India's spiritual sages. Initially, he conceived of gaining some material help from the West for India in return. This, however, evolved into a different mission. He realised that to raise funds, perhaps, would involve him in the acknowledgment of shortcomings of Indian society; the missionaries were making great capital of these already. So he took upon himself extolling the greatness of India's spiritual wisdom. While it is difficult to trace the details of this change of strategy, it is clear that his goal for India had become a more personal, spiritual one. What a message for the West and East did he have, and specifically what he did he have to share from the Gita, which he described as "The best authority on Vedanta", which, he believed, was Hinduism universalized. "The only commentary, the authoritative commentary on the Vedas, has been once and for all by Him who inspired the Vedas-Krishna in the Gita". Returning to

India to a hero's welcome late in 1897, he set out to implement his mission of an updated Hinduism, responsive to human needs.

It is initially surprising to find that Vivekananda's critical observations on the Gita in the West seem more traditionally Indian, and his addresses in India more informed by modern scholarship. We may judge from this that he perceived his western listeners as being less sophisticated in their understanding of Indian texts. By contrast, the novice monks whom he addressed in Bengal were treated to a relatively rather heady fare of critical methodology. But in each case, these four formal discourses frustrate our expectations as to scholarly format. We are never told the versions from which he quotes the Gita; are the translations his own? We have almost no bibliographical data; footnotes, marginalia. They are missing. If there are interpretive sources which he employs, we do not know in what manner he employs them. Only a few are named, let alone quoted. His lecture to the young monks in Bengal, nevertheless, does contain some historical and critical observation. He notes how questions of historicity of the Gita could be clarified considerably if the widely reputed commentary by Bodhyana, antedating Sankara, were not so shrouded in darkness. He states that he could not find a copy of it in the whole of his travels in India in the early 1890s.

But his greater concerns are with the cultic Krishna, spawned by whatever shadowy original may have inspired later legends. "It is human nature to build round the real character of a great man all sorts of imaginary superhuman attributes. As regards Krishna the same must have happened, but it seems quite probable that he was a king". A paucity of information of origins, however, inhibits his quest of the historical Krishna. Vivekananda method is not 'de-mythologizing' to get to the essential, earliest core of the teaching, but, 'multi-mythologizing' to focus attention on the varied strands of the tradition and the vivid manner in which mythic and cultic life has been stimulated by the figure of Krishna. Thus Vivekananda remarks, satirically, "Many of our people think that Krishna as the lover of the Gopis is something rather uncanny, and the Europeans do not like it much. Dr. So-and-so does not like it. Certainly, then, the Gopis have to go! Without the sanction of Europeans how can Krishna live? He cannot!" You are not to know whether Krishna was born in Mathura or in Vraja, what he was doing, or just the exact date on which he pronounced the teachings of the Gita. You only require to feel the craving for the beautiful lessons of duty and love in the Gita". While, Vivekananda's primary counsel from the Gita for India is in the direction of karma jnana and yogic strategies, here he also validates the more characteristically devotional response.

For western readers, however, who were more historically minded, he could oblige with at least some superficial conclusions concerning origins. Every religion, he suggests, must have some economic value to succeedwith the Upanishads. Gita as an Upanishad, there is very little economic value, but tremendous altruism. There is very little kingdom in them, yet they were discovered by kings who held royal power in their hands. "The seed of Buddhism is here, in the ordinary struggle between the king and the priest". Krishna is the reconciler of this struggle, as Buddhism later was, Vivekananda seems intent in the West, to establish the priority of the Gita and the earlier Upanishads, which he dates at about 5000 and 6000 B.C., over Buddhism. Back in India, he would appear to have developed a greater feeling for Buddhism, so that his interest in speculation concerning origins, fades.

Vivekananda once suggested that the two special characteristics of the Gita are reconciliation of paths and work without desire. These seem clearly to have been the most common lessons which he drew from the Gita for his western audience. There are several facets to the first, beginning with his first two-minute oration at the Parliament of Religions, where he is quoted as saying, "The present convention, which is one of the most august assemblies ever held, is in itself a vindication: a declaration to the world of the wonderful doctrine preached in the Gita: 'Whosoever comes to Me, through whatsoever form, I reach him; all men are struggling through paths which in the end lead to Me,. . . I fervently hope that the bell that tolled this morning in honor of this convention may be the death-knell of all fanaticism, of all persecutions with the sword or with the pen, and of all uncharitable feelings between persons wending their way to the same goal."

"Allow me to call you, brethren, by that sweet name, heirs of immortal bliss-yea, the Hindu refuses to call you sinners. You are the children of God, the sharers of immortal bliss, holy and perfect beings, ye are divinities on earth. Sinners? It is a sin to call a man so; it is a standing libel on human nature. Come up, O lions and shake off the delusion that you are sheep."

There were thus areas which he discovered did not allow for facile harmonization. Differing views of human nature and exclusivist claims were two of these. "It does not matter", he states, following the insight of the ninth chapter of the Gita cited above, "whether one approaches the destination in a carriage with four horses, in an electric car, or rolling on the ground. The goal is the same." The theory of incarnation gives Hinduism a basis for toleration of alternate paths; we see in them the workings of various avatars and the human responses to their power. He quotes Gita 4:18, "whenever virtue subsides and irreligion prevails, I come down. Again and again I come. Therefore, whenever thou seest a great soul struggling to uplift mankind, know that I am come, and worship". At the same time, Vivekananda asks, "if He comes as Jesus or as Buddha, why is there so much schism?" if, he would appear to be saying, we find in one of these great persons what we regard as truth, we ought to find echoes of that truth in other such persons, to look for it, and not to demean it or explain it away when it occurs. "You say Uncle Sam is everybody 's uncle. If there is a god, you ought to be able to see him. And, by implication, so should everyone else, in whatever guise. If not, let him go". It is the Upanishadic insight, that Truth is One.

In support of this, he cites several similarities between Jesus of Nazareth and Krishna. Krishna was of royal birth. King Kamsa, hearing that a child who would be king would be born in such and such a family, ordered a massacre of male infants. Krishna's parents were in prison when he was born. A light suddenly shone in the prison and Krishna spoke, saying, "I am the light of the world, born for the good of the world". Sages affirmed that God Himself was born, and they went pay Him homage. Just as he sought to make Krishna familiar by comparison with known circumstances in the life of Jesus, Vivekananda pointed to the Gita as the inspiration of some of America's greatest literary figures. In a lecture to the Shakespeare Club in Pasadena in 1900, he claimed that the Gita was the source of Emersons's inspiration. Visiting Carlyle, Emerson had been presented by him with a copy of the Gita. "The little book is responsible for the Concord Movement," Vivekananda claimed.

The practical problem with the harmonization of religions, lay for Vivekananda in the definitions by most of them of religion as doctrine, with assent to dogma as the mark of belonging. By contrast, he says, religion in India does not consist in doctrine, but in realization, by whatever path. He quotes Gita 3:35 as follows, "Better die in your own path than attempt the path of another". This may not carry the full weight of the meaning of dharma in the original, but he is speaking to Americans. "What do you mean by 'saving people' and all believing in the same doctrine?" he asks. "It cannot be.... We start a religion," he counsels, "enter not the gate of any organized religion. They do hundred times more evil than good , because they stop the growth of each one's religious development."

The answer, for Vivekananda, would appear to be personal confidence in your own insight and strength, and restraint in assuming that your path is better than that of another. In refuting the doctrine that says human beings are sinners because Adam sinned, and are saved because Christ dies, Vivekananda states, "No man's seeing God can help you the least bit except it may excite you and urge you to do the same thing. That is the whole value of the ancient's examples. Nothing more. Just signposts along the way. No man's eating can satisfy another man. No man's seeing God can save another man". Again, in underscoring his appeal that we recognize our identity as lions and not sheep, Vivekananda refers to the Gita, 6:5, saying, "It is a tremendous error to feel helpless. Do not seek help from anyone, we are our own help. If we cannot help ourselves, there is none to help us". He nears the conclusion of his California lectures on the Gita with the following words:

"There is only one sin. That is weakness. When I was a boy I read Milton's *Paradise Lost*: The only good man I had any respect for was Satan. The only saint is that soul that never weakens, faces everything and determines to die game. Stand up and die game! Do not add one lunacy to another, Do not add your weakness to the evil that is going to come. That is all I have to say to the world. Be strong!"

To the other side of the coin, personal strength which does not seek to overpower others, Vivekananda counsels: "Each one thinks his method is best. Very good! But remember, it may be good for you". Citing Gita, chapter 3, verses 26 and 29, he observes; "Even if you here knowledge, do not disturb the childlike faith of the ignorant. On the other hand, go down to their level and gradually bring them up". It is in these various ways that Vivekananda sought to effect, through the Gita's message, a tolerance of paths among Westerners.

They must believe in the validity of the insights of various great teachers. They must have confidence in their own insights, as well. And they must not be so presumptuous as to believe that what has worked for them will be easily tailored for another's spiritual garb.

The other message for the West form the Gita, as Vivekananda sought to teach it, was the lesson of non-attachment to work; calmness in the midst of strife. It was not an exhortation to work; that message was reserved for India. The Western work ethic was visible enough to the outsider, but he could critique, in the spirit of the Gita, the manner in which it was done, and th anxiety which it produced. Krishna, here, is the example. With Krishna, "non-attachment is the central idea. He does not need anything. He does not want anything. He works for work's sake. Similarly, Buddha is the ideal karma yogi, who did not work for any reward. Yet, Vivekananda prefers Krishna as the more representative human example. While Buddha and other spiritual leaders were monastics, with no sympathetic understanding for householders, Krishna fulfilled his roles as a son, king, and a father. For Americans, the symbolism is that Krishna lived the truth in the midst of the battlefield of life. Gita 4:18 is quoted as follows: "He who in the midst of intense activity finds himself in the greatest calmness, and in the greatest peace finds intense activity, that is the greatest Yogi as well as the wisest man".

The battlefield of Kurukshetra had abundant parallels to the American scene for Vivekananda, who was alternately attracted and repelled by its materialism. In Boston once he had planned to speak on the subject of his master, Ramakrishna, but at the sight of a crowd composed of persons of wealth and position and of a civilization represented by foxes and wolves, he was so repelled that he lashed out furiously. Hundreds noisily left the hall and the press was furious. Nikhilananda records the remorse Vivekananda felt after reflecting on what he had done. "His Master had never uttered a word of condemnation against anybody, even the most wicked person; Vivekananda resolved not to discuss him in public or even to write about him again.

A natural affection for the freshness, brashness, and energy of the American spirit also impressed him. Anticipating his first return to India, after several years in the West, he could write to a friend, "It is to America – there is where the heart is. I love the Yankee land. I like to see new things. I do not care a fig about old ruins and mope a life out about old histories and keep sighing about the ancients. I have too much vigour in my blood for that. In America is the place, the people, the opportunity for everything. I have become horribly radical. I am just going to India to see what I can do in that awful mess of conservative jellyfish."

Yet the conservative jellyfish perhaps could teach America something about tranquility. Vivekananda reminded his San Francisco hearers of the message in Gita 2:45 and elsewhere concerning the giving up of all desires. "When he has become perfectly satisfied, he has no more cravings". Such a man lives by different rhythms from the herd. It is this alternative message of Gita 2.65 which the western world needs for balance. The question which Vivekananda seeks to address, then, is how, to channel the West's abundant energy in such a menner as to bring spiritual freedom and not material bondage to its citizens. If non-attachment to work is the central message of the Gita, as Vivekananda asserts variously, then America was peculiarly in need of this work.

Vivekananda's uses of the Gita in India

If work without desire was a hallmark of the Gita's message for the West, Vivekananda's prescription for India was simpler still: "Work". There is more, but this is the karma yogic core of his teaching, the one which he judged that his people most needed to hear from the sacred pages. How to awaken the slumbering giant? Vivekananda interpreted the western spirit of power and energy as natural to the Yavana or Greek temperament; the Arya, by contrast, tends toward quietness and meditation. But then he makes the judgment, "Europe and America are the advanced children of the Yavanas, a glory to their forefathers; but the modern inhabitants of the land of Bharata are not the glory of the ancient Aryas". Although he feels that the ancestral fire will once more manifest itself, it is presently buried latent beneath ashes. These ashes are the delusion of India, who believes that she is pursuing sattva, or truth, when she is actually drowning in a sea of tamas. His powerful indictment continues:

"Where the most dull want to hide their stupidity by covering it with a false desire for the highest knowledge which is beyond all activities, either psychological or mental; where one, born and bred in lifelong laziness, wants to throw the veil of renunciation over his unfitness for work; where the most diabolical try to make their cruelty appear, under the cloak of austerity, as a part of religion; . . . . Where knowledge consists only in getting some books by heart, genius consists in chewing the cud of others thoughts . . . ; do we require any other proof to show that country is being day by day drowned in Tamas?"

He then goes to say that the nation and each person must pass from tamas through rajas to sattva. Where he feels that the West was almost wholly lacking in sattva, it is rajas, the spirit of energy, which was practically absent in India. His oratorical portrait of what India needs is eloquent; these three energy modes of expressions of prakrti found in the Gita, are the categories by which he expresses it:

"What we should have it what we have not, perhaps, what our forefathers even had not-that which the Yavanas had; that, impelled by the life-vibration of which, is issuing forth in rapid succession from the great dynamo of Europe. The electric flow of that tremendous power vivifying the whole world. We want that. We want that energy, that love of independence, that spirit of self-reliance, that immovable fortitude, that dexterity in action, that bond of unity of purpose, that thirst for improvement . . . we want-that intense spirit of activity (Rajas) which will flow through our every vein, from head to foot."

Vivekananda addressed a Madras gathering shortly after his return to India in 1897 urging them, "First of all, our young men must be strong. Religion will come afterwards. Be strong, my young friends; that is my advice to you. You will be nearer to Heaven through football than through the study of the Gita. These are bold words, but I have to say them, for I love you . . . You will understand the Gita better with your biceps, your muscles, a little stronger. You will understand the mighty genius and the mighty strength of Krishna better with a little of strong blood in you. Yield not to unamnliness, O Son of Pritha". This was a keynote for his message on the Gita to the young monastics back in Bengal. "Thou art Atman imperishable, beyond all evil. Having forgotten thy real nature, thou hast, by thinking thyself a sinner, as one afflicted with bodily evils and mental grief, thou hast made thyself so-this doth not befit thee!" He had told a California audience earlier that for Indians the problem is how to become what they really are, to regain their lost selfhood, now he draws on those jnanin aspects of the Gita to reinforce the imperative to strong, karma yogic behavior. A Bengali disciple recorded his instructions in 1898 on several occasions in the monastery in Belur, sometimes linking these two themes from the Gita, but invariably emphasizing these strains of jnana and karma. "Shri Krishna spoke the Gita, establishing Himself in the *Atman*. Those passages of the Gita where He speaks with the word 'I' invariably indicate the *Atman*: "Take refuge in Me alone' means, 'Be established in the *Atman*. This knowledge of the Atman is the highest aim of the Gita". Again the disciple observes, "On the lips of Swamiji were very often heard the words of the Gita, A doer of good never comes to grief, my son. Asked by a disciple how an artist should try to represent the Krishna of the Gita, Vivekananda, after discussing and demonstrating possible battlefield scenes and poses, asked him in return, "Now tell me what idea this picture of the Preacher of the Gita conveys to you?" the response was, "Activity combined with firmness and serenity". Vivekananda replied enthusiastically, "Ay, that's it! Intense action in the whole body, and with a face expressing the profound calmness and serenity of the blue sky".

How is it that the bhakti components of the Gita are de-emphasized, or slanted towards more Upanishadic, Advaitic interpretations, and that the activist flavor everywhere dominates? ("Work is worship", etc.) Again it would seem to be that India, in his judgment, had enough of ceremonials. He addressed his brother monks in 1894 from America, giving them, in one of his first letters back to Bengal, some sense of how he expected them to proceed, and what to avoid, in an eloquent satitical treatise on ceremonials:

"If you want any good to come, just throw your ceremonials overboard and worship the living God, the Man-God-every being that wears a human form – God in His universal as well as individual aspect. The universal aspect of God menas this world, and worshipping it means serving it – this indeed is work, not indulging in ceremonials. Neither is it work to argue as to whether the rice plate should be placed in front of the God for ten minutes or for half an hour-that is called lunacy. Millions of rupees have been spent only that the temple doors at Varanasi or Vrindaban may play at opening and shutting all day long! Now the Lord is having his toilet, now he is taking his meals, now he is busy on something else we know not what . . . And all this, while the living God is dying for want of food, for want for wnt of education! The banias of Bombay are erecting hospitals for bugs-while they would do nothing for men-even if they die! You have not the brain to understand this simple thing – that it is a plague with our country, and lunatic asylums are rife all over . . ."

Later, in a more temperate mood, he could confess to his gurubhais, "I am trying and always trying to keep down the rush of Bhakti welling within me. I am trying to bind and bind myself with the iron chains of Jnana, for still my work not yet fully delivered. So, as soon as I find that Bhakti feelings are trying to come up to sweep me off my feet, I give a hard knock to them and make myself adamant by bringing up austere Jnana".

However, the example of Ramakrishna was often cited as precedent for alternative directions which the Movement might take. It was an ultimate example which had at times resulted in devotion. But given the divine authority of Ramakrishna, who best could interpret Ramakrishna? In one heated exchange, Vivekananda railed at his brother monks:

"You think you understand Shri Ramakrishna better than myself! You think Jnana is dry knowledge to be attained by a desert path, killing out the tenderest faculties of the heart. Your Bhakti is sentimental nonsense which makes one impotent. You want to preach Ramakrishna as you have understood him which is mighty little. Hands off! Who cares for your Ramakrishna? Who cares for your Bhakti and Mutkti? Who cares what the Scriptures say? I will go to hell cheerfully a thousand times, if I can rouse my countrymen, immersed in Tamas, and make then stand on their feet and be men, inspired with the spirit of Karma-Yoga. I am not a follower of Ramakrishna or any one, I am not a servant of Ramakrishna or any one, but of him only who carries out my plans! I am not a servant of Ramakrishna or any one, but of him only who serves and helps others, without caring for his own Mukti."

Despite his disavowals, the priority of karmayoga was a lesson which he had learned earlier from Ramarishna. When he had implored Ramakrishna to show him the way to nirvkalpa smadhi, the state of ultimate release, he was given a surprisingly sharp rebuke by his gentle master. "Shame on you!" Ramakrishna exclaimed. "I never thought you to be so mean as to anxious for your own salvation only whereas you have powers to do so much good to mankind".

The Gita's message authenticated his own deep missionary imperative. It taught a ministry to human need, a ministry activated most vividly by energizing the people of India to claim their own strong, if dormant, identity. Vivekananda noted western objections to Krishna's militant counsel to Arjuna in chapter two of the Gita, and responded by suggesting that all of Arjuna's apparently sophisticated arguments against participating in combat stemmed from cowardice. It was not non-resistance from strength, which would have been true renunciation. The sattvic goal of renunciation can only be pursued after one has passed through the inferno of his passions, has engaged the foe in battle, has exercised the karma yogic imperative of resistance to evil. In support of this, he gives an example of a conversation which he had with a young man in India: who I had known as a very stupid, dull person, who knew nothing and had not the desire to know anything, and was living the life of a brute. He asked me what he should do to know God, how he was to get free. Can you tell a lie? I asked him, 'No' he replied. 'Then you must learn to do so. It is better to tell a lie than to be a brute, or a log of wood. You are inactive; you have not certainly reached the highest state, which is beyond all actions, calm, and serene; you are too dull even to do so something wicked'. That was an extreme case, of course, and I was joking with him; but what I meant was that a man must be active in order to pass through activity to perfect calmness."

This *karma-jnana* blending from the Gita is the mode whereby all persons in India may be energized. It is there for everyone in every occupation of life. These conceptions of the Vedanta must come out, must remain not only in the forest, not only in the cave, but they must come out to work ar the bar and the bench, in the pulpit, and in the cottage of the poor man, with the fisherman that are catching fish, and with the students that are studying. They call to every man, woman and child what ever be their occupation, wherever they may be.

For each, it follows, "if the fisherman thinks that he is the Spirit, he will be a better fisherman," etc. "If you teach Vedanta to a fisherman, he will say, I am as good a man as you; I am a fisherman, you are a philosopher, but I have the same God in me as you have in you". So, for Vivekananda, castes might continue, but not privilege; there is to be equality, but with division of labor. We see in his program, then, a case for social service, but not for social reform. He is impatient, for instance, with questions about what to do with the widow problem and the women question. "Let me answer once and for all – am I a widow that you ask me that nonsense? Am I a woman that you ask me that question again and again? Who are you to solve women's problems? Are you the Lord God that you should rule over every widow and every woman? Hands off! His point is that you do not help others by presuming to identify with their lot, which is impossible. Your help may actually inhibit their own self reliance, their experience of the power resident in their own true identity."

In addressing a Madras gathering which would have been composed primarily of Brahmins, he stated that the Gita advocates true Brahminhood for all. There is to be no doing away with caste, but there is to be no warfare among the castes. Just as in the Mahabharata he observes, there was only one caste at the beginning of the *Satya Yuga*, so in the coming *Satya Yuga*, his vision for India's future, all castes will return to true Brahminhood, the ideal of humanity in India. In the meantime, he states;

"The days of exclusive privileges and exclusive claims are gone, gone for ever from the soil of India, and it is one of the great blessings of British Rule in India. Even to the Mohammedan Rule we owe that great blessing, the destruction of exclusive privilege. The Mohammedan conquest of India came as a salvation to the downtrodden, to the poor. That is why one-fifth of our people have become Mohammedans. It was not the sword that did it all. It would be the height of madness to think it was all the work of sword and fire. And one-fifth – one half – of your Madras people will become Christians if you do not take care. Was there ever a sillier thing before in the world than what I saw in Malabar country? The poor Pariah is not allowed to pass through the same street as the high-caste man, but if he changes his name to hodge-podge English name, it is all right; or to a Mohammedan name, it is all right."

India, after centuries of alien political domination, had become, insists Vivekananda's, a servile, boot-licking race. The mission which he began to intuit from the rock off Cape Comorin, subsequently to be named in his honor and a temple erected upon it, did have a part in energizing India. The tiny surface of Vivekananda Rock became a place of vision from which the conch shell of Kurukshetra might again be heard to awaken the fearful and slothful to engage in life's battle. Vivekananda's use of the Gita, in the West and in the East, and in the insights which ripened from his bridges between them, was active and outward in its intent, and an understanding Vivekananda thought was faithful in spirit to the Gita's own best wisdom.

Vivekauanda felt that Vedic truth was distorted and concealed by various superstitions, practices, and beliefs over the centuries. The universal character of Vedic truth was discredited due to institutional degeneration of all kinds by priest-craft to uphold their superiority over others, which had, in fact, no warrant in the scriptures. He admitted, too, that these could not be defended as appropriate ways of life any longer. He even devoted one of his speeches delivered in America to explain how, contrary to Vedic truth, the brahmins were brutal in exploiting the poor, that they terrorized people by imposing; unfair demands in the name of tradition, and that they should repent for the past sins. According to him, the Upanisads challenged some of these traditions and ceremonies in a significant way but the Gita emerged as a text that would reconcile the conflicting positions in the Vedas and the Upanisads. He argues that these superstitions, rituals, and ceremonies are blind if considered independent of 'truth', or developed not from the real 'self' but from the 'ego', just as fables and stories are meaningless if understood without their true relations with the central truth of the text. If traditions are practised with the higher detachment by the Kumayogi, or with the object of setting an example for the ignorant, these ceremonies and rituals would no longer be 'blind', and could be regarded as the highest truth. Vivekananda finds such a presence in Krishna:

"My regard for him is for his perfect sanity. No cobwebs in that brain, no superstition. He knows the use of everything, and when it is necessary to assign a place to each, he is there. Those that talk, go everywhere, question about the mystery of the Vedas, etc., they do not know the truth. They are no better than frauds. There is a place in the Vedas even for superstition, for ignorance. The whole secret is to find out the proper place for everything."

Vivekananda justified idol worship, or worship of different gods, for instance, on the same ground. Idol worship may be perverse in itself if it is not combined with, or detached from, absolute truth. But if it is derived from the highest realization or done as an example for the ignorant, it is as good as worshipping the imperceptible.

"Even if you have knowledge, do not disturb the child like faith of the ignorant. On the other hand, go down to their level and gradually bring them up. That is a very powerful idea, and it has become the ideal in India. That is why you can see a great philosopher going into a temple and worshipping images. It is not hypocrisy ... Can't you understand that whatever a man has in his own heart is God—even if he worships a stone?"

Vivekananda suggested a relation between such practices and historical investigation. Historical enquiries can be used to recast all these practices, rituals, ceremonies which had come to be invented around the universal truth and to model them as accepted attributes of truth in order to avoid blind and equivocal practices. However, it would not alter the truth in any way.

"Then what is the use of so much historical research, you may ask. It has its use, because we have to get at the truth ... Many of the sects believe that in order to preach a good thing, which may be beneficial to many, there is no harm in telling an untruth... But our duty should be to convince ourselves of the truth, to believe in truth only. Such is the power of superstition, or faith in old traditions without inquiry into its truth, that it keeps men bound hand and foot, so much so that even Jesus the Christ, Mohammed, and other great men believed in many such superstitions and could not shake them off. You have to keep your eye always fixed on truth only, and shun all superstitions completely."

Nishkama Karma as the Moral Foundation

Vivekananda, insists that nishkama karma or non-attachment is the core teaching of the Bhagavadgita. It is central to the text as 'sacrifice and love are central to Buddhism and 'service and love' to Christianity. It is based on the belief that every action in nature produces some effects, good or bad, thus entailing bondage upon the doer. As a mode of seeking release from this bondage, the text does not advocate abstention from the worldly affairs or sannyasa or performance of action with selfish interest. The solution does not on either depend the pursuance of seclusion or self-centred action, but in nishkama karma—working incessantly without attachment and without expecting reward. The Gita explains nishkama karma as letting karma operate naturally and ceaselessly through the soul:

"Every work must necessarily be a mixture of good and evil ... good and bad are both bondages of the soul. The solution reached in the Gita in regard to this bondage-producing nature of work is that, if we do not attach ourselves to the work we do, it will not have any binding effect on our soul. This is the one central idea in the Gita; work incessantly, but be not attached to it."

For Vivekananda, the concept of *nishkama karma* implies four things. First, it implies the necessity of purification of mind. As the mind is the instrumental cause for every good and bad action, its purification is the first necessity. A *nishkama karmi* would, therefore, control his mind from the bondage-producing external objectives and develop a proper perspective:

"How to attain purity living this life? ... If the mind is not under control, it is no use living in a cave because the same mind will bring all disturbances there ... If the mind is under control, we can have the cave anywhere, wherever we are. It is our own mental attitude, which makes the world that it is for us. Our thoughts make things beautiful; our thoughts make things ugly ... Everything in the world is good, is holy and beautiful. If you see something evil, think that you are not understanding it in the right light."

Secondly, it suggests the purification of heart. It is through the heart that one identifies oneself with happenings in the external world. The heart is the root of 'mine-ness' and 'thine-ness' and hence, the basis for all kinds of attachment. A nishkama karmi would keep his heart untainted by not contemplating the results of his actions. 'Attachment to the unreal will' bring misery. There is only one existence that is real... unattached love will not hurt you.'

Third, *nishkama karma* implies the absence of passion and tenderness. Passion and tenderness are the foundations of attachment. Therefore, a *nishkama karmi* would perform his karma for karma's sake, without giving way to any emotionalism and sentimentalism. He is not a feeble person to surrender to the feelings and excitements of the external world but he will be able to master them. Arjuna was not a *nishkama karmi* in the sense that he was not controlled by his real self hut by his emotions and sentiments.

The nearer we are to beasts and birds, the more we are in the hells of emotion. We call it love. It is self-hypnotisation. We are under the control of our emotions like animals. There emotion has no place, nor anything that belongs to the senses— only the light of pure reason. There man stands as spirit. Now, Arjuna is a slave of this emotionalism. He is not what he should be — a great self-controlled, enlightened sage working through the eternal light of reason. He has become like an animal, like a baby, just letting his heart carry away his brain, making a fool of himself and trying to cover his weakness with the flowery names of love and so on.

Four they nishkama karma also implies the concentration of one's full energy on work. A nishkama karmi would work with concentration and a steady mind. It is concentration that nullifies the self-ego and attachment and makes a man's full energy completely focused on action. Hence, Vivekananda regarded this as the most important aspect of nishkama karma.

Vivekananda asserts that actions done continuously and tirelessly with a pure mind and untainted heart, with one's full energy concentrated on the means without attachment to the self, and regarding God as the source of everything is the nishkama karma of the Gita. This has great implications for the nation. In a nation, masses that are equal in a profound sense would regulate their lives and their mutual relations on this foundation. In its application to politics and society, *nishkama karma*, however, has a wider meaning and objectives.

Vivekananda viewed nishkama karma in the text as directed against priest-craft and specifically against brahminism and their religious practices. In different speeches delivered in the West and various parts of India, Vivekananda criticized priest-craft for its repressive and inhuman exploitation of the poor in the name of religion. In one of his speeches delivered in San Francisco he argued that the Vedico-Upanisadic religion, which was originally pure and universal, was subsequently made elitist by priest-craft, keeping it at a great distance from the masses and making it the privilege of a small minority. They maintain this privileged position by fabricating or imposing rituals, and declaring that salvation was the monopoly of a few and that the path of karma with its culmination in jnana, was not equally open to every human being in society. Hence, priest-craft was responsible for making religion and salvation as difficult as possible for the poor and the marginalized, an excluding them from spiritual quest. On another occasion, too, he expressed the same opinion. He thundered:

"Why, you priest-class never let the non-Brahmin classes read the Vedas and Vedanta and all such weighty Sastras—never touch them even. You have only kept them down. It is you who have always done like that through selfishness. It was the Brahmins who made a monopoly of the religious books and kept the question of sanction and prohibition in their own hands. And repeatedly calling the other races of India low and vile, they put this belief into their heads that they were really such. If you tell a man, You are low, you are vile', in season and out of season, then he is bound to believe in course of time that he is really such. This is called hypnotism."

For Vivekananda, *nishkama karma* avowed by the Gita does not make religion the privilege of the few. It is, in fact, directed against vested interests such as the priestly classes. Against the monopolization of the Vedic religion by priest-craft, it attempts to democratize religious participation and ethical pursuits. Hence, it aims to achieve a double purpose of exterminating rituals and ceremonies and universalizing the vedic religion.

It is interesting to compare Vivekananda's understanding of this part of the Gita with Tilak's commentary in the *Gita Rahasya*. For Tilak, society basically consists of two kinds of individuals—one possessing weak reason and the other possessing mental strength. It is the responsibility of the strong-minded, the *sthitaprajnas*, who are well versed in religion, and whose moral practices have an epistemic foundation, to guide and lead the masses. Therefore, the nation is going to be led by the sthitaprajnas, a new brahmin class. Unlike Tilak, Vivekananda completely underplayed the concept of the sthitaprajna that dominates the Gita Rahasya. On the contrary, Vivekananda considered everyone as equal. Those who consider themselves as savants have to prove their claim by putting into practice the ethics of the Gita.

Vivekananda argued that the doctrine of nishkama karma pays greater attention to the masses, particularly the poor in the society. He felt that the ancient scriptures such as the Vedas and Upanisads were more concerned with vituals and care moralist rather than the economic life of the masses. The application of these morals to society by priest-craft, in fact, worsened the position of the poor. But the success of any religious system largely depends on its economic concerns and policies and programmes for the poor.

"There runs an economic struggle through every religious struggle. This animal called man has some religious influence, but he is guided by economy. Individuals are guided by something else, but the mass of mankind never made a move unless economy was involved. Whenever any religion succeeds, it must have economic value. Thousands of similar sects will be struggling for power, but only those who meet the real economic problem will have it. Man is guided by the stomach. He walks and the stomach goes first and the head afterwards. For the religion of the Upanisads to be popularized was a hard task. Very little economy is there, but tremendous altruism."

Vivekananda suggested that the Gita put greater emphasis on economics concerns as central to religion. It overturned the spiritual and altruistic religion of the Vedas into an economic religion through the concept of *daridranarayana*. For the Gita, the highest religion does not lie in *sannyasa* or worshipping various gods in the form of idols or in following the priestly version of the Vedic religion. The highest truth lies in nishkama karma, service of the poor. Therefore, he called on its followers to worship 'daridra' as 'narayana' and seek transcendence in their service. However, this service does not consist of just providing temporary relief to their problems; they need to be addressed religiously:

"Go on and work, without any sorrow, without any misery. See His play in the slums, in the saloons! Work to lift people! Not that they are vile or degraded; Krishna does not say that... My lady goes to the slum ... She gives a few ducats and says, 'My poor men, take that and be happy!' Or my fine woman, walking through the street, sees a poor fellow and throws him five cents. Think of the blasphemy of it! ... Serve the living God! God comes to you in the blind, in the halt, in the poor, in the weak, in the diabolical. What a glorious chance for you to worship!"

It is through the philosophy of nishkama karma that Krishna shows his concern for redeeming the fallen, whom the Vedic texts had ignored. Hence, for Vivekananda, Krishna qualifies as a universal God. Shri Krishna is the God of the poor, the beggar, the sinner, the son, the father, the wife, and of everyone. He enters intimately into all our human relations.

Not only does the Gita make religion accessible to the poor, but it extends an immense psychological and moral support to the weaker sections of the society, Vivekananda regarded Arjuna's weakness, dejection, and timidity as expressions of the weakness of the marginalized and Krishna repeated exhortation as an expression of this psychological and moral support. Krishna did not lambast Arjuna for his cowardice, ignorance, and occasional irrelevant questions and gradually persuaded him to believe that he would not be a sinner if he participated in war. He shows that the poor, the women, the weak, the sudras, or those who suffer from want of courage are not to be suppressed or humiliated, rather they are to be inspired towards the right path. Hence, the highest religion consists not in decrying the poor but in making earnest attempts to draw their attention to the right path.

"It was not that the disinclination of Arjuna to fight arose out of the overwhelming predominance of pure Sattva quality; it was all tames that brought on this unwillingness. Arjuna was afraid, he was overwhelmed with pity ... In order to remove this delusion ... what did the *Bhagavan* says ... you should not decry a man by calling him a sinner, but that you should draw his attention to the omnipotent power that is in him, in the same way does the Bhagavan speak to Arjuna. — 'It doth not befit thee!' 'Thou art Atman imperishable, beyond all evil. Having forgotten thy real nature, thou hast, by thinking thyself a sinner, as one afflicted with bodily evils and mental grief, thou hast made thyself so—this doth nor befit thee!'... Shake off this weakness, this faint-heartedness!

Vivekananda regards this aspect of nishkama karma as the future course of his mission, and appeals to his fellow young persons who decided to take brahmacharya and sannyasa to propagate and fulfill this teaching of the text across the world.

"If you, my sons, can proclaim this message to the world—then all this disease, grief, sin and sorrow will vanish ... go to the mouth of the cannon, fear not. Hate not the most abject sinner, look not to his exterior. Turn thy gaze inward, where resides the Paramatman. Proclaim to the whole world with trumpet voice, "There is no sin in thee, there is no misery in thee; thou art the reservoir of omnipotent power. Arise, awake, and manifest the Divinity within!"

It is worth noting here that nishkama karma emphasizes the economic aspect of religion and insists that the poor and lowly come out of their weakness and realize the universal truth. What is really creditable is that the Gita analyzes the economic conditions of the people while reconsidering Vedic religions, which paid scant attention to this aspect of life. In doing so, it suggests new concerns for the 'spiritual' duties of the priestly class. For Vivekananda, the Indian nation is to be reconstructed on this economic foundation of the Gita religion.

For Vivekananda, the doctrine of *nishkama karma* upholds the universal essence of human beings, thereby proclaiming the equality of all. Each individual, whether poor or weak, learned or brahmin, woman or sudra, represents the same essence. Vivekananda considered this as the central meaning of nishkama karma, irrespective of differences in interpretation and understanding this reality.

"Let every man and woman and child, without respect of caste or birth, weakness or strength, hear and learn that behind the strong and the weak, behind the high and the low, behind everyone, there is that Infinite Soul, assuring the infinite possibility find the infinite capacity of all to become great and good ... Too much of inactivity ... weakness ... hypnotism has been and is upon our face ... Teach yourselves, teach everyone his real nature... Power will come ... if there is anything in the Gita that I like, It is these two verses coming out strong as the very gist, the very essence of Krishna's teaching—He who sees the Supreme Lord dwelling alike in all beings, the Imperishable in things that perish, he sees indeed. For seeing the Lord as the same, everywhere present, he does not destroy the Self by the Self, and thus he goes to the highest goal."

Vivekananda felt that the pursuit of nishkama karma does not confine itself to any one section of the society bur is accessible to everyone — brahmin, kshatriya, vaishya and sudra. In other words, ii does not circumscribe itself to the caste-varna divisions as it can be done from any station in life. He presents the pristine Vedico-Upanisadic religion in a strong popular appeal:

"The Advaita, was its being worked out so long on the spiritual plane only ... time has come when you have to make it practical. It shall no more be a Rahasya, a secret, it shall no more live with monk., in caves and forests, and in the Himaliyas; it must come down to the daily, everyday life of the people ... in the cottage of the poor, the beggar in the street. Therefore do not fear whether you are a woman or a Sudra, for this religion is so great, says Lord Krishna, that even a little of it brings a great amount of good."

Vivekananda argued that Krishna, through *nishkama karma,* was the first, long before Buddha and Christ, to open the door of religion to men and women of all sections of society and make salvation for ordinary men as easy as possible on their own grounds. 'His was the first heart that was large enough to see truth in all, his the first lips that uttered beautiful words for each and all.

Superficially considered, Vivekananda's reading and understanding of the Gita can well be accommodated within the same mode of ethical interpretation as that of his contemporary Tilak. His vision and approaches, however, were significantly different. Vivekananda thought that India, built on the ethical principles of the Gita, can provide an ethical lead to the world. Hence, it was a mission not merely for India but also for the larger world. Moreover, Vivekananda was not a political writer in the sense Tilak was. Tilak used the text of the Gita for political dialogues, particularly for the justification of violent struggle against the colonial administration and the establishment of self-government, while Vivekananda used it for the rejuvenation of the cultural heritage of India's past.

The Bhagavad Gita had a very significant role in the life and work of Vivekananda. Although he did not write a verse-by- verse commentary covering the Gita as a whole, he quoted and explained selected verses from it. In fact, in his short opening address at the Parliament of Religions in Chicago in September 1893, he quoted a verse from the fourth chapter of the Gita to the broad objective of the Parliament of Religions itself. Vivekananda regarded the Parliament as a vindication, a declaration to the world, of the wonderful doctrine preached in the Gita, and quoted the following verse: "Whosever comes to Me, through whatsoever form, I reach him; all men are struggling through paths which in the end lead to Me."

The most significant elements from the teachings of the Gita, which Vivekananda explained to his followers, listeners and readers, and himself utilized in his work, are contained in the 1896 publication entitled "Karma Yoga'. Various aspects of karma, including "The secret of work", "What is duty?", "We help ourselves, not the world", and so on, are discussed by Vivekananda, not only from a theoretical angle but also in relation to life in modern times. One of the main messages which he wants to convey is the supreme importance of being ready to sacrifice himself for others, expecting no personal gain in return. He explains:

"However much the various systems of philosophy and religion may differ, all mankind stands in reverence and awe before the man who is ready to sacrifice himself for others... When you give something to a man and expect nothing – do not even expect the man to be grateful –his ingratitude will not tell upon you, because you never expected anything, never thought you had any right to anything in the way of a return."

Vivekananda spoke about Sri Krisna and the Gita, again in the course of four lectures delivered in April-May 1900. He described Sri Krisna as "the most rounded man" he knew of, wonderfully, developed equally in brain and heart and hand. Every moment of Sri Krisna said Vivekananda, was alive with activity, either as a householder gentleman, as a scholar, as a poet. This all-rounded and wonderful activity and combination of brain and heart, Vivekananda saw in the Gita.

This tremendous activity of Krisna, said Vivekananda, "the first man, way before Buddha, to open the door of religion to every caste." Thereafter, Vivekananda compared these two great personalities: "Buddha's activity was on one plane, the plane of teaching. He could not keep his wife and child and become a teacher at the same time Krisna preached in the midst of the battlefield. It means nothing to this man—the flying of missiles against him. Calm and sedate he goes on discussing the problems of life and death. He practised what he preached in the Gita: He who in the midst of intense activity finds himself in the greatest calmness, and in the greatest peace finds intense activity, that is the greatest Yogi as well as the wisest man.

The Gita verses which Vivekananda explained in the course of the lectures occur mostly in the first six chapters. The ideas that he emphasized were essentially the main elements of "Karmayoga", but in some cases he introduced additional details. For example, he said, with reference to the opening statement of Sri Krisna in the second chapter. The Gita opens with this very significant verse: "Arise, O Prince, give up this faint-heartedness, this weakness. Stand up and fight... Not one step back, that is the idea... Fight it out, whatever comes. Let the stars move from the sphere. Let the whole world stand against us. ... Arise, awake, stand up and fight. Die if you must..."

Analysing the initial arguments of Arjuna in the Gita, Vivekananda sensed in them an attempt "to cover this weakness with the flowery names of love and higher moral ideas." For Vivekananda this is a common human weakness.

Many a time comes when we want to interpret our weakness and cowardice as forgiveness and renunciation. There is no merit in the renunciation of a beggar. If a person who can give a blow forbears, there is merit in that. If a person who has, gives up, there is merit in: that. We know how often in our lives through laziness and cowardice we give up the battle and try to hypnotise our minds into the belief that we are brave. Appropriately, the Gita opens with a strong call to Arjuna to give up faintheartedness, to give up weakness.

Another section of the Gita highlighted by Vivekananda was the one containing the Lokasathgraha-verses of the third chapter (III. 20-26). He translated *Lokasamgraha* as "working for the good of others", and citing the example of Sri Krisna, Vivekananda asked men of knowledge to help the ignorant and gradually bring them up:

"Even if you have known the secret that you have no duty, that you are free, says Sri Krisna, still you have to work for the good of others. Because whatever a great man does, ordinary people will do also. If a great man who has attained peace of mind and freedom, ceases to work, then all the rest without that knowledge and peace will try to imitate him and then confusion would arise."

Behold, Arjuna, says Sri Krisna, there is nothing that I do not possess and nothing that I want to acquire. And yet I continue to work. If I stopped work for a moment, the whole universe would be destroyed. That which the ignorant do with desire for results and gain, let the wise do without any attachment and without any desire for results and gain.

Vivekananda characterised Nishkam Karma as a very powerful idea— which has become the ideal in India Undoubtedly this is one of the powerful forces that had inspired him when he started the Ramakrishna Mission in 1897.

7

Ideal Society

Vivekananda's part in the history of religions can never be overestimated. He was the first who being himself a Hindu introduced in a very convincing way the main thoughts of the Hindu religion to the international public, giving at the same time a new interpretation of traditional concepts and values.

But can we confine his importance to the field of religion? His first words at the Parliament of Religions in Chicago, "Sister and Brothers of America..." can be taken as the expression of his firm conviction of the equality of man regardless of his nationality, faith, sex or colour; but it was also the expression of the self-confidence of a man who, coming from a colonial country, proudly explained to the public that his country downtrodden and starving as it was something valuable to offer.

Vivekananda's several speeches in Chicago clearly give evidence that for all his concentration on spiritual themes he never lost sight of the real conditions his fellow beings lived in. This, for example, can be seen his critical remarks on the activities of the Christian missionaries in India. He himself repeatedly stressed that his first aim was to bring bread to the people; to teach religion should be only the second step. To his mind, a religion which did not aim at the improvement of the social conditions of the poor and suppressed, could not claim to be called religion at all. He did not believe in a religion which did not appease the hunger of the distressed. Thus his challenge to religion was:

"Bread! Bread! I do not believe in a God who cannot give me bread here, giving ,me eternal bliss in heaven! Pooh! India is to be raised, the poor are to be fed, education is to be spread, and the evil of priestcraft is to be removed. No priestcraft, no social tyranny! More bread, more opportunity for everybody."

Religion confined to books and dogma was not recognised by him as religion. In this way Vivekananda took the real social engagement of religion as a criterion for evaluating its sincerity. But the social implication of Vivekananda's philosophical concepts is by no means exhausted by this observation on the relationship between religious theory and practical behaviour of religious people. In order to illustrate this we have to go back into the history of Indian philosophy. In ancient and medieval Indian philosophy there was a general indifference to ethical and social thought. Sankara lived at a time of radical social change, when the feudal features of social development grew more rigid and regional dynasties became stronger. It was a time of all-Indian intellectual and cultural life of the educated: an ideological-cultural unity among the social upper class emerged, but also a feeling for cultural unity amongst the masses.

The intellectual climate was characterised by decline of Buddhism and Vedic ritualism as well as the development of Hinduism into a people's religion with a great number of directions, together with the adoption of new ritual cults particularly in Southern India and by a flourishing philosophical life. These factors produced the need for a synthesis of different religious and philosophical streams which was answered by Sankara's basic philosophical concept. His monistic interpretation of *tat tvam asi* was determined by the idea that the real nature of the world and of man is in the end marked by the sole existence of the all-embracing absolutely spiritual Brahman, which in reality is identical with the individual soul. The result is that from the viewpoint of supreme truth the world in its great variety is only of apparent, illusionary existence, as is the individual soul.

Sankara's philosophy, in the end, has to be understood as a doctrine. of salvation from the impermanence through realisation of one's own identity with the supreme spiritual being. This aim can only be attained after having studied the holy scriptures, which the upper three ranks only are allowed to do. Sankara's philosophical concept was of lasting influence on further. philosophical developments, but the discussion triggered off by it was mainly focused on the relation between God, man, the individual soul and the universe, and not at all on social questions. It was only in the nineteenth century that social philosophy eventually became an inseparable part of philosophy in India, and within this process Vivekananda played by decisive a seminal role.

When in the last century the development of the Indian bourgeoisie began, a philosophy was needed which could correspond to the demands and needs of this new social development while maintaining traditional lines of thinking. Demands, under the conditions of colonial rule, for the unfolding of individuality and the emancipation of the citizens from all feudal restrictions, were connected with the demand for national equality and justice; and its philosophical expression was closely connected with the religiousness of the masses as well as the need for national unity. In addition, this modern development was not the result of its own national historic growth, but largely initiated through foreign rule and was marked by certain disproportions.

But neither Rammohun Roy nor Ramakrishna Paramahamsa developed a social philosophy proper in the sense of systematic philosophizing on social problems. This was achieved only by Vivekananda, who rightly can be named as the first among Indian philosophers for whom social philosophy constituted an integral part of his philosophic system. He was the first who connected his new interpretation of the Advaita Vedanta with the development of a social philosophy that corresponded to the requirements of a modern society.

Of course Vivekananda took over Sankara's concept of the sole existence of Brahman and the relative reality of the phenomenal world; but he emphasised that the time had come for using this knowledge practically. Vivekananda demanded the application of Vedanta to the every-day life of the common man, which Sankara was not able to do in view of the social conditions of his times. That is why Vivekananda explained: "leave this Advaita philosophy in the hills and forests, while I have come to bring it out of those places and scatter it broadcast before the work-a-day world and society."

Tracing this further, we can find in Vivekananda's social teachings two main aspects, namely the demand for equal rights for humen beings as well as for nations and the call for the development of the personality. He stressed also the idea of universal brotherhood: if only the absolute exists with which every individual is identical, then every human being by his very essence is divine and there does not exist any fundamental difference between humen beings. Vivekananda was also the first in the history of Indian philosophy who at least in rough outlines drew the picture of an ideal society, put it in another way, who at first developed a social utopia. Notwithstanding the sketchy character of his concept of an ideal society we can find enough clues in his speeches and writings for completing his sketch.

On one occasion Vivekananda explained: that society is the greatest, where the highest truths become practical. That means, according to him, that an ideal society has to be structured in such a way that the divinity of human beings can be realised. Out of this follows that first of all this ideal society has to guarantee liberty of thought and action, which is the precondition of life and growth in general. 'Where it does not exist, the man, the nation must go'. Liberty means the natural right of human being to use his body, mind and property according to his own will, without doing any harm to other people. All members of the society shall have the same opportunities to acquire education, wealth, and so on. He felt that this natural right of human beings had not been realised in modern society, where the luxury of the wealthy is ensured at the cost of millions of poor people condemned to misery, injustice and ignorance.

Thus equality of human beings can be considered as one of the most important features of his ideal society. But equality, according to Vivekananda did not simply imply the equalisation of all human beings. Human beings are never equal, they always will be born differentiated by their natural capacities. Sameness in physical forms intelligence or social status can never be attained, and to do away with all differences would also bring death and annihilation. The ideals of human beings are different, everyone does the best he can for realizing his own ideal. Unity in variety is the plan of creation. What was asking for was the elimination of privileges: preach neither social equality nor inequality, but that every being has the same rights, and insist upon freedom of thought and action in every way'. Vivekananda's ideas reffect the ideas of Rousseou.

In Vivekananda's ideal society there will be left no space for privileges of force, wealth, intelligence, birth or spirituality. All privileges have to be overcome, and very often he harshly criticised the Indian Brahmins for their clinging to privileges. Who is not ready to give liberty to others does not deserve liberty himself. Vivekananda's social thoughts were always centred on the life conditions of the common man, but especially at the end of his life he stressed that the labouring masses are the backbone of any nation, by their labour they are producing food poor people, the sweepers and labourers, who if they stop work for one day will create a panic in the town. In his opinion we should not trust the so-called wealthy people because they are more dead than alive. Real hope for the future could only rest on the lowly oppressed. that the nation lives in the cottages'.

Vivekananda saw his task in struggling for the improvement of the masses in order to give them back their lost individuality by ensuring their equality, liberty, right to work, education, and so on, thus enabling them to improve their position themselves. There is no space in his ideal society for the tyranny of the minority, worst tyranny in the world. The main reason for the deficiencies of Indian society is that the masses have been downtrodden by the money-owning upper classes and by this they have been deprived of their individuality, their human dignity.

This demand for equality of human beings for overcoming all privileges was philosophically based on the Advaita Vedanta philosophy: "base my teaching on the great Vedantic truth of the sameness and omnipresence of the Soul of the Universe." Vivekananda did not go for another social reform movement whose emphasis would be only on changing the social habits of the upper strata of society; he demanded the practical realisation of the idea of oneness of the world by having faith in oneself, he demanded compassion for fellow beings and universal tolerance: "you and they, the poor and the rich, the saint and the sinner, are all parts of One Infinite Whole, which you call Brahman."

Vivekananda argued that when there exists only the absolute, then everybody is identical with it, man is divine, and there is no difference between one person and another, all beings essentially alike. Thus Vivekananda stressed universal brotherhood and of equality of beings man.

In accordance with this he struggled against all privileges of nations as well as of groups and individuals. 'The idea that one man is born superior to another has no meaning in the Vedanta; that between two nations one is superior and the other is inferior has no meaning whatsoever. Vivekananda did not deal very much in detail with untouchability as one of the worst consequences of the varnasraniadhanna. But he repeatedly expressed his opinion on the caste system as such, which can be summed in the following two points. First, he was of the opinion that the institution of caste was a social necessity to maintain the stability of society and 'to protect us as a nation, and when this necessity of self- preservation will no more exist, they will die a natural death.

Especially in his lectures in Europe and the USA he stressed this point. He was of the conviction that there exist differences of abilities that are the basis for different occupations and professions of human beings but that should not be taken as determined by heredity, as traditionally it was the case in the varna concept. Human beings ate different due to a different mixture of the three gunas within them; but we can distinguish in general four different groups of characteristics toughly corresponding to the four varnas of Brahmin-scholar, Kshatriya-politician, Vaishya-businessman, and Shudra-labourer.

In contrast to this, in his speeches and writings in India he sharply criticised the social tyranny of the Brahmins and their claim of superiority. The false pride of birth on which this claim was based was taken by Vivekananda as a sign of death and of stagnation. It might have been justified, he said, for knowledge to be concentrated at certain times among certain social groups or families due to social circumstances; but the period of time for this should be very much limited, and our whole endeavour should be concentrated on dissemination of knowledge into the whole of society. Otherwise the destruction of society would be the consequence.

Second, he rejected the view that varnasramadhanna was part of the religion of Hinduism; In his view it was a social concept, misused by religion:

"No religion on earth preaches the dignity of humanity in such lofty strain as Hinduism, and no religion on earth treads upon the necks of the poor and low in such a fashion as Hinduism. The Lord has shown me that religion is not in fault, but it is the Pharisees and Sadducees in Hinduism, hypocrites, who invent all sports of engines of tyranny in the shape of doctrines of Paramarthika and Vyavaharika."

He rejected the view that as an institution of religion and to struggle for extirpating religion and caste together. Caste simply a crystallised institution which after doing its service is now filling the atmosphere of India with its stench, and it can only be removed by giving back to the people their lost individuality'. The caste system determined by birth and connected with hereditary privileges is completely opposite to Vedanta and especially the caste system with its social and religious exclusivity should be overcome. An important part of Vivekananda social philosophy is closely connected with the traditional teaching. of the four varnas which he combined with the four Puranic *yugas* and with modern historiography.

He interprets slavery as the rule of the Brahmin, feudalism as Kshatriya rule, capitalism as Vaishya rule and socialism which he thought of coming in the future as Shudra rule: But from a careful study of the history of the world, it appears that in conformity to the law of nature the four castes, the Brahmin, Kshatriya, Vaishya, and Shudra do, in every society, one after another in succession, govern the world. Whereas Brahmins and Kshatriyas ruled within their respective nations, Vaishya rule has become international. He described the ruling Vaishya at whose command, electricity carries messages in an instant from one pole to another, whose highway is the vast ocean. - at whose instance, commodities arc being carried with the greatest ease from one part of the globe to another.

This Vaishya rule has started in the West. Among the modern Western nations, with England at their head, this power of controlling society has been, for the first time, in the hands of the Vaishyas or mercantile communities, made rich through the carrying on of commerce. India, according to Vivekananda, was ruled by the British Vaishyas, whereas in relation to them all Indians independently of their former caste status had become Shudras.

Each historical epoch had its positive and negative aspects. During the Brahmin rule the foundation of science was laid, but access to knowledge was confined to a privileged group, determined by birth. The rule of the Kshatriyas promoted the development of art and culture; this rule was not so much exclusive but cruel and tyrannical. The Vaishyas by their money and their international connection spread science and culture all over the world. Their commercial rule is awful in its silent crushing and bloodsucking power. Its advantage is, as the trader himself goes everywhere, he is a good disseminator of ideas collected during the two previous states. They are still less exclusive than military, but culture beings to decay. Last will come the labourer (*Shudra*) rule. Its advantage will be the distribution of physical comforts but its disadvantages, will be perhaps the lowering of culture. There will be a great distribution of ordinary education, but extraordinary genuiness will be less and less.

In his ideal society there will exist only one caste, for the lower strata will be raised to the level of the higher ones. That means that all social differences will be extinguished in so far as all the people will be elevated to the level of Brahmins, as it was the case in the *Satyayuga*. In this ideal society the positive aspects of all the four preceding societies will be kept but their negative features will have been overcome: 'If it is possible to form a state in which the knowledge of the priest period, the culture of the military, the distributive spirit of the commercial, and the ideal of equality of the last can all the kept intact, minus their evils, it will be an ideal state'. There would be peace and harmony everywhere. Vivekananda added a question mark on this by asking: 'But is it possible?'

Vivekananda conceived the demand for the reconstructing of society in such a way that each and everybody has the opportunity for the development of his personality. This concerns most of all the downtrodden masses, caused whose lack of opportunities for developing their abilities, the decline of India. India in his opinion had lost her identity because the masses have been trampled under foot, and they should be raised in order to gain back their dignity and individuality.

But out of this belief in the fundamental or potential divinity of man follows the relationship between man and man. It should not be determined by money or the principle of utility of each and everything. Very often he criticised the worship of mammon of gold as well as the spirit of competition moulding the whole life and value system in the West, and he admonished the West:

No nation however strong, can stand on such foundations, and the history of the world tells us that all that had such foundations are dead and gone. Vivekananda said:

"The more I study history, the more I find the idea of competition to be wrong. Some say that if man did not fight with man, he would not progress.... but I find now that every war has thrown back human progress by fifty years instead of hurrying forward. The day will come when men will study history from a different light and find that competition is neither the cause nor the effect, simply a thing on the way, not necessary to evolution at all."

Vivekananda dreamt of a future society as resulting from a synthesis of the value system of the East and the scientific-technological achievements of the West. He hoped that religious liberty and tolerance should be guaranteed everywhere. He expressed his hope that the Parliament of Religions in Chicago in 1893 would become the death-knell of all religious fanaticism, of all persecutions by the sword or by the pen. On the other hand the Indian society was in the past not able to grow due to the bondage of caste system. Therefore the ideal of social liberty should be taken over from the West. This synthesis should consist of the realisation of western concept of social equality and democracy and the Indian value system based on the belief in the fundamental divinity of everything. The bondages of both societies would then be thrown off. Therefore there would be no need for India to give up her religion, but religion within its proper limits and give freedom to society to grow.

Closely connected with his demand for mutual understanding is his call for charity, for loving devotion and service of men which we can take as another fundamental feature of Vivekananda's future society: 'God is present in every *Jiva*; there is no other God besides that. "Who serves Jiva, serves God Indeed".

In order to realise his ideal society, Vivekananda insisted that the first requirement is education. Education of the masses is the precondition of every social change, for by education the downtrodden and poor get the means to solve their problems themselves. Vivekananda understood education in the sense of putting chemicals together, to give the stuff out of which the masses themselves will get the strength to change their life conditions. Through education the masses will acquire faith in their own selves, they will get self-awareness and self-confidence. That was one of the reasons why Vivekananda founded the Ramakrishna Math; he wanted to form a group of brave men and women who be ready to spread the spirit of equality all over the country together with general knowledge. He knew that this would be a rather difficult task. He criticised the traditional Indian society in which the poor had had been trampled upon. He demanded that given the greater aptitude for learning among Brahmins than among Pariahs, no money should be spent any more for the education of the Brahmins, so as to have enough resources for raising the Pariahs to the level of the Brahmins. This has to be done by the Brahmins themselves: it is the duty of every aristocracy to dig its own grave; and the sooner it does so, the better for all.

Vivekananda asked for courage and energy in trying to carry through social change, even at the cost of committing errors, by pointing at the fact that trees, far example, are not able to commit errors, it is only human who is able to do that: mistake makes a man a genius, a sage. Isn't it because he thinks, reasons, he wills Without exercise, the power of deep thinking is lost. Tamas prevails. By this, Vivekananda's understanding of karma is touched. There is no doubt about the fact that he understands karma not at all in the sense of fatalism. Karma, according to Vivekananda, determines what man is, but what one wants to be depends on his own endeavour. Once, in Almora, Vivekananda was asked by an old man what one could do in use of the suppression of the weak by the strong. Was it not justified by the law of karma? Vivekananda emphatically answered: thrash the strong, of course! You forget your own part in this Karma: yours is always the right to rebel'.

Vivekananda who had been working for the national rebirth of India in a patriotic way, had expressly been opposed to national isolation. In order to be lasting, progress had to be of global character he said: "Even in politics and in sociology, problems that were only national twenty years ago can no more be solved on national grounds only. They can only be solved when looked at in the broader light of international grounds."

Science and Sanskrit encapsulates Vivekananda desire to bring together the best aspects of both the traditional Hindu and Western systems of education. The notion of an equal, reciprocal exchange of Eastern spirituality and Western materialism and their synthesis within modern Hinduism was a key feature of Vivekananda thought. Vivekananda ability to employ apparently modern Western ideas to justify traditional Hinduism and, conversely, use aspects of the Indian tradition to introduce modern Western concepts can be seen at play in his approach to education. The call for mass education and national identity is the justification for a religiously oriented system of education led by sannyãsins (wandering ascetics) and the highest goal of spiritual endeavour, realization of Brahman, is redefined to include scientific and technical knowledge. Vivekananda's interpretation of Vedanta, Practical Vedanta, was an attempt to establish a justification for the pursuit of such knowledge as a religious duty on the grounds that scientific enquiry would lead to Brahman. He offers a definition of science which takes it in its most general sense and perceives its focus as being the search for the underlying principle which explains all apparent diversity. Rammohun Roy, in his defence of Hinduism, had offered an interpretation of Vedanta which he believed to be consistent with the conclusions drawn by rational theists such as Paley that God could be known through the study of nature. For Vivekananda, gross melts into the fine, physics into metaphysics, in every department of knowledge. Consequently, he saw no need for a disjuncture between the transcendent state of spiritual awareness and the knowledge of material reality which is described informal Vedantic thought as avidya (ignorance): this is the real, practice side of Vedanta. It does not destroy the world,, but explains it.

'Science and Sanskrit' is a striking and resonant phrase; today we might call it a slogan. Its use by Vivekananda serves as an illustration of the way in which he could take a symbol and use it to convey an idea in a way that had great impact whilst remaining conveniently vague. The need for a programme of national education to promote the regeneration of India was a recurrent and consistent theme in Vivekananda speeches and letters throughout his life; that it should be so is not surprising. The issue of what form public education should take in India had exercised both the British administration and Indian leaders for at least seventy years prior to Vivekananda visits to the native princes.

The salient features of thinking on education are discerned in a letter "Education That India Needs" written to Shrimata Saralala Ghosal, editor of *Bharati*, in April 1897. For Vivekananda, the key to social reform and economic development is the education of the people: nation is advanced in proportion as education and intelligence spread among the masses. Education consists of uncovering, or releasing the potential lying within each individual; as such, it is a case of removing barriers rather than instilling knowledge. This is consistent with his view of evolution as the gradual expression of what was already present and simply needed to be realized : "Through education comes faith in one's own self, and through faith in one's in one own self the inherent Brahman is waking up. Once the full capabilities of people are realised through education, they will take control of their own affairs and achieve such social and economic change as they desire. They will also be possessed of the energy and concentration of purpose to ensure success."

Vivekananda is critical of the Western education the current, generation were receiving: 'The schoolboy learns nothing, but has everything. As he makes clear elsewhere, education must take a form which is compatible with the national character. For India, this means that it should retain a religious orientation and maintain links with the past. It is also essential if education is to release the power of Brahman from within. Vivekananda also criticised the emphasis on the amassing of facts which predominated in the textbook culture of 19th century India, sentiments which he voiced in a lecture in Madras earlier in 1897:

"Education is not the amount of information that is put into your brain and runs riot there, undigested, all your life. We must have life-building, man-making, character-making assimilation of ideas. If you have assimilated five ideas and made them your life and character, you have more education than any man who has got by heart a whole library."

Vivekananda was not anti-intellectual and insisted that religion must be compatible with reason. He said "it is better that mankind should become atheist by following reason than blindly believe in two million of gods on the authority of anybody." However, experience an important source of knowledge and education should be an active process which fully engages the learner. In his own spiritual search, Vivekananda had not been interested in intellectual debate and had simply posed the question, have you seen God? It was Ramakrishna direct reply as clearly as I see you standing there that had drawn Vivekanand to become his disciple. Vivekananda makes it clear that access to education should be open to everyone with men and women treated equally and goes on to outline how the system is to be organised. Sannyasins are to be recruited to teach both secular and religious knowledge; centres should be established in the major cities to train them. The goods produced in the practical workshops, which would form part of the education process, could be sold abroad to raise funds. Further funding for the project would come from an exchange of religious teaching from India for financial support from the West.

The official history of the Ramakrishna Mission mentions Vivekananda's support for the gurukula system and within the Arya Samaj there was a faction that advocated a revival of this traditional form of education whilst incorporaing into itself all that is best and assimilable in Occidental thought. The ideal of education within traditional Hinduism was expressed in the *gurukula* system. Teachers would take only a few pupils at a time who would live with them and attend to their daily needs; collecting firewood, cooking and even begging for food if necessary. No fees were paid but the student would present a gift to the teacher at the end of his stay. In return, the teacher acted as a role model, embodying wisdom and spirituality, and passed on the closely guarded oral tradition of sacred teachings. Learning was by rote and students developed the capacity to memorise accurately complex rules and teachings. During their education students must be completely obedient to their teacher and also, as brahmacaryas, be celibate and exercise self-discipline. The gurukula system was intended to form the character of the student; to encourage the fulfilment of dharma and direct his aspirations towards the highest end of human life, the saving knowledge which leads to liberation (*moksa*).

Within the concept of *dharma*, morality and spirituality are closely intertwined. The student was removed from the world of everyday family concerns and encouraged to live close to nature. Stress was placed on experience, doing and feeling, as well as on intellectual knowledge. The practice of self-control promoted the accumulation of energy (*tapas*) which could be channelled into learning so that remarkable feats of concentration could be performed. The product of this system of education was a young man of strong character, schooled in the sacred teachings who was ready to fulfil his dharma as a householder, contributing to the welfare of society and rearing the next generation, before returning to the ascetic way of life in his pursuit of moksa.

Essentially, access to the gurukula system was restricted to born Hindus members of the first three varnas: Brahmins, priests and teachers; Kshatriya, (rulers and warriors;) Vaishyas, merchants.

However, there is some evidence of women participating in education in ancient times. Mention is made in texts to both women teachers and students. It is unlikely that women ever studied in great numbers but those who did appear to have enjoyed parity with men. The status of women deteriorated over the centuries and the Laws of Manu contains proscriptions against women studying at all.

The *gurukula* system served as an ideal, it is probable that only a minority ever followed this route in its classical form. Kshatriyas would also follow courses of instruction in statecraft and military affairs and Vaishyas would often follow an apprenticeship system to learn their trade. Sometimes the students were not brahmacarayas but householders who lived at home and attended the teacher on a daily basis. The towns of Kashi, Kanchi and Taksila evolved in contravention of the prescription that teachers should only take a few students and live apart from others. With the emergence of Buddhism, monasteries became centres of learning and this development was emulated within the maths of the various Hindu orders.

There was, for Vivekananda, within the *gurukula* system much that was worthy of emulation. The emphasis on the religious teacher who was responsible for the pupils' spiritual, moral and intellectual development was something he hoped to recreate in the residential schools of the Ramakrishna Mission. Vivekananda seemed to be importing a sutra that would become the twentieth century humanistic, social philosophy. It expressed his firm conviction of the equality of human beings, no matter what his nationality, faith, sex, colour, etc., and it also expressed the self-confidence of a human beings who, coming from a colonial country, proudly announced to the public that his country, poor, downtrodden, and starving as it was, had something valuable to offer the world. Vivekananda speeches delivered in Chicago give clear evidence of his great interest in spiritual themes, but he never lost sight of the wretched conditions his fellow countrymen lived in. This can be seen in his critical remarks on the activities of the Christian missionaries in India. He emphatically said that it was not religion what India needed most:

"You erect churches all through India, but the crying evil in the East is not religion we have religion, enough it is bread that the suffering millions of burning India cry out for with parched throats. They ask us for bread, but we give them stones. It is an insult to a starving people to offer them religion; it is an insult to a starving man to teach him metaphysics. I came here to seek aid for my impoverished people, and I fully realised how difficult it was to get help for heathens from Christians in a Christian land." He himself repeatedly stated that his first aim was to bring bread to the people; to teach religion should be only the second step: 'First bread and then religion'. He thundered that religion which did not aim at the improvement of the social conditions of the poor could not claim to be called religion at all. He did not believe in a religion which did not appease the distressed people hunger. He said:

"Bread! Bread! I do not believe in God who cannot give me bread here, giving me eternal bliss in heaven! Pooh! India is to be raised, the poor are to be fed, education is to be spread, and the evil of priestcraft is to be removed. No priestcraft, no social tyranny. More bread, more opportunity for everybody!"

Religion confined to books and dogmas was not recognized as true religion by him: 'I do not call it religion so long as it is confined to books and dogmas'. In this way Vivekananda took the social engagement of religion as a criterion for evaluating its sincerity. These remarks on the relationship between religious theory and. practical behaviour of religious people are still valid today.

In ancient and medieval Indian philosophy there was a general indifference to ethical and social problems. To explain this, we can mention several factors : First of all, the dominating role of religion in ancient Indian culture: the idea of the Eternal and Divine dominated every aspect of social life. The varna system was regarded as the eternal structure of society and was fixed by the religious doctrine of dharma, which was considered as inviolable by nature and universally valid. But what was perhaps more decisive was the fact that Indian society apparently remained static; social conditions changed so slowly in the course of Indian history that philosophers were not forced to think and talk about social problems as such. Questions concerning ethics or social or political problems were settled by the authoritative scriptures, or were dealt within the epics or Puranas, but very rarely in philosophical literature proper. Closely connected with this is the lack of historical knowledge in ancient India which further hampered the development of any social philosophy. But this does not mean that social questions were totally excluded from the philosophical thinking. Philosophically, the varna system was justified by a number of thinkers obviously reacting to some criticism, but, this was mostly done apologetically rather than philosophically.

Sankara did not philosophize on society as such, or on certain social questions in the sense of a systematic development of thought. His thinking was centred around self-realization: how to reach paramartha, the highest good, the realm of the identity of Atman and Brahman. Starting from the Advaitic concept of the metaphysical unity of the world, he did not reach the conclusion of social equality in the empirical realm. The ideal of *jivanmukti* developed by Sankara did not include charity or service of man, for the world with its diversity, social diversity included, vanishes after the realization of the Absolute Oneness what Sankar calls a *jivanmukta*.

In the theistic philosophy of the Middle Ages, which was influenced by Sufism and the Bhakti movement, equality, of men in the eyes of God was admitted: all men are equal for they have been created by God or are part of his being, therefore God has to be seen in every human being. Loving God means loving his creatures. But the relationship between man and society was not taken up as a philosophical question, and no social philosophy was contemplated. In the nineteenth century Indian philosophy got a completely new dimension, and within this process social philosophy became an inseparable part of philosophy for whom social philosophy constituted an integral part of any philosophy or world-view, and for whom the analysis of the urgent philosophical questions of the nineteenth and twentieth centuries was possible through the use of the theoretical language of the Vedantic tradition.

Even Ambedkar stressed the point that the teaching of *tat tvam asi* ('You are that, the Supreme Reality') '...makes democracy an obligation for one and all because it teaches that all men are part of the same cosmic principle. Ambedkar harshly criticized the caste system of Hindu society and rejected especially the cruel custom of untouchability. He regretted very much that this interpretation of one of the most important mahavakyas of Hinduism (tat tvam asi) had unfortunately not yet created any impact on society .and had not become the foundation of dharma. Like Vivekananda Ambedkar wanted to put into practice the doctrine of Vedanta which emphasizes universal unity: it is not enough to know. Those who know must endeavour to fulfill.

The question we have to ask today whether it is possible to have a utopia, to put into reality the dream. Man always hopes for a better future, and in the history of mankind we find that many different concepts of a better society have been developed by Plato Rousseau. More, Marx including concepts of an ideal society where all human beings are equal and live a happy life, free from exploitation and oppression, free from all kinds of misery and suffering.

Thus, we can conclude that in Vivekananda ideal society the relationship of samasti, the whole, and vyasti, the individual as part of the whole must be balanced. This relationship is based on the fundamental oneness and divinity of the universe. Everyone should try to manifest the divinity within himself. From this belief in the fundamental divinity of man follows Vivekananda's insistence that the relationship between man and man should not be determined by money. He criticizes the worship of mammon, of gold, as we as the spirit of competition moulding the whole life and value-system in the West. He admonishes the West: nation, however strong, can stand on such foundations, and the history of the world tells us that all that had such foundations are dead and gone.

Vivekananda contemplated a synthesis of the Western concept of social equality and democracy, and the Indian spiritual values based on the belief in the fundamental divinity of everyone everything: are falling off the shackles from the feet of Eastern society as from those of Western religion. Therefore there is no need for India to give up her religion, but religion within its proper limits and give freedom to society to grow. Viewing the terrible conflicts all during the twentieth century all over the world we can grasp the importance of Vivekananda plea for mutual understanding which was based on a belief in the fundamental unity of the universe.

Vivekananda views on social questions and his picture of an ideal society impel us to look critically at the social and political conditions we live in, and not to lose hope for a better future for all. He once declared himself to be a socialist: "am a socialist not because I think it is a perfect system, but half a loaf is better than no bread. The other systems have been tried and found wanting. Let this one be tried for nothing else, for the novelty of the thing." On the eve of the twenty-first century we see that the first experiment of building up a socialist society has failed. One of the most decisive reasons for its failure was the fact that real democracy as well as liberty of thought and action were not practised. But the capitalist society is also obviously not able to solve the problems mankind is confronted with. Market economy based only on monetary principles and having competition as its main driving force rejects the ideal of the fundamental unity of mankind. The vision of an ideal society such as Vivekananda conceived of may give impetus to further human endeavour, and strengthen man's belief in man, which is a precondition for the survival of the human race. At the beginning of his public life, in a letter dated 20 September 1892, Vivekananda asked: "When, O Lord, shall man be brother to man?" This question is still being asked.

8

Vivekananda's Social and Political Philosophy

Narendranatli Datta, the secular name of Swami Vivekananda was born in the family of a highly educated and seemingly rich attorney of Calcutta. His father passed away, leaving behind only debts, when Narendranath was still studying in a college where he displayed extraordinary capabilities. The family was on the verge of poverty, and the young boy had to pass through days of semi-starvation. Still earlier, spritual quests, associated, with questions of religion, had brought him to Ramakrishna whose cottage in a temple near Calcutta attracted even some Calcutta intelligentsia. Now he came still closer to Ramakrishna and later became his disciple. In 1891 he went wandering all over India as a sannyasi, adopting the name of Vivekananda. During these wanderings of about two years, he suffered, as he put it, sharpest pain on seeing the monstrous poverty and suffering of the common people.

Apparently, it was then that he conceived his naive plan of turning to the rich countries of the West for material aid to India in exchange, so to say, for her spiritual values. This led to his journey to the USA. which he undertook on modest means provided by an Indian prince. The immediate purpose of his journey was to take part in the World Parliament of Religions at Chicago in 1893. In his speeches Vivekananda rebuffed the attacks of the missionaries on the beliefs of the Indians and showed that Indian religious philosophical and ethical conceptions were not inferior to such types of systems existing in Europe and America. His brilliant speeches, imbued with humanist spirit and affirming national dignity of Indians, attracted attention in the West, and in India these were construed as a national success. His stay in the USA and Europe in

1893-1896 brought a turning point in many of his views, and on returning home he devoted himself to active preaching work. He set up a socio-religious body of its own type with the features of a religious fraternity Ramakrishna Mission, which, as per his ideas, was to carry out the work of enlightening the people. In 1899-1900 he once again visited the U.S.A. and Europe.

The growing democratism and along with it the criticism of bourgeois relations combined with religious-moralist preaching were specially perceptibly seen in the views of Swami Vivekananda. His personal destiny was unusual, but reflected in it were some characteristic features of India of that time. In the West Vivekananda was known mainly as a religious philosopher, a moralist-preacher, and a yogi. But his interests were not confined simply to religious-philosophical problems, and his work was not limited merely to moralist preaching and popularization of yogic practices. All this coexisted and remained in Vivekananda associated with social and political problems primarily of India herself, which concerned him as a thinker and social leader.

The social-political ideas of Vivekananda played an extremely important role in the development of Indian social thought and growth of national liberation movement, and influenced not simply one generation of its participants, specially in Bengal. Vivekananda, with a greater awareness than Bankimchandra, rejected the notions of the British power being a blessing for India. He saw in colonial dominance not only the manifestation of national oppression in general but also a main obstacle in the material and cultural development of India, a cause for the monstrous poverty of the Indian masses. Vivekananda also sensed most acutely the weight of political oppression by colonial powers, as also the need for fighting against it. He wrote: "few hundred of modernized and half educated people who have lost their nationality, this is all that modern British India can boast of, and nothing more.... The monstrous hunger, involving millions of lives, five times more people than her present population if everything would not have been taken from the people right at the roots... Lately the country is being dominated by terror. The British soldiers kill our men and use force on our women, they are sent back home on a pension which, like the passage money, is also paid to them at our expense". 'Freedom is the first prerequisite of growth and development... 'O India! Will this shameless cowardice really give you freedom which can be worthy only of a hero! The demands of the poor will never be satisfied.'

The most important, progressive feature of social-political views of Vivekananda was that he considered national liberation of India and democratic social emancipation of its masses as mutually related and the two-fold goal. He regarded the education of the working people as the first step on the way to this goal, called upon the youth to go to the people and try to work in this direction. He undoubtedly showed interest in Russia and is known to have met Kropotkin in Paris. Here are a number of Vivekananda statements on the masses and on the need of awakening them: "Our aristocratic ancestors went on treading the common masses of our country under foot till they became helpless, till under this torment the poor, poor people nearly forgot that they were human beings. ... consider that the great national sin is the neglect of the masses, and that is one of the causes of our downfall. No amount of politics could be of any avail until the masses in India are once more well educated, well fed, and well cared for. They pay for our education, they build our temples, but in return they get kicks. They are practically our slaves. If we want to regenerate India, we must work for them.. . most important thing which I wish once again to remind you about, is the need for practical work, and practical work consists above all in that you must go to the suffering millions of Indians and take them with you to their huts, from door to door, at noon and in the evening, at any time, and open their eyes... . Give them ideas, open their eyes to the world surrounding them, and then they will themselves bring about their salvation... Your task is to give the masses their rights, and let them defend these ... . The only hope of India is from the masses. The upper classes are physically and morally dead. "Although Vivekananda saw the hope of India in the common people, he considered the middle class the leading force of social movement, obviously having in mind mainly the intelligentsia. He contrasts this middle class to the rich in any country where the rich persons ever helped anyone." It is the middle classes in all countries who carry out great tasks .... I expect nothing from the rich people of India.

In his own way Vivekananda already realized the class character of the position of the propertied classes in the work of national liberation. While Bankimchandra still hoped that zamindar (landlord) also play some positive role in this, Vivekananda clearly had no such illusions. He regarded the national freedom itself not only impossible without political mobilization of the masses but also unthinkable without their social emancipation. Upset, like also Bankimchandra, over political ineffectiveness of liberal leaders in the face of colonial power, he saw in their position class interest hostile to the working masses. He wrote: "Our young fools hold meetings to gain more power from the British. They only laugh. He who is not ready to give freedom to others is not worthy of it. Suppose that the British hand over to you all power. What then ? You will use it to hold the people at the low level. Then let this freedom be not there. The slaves thirst for power in order to enslave."

The growing democratism in Vivekananda is combined with an intensification of criticism of the bourgeois society. The Indian thinker now criticized not only the colonial policy of capitalist powers but also their social structure itself-social inequality and omnipotence of the rich dominant there. He saw in the power of money concrete political power of the exploiters in the bourgeois society, having at its disposal the destinies and lives of common people for the sake of their own avidity.

The process of evolution of his ideas on bourgeois society in the West is interesting. It was a typical reflection of the movement of the nineteenth-century progressive Indian social thought from enlightening idealization of bourgeois society to its subjective criticism. At the time of his first visit to the U.S.A. in 1893 Vivekananda clearly perceived the conditions of life and the manner of living of those circles with whom he came in contact while taking part in the World Parliament of Religions. He felt affected by trivial-bourgeois notions of this environment. In the background of the monstrous poverty of the Indian masses, of the Indian life, the western society first appeared to him a society of opportunities for all and the poverty of that place lot of the lazy and the immobile'. There was really a big difference between the conditions of life in a colonial country where millions of people daily saw the face of death by starvation, and in the developed capitalist countries which had made bourgeois progress, exploiting the colonies. He did not find all these .associations revealed at once, and the illusions appeared far more modest and simpler. Nevertheless, in the ultimate end, he did, as he said, come the essence of things in all probability, he was helped by his own penetrating sense of a patriot-democrat and by his familiarity with the advanced social thought of the West. Having visited the U.S.A. twice, he had high appreciation of the energy, hardworking temperament, and democratic spirit of the American masses, of their readiness and capacity to defend their rights; and he was also impressed by their scientific and technological achievements. But, at the same time, he sharply criticized the social structure in the U.S.A. and in the West in general. All the criticism of the westerners against our caste, they have a worse one of money. The almighty dollar, as the Americans say, can do anything here' Vivekananda was particularly disturbed by racism. He said that the position of the Negroes hardly improved after the abolition of slavery: lives are of no value; they are burnt alive on mere pretences. They are shot down without any law for their murderers; for they are niggers, they are not human beings, they are not even animals. Like the social inequality, Vivekananda compared the racial discrimination in the U.S.A. with the hateful caste system in India. Going through the racial discrimination in America, he wrote: "It has begun to appear to me somewhat familiar, something like my own country, defiled by castes."

Notwithstanding all this, Vivekananda directs the main fire of his criticism against the dominance of the rich whose autocracy the institutions of bourgeois democracy were not able to conceal from him. The force with which he exposed the bourgeois structure retains its significance even till this day rich who have money, he said, hold the government of the land under their thumb, plunder the people, drink their blood, depute common people to far-off countries to fight, so that in case of victory they may fill their bags with gold obtained with the blood of these simple people. As regards the common people, they are only to shed their blood Vivekananda spoke also of the of people who in the name of politics plunder others and go on fattening, sucking the blood of the masses, the present-day politicians act, plunder in mid-day light, the real dance of the devil in man'.

Vivekananda could feel also the growth of antagonisms in the bourgeois society and its impending crisis. There never was a time in the world history when there was so much robbery, and high-handedness, and tyranny of the strong over the weak, as at this end of the nineteenth century. He showed great insight while cautioning in 1900 about the imminent military catastrophic war in which countries will take part and which will disintegrate very fast The whole western world appeared to him as being a volcano which can start erupting, and tomorrow itself this world will fly off into dust'.

Despite the criticism of western civilization, Vivekananda understood in his own way the positive significance of European ideals of enlighteners. But the main conclusion he drew was that neither the feudal orders, becoming a thing of the past, nor the bourgeois relations on the whole now affirming themselves in India could be accepted. In a certain sense, materialism came to save India, opening the doors of life for every person and destroying the exclusive privileges of the caste', wrote Vivekananda. "We fight for establishing political institutions in India which have already been long existing in Europe. These were tested in the course of centuries and have been admitted to be imperfect. Various institutions of political trend were condemned one after the other as not justifying their existence, and now Europe is caught in confusion and does not know what to do. The material tyranny has become truly monstrous. Wealth and power are everywhere concentrated in the hands of the few people who do not work but have at their disposal the labour of the millions. Possessing the power, they can fill the whole world with streams of blood. Religion and generally everything is under their thumb. They are the rulers, they are the top masters. The western world is ruled by a handful of Shylocks. Constitutional rule, freedom, parliament, these things you hear about are only a fun. The West groans under the tyranny of Shylocks and the East from the tyranny of the priests... There are two great obstacles on our way: The Scylla of old orthodoxy, and the Charybdis of modern European civilization."

Vivekananda undoubtedly knew about the ideas of scientific socialism. It is probable that he was the first among the Indians to expound the ideas of systematic change in social formations and to declare that feudalism and capitalism, as also the dominance of the exploiters, would inevitably give way to the power of the Shudras working people to socialism.

In 1899, in an article on India he wrote: "time will come when there will be the rising of the shudra class, with their shudra-hood; that is to say, not like that as at present, when the shudras are becoming great by acquiring the characteristic qualities of the vaishya or the kshatriya, hut a time will come, when the shudras of every country, with their inborn shudra nature and habits becoming in essence Vaishya or Kshatriya, but remaining as *shudras* gain absolute supremacy in every society".

Speaking of absolute inevitability of impending power of the working people, that is, of socialism, Vivekananda at the same time shared the naive ideas of the nineteenth-century western intelligentsia that socialism, as a result of uniform distribution of material wealth, at its low level, will possibly lead to undermining of culture. In the context of these ideas he who was the first Indian to call himself a socialist He wrote: "I am a socialist not because I think it is a perfect system, hut half a loaf is better than no bread."

The familiarity with the socialist movement in the West made it possible for Vivekananda to take a perceptible step forward compared to his predecessors in the understanding of the development of class conflicts in India herself. Already in the 90s of the nineteenth century, he showed that the class struggle of the working people, peculiar only to the modern, that is bourgeois, society, had also started developing here. In the totally legitimate strikes of those years he could discern the phenomenon taking shape of the same order as the organized working class movement in the West. As a confirmed democrat, he welcomed these mass actions, seeing in them the awakening of the working people. 'They have worked so long uniformly like machines guided by human intelligence, and the clever educated section have taken the substantial part of the fruits of their labour; said Vivekananda in 1898, in every country this has been the case. But times have changed. The lower classes are gradually awakening to this fact and making a united front against this, determined to exact their legitimate dues. The masses of Europe and America have been the first to awaken and have already begun the fight. Signs of this awakening have shown themselves in India, too, as is evident from the number of strikes among the lower classes nowadays. The upper classes will no longer be able to repress the lower, try they ever so much.

Sympathizing with the idea of establishment of the power of the working people, and even considering it inevitable in all countries of the world, Vivekananda, like Bankimchandra, regarded socialism only as an extremely remote possibility. Fighting for the awakening of the masses and welcoming its first signs in India, he however, did not any more raise the question of organization of the working people on class basis. He criticized the bourgeois structure precisely from the stand point of a democrat and a humanist sincerely sympathizing with the working people, and protested against social inequality and oppression, though not comprehending the objective laws conditioning the exploitation and very omnipotence of the rich in a capitalist society. This lack of understanding of the objective laws of bourgeois relations on the one hand and the tendency of securing national unification of Indians on the other led Vivekananda to utopian endeavours to eliminate social and class conflicts without liquidating the material basis of class society.

Extremely important also is the following circumstance acquiring a special vehemence and significance in the conditions of economic dominance of foreign capital. Vivekananda, and also Tilak and a number of other radical nationalists like such enlighteners as Rammohun Roy, saw that the British dominance was obstructing the economic, above all industrial, development of India, condemning it to backwardness. At the same time, following essentially the advanced traditions of enlightenment he distinctly understood that national revival of India required development in the country of modern industry, science, education, etc.

Defending objectively nothing else but accelerated development of capitalism, Vivekananda, more than anyone else in India, realized the growth of social contradictions conditioned by this development. As a democrat, he sincerely desired the awakening of the working masses, their social emancipation. At the same time, as a nationalist, he strove to remove social conflicts, and to achieve some compromise between the exploiters and the exploited and thereby to secure national unity.

'In the next fifty years we must have only one slogan: great Mother-India, let all other deities go away from our consciousness during this time.' All this gave rise to profound, truly pressing contradictions which showed themselves in his quests for a social ideal. Rising against feudal oppression, Vivekananda at the same time, from the very beginning, tried to find the ideal of social organization in the institutes of ancient India, particularly in the caste system. He presumed to bring out some reform in them. Categorically rejecting castes on the basis of birth, as embodying social injustice, he put forward the idea of organization of peoples in castes according to their capacities and to society, what he called 'caste on merits.' However the democratism inherent in the thinker demolished his own social formulation. 'The conviction is daily gaining on my mind', he wrote in 1897, the idea of caste is the greatest dividing factor and the root of maya; all caste either on the principle of birth or of merit is bondage. Some friends advise, that at in the world of relative experience, distinctions like caste must needs be maintained.

Vivekananda's moralistic sermon acquires a great social-political trend, as a completely conscious attempt, on the one hand, to make the propertied classes yield concessions to the working lower classes and, on the other, to restrict within definite limits further development of class struggle of the working people. Welcoming the awakening, now set in, of the working people, the first signs of which appeared in India, speaking of the impossibility of stopping this process, he, however, clearly does not want that matters reach revolutionary struggle. He would have liked the oppressed to be liberated without it so that classes the lower should somehow solve matters peacefully. Here, while Bankimchandra simply appealed to the conscience and patriotism of the propertied classes, Vivekananda introduced also a new element of threat of its own kind. He cautions: "well- being of the higher classes now lies in helping the lower to get their legitimate rights."

The power of putting a curb on the exploiting and oppressing tendencies of the properties classes and at the same time restricting the class struggle of the working people, in other words capable of securing social compromise and national unification, was seen by Vivekananda in moralistic religion. He, more consciously than many other Indian nationalists of the late nineteenth and early twentieth centuries, sought in religion not only a national banner in general, not only the means of unification of various peoples inhabiting India, but above all a weapon of social compromise and of creation of an ideal society, remaining a class society, but free from exploitation, and, more correctly precisely from oppression. Such kind of views, inherent in the various so-called versions of socialism, seemed in India rather a nationalistic utopia. Created largely by Vivekananda, it most fully expressed the social aspirations of radical nationalists of that period and appeared in some measure or the other in the views of many leaders of Indian national liberation movement even later.

Vivekananda's religious views reflected the tendency peculiar to capitalism of filling the religious ideology with the norms of morality which the bourgeois ideologists call universally human.

Of such ethical norms some reflect class interests of the exploiters particularly, the acceptance of private property as sacred, and others are positive norms of human relations. But at the same time the working masses strive for affirming the positive norms of human mutual relations. In the conditions of dominance of religious consciousness these aspirations, reflecting in their own way the struggle of the working masses against oppression and exploitation, also partly acquired religious forms.

In India this tendency manifested itself in the views of the earliest enlighteners, for instance, Rammohun Roy. But in Vivekananda and some other Indian thinkers of the late nineteenth and early twentieth centuries, the idealized notions of religious morality as a morality universally human were contrasted not only to the morals of the dominant classes of a feudal society, justifying the caste-position, inequality, and the power of the feudal society but also the inhuman moral of making money and money-grabbing inherent in bourgeois society itself, which justified social inequality based on private property. Being incapable, because of its social-historical constraints of actually rising against the first cause of evil, viz. private property, Vivekananda attacked its consequences, which he wanted to fight against by means of moralistic sermon, using a number of traditional positions of Indian religious-philosophical thought. Accordingly, religion is in him a theory and practice of its own kind of moral perfection. If he regarded the concept of God or realization as the essence and meaning of religion, then moral perfection precisely was virtually the main content of the very concept of 'realization'. In this context Vivekananda interpreted the positions of Hindu religious- philosophical system of Vedanta, stating that it revealed the secret of selfless work.

As the starting-point, Vivekananda took the positions of Vedanta about the top hierarchy of Brahmins and of soul as manifestation of Brahman in man. According to these positions, the divine soul in its nature possesses an initial purity which, however, is destroyed under the influence of prakriti (material world). The original purity of the soul can be restored, if a man renounces the material world, worldly activity, passion and ties, and leads a monastic form of life. The renunciation thus creates conditions for the confluence of soul with Brahman. Vivekananda gave to these positions such interpretation that in the ultimate count served as the foundation of his social philosophy. The concepts of divine nature of soul and of restoration of its original purity were used by him for showing the very possibility of moral perfection, and the concept of confluence of soul with Brahman was treated as an attainment of this goal in the spirit of the formula: divine kingdom is within us. Soul, he said, divine in its potential. The aim is to reveal this divine source within us, controlling both inner and outer nature. This concept was also. interpreted by him quite differently from the traditional medieval interpretation. Renunciation was treated by him not as a denial of or isolation from day-to-day work as a denial of self-interest in this work and devoting it to the common well-being. The thinker regarded such routine but selfless work of the householder concerned over his home and over those who may need his care, as the highest virtue and the most important way of God. This was the main theme in all his religious- moralistic sermon. He said: "refuse to have any attachment to work. Let your soul remain free..... Do not bring in egoism into it: I... My."

The position about the householder, selflessly working and naturally fulfilling his duty of care for the near and dear ones, obviously reflected the traditional notions of the peasant community about work and virtue. Vivekananda revealed these aspirations and dreams in precise religious-philosophical garb and at the same time introduced into these something from contemporary trivial, bourgeois notions. The latter are particularly felt in some of his lectures meant for the American audience. But the pre-eminent mood, the pathos of his sermon of selfless work and concern for the near ones was a call for working for the welfare of the country and for the well-being of the poor. It was embodied in Vivekananda's famous formula of impoverished God which later became one of the symbols of faith in the doctrine of M. K. Gandhi. "Only God who exists, the only God in whom I believe. O my God, said Vivekananda, the unfortunate ones, the poor of all nations!"

Vivekananda, like many others in his time, declared India a peculiar of religion different thereby from tile West. . Above all, India is the land of religion, he wrote. Religion is the vitality of India.

Turning to religion sharply deepened the contradictoriness of Vivekananda's social position. To the contradictions which were inherent already in Bankimchandra, Vivekananda added some more. The criticism of the medieval period and of semi-feudal social oppression, including that of orthodox religion, was combined in him. with assertions that India has inherent in her, from times of past, particularly noble ethical norms and social regulations which guard against oppression and are sanctified by religion. There was, on the one hand, confusion because of centuries-old exploitation and oppression of the working people by the other, assertions of the following type : 'In Europe, it is everywhere victory to the strong and death to the weak. In the land of Bharata every social rule is for the protection of the weak.' On the one hand, there is a call for the awakening and enlightenment of the masses, and on the other, a tendency to restrict and avert the development of class struggle by preserving religiosity in the masses, which generates humiliation and shame. Rising against this humiliation of working people, medieval in nature, and fighting for their awakening, Vivekananda at the same time firmly reiterated that the enlightenment of the people must be combined with propagation of 'indirect truths of religion'. 'Keep the motto before you of masses without injuring their religion…", he wrote. 'Before flooding India with socialistic or political ideas, first deluge the land with spiritual ideas'.

It is extremely important that Vivekananda already foresaw the future of India with socialistic ideas and wanted to link these to religious-moralistic sermon, and thereby to avert the danger of class struggle. The democratic social emancipation of masses and creation of a modern society, but without the antagonisms and class struggle inherent in it main position of his nationalistic utopia was formulated by him like this: 'Create European society with the religion of India'.

"If the many and the One he indeed the same Reality, then it is not all modes of worship alone, hut equally all modes of work, all modes of struggle, all modes of creation, which are paths of realization. No distinction, henceforth, between sacred and secular."

Everything in life is sacred, every activity is a form of yoga. Religion is not restricted to a special mode of life but applies to total life. Everything that helps in the manifestation of the inner divinity. Brahman, is religion. Another equally important implication is the resolution of the conflict between the ethics of conduct and the ethics of virtue. The earlier attempts in this direction that had been made by Western thinkers were superficial; Vivekananda brought about a true integration of the two ideals at a deeper level. He made an expression of the true Being, the inner Self. As he put it, ideal, indeed can be put in a few words, and that is: to preach unto mankind their divinity, and how to make it manifest in every movement of life. Self-realization is the rationale of all human activities. We should work not out of any social or individual compulsion, or to seek pleasure, but as a spontaneous expression of the joy, unity and love inherent in the Self.

Why Be Moral?

This another important issue in meta-ethics: why should we be moral?

We usually take moral life for granted, so much so that we hardly ever pause to ask ourselves why we should be moral or why we should do good to others. Almost all the ethical speculations, in the West and in India centred around the question of what morality is. In the history of ethics the first thinker to raise the question, why we should be moral, was the Confucian philosopher Mencius who lived in China in the third century BC. Though this question may not be found so explicitly stated in other systems, their probable answers may be surmised from the available premises. Greco-Roman ethics may give the answer as a hedonistic or utilitarian motive. The answer found in the Judeo-Christian tradition is, we should be moral because that is the Commandment of God. Islamic tradition may attribute it to fear of God. The answer provided by Buddhism and traditional Hinduism is that fear of karmic consequences is the reason for being moral. All these answers have one thing in common: they all make morality a compulsive act.

The answer provided by Mencius is unique in that it makes morality natural and spontaneous. According to him, we should be moral because our nature is good. To be good is our true nature. Mencius, however, says that this nature is present only in a potential form in most people. Morality is the development of this potential goodness in us; immorality is its inadequate development. But then, what exactly is this nature of man? A satisfactory answer to this question is not found in the works of Mencius. The true answer is found in the ancient Hindu scriptures known as the Upanisads. The Upanisadic sages discovered that the mind, which consists of subtle matter and is ever-changing, cannot be the real, eternal nature of man. Beyond the mind there is the uncreated, unchanging, ever-pure, ever-blissful Self known as the *Atman* and this is the real nature of man. Unfortunately, this truth, although found in the Upanisads, was never made the basis of morality until Vivekananda did it. More than two thousand years after Mencius, Vivekananda asked,

Why should we do good?... Why should I do good to other men, and not injure them? If happiness is the goal of mankind, why should I not make myself happy and others unhappy? He showed that the answer to this question could be found in the Upanisads. Goodness is not an external attribute to be acquired or infused into the soul. Rather, it is the manifestation or unveiling of the inherent purity and unity of the true Self. This is a basic principle of ontological ethics.

This, however, raises the question, what then is immorality? If the real inherent nature of man is good, why do people do evil? The sages of the Upanisads saw nothing but the goodness and bliss of Brahman everywhere. By contrast, Buddha regarded existence itself as duhkha, that is, evil. Between these two extreme position come Zoroastrianism, Judaism and Islam in which evil is conceived as an external force, often personified as Ahriman or Satan. Christianity also shares this belief; in addition, it holds that Adam internalized evil by his disobedience and this sin has been transmitted to all humanity. This evil is an inborn trait in the human soul which can be removed only through divine grace. The main drawback of the above views is their failure to integrate evil into their conceptual framework of Reality. Hegel and, following him, Karl Marx, attempted this integration through their theory of dialectics. In India the Sankhya philosophy also attempted a similar integration of evil with the help of the theory of the three *Gunas*. The most successful attempt was Sañkara's introduction of the theory of maya or ajnana, ignorance. However, for centuries, the concept of maya had served only a negative purpose. For a defeated, demoralized and exploited people, maya became a dope, a means of escape from individual and social responsibilities. It was Vivekananda who worked out the positive ethical implications of the theory of universal ignorance: He saw that it was a much better explanation for evil than the theological concept of sin. He said we have no theory of evil. We call it ignorance'. Evil is nothing but ignorance which can be removed through true knowledge. So true knowledge, knowledge of the *Atman*, should be the basis of ethics. Vivekananda asserted:

"Instead of telling them they are sinners, the Vedanta takes the opposite position, and says, You are pure and perfect, and what you call sin does not belong to you. Sins arc very low degrees of Self-manifestation; manifest your Self a high degree. That is the one thing to remember; all remember; all of us can do that." Hindu sages developed a unique concept of the ultimate Reality as the Supreme Self. Basing himself on this concept, Vivekananda laid the foundation for a true ontological ethics. Conventional morality is based on social compulsion or obligation, and consists of do and don't it does not appeal to modern youths. Ontological ethics is based on freedom, but it gives a new meaning to freedom. In Western ethics moral freedom is meant the freedom to choose between good and evil by an exercise of the will. In ontological ethics moral freedom is derived from the ever-free nature of the Atman. In India this freedom had been regarded only as the ultimate goal of life, called moksa or mukti. Vivekananda made it an existential motivation behind all human activities. The difference between good and evil lies in their results: good actions lead to true freedom, whereas evil deeds lead to greater bondage.

According to Vivekananda, selflessness is the main criterion of true freedom. Freedom does not mean liberty to do whatever we like. True freedom means one should be free from our limited individuality, the ego. The only definition that can be given of morality is this : "That which is selfish is immoral, and that which is unselfish is moral. This real Self is a unitary principle dwelling in all beings; its cosmic dimension is known as Brahman. It is this unity of Self that is the basis of all love. This is clearly stated in the famous Yajnavalkya-Maitrey dialogue in the Brhadranyaka Upanisad where the sage teaches his wife that the husband is loved not for the sake of the husband but for the sake of the Self; similarly, children, friends and others are loved not for the sake of them but for the sake of the Self."

But this wonderful doctrine had been for centuries interpreted only to provide a rationale for either renunciation or man's love for God. It could have served equally well as the basis of man's love for man. Though this point also had been understood, it did not find proper social expression. It was Vivekananda who made the doctrine of the unity of the Self the basis of man's love for his fellowmen. He converted it into a new social philosophy which may be described as spiritual humanism. This expression of oneness is what we call love and sympathy, and it is the basis of all our ethics and morality.

This is summed up in the Vedanta philosophy by the celebrated aphorism, Tat Tvam Asi, 'Thou art That'.

In western countries the ideal of service to the poor, popularized mainly through scular humanism, has become a part of collective social imagination. But in India service was usually understood to mean service to one's elders, teachers and holy men. Owing the lack of enlightened humanism, service to the poor as a means of social uplift did not become a part of collective awareness. Hence Vivekananda emphasized social service in his work in India. He also gave a theistic turn to the ontological basis of service by describing it as *Sivajnane jiva-seva*, 'Serving man as Siva.' This naturally leads to another tenet of ontological ethics. This has immense social implications especially for Indian society with its permanent stratification into castes, exploitation of the poor, and other forms of social injustice. He also stood for the equality of the sexes.

"I shall not rest till I root out this distinction of sex. Is there any sex distinction in the *Atman*?" The sameness and unity of the Atman provides the only satisfactory basis for all forms of social equality. In his talks delivered at Thousand Island Park in America Vivekananda said, that in the universal melody three ideas stand out: freedom, strength, sameness. Strength is one of the most important, but often misunderstood concepts in Vivekananda message. He laid much stress on strength and in oneself no doubt, but he did not use these terms in the sense of aggressive, mascalinist egoistic self-assertion. In several contexts, by strength he meant the courage to face the problems of life. It is quite similar to what the liberal Protestant theologian Paul Tillich has described as courage to remain unaffected by meaninglessness, anxiety, guilt, loneliness and other existential problems by holding to one true Being. Vivekananda's idea of strength means self-mastery, acquisition of mental strength to follow the moral path, to hold on to the moral ideal, at all times. This needs the practice of the system of self-discipline known as yoga. Yoga alone enables us to carry into practice of the teachings of morality. The practice of self-discipline, yoga as it may be called, represents the practical aspect of ontological ethics.

Lastly, ontological ethics does not posit morality as an end in itself; it is considered only a means to a higher end. That end is the transcendental experience of the ultimate Reality. When morality is made an end in itself, as is done in popular religious traditions and secular life, it has to be enforced with the help of rules and regulations. But when it is understood as a means to higher joy and peace, it will be willingly accepted and followed.

Patriotism

Vivekananda was markedly different from the nineteenth century leaders preceding him, both in the critical, negative aspect of his teaching as well as in the constructive, positive aspects. His teaching reflected a qualitatively new stage of bourgeois reformation, whose means, methods, and objectives underwent considerable changes. He focussed attention on the social aspects of Hinduism, on expansion of the scope of religion by its assimilation of a whole complex of progressive ideas and concepts. Vivekananda's works do not have that critical approach to Hinduism which was the characteristic of the reformers of the early period and which had etokcd negative reaction from Vivekananda. He explains his differences with his predecessors like this: "The difficulty seems to be that we are losing faith in ourselves day by day. That is my objection against the reformers. The orthodox have more faith and more strength in themselves, in spite of their crudeness; but the reformers simply play into the hands of Europeans and pander to their vanity."

He tried not to make the differences of opinion subject of wide discussion, but in his private correspondence with those caring for his views he unambiguously dissociated himself from the Brahmo Samaj. "The Brahmo Samaj...died out', says Vivekananda, 'and I am not sorry, neither glad that it died. It has done its work, viz. social reform." Its religion was not worth a pie for him. Our modern reformers are very busy about widow remarriage. Of course, I am a sympathiser in every reform, but the fate of a nation does not depend upon the number of husbands their widows get, but upon the condition of the masses. It is interesting that Vivekananda had a more benign attitude towards the reformers. He firmly refused suggestions to criticize them publicly. Obviously, he was concerned more with the upholding of Hinduism, than with attacks on it from the side of Brahmo Samaj. Many questions which agitated the reformers were simply ignored by him, not particularly bothering to enter into arguments. For instance, he categorically declared: '...there is no polytheism in India', and had the same attitude towards idol worship too. Vivekananda as though deliberate, closed his eyes to the said questions.

He was worried, though, not so much over religious problems as over the position of India of his time. And how so much he might have stayed away from politics, his entire activity was undoubtedly anti-colonial and for the good of the country and to awaken in them a confidence in the great future of India, to generate in them a sense of dissatisfaction over the dependent position of the country, and did also at the same time reprimand them for apathy, defeatism indifference, and passivity. In many works of Vivekananda, and specially in his speeches in the USA and Europe, the Indian national character appeared as the focus of all virtues; however, in his sermons 'for internal use', he assigned these virtues to the field of the ideal. In his private correspondence with like-minded persons he did not hesitate to express himself openly. He called India a 'country of beggars', a 'country of women and eunuchs', etc. The psychological portrait of a contemporary Indian created by him included such traits as weakness, fear, lack of confidence in himself and his powers. However, when Vivekananda glorified the virtues, nobility, and religious toleration of the Indians, and when he abused them for their cowardice and weakness, he was, undoubtedly, guided by a passionate love for his country and his people. His purpose was to awaken in his coutnrymen a sense of national pride and sense of shame for their denigrated position, a shame which, however, had, in its turn, to awaken a desire to change life.

What exactly, in his view, was the cause of the 'degradation of the nation'? The main reasons, according to Vivekananda, were the poverty of wide sections of population, their illiteracy, and the indifference of the propertied classes to the needs of the poor people. 'I consider that the great national sin is the neglect of the masses', he said in an interview, 'and that is one of the causes of our downfall'. And at another place : "Who will bring the light to them—who will travel from door to door bringing education to them'? 'India must rise, the masses and the poor are to be made happy."

Another reason of the downfall as seen by him was in the isolation of the country in the rigidity of the prejudices, particularly in the oddness of the injunction prohibiting the Indians from crossing the sea. Here he usually cited the example of Japan. "I want that numbers of our young men should pay a visit to Japan and China every year. Especially to the Japanese, India is still the 'dreamland of everything high and good. And you, what are you?... talking twaddle all your lives, vain talkers, what are you ? Come, see these people, and then go and hide your faces in shame. A race of cowards, you lose your caste if you come out! Sitting down these hundreds of years with an ever-increasing load of crystallized superstition on your heads, for hundreds of years spending all your energy upon discussing the touchableness or untouchableness of this food or that.. .what are you ? And what are you doing now?"

The two ideas which were the object of constant, uncompromising criticism from the side of Vivekananda were man's inborn sinfulness and non-resistance to evil. While the former in its pure form was on the whole alien to Hinduism and was present only in the form of 'law' of Karma and dogma of transmission of souls the latter was an integral part of the religious ethics of India. Vivekananda did not wish to reconcile himself with its weakening influence. He did not totally discard it or shift it to the category of the ideal, but showed that this ideal could be attained by means directly opposed to it—non-resistance must be arrived at through active non-acceptance of evil in all its manifestation. In his work Karma-yoga, Vivekananda wrote: "Before reaching this highest ideal, man's duty is to resist evil; let him work, let him fight, let him strike straight from the shoulder. Then only, when he has gained the power to resist, will non-resistance be a virtue".

One who has not learnt to resist evil violates his religious duty. Vivekananda asserted: 'He [the householder] must not sit down in a corner and weep, and talk nonsense about non-resistance'. And further : 'Inactivity should be avoided by all means. Activity always means resistance. Resist all evils, mental and physical; and when you have succeeded in resisting, then will calmness come. It is very easy to say, "Hate nobody, resist not evil', but we know what that kind of thing it generally means in practice."

Vivekananda regarded Hinduism as the means of social emancipation; turning to religion with this object was for him a specific trait in India : "The Englishman can understand religion through politics, the American through social reforms; but we can understand even politics and sociology through religion. This is the theme, the rest are only variations in the national life-music". Together with this, he tried to apply this method also across the borders of India : 'We shall address all people in the language of their own orthodoxy'.

On the other hand, Vivekananda knew that the need for making use of religion was related simply to a definite historical stage and that other approaches were also possible in future. For the religion to be an effective instrument in the fight for progress of the country and emancipation of the masses, he very firmly shifted the inner accents in Hinduism and broadened the scope of religion, associating it with the field of practical work, and not of abstract judgements: "Religion is not words and not theory."

Work, according to Vivekananda, was of the nature of religious duty and was contrasted by him with asceticism : "It is useless to say that the man who lives out of the world is a greater man than he who lives in the world; it is much more difficult to live in the world and worship God than to give it up and live a free and easy life".

However, when one ponders, one finds between Ramakrishna's and Vivekananda's views far greater dissimilarities than similarities. This is accounted for by their subjective differences as well as the changed social-political conditions, and, chiefly, by the different objectives which both the preachers had before them. Soon after the return of Vivekananda from his first visit to USA, the other disciples of Radhakrishna openly turned against him, accusing him of not conforming his work to the tenets of the teacher. "Hands off!" — Vivekananda told them. "Who needs your Ramakrishna? Who needs your *bhakti* and *mukti*? Who bothers what the texts say? I would gladly go to hell a thousand times if I can lift my countrymen immersed in tamasa, if I can put them on their feet, make them people, inspired by the spirit of Karma-yoga. I am not a follower of Radhakrishna or whoever it is, I am a follower of these who carry out my plans."

For the rationalist Vivekananda, it is like science, with no place for anything secret, mystical, and; supernatural. He explains : "The chemist never requires demons, or ghosts, or anything of that sort to explain his phenomena ... And this is one of the features of science which I mean to apply to religion." The idea of supernatural beings may rouse to a certain extent the power of action in man, but it also brings spiritual decay. It brings dependence; it brings fear; it brings superstition. It degenerates into a horrible belief in the natural weakness of man. And further : "Believing certain things because an organized body of priests tell him to believe, believing because it is written in certain books, believing because his people like him to believe, the modern man knows to be impossible for him."

While Ramakrishna preached the principle of salvation by faith, Vivekananda gave firm preference to reason: "It is wrong to believe blindly. You must exercise your own reason and judgment; you must practise and see whether these things happen or not. Just as you would take up any other science, exactly in the same manner you should take up this science for study. 'Are the same methods of investigation which we apply to sciences and knowledge outside, to be applied to the science of Religion'—he wrote a few years after the death of the teacher.— "In my opinion, this must be so, ...If a religion is destroyed by such investigation it was then all the time useless unworthy superstition; and the sooner it goes, it will become a thousand time stronger."

Humanism

It is in the background of this idea that Vivekananda's singular interest in the needs of the masses of India should be perceived. His thoughts in this regard are also expressed in the form of religious moralistic precepts and advice to his disciples. 'Where have you to go, where to search for God',— he asked,—'are these poor, these unfortunate, these weak people not really the gods ? Why not first pray to them ? Why dig a well at the banks of Ganges' ? Turning to his followers, he appealed for working in the name of spiritual liberation and material progress of the masses: 'Swear to devote all your lives to the work of saving these 300 millions, going lower and lower each day'. He considered their emancipation the foremost task and, religion had to fulfil this task that is, the aim of religion was understood by Vivekananda in a reformer's spirit—not the entertainment of the sufferers, not passive accumulation of good deeds in the expectation of a reward in future existence, but active day to day help, called upon to assist in spiritual growth of the nation and improvement of material position of the people. He consistently stressed the need for practical work, and appraised religion just from the standpoint of its social advantage : 'I do not believe in God or in religion which cannot wipe out the tears of widows or give a piece of bread to the orphan'. And at another place: 'Bread ! Bread ! I do not believe in a God, who cannot give me bread here, giving the eternal bliss in heaven'.

The record of a wonderful dialogue between Vivekananda and a preacher of a Society for Protection of Cows, which took place in Calcutta in 1897, soon after former's return from his first visit to

USA and Europe suggests the clash of the orthodox and the reformist points of view.

Vivekananda : What is the objective of your association ? Preacher: We save our *Gomata* from the butchers, acquire them, organize special enclosures where we look after the old, sick and helpless cows.

Vivekananda : Splendid idea ! The Central India is in the grip of terrible famine. The government reports mention that nine hundred thousand have died of starvation in your Society doing something to save these starving persons from death ?

Preacher: We do not give any help at the time of famine etc. Our objective is to save only Gomata.

Vivekananda : When hundreds and hundreds of thousands of your countrymen, following the same religion as you, are dying of hunger, do you not think it your duty to help these unfortunate persons ?

Preacher : No. Hunger is the result of their karma, their sins. Here is an example of "like karma, like results".

Vivekananda thundered at the preacher that he had no sympathy for such societies that have no concern for man and, seeing thousands of starving brothers, dying from famine, do not bother to save them, do not offer them a single piece of bread, but waste millions on the protection of birds and animals.

With all his religious outlook, Vivekananda did not at all consider religion the determining source in the life of a man. On the other hand, preaching the grandeur of Hinduism, he did at the same time, limit the sphere of influence and application of religion, specially in the field of public education, to the limits of social relations. Turning to those engaged in the service of the cult he said: "We insist that religion has no right to be the law giver of the public. Keep your hands off! Keep yourself within your limits, and all will be well."

Vivekananda sharply criticized religious fanaticism regarding it as an obstacle in the way of human progress. "If there were no fanaticism in the world, it would make much more progress than it does now. It is a mistake", 'to think that fanaticism can make for the progress of mankind. On the contrary it is a retarding element. "He also sharply criticized asceticism, the fanatic mortification of flesh.

'I need sappers and miners in my religious army', he said, 'work up your muscles, boys ! The mortification of flesh is all right for ascetics, but the workers need muscles of steel and well developed body!"

Characterizing Vivekananda's ideas of enlightenment, it must be specially stressed here that their decisive features are a steadfast faith in people, in their great constructive powers, and an ardent love for the working masses, sympathy for their wants and sufferings, and a fervent urge to free them from colonial and social oppression. Dividing the Indian society into two categories of classes—the higher, that is the rich, and the lower, that is the working people,—Vivekananda, for the work of resurrection of India, pinned all his hopes on the latter. He said directly: "The masses are the only hope of India. The higher classes are physically and morally dead. 'Millions of poor people from the lower classes are the ones who build up the real life of the country'."

'Our proletariat',—he asserted,—are doing their duty. . .day and night...well, is there no heroism in this ?. .. Ye evertrampled labouring classes of India! I bow to you. It is, therefore, not surprising that Vivekananda's democratic convictions led him in the ultimate end to the bold thought of the inevitable coming of the period of rule by Shudras, that is, of the emergence of such a society in which the workers themselves would be the ruling and the guiding force.

Vivekananda's ideas of enlightenment retained the stamp of contradictions and inconsistency, inherent in his whole world outlook. Regarding enlightenment as one of the decisive means of awakening the people, he essentially rejected the political struggle and generally remained away from politics. He directly declared: "Nothing I say or write should be given any political interpretation"; "I do not wish to have anything to do with political follies, I do not believe in any politics. God and truth—these are the only politics in the world. Everything else is absurd."

Seeking to restrict the spheres of influence of religion, Vivekananda at the same time asserted that in India religion was the basis of national unity. Therefore, along with caution against interference of religion in the field of social relations, one also finds in him statements of a directly opposite nature. For instance, he stated that political and social reforms must always be carried out in India, proceeding from her religious life.

The idealistic understanding of social life did not make it possible for Vivekananda to discover the real principles of social development; and in this context he did not discern the actual role of the masses in history. Resting his hopes on the working people in the matter of transformations in India, Vivekananda also at the same time allowed subjective-idealistic exaggeration of the role of the individual in historical process. "The history of the world",—he said,—"is the history of a few people having confidence in themselves. This confidence evokes the deity hidden deep within.. .a handful of strong people will move the world."

Rationalism

In the conditions of India of that time, this thesis of priority of reason in relation to faith was undoubtedly of great positive significance. Depending upon it, Vivekananda actively opposes various types of prejudices, superstitions, ignorance. In his lectures on 'Practical Vedanta', addressing a wide audience, he says : "You know in your inmost heart that many of your limited ideas, this humbling of yourself and praying and weeping to imaginary beings, are superstitions. Tell me one case where these prayers have been answered. All the answers that came were from your own hearts. You know there are no ghosts but no sooner are you in the dark than you feel a little creepy sensation. That is so because in our childhood we have had all these fearful ideas put into our heads".

At the time of his stay in America, Vivekananda had to come in clash with the theosophists. The fight against them turns out to be long, hard, and persistent. Vivekananda constantly stresses the damage which the theosophists do to the task of enlightenment and progress in India by misguiding the people and making their minds weak: "Mystery-mongering and superstition are always signs of weakness. These are always signs of degradation and of death'. Speaking, however, of the activity of the theosophists in the West, he distinctly observes that their 'successes' rest on the craving for the 'unusual', for the 'sensational', which destroys the monotony of the course of life: "It is a tendency in Western countries, in these modern times, to make a hotchpotch of the brain. ..it becomes a sort of disease, but this is not religion. Then some want a sensation. Tell them about ghosts and people coming from the North Pole or any other remote place, with wings or in any other form, and that they are invisibly present and watching over them... then they are ' satisfied and go home; but within twenty-four hours they are ready for a fresh sensation. This is what some call religion. This is the way to the lunatic asylum".

Vivekananda criticized not only the imaginary 'miracles' of the theosophists but also miracles in general, considering that the violation of natural courses of events in nature, or the interference of outside forces etc. in it, was not possible. 'I consider miracles the greatest hurdles on the path to truth'.

In the context of India, however these 'hurdles', from Vivekananda's viewpoint, are associated not so much with the 'Scripture'— Sruti—as with 'tradition'—Smriti: In works ascribed to 'tradition' the ideas of Sruti are popularized, adapted to the level of understanding of the ordinary Indian, but are also at the same time distorted. As regards Sruti, the 'main nucleus' of the views contained there, as Vivekananda assumes, does not in any way conflict with reason and science; besides, the main principles and positions which the modern scientific knowledge rests on, were formulated in Sruti even more distinctly and lucidly than in the most modern science.

But in the specific conditions of late nineteenth-century India, Vivekananda's ideas of enlightenment, as also his entire outlook, were significantly greatly progressive. His teaching had an effective influence on the formation in India of democratic and liberation ideas, advanced for their time. Jawaharlal Nehru names Vivekananda amongst those who laid the 'beginning of new trends of thought'. Vivekananda's ideas influenced also such eminent thinkers and social leaders of India as Aurobindo Ghosh, Rabindranath Tagore, Mahatma Gandhi.

But the main significance of Vivekananda's outlook was in the influence which his ideas wielded on the awakening national self-consciousness in the Indian people. The life of this eminent Indian thinker came to an abrupt end a little before the onset of the period of 'awakening of Asia', under the influence of the first Russian revolution of 1905-1907. His social-political and specially enlightening ideas objectively helped in the awakening of the wide masses of India and prepared them for the subsequent growth of national-liberation movement, which, as a result of the heroic efforts of the Indian people, culminated in the historic victory, in the creation of the independent Republic of India.

The reformist tendency was from the very beginning intertwined in India with the tendency of enlightenment. In the ultimate end the familiarity with the ideas of European elightenment left the most profound mark on this entire work the first Indian philosopher of the new times—Rammohun Roy. The faith in the great 'cleansing' and 'liberating' role of reason and science became the characteristic feature of the outlook of the majority of the vanguard thinkers of India of this period. All of them saw in the wide dissemination of knowledge the radical means of struggle against hunger, diseases, prejudices, and barbarian customs inherited from the medieval times. But here enlightenment was for them usually fully compatible with religion—true 'cleansed' and 'rationalized'. And this 'rationalized' religion was also, in their view, called upon to play a special historical role.

In the conditions of India of that time, Vivekananda's teaching on religion undoubtedly had a number of positive features. Above all, his constant statements in defense of tolerance, against fanaticism and inflammation of religious community differences were historically progressive. The actions of the Christian missionaries, fighting tooth and nail to implant Christianity in various countries of the world are, according to Vivekananda, those of a 'tiger thirsting for blood'. But no less sharply does he stand in opposition to the Hindus who condemn the believers of other faiths particularly, Muslims for using meat in their food: "Is God indeed such a great fool like you that the stream of his noble acts would stop just because of a piece of meat?" Vivekananda censures at the same time all other forms of persecutions of people for their religious affiliation. In his words, "besides the sword, besides the material weapon, there are weapons still more terrible — contempt, social hatred, and social ostracism. Now, these are the most terrible of all inflictions that are hurled against persons who do not think exactly in the same way as we do". And this, Vivekananda stresses, can make country look like a graveyard.

It is true that the rituals and the symbols and images associated with them are accepted by Vivekananda as quite essential, and sometimes he even calls the Universe a gigantic idol and the object of ritual action, but the rituals for him are simply a means and in no way the end. In the course of evolution of religions, however, the means are frequently absolutized and hypertrophized to the detriment of the end: 'The spiritual ideas are developed in arithmetical progression and the ritual—in geometric'. It is against this absolutization that Vivekananda's famous aphorisms are directed: 'it is very good to be born in a temple, but very bad to remain there up to death'; 'temples and churches are merely kindergartens of religion'.

The relativity and conventionality of mythology, their dependence on the image of the personality of their builders, are lucidly shown by Vivekananda on the example of varied, contrasting notions of paradise. Thus, for the Arabs living in a desert paradise means first of all abundance of water lakes and rivers of paradise; there is a directly opposite image of ' paradise in mythologies of residents of those areas of India which suffer from constant inundations. If the paradise of the peaceful agricultural tribes is an idyllic existence alien to all struggle, the paradise of the militant tribes is a place for waging contant war in the course of which the 'dead' resurrect again and again and everything repeats itself over again. Vivekananda not only criticizes the idea of paradise, he considers the very idea of paradise first internally unfounded, for it presupposes the possibility of discerning the good in 'pure' form. From Vivekananda's point of view, paradise and hell are nevertheless contrasts which are thinkable only in their unity with and struggle against each other like light and shadow. The 'paradise' is thus a 'castle in the air'. But it is the idea of hell that Vivekananda particularly condemns because he considers it not only unfounded but also derogatory to man's dignity. In this context, he has a fairly heated argument with the Christian opponents who object to him and say that without the fear of the sufferings of hell people cannot be subjected to the requirements of religion and morals. 'Man who is pushed to religion by fear, docs not have any religion!' Vivekananda affirms. It should be noted that, with all his tolerance and his constant stress on values of'internal nucleus' of all religions, including also Christianity, Vivekananda is steadfastly opposed to a number of ideas characteristic of the Christian religion.

But the main target of his criticism are the Christian notions of sinfulness of human nature, of pre-determination, 'noble deeds', need for 'conciliation', etc. The cultivation of these notions, in his view, makes a man a slave, injects into him lack of trust in his own powers. Nevertheless, it is necessary to make a man to trust his own powers. Equally constantly occurring in Vivekananda's work is the following brilliant formulation: 'Vedanta believes only in one sin, the only one in the world,! and it is this: 'The moment you think of yourself or of any other person as a sinner, you are sinning'.

Conclusion

This is an intensely political book that seeks to unravel the intellectual lineage and legacy of Swami Vivekananda.

For successive generations, assessments of Vivekananda have remained polarized and polemical, alternating between images of the speculative monk and fearless social crusader, world-renouncer and social activist, fiery patriot and gifted prophet. People have at given moments of time, paid attention only to selective aspects of his personality or appropriated specific ideas or suggestions in his writings or speeches. In recounting the histories of individuals or of mentalities, we often search in vain for typologies whereas our focus, if any, ought to be on the fluidity of mental boundaries. In a sense, a widening of points of reference would be a more faithful echo of the flexibility and dynamism in Vivekananda's life and message: providing legitimate space for diverse viewpoints, attempting to see many in the one, one in the many.

I have a case through the writings and speeches of Vivekananda, and, of course, his guru, Sri Ramakrishna, that the worlds of the sishya and the guru, despite a shared beginning, diverge vastly in their pursuit of God. The rupture was inevitable, for the guru was a mystic whereas the *sishya* saw himself not only as a Hindu missionary, but also as a monk with a man-making mission, a nationalist. The roles converge in Vivekananda to produce a philosophy, even if ridden with contradictory statements that sought to project Hinduism as "the grandest religion of the world". This carefully constructed vision of Hindu religion, Sharma says, makes Vivekananda "the father and preceptor of Hindutva", "the dominant expression of Hinduism in our times, though not the only way in which Hinduism articulates itself". The political import of this argument is that the presence of Vivekananda in the pantheon of

Hindu nationalists is not a case of appropriation by the latter to further their political agenda but the monk, perceived by many to be a liberal religious thinker, finding a place in the appropriate ideological platform.

I have tried to construct an image of Vivekananda by exploring three themes that distinguish his outlook. I begin by identifying the point where Vivekananda breaks away from Ramakrishna's vision. He picks up a story popularised through Sri Ramakrishna Kathamritha, the seminal text that contains the life story and message of Ramakrishna, and told by Vivekananda to his *guru-bhais*. A few days before Ramakrishna's death, Vivekananda says the guru summoned him and fell into a trance. A subtle force like an electric force, Vivekananda says, passed through his body, empowering him. Ramakrishna then wept and told Vivekananda that he has passed on all his power to his disciple, which will now enable him to work for the world's good.

This story, is incongruous with Ramakrishna's philosophy, especially his idea of God (in this case, Kali) and power and the idea of work, and Vivekananda's own approach to the prophetic and revelatory traditions in religions. Vivekananda gave Ramakrishna's faith a theological face and a preacher's energy, shedding all the intricate complexity and intense religious emotion that is the hallmark of Ramakrishna's pure devotionalism. How Vivekananda stands apart from Ramakrishna's world of bhakti, which is ecstatic love for God that demands total surrender and devotion, is explained by a close reading of the language and vocabulary the guru and sishya deploys to explain the path to God. The idea of a distinct Hindu identity is absent in Ramakrishna Kathamrita. Vivekananda's interpretation of Ramakrishna is a simultaneous act of fidelity and distortion. In every instance, the skeleton of Ramakrishna's thought is kept intact but the flesh and blood imposed on the skeleton often bear little resemblance to the original. Considering the goals that Vivekananda sets for himself, this departure from Ramakrishna's path was inevitable. One question that the missionary in Vivekananda framed for himself was whether it was possible to make a European society with India's religion. He concluded that it was possible. He now had to propose what he meant by a European society and India's religion. This clearly is more a political project than a spiritual quest.

Vivekananda admires some aspects of the European civilisation that has arrived in India but also is worried that it will sweep Hindu society away, which, due to an excessive preoccupation with the *satva guna*, was drowning in an ocean of tamas or dark ignorance. India desperately needed to possess more rajas to save itself from the brutal embrace of tamas. Religion that sought to provide bread to the needy and remove property could provide the necessary rajas. Ramakrishna and Vivekananda understood the balance or interplay of the gunas very differently.

India's religion — for Vivekananda was synonymous with Hindus, — had to be restated so that it fitted his prescription of what ought to be the real religion. So, he said: "I do not believe in a god or religion which cannot wipe the widow's tears or bring a piece of bread to the orphan's mouth." Out of all this emerges the idea of a masculine Hindu religion and society, one that has Vedanta's brain and Islam's body, to paraphrase Vivekananda.

Many scholars have argued what Vivekananda created was "a Hindu self-image that endures in its self-righteousness, revels in its historicity, and remains smug in its designer victimhood". Vivekananda crafted the idea of Hindus as gentle, tolerant and spiritually inclined among other things. This image is frequently contrasted with Muslims and Christians. This Hindu religion had to be the bedrock of national unity and, hence. He glided over the religious diversity, practices, rituals and customs that persisted in India. In his search for a unified religion he privileged vedic and vedantic traditions over popular representations and beliefs and ignored non-Sanskritic, non-elite and marginal representations of religion. And, the social order Vivekananda upheld privileged the one ordained by the orthodoxy, including the caste system. Despite the occasional criticism of Brahmins and the practice of untouchability, Vivekananda wanted caste to be reinstated and strengthened. Here again, Vivekananda was walking a path different from Ramakrishna, whose spiritual world did not include caste.

The privileging of the vedic-vedantic tradition too was a departure from Ramakrishna for whom bhakti overrode jnana and karma. Ramakrishna sought to protect the faith from being contaminated by worldly things, while Vivekananda circumscribed every aspect of human life with his brand of religiosity. In redefining the centre/ core and the marginal, Vivekananda was forsaking an idea of the 'centre' that existed in India which signified movement, ambiguity, doubt and transformation. Out of the restatement of India's religion emerged what Vivekananda called practical Vedanta, a faith for the world. He explains it thus: "It does not destroy the world, but explains it; it does no destroy the person, but explains him; it does not destroy individuality but explains real individuality. It does not show that this world is vain, and does not exist, but it says, 'Understand what this world is, so that it may not hurt you....' The theme of Vedanta is to see the Lord in everything, to see things in their real nature, not as they appear to be."

Vivekananda died young at 39. He was a product of the heady times he lived in, but certainly not a finished one. However, Sharma's study, cautions us that the charismatic Swami needs to be interrogated for the Hindu self-images he created, which continue to influence the making of modern India.

A more familiar line of argument discards the notion of secularism as a rationalist worldview, according to which religion is excluded from societal space or, at best, granted legitimacy only in the privacy of individual lives. This argument adopts the idea of secularism as religious pluralism, which stands for non-preferentialism as state policy and of inter-religious tolerance as social philosophy. Religious pluralism was revived and restated by Hindu social reformers of the late nineteenth and twentieth centuries. Swami Vivekananda was perhaps the first modern intellectual to vigorously present tolerance, and indeed acceptance, as the correct Hindu position on the phenomenon of religious difference. Addressing the Parliament of Religions at Chicago in 1893, he declared:

"I am proud to belong to a religion which has taught the world both tolerance and universal acceptance. We believe not only in universal toleration, but we also accept all religions as true. I am proud to belong to a nation which has sheltered the persecuted and the refugees of all religions and all nations of the earth."

Vivekananda's spiritual mentor, Sri Ramakrishna, had in his own life and teachings tried to realize the oneness of the religious quest, not only by affirming the truth of all available paths of spiritual realization within the Hindu world, but also by temporarily suspending his Hindu identity and living the life of a practising Muslim. Needless to stress, there is a continuity from Rammohun

Roy's consensual theology to Vivekananda's universalist praxis via Ramakrishna's pluralist personal experience. In fact, Roy's early endeavour appears modest in retrospect compared to the immensity of Ramakrishna's spiritual quest and the vast scope of Vivekananda's mission, which was to establish the supremacy of Vedantic Hinduism on a worldwide basis.

In his younger years as a temple priest and religious devotee, Ramakrishna had shown an amazing openness of mind in respect of religious beliefs and practices, embracing Vedic-Puranic texts and rituals, tantra, and even obscure rustic cults. But, as he grew older, and emerged as a revered guru among the gentry of Calcutta, he tended to be more selective, and favoured the higher tradition of Brahminism and bhakti. The seer's familiarity with other religious traditions, his foray into Islam notwithstanding, was fairly minimal. In other words, inter-religious pluralism was not a dominant theme of Ramakrishna's religious quest: he was indeed eclectical in his approach but primarily within the Hindu fold.

Vivekananda's message of tolerance and indeed acceptance was formally addressed to the followers of all religious faiths, but it was given from a Hindu platform, as it were:

"We not only tolerate, but we Hindus accept every religion, praying in the mosque of the Mohammedans, worshipping the fire of the Zoroastrians, and kneeling before the cross of Christians, knowing that all the religions, from the lowest fetishism to the highest absolutism, mean so many attempts of the human soul to grasp and realise the infinite, each determined by the conditions of its birth and association, and each of them marking a stage of progress."

As a statement of ideals which Vivekananda may have truly held dear, the foregoing declaration is indeed laudable; but as a statement of prevailing Hindu practice of the time, it was inaccurate and misleading. Vivekananda's specific references to religions other than his own were not always flattering. In his paper on Hinduism presented to the Parliament of Religions, he proclaimed that there was a place for the agnosticism of the Buddhists and the atheism of the Jains in the Hindu's religion. Exactly a week later, he clarified at the same forum that the Buddha had taught 'nothing new', that 'he was the fulfilment, the logical conclusion, the logical development of the religion of the Hindus'. He complained that the Buddha 'was not understood properly by his disciples', and called for a rapproachment: 'Hinduism cannot live without Buddhism, nor Buddhism without Hinduism'. Else where he clarified that, like 'everything else in India', Buddhism was based on Vedanta and had, in turn, influenced developments in the latter.

Needless to emphasize, the foregoing views are not of tolerance or acceptance but of absorption or inclusion. It may be added that Vivekananda held similar views about Jainism and Sikhism. Actually he was kinder to the Sikhs than to the Buddhists and Jains, obviously because he considered them a Hindu sect, an attitude common to most Hindus of the time. Vivekananda deplored the influence of the Buddhists and Jains as conducive to passivity inaction and, worse; ignorance. Some of his most negative remarks were reserved for the Buddha, he 'ruined us' by his stress on nirvana and the Buddhists for want of right means have degraded India.

It is remarkable that Vivekananda once spoke on the Prophet Muhammad in the course of his travels in America, but the remarks he made, while respectful, do not reveal a close familiarity with the basic teachings of Islam. What is more, the idea of Hindus learning from Islam is politely brushed aside: 'the great messengers of light are our great teachers, our elder brothers. But we must go our own way!'. Elsewhere he paid rich tribute to Islam, for 'the peculiar excellence of Mohammedanism', namely its message of equality among the believers, and for its patronage of learning. The attitude is patronising, however, and sometimes even critical and paradoxical as, for instance, when he disapproves of the Islamic doctrine of 'the same law and the same rule for all'. He obviously preferred the context-sensitivity characteristic of Hindu society. He is said to have prayed that India may have 'an Islamic body and a Vedantic heart'. The reference presumably is to the egalitarian Muslim social-organization, but he was rather ambivalent about the Islamic ideal of all beings made equal by the confession of faith.

Vivekananda's attitude to Christianity was more complex, being influenced by his keen awareness of the threat of Christian evangelicalism and Western cultural domination. How deep Christian influence could penetrate, even without the efforts of the missionaries, was known to him from his personal contacts with Brahmos such as Keshub Sen. The attitude he adopted could be simply but not inaccurately described as aggressive. At the broadest level, he considered the East and the West irreconcilably different in their core values. The West, he said, was unable to rise above the notion of the 'mind' (*manas*), while the Hindus knew the higher reality of 'the inner self (*atman*). While Indians should learn, he advised, from the West her arts and sciences, in the domain of religion, 'Hindus must believe that we are the teachers of the world'. His assessment of Christianity was that it was an inferior religion: 'with all its boasted civilization it is but a collection of little bits of Indian thought', 'a very patchy imitation' of our religion. He even believed that the veneration of Virgin Mary had been borrowed from Hinduism's Kali worship. Vivekananda considered the Bible a text suitable for ordinary devotees, preferring Vedanta for the spiritually advanced.

Vedanta was indeed, in Vivekananda's judgement, India's gift to the world. He called it 'truer than any other religion, because it never conquered, because it never shed blood, because its mouth shed on all words of blessing, of peace, words of love and sympathy'. He exhorted his Indian followers to 'go out' and 'conquer the world through our spirituality and philosophy. There is no other alternative, we must do it or die',

In view of Vivekananda's patroising views on other religions there is contradiction in his speeches and writings of the Rigvedic aphorism about the Absolute being one despite it being described variously. To cite but one example:

"In India the same competing gods had been struggling with each other for supremacy, but the great good fortune of this country and of the world was that there came out in the midst of the din and confusion a voice which declared [ekam sad vipra bahuda vadanti] "That which exists is One; sages call it by various names". It is not that Shiva is superior to Vishnu, not that Vishnu is everything and Shiva is nothing, but it is the same one whom you call either Shiva, or Vishnu, or by a hundred other names.

Vivekananda's highest concern was to purify Hinduism and to unite Hindus. He found the emergence of 'sects' understandable. The almost infinite mass of energy in the world cannot be managed by a small number of people. He disapproved of contentions and divisive sectarianism. Besides, he envisaged an 'eternal' and 'infinite' religion, based on 'the wonderful truth' that he said he had learnt from his master, namely 'that the religions of the world are not contradictory or antagonistic'. Judging by the spirit of his overall position, one may safely conclude that Vedanta was this 'eternal religion' or, at least, the basis for it. And the moral of the discourse was: 'we must respect all religions and we must try to accept them all as far as we can. The qualification with which this sentence concludes is noteworthy.

Vivekananda's notion of tolerance, it is reasonable to conclude, was hierarchical in as much as Vedantic Hinduism was regarded as the foundation of all religious ideals of all times. He declared in a speech delivered in India:

"Ours is the universal religion. It is inclusive enough, it is broad enough to include all the ideals. All the ideals of religion that already exist in the world can be immediately included, and we can patiently wait for all the ideals that are to come in the future to be taken in the same fashion, embraced in the infinite arms of the religion."

It is obvious that Vivekananda's ideas of tolerance, acceptance and harmony, and of the conquest of the world by Hindu spirituality, are more inclusive or synthetic than pluralist. Pluralism requires a transcendental referent in the absence of which either rank relativism will prevail or hierarchy will rule. Vivekananda clearly believed Vedanta to be "the transcendental religion; but surely one of the existing religions cannot be so regarded. Gandhi knew this and maintained that the religion which he considered the source of value was not Hinduism or any other known religion, but one that transcended them all.

Apart from the issues of tolerance and pluralism, it may well be argued that largely in response to the challenge of the West and the nobler aspects of Christianity, Vivekananda gave a secularist orientation to Hinduism through his notion of 'practical' or socially engaged Vedanta. This stood for applying the truths learnt from the Vedic tradition to an active engagement in social ameliorative and emancipatory activities. He called for a marriage of renunciation (*vairagya*) and service of humanity (*jivanseva*)'. His concept of service was constituted of several, hierarchically-arranged strands beginning with material needs 'It is an insult to a starving people to offer them religion': but eventually rising above them to the spiritual level. Going beyond orthodox Vedanta and the immediate teachings of Ramakrishna, which focused on the illusory character of the world (maya) and self-directed salvation (mukti) respectively, Vivekananda was responsible for introducing the ethic of altruism into modern

Hinduism. He wrote: 'The universal aspect of God means this world, and worshipping it means serving it this indeed is work, not indulging in ceremonial'. The Ramakrishna Mission, founded in 1897, became the organizational means through which Vivekananda sought to achieve his objectives. All this is important: in it only highlights the fact that the Vivekananda was an innovator and not an agent of tradition.

Vivekananda knew the importance of spiritual in building a strong foundation. He said: "If any nation attempts to throw off its national vitality, that nation dies. In India, religious life forms the centre". But for occasional lip service, nothing was done to construct the nation from within. The decision makers paid no heed to Vivekananda's sane advice that "a nation in India must be the union of those whose hearts beat to the same spiritual tune". Vivekananda called her, had woken her up but she started moving in the wrong direction. Only another Vivekananda can help her get back on the right path, towards founding "the greatness of the future on the greatness of her past".

Making an objective assessment of Vivekananda's contributions to world culture, the eminent British historian A L Basham stated that "in centuries to come, he will be remembered as one of the main moulders of the modern world..." One of the most significant contributions of Vivekananda to the modern world is his interpretation of religion as a universal experience of transcendent Reality, common to all humanity. He met the challenge of modern science by showing that religion is as scientific as science itself; religion is the 'science of consciousness'. As such, religion and science are not contradictory to each other but are complementary. This universal conception frees religion from the hold of superstitions, dogmatism, priestcraft and intolerance, and makes religion the highest and noblest pursuit – the pursuit of supreme freedom, supreme knowledge, supreme happiness.

Vivekananda's concept of 'potential divinity of the soul' gives a new, ennobling concept of man. The present age is the age of humanism which holds that man should be the chief concern and centre of all activities and thinking. Through science and technology man has attained great prosperity and power, and modern methods of communication and travel have converted human society into a 'global village'. But the degradation of man has also been going on apace, as witnessed by the enormous increase in broken homes, immorality, violence, crime, etc. in modern society. Vivekananda's concept of potential divinity of the soul prevents this degradation, divines human relationships, and makes life meaningful and worth living. He has laid the foundation for 'spiritual humanism', which is manifesting itself through several neo-humanistic movements and the current interest in meditation, Zen etc. all over the world.

The prevalent morality, in both individual life and social life, is mostly based on fear – fear of the police, fear of public ridicule, fear of God's punishment, fear of Karma, and so on. The current theories of ethics also do not explain why a person should be moral and be good to others. Vivekananda has given a new theory of ethics and new principle of morality based on the intrinsic purity and oneness of the *Atman*. We should be pure because purity is our real nature, our true divine Self or *Atman*. Similarly, we should love and serve our neighbours because we are all one in the Supreme Spirit known as *Paramatman* or *Brahman*.

Another great contribution of Vivekananda was to build a bridge between Indian culture and Western culture. He did it by interpreting Hindu scriptures and philosophy and the Hindu way of life and institutions to the Western people in an idiom which they could understand. He made the Western people realize that they had to learn much from Indian spirituality for their own well-being. He showed that, in spite of her poverty and backwardness, India had a great contribution to make to world culture. In this way he was instrumental in ending India's cultural isolation from the rest of the world. He was India's first great cultural ambassador to the West. On the other hand, his interpretation of ancient Hindu scriptures, philosophy, institutions, etc prepared the mind of Indians to accept and apply in practical life two best elements of Western culture, namely science and technology and humanism. He has taught Indians how to master Western science and technology and at the same time develop spiritually. He has also taught Indians how to adapt Western humanism especially the ideas of individual freedom, social equality and justice and respect for women to Indian ethos.

In spite of her innumerable linguistic, ethnic, historical and regional diversities, India has had from time immemorial a strong sense of cultural unity. It was, however, Vivekananda who revealed the true foundations of this culture and thus clearly defined and strengthened the sense of unity as a nation. He gave Indians proper understanding of their country's great spiritual heritage and thus gave them pride in their past. Further more, he pointed out to Indians the drawbacks of Western culture and the need for India's contribution to overcome these drawbacks. In this way he made India a nation with a global mission.

Sense of unity, pride in the past, sense of mission – these were the factors which gave real strength and purpose to India's nationalist movement. Several eminent leaders of India's freedom movement have acknowledged their indebtedness to Vivekananda. Free India's first Prime Minister Jawaharlal Nehru wrote: "Rooted in the past, full of pride in India's prestige, Vivekananda was yet modern in his approach to life's problems, and was a kind of bridge between the past of India and her present ... he came as a tonic to the depressed and demoralized Hindu mind and gave it self-reliance and some roots in the past." Netaji Subhash Chandra Bose wrote: "Vivekananda's harmonized the East and the West, religion and science, past and present. And that is why he is great. Our countrymen have gained unprecedented self-respect, self-reliance and self-assertion from his teachings."

Vivekananda's most unique contribution to the creation of new India was to open the minds of Indians to their duty to the downtrodden masses. Long before the ideas of Karl Marx were known in India, he spoke about the role of the labouring classes in the production of the country's wealth. He was the first religious leader in India to speak for the masses, formulate a definite philosophy of service, and organize large-scale social service.

It was Vivekananda who gave to Hinduism as a whole a clear-cut identity, a distinct profile. Before he came Hinduism was a loose confederation of many different sects. He was the first religious leader to speak about the common bases of Hinduism and the common ground of all sects. He was the first person, as guided by his Master Sri Ramakrishna, to accept all Hindu doctrines and the views of all Hindu philosophers and sects as different aspects of one total view of Reality and way of life known as Hinduism. Speaking about his role in giving Hinduism its distinct identity, Sister Nivedita wrote: "... it may be said that when he began to speak it was of 'the religious ideas of the Hindus', but when he ended, Hinduism had been created."

Before Vivekananda came, there was a lot of quarrel and competition among the various sects of Hinduism. Similarly, the protagonists of different systems and schools of philosophy were claiming their views to be the only true and valid ones. By applying Sri Ramakrishna's doctrine of Harmony (*Samanvaya*) he brought about an overall unification of Hinduism on the basis of the principle of unity in diversity. Speaking about his role in this field K M Pannikar, the eminent historian and diplomat, wrote: "This new Shankaracharya may well be claimed to be a unifier of Hindu ideology."

Another important service rendered by Vivekananda was to raise his voice in defence of Hinduism. In fact, this was one of the main types of work he did in the West. Christian missionary propaganda had given a wrong understanding of Hinduism and India in the Western minds. He had to face a lot of opposition in his attempts to defend Hinduism. At the end of the 19th century, India in general, and Hinduism in particular, faced grave challenges from Western materialistic life, the ideas of Western free society, and the proselytizing activities of Christians. Vivekananda met these challenges by integrating the best elements of Western culture in Hindu culture.

A major contribution of Vivekananda to Hinduism is the rejuvenation and modernization of monasticism. In this new monastic ideal, followed in the Ramakrishna Order, the ancient principles of renunciation and God realization are combined with service to God in man (Shiva jnane jiva seva). Vivekananda elevated social service to the status of divine service.

Vivekananda did not merely interpret ancient Hindu scriptures and philosophical ideas in terms of modern thought. He also added several illuminating original concepts based on his own transcendental experiences and vision of the future. He said: "My ideal, indeed, can be put into a few words, and that is: to preach unto mankind their divinity, and how to make it manifest in every movement of life. Education is the manifestation of the perfection already in man. We want that education by which character is formed, strength of mind is increased, the intellect is expanded, and by which one can stand on one's own feet." He further complained: "So long as the millions live in hunger and ignorance, I hold every man a traitor who, having been educated at their expense, pays not the least heed to them. Whatever you think, that you will be. If you think yourselves weak, weak you will be; if you think yourselves strong, strong you will be.

He warned: "If you have faith in all the three hundred and thirty millions of your mythological gods, ... and still have no faith in yourselves, there is no salvation for you. Have faith in yourselves, and stand up on that faith and be strong; that is what we need." He thundered: "Strength, strength it is that we want so much in this life, for what we call sin and sorrow have all one cause, and that is our weakness. With weakness comes ignorance, and with ignorance comes misery."

He felt: "The older I grow, the more everything seems to me to lie in manliness. This is my new Gospel. Purity, patience, and perseverance are the three essentials to success, and above all, love."

He defined religions: "Religion is realization; not talk, not doctrine, nor theories, however beautiful they may be. It is being and becoming, not hearing or acknowledging; it is the whole soul becoming changed into what it believes."

Religion is the manifestation of the Divinity already in man. Teach yourselves, teach everyone his real nature, call upon the sleeping soul and see how it awakes. Power will come, glory will come, goodness will come, purity will come, and everything that is excellent will come when this sleeping soul is roused to self-conscious activity. "They alone live who live for others, the rest are more dead than alive. This is the gist of all worship – to be pure and to do good to others."

"It is love and love alone that I preach, and I base my teaching on the great Vedantic truth of the sameness and omnipresence of the Soul of the Universe."

One greatness of Vivekananda's thought lies in its bringing together the people of upper castes and the Dalits through the philosophy of Advaita Vedanta. According to Advaita it is the same Atman that is identical with Brahman, the Innermost Reality in a Brahmin and a Dalit. All are one in 'the One Supreme Brahman *Atman*: if each individual soul is part of the One Universal Soul, in injuring one's neighbour, a person actually injures- oneself. In the *Atman* there is no distinction of sex or *varna* or *asrama*, so there should not be any privilege given to anyone. It is thus Advaita Vedanta which gives a philosophical basis for equality and social justice. Advaita Vedanta cannot but be practical because it forces us to love our neighbours as our Self. Also, if all the jivas alike are the embodiments of the *Atman*, then service to the jivas is service to Siva. The practical Vedanta of Vivekananda thus stands for the cause of Dalits.

There is no need for the Dalits to revolt 'against the Upanisads and Advaita Vedanta, which in reality stand for their rights, dignity and honour. The revolt of the Dalits has to be against those upper castes who are ignorant of the teaching of equality found in the Upanisads and its systematisation in Advaita Vedanta. There is much possibility for synthesis of Vedantic and Dalit theologies and this insight was implicitly proclaimed by Vivekananda as early as the end of the nineteenth century. Today the Dalit theologians and those who fight for the cause of Dalits can be greatly enlightened by this. If the Dalit theologians hold that the sufferings of the Dalits should be the basis or starting point of Dalit theology, Vivekananda is inspiring them to add to it the basis of the One Innermost Atman shared by all alike. Here again Vivekananda stands for harmony in a glorious way. Also, if what he taught was a practical Vedanta of equality and unity of all, it would be missing the point to brand him as an inchisivist.

Vivekananda stands in the line of the glorious tradition of religious harmony in the long history of India. When we analyse the history of India from the perspective of harmony, we perceive that in the thought of Hinduism, religious pluralism is theologically and epistemologically accepted. The Indus Valley religious ideas were absorbed in Hinduism. The Buddhist or Jain teachings did not claim to break away from the Aryan tradition. Buddhism in its Mahayana form became more and more a theistic religion, and by the ninth century A.D. the line dividing Buddhist lay-people from ordinary Hindus became less and less marked in India. The Syadvada of Jainism, emphasised the theory of relativity of knowledge and thus stood for openness and catholicity.

The medieval Hindu bhakti was eclectic by its combination of Hindu and Muslim ideas. The bhakti movement in Hinduism and the Sufi movement in Islam brought Hinduism and Islam closer to each other. Then Sikhism was bora out of the wedlock between Hinduism and Islam. The Indian tribal vision of life emphasises harmony, equality, collectivism, accommodation, and democracy. Indian Christian theology and worship are influenced by Hinduism culturally, philosophically, and religiously. Also, it should be noted that in India there were many kings who were tolerant towards all religious traditions, for example, Asoka, Harsha Vardhana, Akbar, and the kings of the Gupta dynasty; in the south there were the Satavahanas and the Kerala kings such as Ayyan Atikal Tiruvatikal," Bhaskara Ravi, and Vira Raghava. In India much cross fertilization of religious ideas has taken place and this has resulted in the evolution of a composite culture which upholds unity in diversity. Vivekananda is truly the modern representative of this Indian religious harmony and integration and composite culture.

Thus in the overall analysis of Vivekananda's contributions to the harmony of religions, we could identify him only as a pluralist who affirmed the validity of different religious paths to the One God. The inclusivist tendencies which seem to appear here and there in his projection of Advaita Vedanta as the supreme possible religious experience have to be understood as attempts to counter-attack the inclusivist Christian missionaries. Also, a universal religious principle like Advaita cannot plead for inclusivism, but only for pluralistic inclusivism. Again, the Christology of Vivekananda is having a positive influence on Indian Christian theologians.

The ideology articulated by Vivekananda shared the suppositions that can be found among both reformist and traditionalist thinkers, namely that Hinduism was in a degenerate state and such had fallen from the condition of its past glories. All was well once, but no longer. Vivekananda saw this decline as stemming from failures within the Hindu community. Degeneration of India came not because the laws and customs of the ancient were bad, but because they were not allowed to be carried to their legitimate logical conclusions "This decline in the observance of the proper Hindu behaviour had resulted in a degraded people, whole national character is one of childish dependence. They are all ready to enjoy food if it is brought to their mouth, and even some want it pushed down" You do not deserve to live if you cannot help yourselves... Their competitiveness made concerted efforts for improvement extremely difficult:

"Three men cannot act in concert together in India for five minutes. Each one struggles for power and in the long run the whole organisation comes to grief. Lord! Lord! When will we learn not to be jealous."

With the vision of a degraded Hindu character, it was difficult to find examples of past achievement. According to Vivekananda, Hindus could find one impressive achievement by their community, namely, that ancient nations have come and gone, but Hindus remained:

"But we live, and if Manu came back he would not be bewildered and would not find himself in a foreign land. The same laws are here, laws adjusted and thought out through thousands and thousands of years; customs, the acumen of ages and the experience of centuries, that seem to be eternal; and as the days go by as blow after blow of misfortune has been delivered upon them, such blows seem to have one purpose only, that of making them stronger and more constant. And to find the centre of all this, the heart from which the flood flows, the main-spring of the national life, believe me when I say that the experience of the world is that it is here."

In spite of all its difficulties Hinduism survived, even if it was in a somewhat diminished state and without its past glories.

The reasons given for Hinduism's decline lay partly outside the Hindu community and were attributed to foreigners and foreign religions. Hindus had to face the most immoral of all religions, Islam:

"The more selfish a man, the more immoral he is. And so also with the race. That race which is bound down to itself has been the most cruel and the most wicked in the whole world. There has not been a religion that had clung to this dualism more than that founded by the Prophet of Arabia, and there has not been a religion which has shed so much blood and been so cruel to other men. In the Koran there is the teaching that unbelievers should be killed; it is a mercy to kill him! And the surest way to get to heaven, where there are beautiful houses and all sorts of sense-enjoyments, is by killing these unbelievers. Think of the bloodshed there has been consequence of such beliefs!"

Having survived the terror of Islam, Hindus faced a new threat to their religion and ancient culture, again from an intrusive and aggressive religion carried by British conquerors. In dealing with Christianity and the British, Vivekananda walked a thin line between outright rejection of Western concepts and religion as presented by

Christian missionaries and any open condemnation of the British Indian government. After travelling to the United States, Vivekananda saw missionary movement from two different perspectives, both negative:

"It is not true that I am against any religion. It is equally untrue that I am hostile to the Christian missionaries in India. But I protest against certain of their methods of raising money in America. What is meant by those lectures in school books for children where the Hindu mother is painted as throwing her children to the crocodiles in the Ganga? The mother is black, but the baby is painted white to arouse more sympathy and get more money."

Vivekananda was furious against the propaganda of the Christian missionaries for their false reporting that women, being burnt at the stake by their husbands, cars crushing over human beings', and villages where 'there is a pond full of the bones of little babies'. He is disturbed by what appears to be a difference between missionary attitudes towards Hindus and Muslims respectively:

"One thing I would tell you, and I do not mean any unkind criticism. You train and educate and clothe and pay men to do what? To come over to my country to curse and abuse all my forefathers, my religion, and everything. They walk near a temple and say, 'You idolators, you will go to hell'. But they never dare to say that to the Muhammadans of India; the sword would be out. But he Hindu is too mild; he smiles and passes on and says, 'Let the fools talk'. That is the attitude."

Both Islam and Christianity are religions of error and abuse; they damaged Hinduism in the past and still threaten it in the present. Also Christianity carried the values and concepts of Western civilization that were undermining Hinduism:

"Children brought up and educated in the new schools started on the occidental plan, drank in these idea from their childhood; and it is not to be wondered at that doubts arose. But instead .of throwing away superstitions and making a real search after truth, the test of truth became what does the West say. The priests must go, the Vedas must be burned, because the West has said so."

There is here a double negative in that what the West brings is of no real help and Hindus do not have the ability to say no to it. This situation has been exacerbated by the education system imported from and conducted by the British. The same system that he experienced and now rebuffed:

"...and you too understand full well, I mean those of our countrymen who have become thoroughly Europeanised both in external habits and in way of thought and ideas, and who are continually crying their eyes out, and praying to the Europeans to save them ye European people, you are our saviours, have pity on us and raise us from this fallen state."

For Vivekananda self-action on the part of the Hindus was the only so solution to their present dilemma. They had to cease being weak, return to their own religion, their own gods, and seek the strength that was inherently in them:

"Say: 'The soil of Bharat is my highest heaven, the good of Bharat is my good and repeat and pray day and night, Thou Mother of the Universe, vouchsafe manliness unto me! O Mother of strength, take away my weakness, take away my unmanliness, and make me a Man!"

Vivekananda's cry for manliness sums up the different trends of his writing. Hindus were degraded, under attack from other religions and principles of Western civilisation, even from the actions of Christians in distant America. Their only hope was to find the strength, the virility, the will to return to their own religious traditions and spirituality. Such actions would, he felt, give them the ability to resist alien pressure and temptation. Thus Hinduism would rise once again above all other religions. This is a Nickchean "will to power".

Looking back over the writings and actions of orthodox defenders of Hinduism, Vivekananda saw contemporary Hinduism as degenerate and filled with error, as each defined that term. The Hindu community was perceived as weak, divided, sunk in controversy and thus unable to defend itself from more aggressive religions. Each group offered solution to the problems of the present, but by opposing forms of action. Reformers called for radical changes within Hindu religious practices in order to cleanse Hinduism of all accumulated garbage. From the orthodox perspective, these reformers in attempting to purify Hinduism had achieved nothing and instead became part of the overall problem.

Vivekananda contended the rituals, beliefs, sacred texts, and social structure of contemporary Hinduism were correct, proper, and even divinely inspired. Their authority lay in the ancient scriptures, the Vedas, Sruti, Smrti, the Puranas and the laws of Manu. These texts were not to be challenged by human reasoning, foreign religious doctrine or concepts of Western science. The revival of Hinduism and Hindus lay in inculcating respect for the ancient texts, for Brahmins, and the system of social structure with all its implications. Acceptance of the varna system and all it meant, even untouchability, was deemed necessary and good for the moral condition of Hindus. Progress would be made by a return to belief in sacred authority and the practice of all religious acts, such as respect for the holy Ganga, Brahmin priests, idol worship, pilgrimages, and proper diet. Together they comprised sanatan dharma, the Eternal Religion, adherence to which would restore Hinduism to its proper place as the leader and teacher of all religions. True, each of these Hindu leaders had his own particular points of emphasis, but all shared the basic supposition as to what was wrong in Hinduism and what should be done to make it right again.

Other religions, particularly Islam and Christianity, were declared enemies, their doctrines and practices untrue, at times cruel, and above all, through conversion a threat to the Hindu community. At times competition took the form of violence, at other times missionaries challenged the beliefs and customs of Hinduism by presenting their alternative systems of belief and conduct. In addition Hindu youth faced an English education that taught both the language and culture from another civilisation, thus directly and indirectly supporting the campaigns of Christian missionaries. At times Vivekananda condemned both Islam and Christianity, specifically the activities of Christian missionaries in India and the United States. In his writing and speeches, however, he primarily championed Vedantic Hinduism. Vivekananda achievement marked him as different from all other religious leaders, for he also brought a new dimension to Hinduism by transforming the traditional Hindu institutions of the Hindu ascetic and monastery into vehicles of social service. He established the Ramakrishna Math and Mission that provided religious training and housing for Hindu ascetics. It also became a base for the management of social welfare institutions, which conducted forms of medical service and emergency relief. In so doing Vivekananda added to Hinduism a social gospel, whereby the tradition of Hindu monks followed a doctrine of action, karma yoga, that stressed action within the world rather than attempting to retreat from it, thus offering to both monks and laity a new path to the traditional goal of release from the cycle of rebirth.

Vivekananda is remembered today as a highly successful spokesperson for Hinduism in North America and Europe and as an exponent of religious tolerance. He was also a defender of orthodox Hinduism. It is clear that Vivekananda cannot be placed in a single category, for he was both complex and, at times, contradictory. A full understanding of Vivekananda a requires of historians and students of religion that they explore the totality of his writings and speeches as well as other available historical sources. Many Dalit scholars have made serious charges againt Vivekananda.

Vivekanand made few controversial statements in speeches at the World Parliament of Religions in 1893. Dalit scholars accuse him that anyone with a basic knowledge of Hinduism and the history of British India will find that his speeches are not only strewn with errors but also carries a plethora of deliberate lies.

During his heydays of Hindu revivalism and nationalism, he introduced a new gospel: "Do even evil like a man, Be wicked, if you must, on a grand scale". He remained oblivious to the repercussions of his often misinformed, misunderstood speeches that will cause havoc to an already violence-ridden Hindu populace, Ceremoniously, he would proclaim to the Hindus: "Sin is impossible; there is no such thing as human responsibility, man can do no wrong".

How about Hindu men can do no wrong? After all, his Hindus are the descendants of a glorious race the Swami would retort repeatedly. This "glorious" Hindu race concocted the most evil system of Apartheid the man has ever envisioned: the caste system. Vivekananda spared no effort to justify that: "...Caste is good. That is the only natural way of solving life".

At other references his explanation of caste system was grossly wild and converged on somewhat Hindu version of marxist's view of history, as recorded by a disciple:

"The *vaisys*, or the merchant, and the *sudra*, or the worker, represent the third and fourth castes in Hindu society. The four castes, by turn, governed human society. The brahmin dominated the thought-current of the world during the glorious days of the ancient Hindu civilization. Then came the rule of the kshatriya, the military, as manifested through the supremacy of Europe from the time of the Roman Empire to the middle of the seventeenth century. Next followed the rule of the vaisys, marked by the rise of America. Then the coming supremacy of the sudra class. After the completion of the cycle, he said, the spiritual culture would again assert itself and influence human civilization through the power of the brahmin. Swami Vivekananda often spoke of the future greatness of India as surpassing all her glories of the past".

"I am a socialist", he proclaimed of himself. Even though he showed many inconsistencies, he remained somewhat stuck to his version of the marxist ideology as he understood it; he prophesied about the coming the proletarian culture of the future. In 1896, he said to Sister Christine: "The next upheaval will come from Russia or China. I cannot see clearly which, but it will be either the one or the other. The world is in the third epoch, under the domination of the vaisya. The fourth epoch will be under that of the sudra."

At the spur of a moment, he would mix multiple, often contradictory, political ideologies, both foreign and domestic; with the result the end-product, his political ideology, looked irrational and beyond any comprehension.

His achievements at the World Parliament of Religions paved the way for his triumphal return. The Hindu masses were in state of ecstasy; they heard that because of him the people of America and England are rapidly converting to Hinduism. However, the were not told that while in Chicago he also truly enjoyed eating beef delicacies, provided freshly prepared. On the positive side, Chicago received immense publicity and became a "Holy City-Chicago" among the Hindus as recorded by Mark Twain when the later visited India in 1895. In the midst of hulabaloo, Vivekananda landed in India on Jan.26, 1897. He received many honors, although his love somewhat faded when less then three years later, he recalled the implications of the warm Hindu reception accorded on him; But, now at the height of popularity in India, people waited eagerly to see him; hear him; hear his message of new India, new vision, and a new sense of direction. Among the few speeches that he delivered, the one at the Victoria Hall, Madras, in February 1897 stands slightly better than his standard regular huggermugger under the heading- My Plan of Campaign. He made clear his prescription.

Evil is everywhere; it is like a chronic rheumatism. Drive it form the foot, it goes to the head; drive it from there, it goes somewhere else. It is a question of chasing it from place to place; that is all. Ay children, to try to remedy evil is not the true way. Our philosophy teachers that evil and good are eternally conjoined, the obverse and the reverse of the same coin.

In other words, the evil which spreads to every labyrinth of Hindu society is essential and therefore must be left intact. You suppose, the people did not come to hear him say that sort of a sermon! Smart elusive Hindu that he was, he stressed the idea of preserving the evil and immediately augmented his visionary statement by providing the prime example of the Afro-Americans. Had the Negroes been kept slaves in America, they would have been better off the evil of slavery should have been kept intact rather than destroying it, as America did. Which is too bad, really!

"The history of the world teaches us that wherever there have been fanatical reforms, the only result has been that they have defeated their ends. No greater upheaval for the establishment of right and liberty can be imagined than the war for the abolition of slavery in America. You all know about it. And what has been its results? The slaves are a hundred times worse off today than they were before the abolition. Before the abolition, these poor Negroes were the property of somebody, and, as properties, they had to be looked after, so that they might not deteriorate. Today they are the property of nobody. Their lives are no value; they are burnt alive on mere pretenses. They are shot down without any law for their murderers; or they are niggers, they are not human beings, they are not even animals;"

Vivekananda's fixation on preserving evil quite never left him and it had the roots in Hinduism, especially in the Vedanta on which he lectured quite extensively. With roughly two and one-half years of hardly any worthiness to his stay in India, he left again for the West on June 20 1899. This time he made it to west coast-in California, where he found a mere receptive audience. Some of his speeches of this time got lost; however, one speech that clearly stands high is 1900 at the Shakespeare Club, in Pasadena.

Swami Vivekananda returned to India in 1897, he was received by the people as a conquering hero. He was driven through the cities in decorated coaches drawn by admiring crowds. In one instance, the ruling prince of a state with his court officials joined the people in drawing the coach. The story was the same wherever he went. He travelled from Colombo to Almora, inspiring people. The nation had long been asleep. Now it awoke at his call, 'Arise, awake, and stop not till the goal is reached. He had set an agenda for India. She has to be herself, not merely a copy of the West as she was then trying to be. India should assimilate whatever good there is in the West, but surely not at the cost of what she now possesses and what has served her well through the centuries. India has much to take from the West-science and technology, for instance but she can also give much to the West in return-religion. Through science and technology India can prosper materially, but she has to hold on to her spiritual traditions so that her growth may be well balanced. It is interesting to note that Vivekanand had an ambivalent attitude to modernity. He was impressed by Western progress, but he did not mince matters in pointing out how the craze for money and the comforts it bought could someday boomerang. In talking to his own people he was equally blunt: He saw no special merit in a starving people indulging in moral and dialectics. His teacher, Ramakrishna, used to say that there could be no religion for any empty stomach. Vivekananda also thought that what India needed first and foremost was bread. He had travelled extensively through India, mostly on foot, before leaving for the West. He had firsthand experience of India's poverty. This is why he had once seriously considered raising funds in America for the poor of India.

Along with poverty, the heinous caste system of India troubled him. No one else attacked it as strongly as he did. He said India's downfall began from the day she coined the word 'untouchable'. In theory, man is divine in India, but in practice, he can be brute. This is the irony. How it happened is difficult to understand. He condemned Indian society as being too restrictive. This was a strange contrast to the freedom India allowed in matters of religion. In the West it was just the other way about: In social matters man was absolutely free, but where religion was concerned, man had little freedom.

The next problem he talked about was education. He found the prevailing system of education turned out only clerks. He did not care for this kind of education. He wanted 'man-making' and 'character-building' education. India had many problems, most of them socio-economic. The root of those problems was in the country's allen rule. He blamed the British, but he blamed more the so-called educated Indians whose only ambition in life was to prosper under the British. He called such people cheats, for, according to him, they had their education at the cost of the poor, but now that they were well-off, they did not care what happened to the poor.

Vivekananda felt that India had greatly harmed herself by neglecting the masses. He described this as a national sin. The common people by and large, have remained poor and backward. He was no politician, but he had no doubt in his mind that the British had no right to impose their colonial in rule over India. He is said to have predicted that India would be independent in a most unpredictable manner within the next fifty years. He said this sometime in1897. Exactly fifty years after this India became independent. The Second World War had completely exhausted England. She had her hands full rebuilding herself and had not the power or inclination to keep under check a disgruntled giant of a country like India.

Vivekananda also predicted the emergence of the Sudra power, that is, the power of the working people, in India. It would be a new India then, the India of the toiling masses. He was sure that this would happen. Lest this be preceded by bloodshed, he wanted the country to be first deluged be spiritual ideas. He appealed to the higher causes to share with the lower castes all the idealism they had so long cherished for their own use. In other words, he wanted all castes barriers to go. He did not want any sort of 'leveling down'. He wanted 'leveling up. He wanted the gap between the high castes and low castes bridged by universal education. Education was the panacea for all evils, according to him. He wanted a classless, casteless society. He visualized the future society as being 'a junctionof the two great systems, Hinduism and Islam-Vedanta brain and Islam body. All will have an equal social status, but they will also aspire to the highest spiritual development possible, as found in Vedanta.

There is hardly any problem he did not touch upon. He was distressed by the neglect to which Indian women were subjected. They were not even allowed to go to school. They were given away in marriage before eight and by fourteen they became mothers. He was prepared to 'murder' people responsible for child marriages.

Women should have the same status as men in society. If they cannot contribute their share towards social growth, society is the loser to that extent. Giving a picturesque simile, he said, "It is not possible for a bird to fly on only one wing." He was struck by the poverty and ignorance. At Cape Comorin sitting in Mother Kumari's temple, sitting on the last bit of Indian rock-he hit upon a plan: We are so many sannyasins wandering about and teaching the people metaphysics- it is all madness. Did not our Gurudeva use to say, 'An empty stomach is no good for religion? That those poor people are leading the life of brutes is simply due to ignorance. He said: We have for all ages been sucking their blood and trampling them under foot... we as a nation have lost our individuality, and that is the cause of all mischief in India. We have to give back to the nation its lost individuality and the raise the masses. The Hindu, the Mohammedan, the Christian, all have trampled them under foot. Again the force to raise them must come from inside, that is, from the orthodox Hindus... Religion therefore is not to blame, but men. To effect this, the first thing we need is men, and the next is funds. Through the grace of our Guru I was sure to get from ten to fifteen men in every town. I next travelled in search of funds, but do you think the people of India were going to spend money? ... Therefore I have come to America, to earn money myself, and then return to my country and devote the rest of my days to the realization of this one aim of my life."

"We are neither Vedantists nor Puranics, nor Tantriks. We are just "don't touchists". Our religion is in the kitchen; our god is the cooking pot. Neglect of the masses had been our national sin. And, as for women? 'Writing down the Smritis, etc..., and binding them by hard rules, the men have turned the women into mere manufacturing machines!' Who can ever forget the impassioned end of the Bartaman Bharat, or when he calls the poor and the afflicted 'the only god that is awake, our own race-everywhere his hands, everywhere his feet, everywhere his ears, he covers everything.' As Bankimchandra equated the Motherland with the Divine Mother, Vivekananda equated the Indian people with the Purusa of the Vedas. He expressed his Indian mission in one sentence- 'We have to bring the Vedanta of, the forests back home. He invited some of them to come and work in India. The most notable among them Nivedita who served India till her death, working in every field of the country's life. India still remembers Nivedita with gratitude.

Vivekananda loved India for her idealism, but her failure at the practical level disgusted him. India says that man is divine but in practice she simply treats him as a brute. The West is more practical: It does not give a man a divine status, but treats him exactly he is-human. He was impressed by Western efficiency. He felt India ought to learn this from the West just as the West ought to learn idealism from India. The solution lies in combining idealism with efficiency, that is, religion with science. What every society needs is good human beings, but it needs good living conditions too. It was his hope that India would show how religion and science could be combined to promote material prosperity and moral excellence. The purpose of life is to improve, both materially and morally.

India owes much to Vivekananda, but so does the world. He was a true citizen of the world. Of all countries India was the dearest to him, but that was because India was the land where the highest thoughts had been thought. India was Truth itself to him. 'Shall India die? Then from the world all spirituality will be extinct, all moral perfection will be extinct...he said. India should live for the sake of the world. In fact, man everywhere was his concern. Man was God Himself to him. This is not humanism but it is only Vedanta, which sees God everywhere and in everything. Man is the very image of God, for God is most manifest in man. Since God is the same everywhere, man is the same everywhere. Color, country, or religion makes no difference. There is only one human family and there is also only one world. To a Vedantin, there is no East or West. It is all one. Vivekananda was at home everywhere-in the East as well as n the West.

Weakness is the root of all problems, both for individuals and nations. He wanted strong men and women everywhere. Atman is not accessible to the weak; he used to say, quoting the Mundakopanisad. He had no sympathy for that religion which robbed people of their faith in themselves. Nothing can be more degrading than losing faith in oneself. A man may have faith in all gods and goddesses, but if he has no faith in himself, he is doomed. Vedanta, which says man is divine, everything is divine, is the message that needs to be preached and not the debilitating creeds and dogmas which make people depend upon an arbitrary God. Vedanta had long remained the monopoly of a handful of scholars. He wanted to carry it to everybody, scholar or no scholar. The West, as much as India, remains grateful to him for unraveling this closely guarded secret, fully, freely. More important, he lived what he preached. His greatest contribution is that he brought the East and the West closer to each other. In fact, he pulled down the artificial barriers that divided them. He demonstrated that man was the same everywhere; distinctions of race, religion, color, gender, nationality were irrelevant.

In 1884 the Master was talking of Vaishnavism. 'Constant repetition of God's name for Jiva and worship of all. Suddenly stopped short to chide himself: 'Pity for Jiva? A worm of worms, who are you to pity? No, service to Jiva, knowing him to be Siva.' Vivekananda was to comment later, "What wonderful light these words of throw on man's duty! How he reconciled the dry knowledge of the Vedanta with bhakti! What he said in a trance convinces me that the Vedanta of the forests can brought home. And as long as you do not see god in all creatures, you won't attain real bhakti either. Even those, who have been proceeding by way of karma-yoga or raja-yoga, can find enlightenment in this. Anyway, if God gives me an opportunity, I will preach this wonderful truth everywhere-overwhelm the scholar and the fool, the rich and the poor, the Brahmin and the chandala alike."

In the first half of the 19th century, particularly in Bengal, patriotism was not grossly inconsistent with an undisguised support for the continuation of British rule. Bengali writers of this period made repeated references to how the British had rescued India from many centuries of 'tyrannical' and 'unprogressive' Muslim rule. Many people of this time, in fact, made an important distinction between the pragmatic gains to be made from a short-term tutelage under British rule and a long-term objective of securing independence from it. Though such thoughts ultimately proved to be naive and over-optimistic, in the 1820s and 1830s, the , advantages of British rule seemed to outweight its disadvantages. Raja Rammohun Roy (1774-1833) opposed an official move to open a Sanskrit College on the grounds that it would produce no positive or progressive influence on the educated Hindu. Rather than indulge in abstract metaphysical speculation as was likely to be the result of a purely Sanskritic education, Indians would profit far more by imbibing the best of modern European civilization—pragmatism and a rational, scientific outlook. Social usefulness, more than anything, else, was now to be the true measure of things. Rammohun's emphasis on rationality and a common sense approach to religion led some of his friends and admirers to call him a 'religious utilitarian'. This was an unfair assessment of his religious views because he also spoke of God and revelation. Nonetheless, it is difficult to overlook the symbiotic connection between the European penetration of India, a rational—utilitarian outlook and consequently, a critical revaluation of Indian life, both present and past.

Rationalism, however, was never the sole preserve of the European: Rammohun's critique of Indian religion and society began at a rime when he hardly knew any English and was quite unfamiliar with the colonial city of Calcutta which was subsequently to become the centre of his intellectual activities. And yet, because this rationalism was rooted in pre-modern sources and quite unrelated to other major developments in the modern world, it did not produce the brilliant flowering of Indian thought as occurred among those educated in English in the mid-nineteenth century. It was only through his newly acquired knowledge of English and an extended dialogue with European friends and acquaintances that Rammohun was exposed to the raging controversies in contemporary Europe.

The early Orientalist movement and the rapid growth of English as the principal medium of instruction after the 1830s, considerably enhanced the educated Indian's familiarity with his tradition. But, perhaps equally importantly, it also fostered a sense of shared culture. Rammohun may have been the first Hindu to have used the term 'Hinduism', thereby indicating some degree of cultural or perhaps even ethnic essentialism. These developments were also facilitated by the coming of the printing press. Texts were more easily available and cheaply priced. Over time, the success of print-culture enormously increased the importance of written texts within a tradition that had hitherto greatly relied on Smriti and Sruti. Perhaps this strengthened the hands of some writers who, particularly towards the end of the nineteenth century, began to emphasize a common cultural base for Hinduism. In the religious sphere, for example, there was now a far greater emphasis on the Vedas as a unified source of Hinduism, the prime determinant of a Hindu identity.

The success of the printing press is also tied up with certain extremely important shifts that began to occur in the social and religious thinking of early nineteenth-century Bengal. Hitherto, texts considered to be the most important in Hinduism had been zealously guarded by a class of Brahmins which prevented their wider circulation. Women and *Sudras*, for example, had traditionally been barred from Vedic knowledge. More importantly, these Hindu scriptures were composed in Sanskrit which meant that many other social groups besides women and *Sudras* had practically no access to the Vedas. Early reformers like Rammohun addressed these issues simultaneously. On the one hand, Rammohun bravely challenged the tradition by attempting to open up Vedic knowledge to all those who might be moved to seek it, irrespective of their social origin and location. This was the impulse behind his publication of Bengali translations of Hindu religious classics like the *Vedanta Sutra* (Brahma Sutra), and subsequently, some important Upanishads. This is also precisely why Rammohun became such a controversial figure. While orthodox opponents were in agreement with him when it came to suggesting the ineffable nature of God-realization, they were scandalized by his extending 'revealed' knowledge to the common man.

Rammohun was strongly critical of the excesses committed in the name of social and religious custom. Although a Brahmin himself, he blamed the members of this caste for the deep-seated problems in contemporary Hindu society. In this, he was clearly the forerunner of Vivekananda. In the course of his religious research, Rammohun came to believe that the true worth of Hindu social and religious life could not be gauged from the society of his day. He believed that over centuries, true Hinduism had been buried under a mass of irrationalities and superstitions by those who stood to profit from such acts. From this he concluded that, shorn of its excesses, Hindu life and thought were as rewarding and pure as any other. Rammohun was as much guided by feelings of patriotism. He reacted strongly to charges of 'Asian-effiminacy'; the notion of a 'true' Hinduism and a renewed cultural pride informed the nationalist consciousness of the educated Bengali and were perhaps most aggressively manifest in Swami Vivekananda.

The latter half of the nineteenth century marked a significant shift in the British policy towards India. India was henceforth to be directly administered by the British crown but more importantly, this period also coincided with the country becoming crucial to the interests of British capitalism. As India began to occupy a pivotal position within the far- flung British Empire, it also began to be subjected to greater political and bureaucratic control. More money was spent on maintaining an army, police and the civil service. Such a policy excluded Indians from key positions of power. It did not aim at improving agriculture or industry. Because the productive base of the economy was not adequately expanded and production itself very unevenly distributed, the standard of living in India fell quite sharply by the end of the nineteenth century. British control over many key sectors such as trade, finance and industry left very little room for Indian enterprise. A large number of English-educated Indians remained jobless or else were doomed to the demeaning life of petty clerks.

These developments produced a series of shifts in the Indian response to British rule. For one, the earlier optimism of Indians was replaced by a more realistic assessment of British rule. Further, the enemy was now seen to lie as much within. The growth of militant, anti-British movements did not altogether blind Indians to the existing ills in Indian society. In fact, one of the classic introspective statements of this period comes from the militant political and spiritual leader, Aurobindo Ghosh (1887- 1950):

"Our actual enemy is not any force exterior to ourselves, but our own crying 'weakness, our cowardice, our selfishness, our hypocrisy, our purblind sentimentalism."

In hindsight, it is not too difficult to see how such sentiments echo Vivekananda's call for inner strength and manliness and go on from there to the Swadeshi gospel of '*Atmasakti*' (inner strength). Many educated Hindus were also beginning to react to what they considered to be an excessive leaning towards the West or western values. In the 1830s, for example, simultaneous exposure to. rationalism and Christian ethics had produced a crop of radical young men who took a perverse pleasure in shocking orthodox opinion. There is, for instance, that well-known legend about Young Bengal greeting the goddess Kali with 'Good Morning Madam!' Stung by such youthful irreverence, the Hindu orthodoxy of Bengal soon began to rally its forces. In the 1820s, Rammohun had successfully defended himself against charges of heterodoxy and innovation by pointing out that his orthodo opponents, such as the pandits from Fort William College, had themselves been guilty of entertaining those whom they otherwise despised as mlecchas (outcastes).

An important development that followed from this was the visible disintegration of the nationalist agenda. Whereas before the 1880s, political demands could happily combine with the social reforms hereafter patriotism in many circles implied an irrational defence of the social status quo. The late nineteenth century, in fact, witnessed sharpening polarities. By the 1880s, there were at least six Bengali journals exclusively devoted to the propagation of popular science; on the other hand, irrational claims were made during this time about the knowledge of electricity among Vedic Aryans. While professional journalism flourished in Bengal, creating greater awareness of the home and the world, the vernacular had been led to believe, that Vivekananda was indeed the 'Karma Yogi'—activist par excellence—it would indeed be hard to accept the fact that he himself had on many occasions denigrated work and activism. This ambiguity derives from the fact that Vivekananda looked at this question both from an abstract, philosophical aspect and from the worldly point of view. His attitude to caste may he here taken as a case in point. Vivekananda was often critical of the divisive effects of caste but on the whole defended it as an institution. This defence however rests not simply on his conservatism but also on the belief that caste was exclusively a social institution on which, he, as a religious preacher, had no locus standi. Not surprisingly then, with respect to work and the changes it was expected to produce, Vivekananda also took radically opposed stands. These in turn were shaped by the two strongest facets of his personality, the deep commitment to this world and its very opposite, the strong penchant for world renunciation.

His rather cynical attitude towards work and its social value emanated from the typically Advaitic standpoint which held that while their respective proportions may change from time to time, the sum-total of good and evil in the world essentially remained unchanged. This, in turn, rested on the belief that changes occurred only at the cognitive level, not at the social or institutional. 'When a disciple expressed the desire to be born again and again so as to be able to complete his social mission, Vivekananda is known to have only rebuked him: 'That is because you cannot overcome the idea of progress,' he said. 'But things do not get better. They remain as they are, only we get better by the changes we make in them.'

Unlike Ramakrishna, Vivekananda neither scoffed at the philanthropic efforts of the Calcutta rich nor did he affirmed as clearly the view that the power to change or reform was essentially something that God in his wisdom conferred on the chosen few. On the other hand, like a true Advaitin, he found the idea of free will to be self-contradictory. Will is only what we have knowledge of and knowledge gained in this world is conditioned by elements of time, space and causation. In Vedanta, what really distinguished the Brahman (the Cosmic Soul) from Jiva (the Earthly Soul) was the former's state of perpetual 'freedom', above and beyond the effects of any natural laws. On the other hand, given the apparently real nature of the world, changes occurring within it were only cosmetic in nature and could not dislodge the inner unity of all forms of life and consciousness. Human intervention, Vivekananda argued, was not entirely infructuous but it did not have the power to create anything anew. In an absolute sense therefore, society could not be made any better or worse than what it already was. 'The world is like a dog's tail that cannot be straightened,' asserted Vivekananda.

The heart of his social agenda did not necessarily comprise the much debated questions of his day. 'Do you think a nation is saved by the number of husbands its widows get?' Vivekananda asks. On questions such as widow marriage, or the general place of the woman in the household, Vivekananda in fact took a fairly traditional conservative position. On the other hand, possibly because of its less controversial nature, he paid far greater attention to issues like mass education. Education was in any case vital to his Indian mission, irrespective of any controversy that might come to be associated with it. Education prepared men and women for their social responsibilities and also instilled in them the courage, self-confidence and power of introspection that was so crucial to their mental and physical growth as individuals. Vivekananda also had great faith in the levelling qualities of education, in his opinion the only practical means through which the lower stratas in society could be brought up to the level of the upper castes without generating a violent class war.

The late nineteenth century was infected and confronted by a controversy over whether social reform should take precedence over the political. Generally speaking, Hindus who were relatively unaffected by the insularity and cultural nostalgia of these years, considered the eradication of social evils a more pressing question. The opponents of this view obviously did not feel that existing social fissures could act as an impediment to political unity. As a major political body, the Congress had temporarily shelved this problem by refusing to entertain uncomfortable social and economic issues like the question of rural landownership or the burden of agrarian rents or taxes, thus allowing as it were, the landlord and the landless peasants to come together on a common political platform. However it was increasingly becoming evident that this was but an uneasy temporary truce and that the basis of politics itself could not be widened without also seriously addressing issues that touched the daily lives of masses. Vivekananda was not among those who even for a moment believed that the glaring social evils internal to Indian society could be glossed over by some overraching nationalist utopia. However, social reform questions could be extremely sensitive in nature and required careful handling. This meant that while moral and social abuses had to go, such work had to be suitably paced and made to work on the lines of a national consensus.

In hindsight it would appear that there were three areas over which Vivekananda seriously disagreed with contemporary social reformers and the nature of ongoing reform. He had no personal quarrel with reformers, most of whom he took to be good and well-meaning individuals. He had doubts however, about whether, given the source of their inspiration and the style of functioning, social reformers had been able to correctly identify the most fundamental problems. His first objection was that no work of reform had truly touched the masses. The widow-marriage campaign, for example, had really no relevance because numerous low jatis among whom such marriages were in any case permissible.

Secondly, modern social reformers, he felt, attempted a piecemeal reform, failing to see the significant inter-connections between one social issue and another. Caste could not be abolished unless there first evolved a new division of labour and a new approach to life and work. What was woman's education really worth if it did not have the power to enable her to rightfully exercise her choices in social matters? Vivekananda was unhappy to see that in many cases, reformers were only self-seeking individuals whose personal integrity was itself under some cloud. He refers, for instance, to the hypocrisy of the leaders of the reform party in Calcutta whose radical public postures were never replicated in the privacy of their homes. More tragic was the fact that the inspiration for reform came from sources that were alien and culturally unrelated to the reformer's agenda. The western guru could not really help Indian pupils to identify the most critical areas of reform, far less to instruct them in the most appropriate methods.

Vivekananda was certain that social reform would leave lasting effects only when founded on popular will. In so arguing, he was presumably hinting at the fact that reform effected through state legislation was bound to be unenduring and ineffective. But these characteristics, Vivekananda also indirectly tells us, were intimately tied up with the alien and unpopular nature of British rule. It is not difficult to see that he was trying to suggest that the power to set one's house in order rightfully belonged to the people and not to alien governments. Vivekananda felt that problems that were more sensitive and deep-rooted were best tackled as long-term projects. Under his leadership, the Rarnakrishna Mission joined wholeheartedly in the work of nursing the sick and feeding the starving people from drought-affected areas; its involvement with reform work touching upon jati or gender however, is practically non-existent.

Vivekananda thirdly argued that every country had its measure of good and bad. He rebuted the Europeans who saw nothing but irrationality and superstition in Indian culture and had themselves been no less guilty on these counts. He reminded had not the medieval Churchmen of Europe put every conceivable obstacle on the road to modern scientific progress? 'You say we ill-treat our women', asks Vivekananda of his western audiences. 'What nation has not?' That he was not averse to reform per se is beyond doubt. He welcomed reform that was positive and opportune; his own journey to the West, he hoped, would break the age-old Hindu taboo on voyages. He was also futuristic and believed that many positive changes were bound to occur with time. Western education itself was breaking down traditional privileges as a river in spate breaks its bank. And caste did not have to be pulled down; modern competition would kill it anyway, he prophesized.

Though Vivekananda commented on a wide variety of social issues, a fairly large part of his writings was devoted to the problems concerning two social groups—women and *Sudras*. In Vivekananda's perception, there appears to be a clear divide between understanding the woman as woman and understanding her as mother or wife.

While he said practically very little on the first, his comments on the other were traditional and conservative. The ambivalence towards the woman is clearly discernable in Bankim Chandra. On the one hand, especially in his essays Bankim has passages deploring the abject social status of the Hindu woman and in his many writings and utterances, Vivekananda has conceded much the same. On the other hand both were also capable of fairly conservative positions.

Although he broadly shared Ramakrishna's inhibitions regarding sexuality, Vivekananda also disagreed with him in certain respects. In the first place, he saw the problem of kam literally sexuality but applied more to female sexuality than male from a somewhat different perspective. Like Ramakrishna, Vivekananda held a woman's pining for her beloved as the most sublime metaphor for the love of God. The selfless love of the Gopis for Krishna as depicted in the Bhagavat Purana was thus a very high religious ideal. At the same time, he was only too aware that taken out of this idealistic context, the expression of intense emotional love between man and woman could easily lapse into debauchery. It was this aspect that worried him most. Vivekananda argued that woman symbolized lack of courage and weakness in every form, in short, everything that a man was not. Therefore, he always rested his hopes on young, unmarried men. Once writing from America, he threatened to disown his brother Mahendranath Dutta in case he married. His 'man-making' mission had no place for females, far less for feminine sentimentality. *Ojas* (spiritual power), Vivekananda maintains, was born only of a lifelong continence. Vaishnav devotionalism in Bengal, he thus complains.

"...this jumping about with the accompaniment of the *khol* and *kartal* (musical instruments) has ruined the the nation. Do we not have the drum and the bugle? Let our children hear their sonorous, soul-stirring sound...listening to womanish kirtan has rendered this country into a country of women."

Arguably, Vivekananda endorsed traditional Hindu binary stereotypes of 'man' and 'woman', 'manliness' and 'effeminacy'. This might appear somewhat odd because there are occasions when Vivekananda is also known to have admired the qualities of courage and heroism in women. Compared to his Guru, Vivekananda had fewer inhibitions about the mixing of genders. Uncritically accepting renouncing the world was also held as a means of gaining greater control over it. The higher one advanced in sadhana, the more free and unrestrained he became with respect to society. In Vivekananda's case however, this relative liberality may also be explained with reference to his exposure to western society, where, more women than men entertained him and ultimately accepted him as Guru. Of his early days in the West, Vivekananda writes, 'American women, a hundred lives would not be sufficient to pay my deep gratitude to you!' American women cast a spell on Vivekananda as indeed he had upon them. It was thus that he may have been led to the remark which many will undoubtedly find rather harsh, and uncharitable: "even the most beautifu1 of our women would look like a black owl here!" In America, he was quite delighted to find women at work places and performing roles that their Indian counterparts would not even contemplate. He writes in a letter of 13 November 1898: "I am at my wit's end to see the women of this country.. .they do all sorts of work...I cannot do even a sixteenth part of what they do."

European and American woman performed 'unwomanly acts' and yet it was their courage and unbounded energy that further inspired the 'manliness' in their men. However, over time, certain 'unsavoury' aspects of western life also became clearer to Vivekananda. He was plainly amused at the American woman's 'mania' for romance, especially when directed at so 'unromantic' a person s as he and her obvious discomfiture on being called 'Mother'. However impressed he might have been by sexual freedom in the West, Vivekananda did not think that conditions that existed there produced ideal women: "nowhere have I found such character, the sense of integrity and devotion, the kindness as I have in India...women in the West do not appear to be women at all'."

Vivekananda was also careful to point out that in India, unlike in the West, it was nor the wife who was the ideal of womanhood but the mother. Here the husband could not be expected to love his wife more than he loved his mother. Conversely, it was only when she herself became a mother that the wife got the greatest respect and recognition from her family. In so highlighting the glories of motherhood and the exalted social status of the mother, Vivekananda embraced older Hindu Brahminical viewpoint which glorifies the mother-figure. The woman as mother was the keeper of progeny; only good mothers produced great sons, Vivekananda would say.

At the same time, a mother figure represented the woman in her most bountiful and affectionate aspect.

Not surprisingly then, Vivekananda's thoughts about the ideal Indian wife focus on her fidelity and single-minded devotion. And here, he recalled the saga of the brave Rajput queen, Padmini. The Rani's heroism and self-sacrifice emanated from her sattiva wifely chastity, every woman of that chivalrous race would rush to meet death', Vivekananda would narrate to his western audiences, with emotion. The greatest embodiment of wifely virtues was Sita and Vivekananda wrote how no attempt to modernize the Indian woman could overstep that ideal. In glorifying satitwa, he also cited the examples of mythical Savitri whose immense power born of chastity forced the Yamaraj to miraculously revive her dead husband, and the medieval mystic poetess, Mira. The inclusion of Mira is a trifle surprising, for this princess, even when married, rebelled against Rajput patriarchy and refused to be tied down by the burden of domestic chores.

Of the several issues of this period specifically concerning women, Viveknanda showed genuine interest in only some. it was here that he also deliberately chose to overlook even evade important inter-connections between various facets of reform. One such instance is his eagerness to discourage early marriages among boys more than among girls. This is not only a strange exception but also inconsistent with his own position with regard to the social and sexual exploitation of child-brides. It does appear as though with the passage of time, Vivekananda 's attitude towards marriage and related questions grew more conservative, no doubt partly because of mounting orthodox pressure but perhaps also on account of his growing detachment from worldly activities. In 1891-92, he had severely condemned the orthodox outcry against the Consent Bill, clearly identifying the several problems that resulted from premature marriges-sickly mothers and children and higher infant mortality. Only four years later, he sounds far more cautious and uncertain: "teach against the marriage of boys; no scripture ever sanctions it but for the present say nothing against little girls being married."

Vivekananda was consistently hostile and simply apathetic to the question of widow marriage. He who otherwise thought that religions would flounder if they could not wipe the widow's tears, does not seem to accept the fact that in many cases, they may be wiped off simply by allowing the widow greater freedom to remarry, whenever possible or desirable. It is also important to remember that the Hindu orthodox as a group were not always opposed the idea of widow marriages.

At Oakland, USA, Vivekananda was harsh and insensitive when he argued that as Hindu marriage was a sacred duty and not a privilege that could be excercised at will, denying the child widow the right to marry caused no particular hardship. The social disapproval of widow marriage, he also quite dubiously attributed to 'socialism' in Hindu society which in his view preferred that virgins be married off before the widow could even entertain thoughts of a second marriage. Social equity demanded that widows be denied the first claim, since, to use Vivekananda's own words, 'they have had their chance'. Vivekananda maintained that upper class widows were rarely able to marry because of the scarcity of men.

It is only fair to add however, that what Vivekananda says on the subject of widow marriage also reflects a general and deep-seated prejudice in contemporary upper-class society. Even in his essay *Samya* (Egalitarianism), generally considered his most radical piece of writing, Bankim Chandra does not admit widow marriage as readily as say, woman's education. The essays in fact argues that a widow who was chaste and loved her deceased husband could hardly marry a second time, an argument not without sinister implications. For by such a logic, a widow who married was both uncaring and unchaste. Vivekananda admits to being horrified by the idea of the 'unfaithful' widow. This indeed may also explain his rather ambivalent position vis-a-vis being married off prematurely. Such marriages were bad but they also helped to preserve the 'chastity of the race'. Vivekananda considered the faithfulness of the widow to be 'the very pillar on which society rested'. He actually supported Sasipada Banerji's 'Widow Home' at Barahnagar, a suburb of Calcutta. He was obviously happier with such institutions because rather than focus exclusively on marriages, they were trying to give helpless widows some dignity and social resettlement.

His general conservatism notwithstanding, there is one progressive suggestion that is perhaps unique to Vivekananda. In the history of social reform in nineteenth-century Bengal, no one however suggested, as clearly as Vivekananda did, that the problems related to the woman were best solved by women themselves. He said that no man shall dictate to a woman nor woman to a man, women will work out their destiny better than men can ever of for them. All mischief has come because men undertook to shape the destiny of the woman. This is simply a patriarchal bias and prejudice.

This line of argument has interesting overlaps with strategies devised by modern feminist movements. Vivekananda, insisted that self-reform had to precede reform of the community and here the role of education was considered to be extremely important. Education would eventually produce great souls among women just it had among men. Vivekananda himself proposed to remedy such grievances by providing new institutional facilities for self-development among women. From the day Nivedita arrived in India, she was entrusted with the task of starting a girls' school. By 1895, the idea of starting a Math for women was high on the agenda of Vivekananda. The members of this Math were to be recruited from among unmarried women, 'chaste' widows and devoted housewives. The curriculum was by and large to be traditional without being obsolete. Apart from training in domestic crafts and the upkeep of children, women were also to be introduced to basic science. Vivekananda also tried to incorporate certain progressive elements of reform into such projects. In the proposed women's Math for instance, parents and guardians were to give an undertaking to the effect that they would not get their children married until they reached the age of fifteen. The Math for women unfortunately could not be started during Vivekananda's lifetime. The Sarada Math, as it is known today, was set up only in 1954.

Though Vivekananda eventually made a number of female disciples, he was a trifle uneasy about radically altering the framework of man-woman relationships. He sensed that among those who demanded greater freedom in this respect, were starry-eyed reformers who were misguided in their ideals and impractical in their approach. He took a dual stand in respect of the social upliftment of women. While he was rather severe on fellow Indians for any act of injustice they perpetrated on their women, outside India he would deliberately overlook these issues. More than simply defend Indian society against harsh criticism, Vivekananda often counterattacked his critics. He was quick to point out that higher education among women had arrived earlier in India than in the prestigious universities of Europe and America. Vivekananda's attitude to woman was coloured by the bias and prejudice of his caste towards woman.

The first step to counter the spell of maya is to identify and name it. 'If maya is once recognized,' says Ramakrishna, 'it feels ashamed of itself and takes to flight.' This is more easily accomplished by practitioners of spiritual discipline than by householders. Householders seldom know whether their wives are vidyashakti or avidyashakti. A wife embodying the characteristics of vidyashakti sleeps little, has no anger or lust, is affectionate, kind, devoted and modest. Such a woman pushes her husband away from herself and in the direction of God. She treats all men like her children. More than anything else, she spends little money, so that her husband doesn't have to work too hard and has all the leisure to aspire for the spiritual path. The traits of a woman who exemplifies avidyashakti are described by Ramakrishna as 'mannish', along with other bad traits as squint eyes, hollow eyes, catlike eyes, lantern jaw like a calf's jaw and pigeon breast. It is remarkable that all the traits of wives who embody avidyashakti are physical unlike those who display the virtuous signs of vidyashakti.

For householders following the path of vidya or knowledge, enjoying conjugal happiness with their wives occasionally is part of satisfying natural impulse, a bit like enjoying 'a sweetmeat once in a while'. But a householder also has to surmount impediments that lie in the way of practising spiritual discipline. Ramakrishna lists these as disease, grief, poverty, misunderstading with one's wife, and disobedient, stupid, and stubborn children. After producing one or two children, the ideal way forward for the husband and wife is to live like siblings. In doing so, they can continue to practise seven kinds of sexual intercourse. Sitting with a woman, talking to a woman for a long time, listening and enjoying a conversation with a woman, to speak about a woman, to whisper to her privately, to keep something belonging to a woman, and enjoying it and touching a woman are the seven kinds of sexual intercourse Ramakrishna permits householders. The eighth kind is actual sexual intercourse resulting in coitus, which he recommends, must stop after the birth of children.

In contrast, one is a sanyasi in the true sense only when he has renounced 'Mani' and 'Kanchan' (woman and gold) and does not regard women with the same gaze with which a worldly person would look at them. The company of young women can make a lustless man lusty. Ramakrishna likens this to staining one's body in a room filled with soot.

But satisfying one's sexual impulse is extremely harmful for a sannyasi. He must not look even at the portrait of a woman. A monk enjoying a woman is like a man swallowing the spittle he has already spat out. A sannyasi must not sit near a woman and talk to her, even if she is intensely pious. It is bad for him even to keep money near him, for it brings in its train calculation, worry, insolence, anger, and such evils. Ramakrishna is clear on the question of women: they are a part of the Divine Mother, but as far as men are concerned, especially if they happen to be snyasis and spiritual practitioners, they must shun women. Ramakrishna aversion to women is personal. In the *Gospal* we read:

"I am very much afraid of women. When I look at one I feel as if a tigress were coming to devour me. Besides, I find that their bodies, their limbs, and even their pores are very large. This makes me look upon them as she-monsters. I used to be more afraid of women than I am at present. I wouldn't allow one to come near me. Now I persuade my mind in various ways to look upon women as forms of the Blissful Mother."

As a sanyasi, who also had a wife, the personal and the public easily get conflated in Ramakrishna in the form of the code of conduct desirable for a sanyasi. 'Don't let yourself touch the air near a woman's body, he advises, and counsels those engaged in spiritual practices to see women as a raging forest fire or a black cobra. There were other reasons for Ramakrishna's injunctions against 'women and gold'. A major part of a man's mind is monopolized by a woman. After a child born, the whole mind is 'frittered away' on the family and nothing or little is left for thinking about God. Some men shed the last drop of their blood in order to keep their wives out of mischief.

It is difficult for a man to escape being stained, even if slightly, by 'woman and gold' if he lives in the midst of these two snares created by avidya. One way was to acknowledge that every man has two metaphorical wives, 'dispassion' and 'worldliness'. He must only take dispassion on the journey towards the knowledge of God. But the walk was not an easy one and the seekers will have to ask help from discrimination, who is dispassion's son, and he is the one who will guide the genuine seeker towards God. Neither Ramakrishna nor Ramprasad tells their readers and listeners anything about the patrimony of discrimination. Another way of avoiding the stain was maintaining physical distance: "Keep yourself eight cubits, two cubits, or at least one cubit away from all women except your mother."

A sanyasi, then, must always look upon a woman as his mother. If he happens to be near a woman, he must offer her his worship. This was the pure way of worshipping Adyashakti, who manifests also as avidya and has to be propitiated. Ramakrishna invokes an unusual metaphor to explain the 'pure' way of perciving women. Drawing upon the tradition of observing a fast on *ekadashi*, he lists the various ways in which the ekadashi fast could be observed. One was to eat only fruit and, perhaps, drink milk during the fast. Another way was to eat luchis and curries. His own way was to observe the fast without even drinking a drop of water, leave alone food: 'Looking on woman as mother is like fasting on the ekadasi day without touching even a drop of water; in this attitude there is not the slightest trace of sensual enjoyment.'

Sanyasis ought not to sit with women devotees or even speak to them. Those who reject the world of passion, and yearn for God are part of an 'unsullied aristocracy'. To develop true renunciation they must keep themselves very far away from women and do not fall into the clutches of women. Having attained this exalted level of meditative depth, Ramakrishna saw 'the inside and outside of the woman'; what he saw was 'entrails, blood, filth, worms, phlegm, and such things'.

Despite the warnings to sanyasis regarding 'woman and gold', Ramakrishna was clear that it was Adyashakti who has assumed all female forms and had to be propitiated. While looking upon all women as mother was the pure way he had chosen, Ramakrishna was once a practitioner of another way of appeasing the avidya aspect of the Primal Energy, namely, Tantra. There are instances in the Kathamrita when he rejects the efficacy of what he calls 'the path of the Vedas' in Kaliyuga for spiritual advancement and instead prescribes Tantra. Admitting that the rites of Shakti worship are very difficult and that he had been initiated into performing these rites he also warns against the vamachara method prescribed in the Tantra. It was, he says, the 'dirty' method of spiritual discipline, a bit like 'entering a house through the back door by which the scavengers come'. Vamachara inevitably led to a spiritual aspirant's downfall because of the proximity of 'an object of enjoyment', namely women. In Tantra, then, a devotee can propitiate Shakti by assuming the attitude of a mistress or of a hero or of a child. In the heroic attitude, the idea is to please Shakti in the same way as a man sexually pleases a woman, and in which instance a woman is seen to represent Shakti or Kali. Ramakrishna rejects the need for Tantric practices that involve the company of women.

Elsewhere, he calls this his natural attitude, it helped hm regard 'the breasts of any woman as those of my own mother and impelled him to worship all parts of the body of the Shorashi, a sixteen-year-old, in a tantric ritual as that of his mother. He also wonders what happiness could there be in sexlife with a woman. Instead, in ecstatic love of God 'all the pores of the skin, hair, become like so many sexual organs, and in every pore the aspirant enjoys with the Atman. In a unique and distinctive gloss on the purusha-prakriti dualism, Ramakrishna prescribes that spiritual aspirants cultivate 'the attitude of Prakriti in order to realize Purusha — the attitude of a friend, a handmaid, or a mother'.

One way of conquering lust and sexual passion was to assume the guise and attitudes of a woman. Ramakrishna speaks that he is handmaid of God. He dressed in women's clothes, put on jewellery and covered the upper part of his body with a scarf. Explaining this by talking about the peacock feather in Lord Krishna's crest, he suggests that the feather bears the sign of female sex. Its significance is that Krishna sports the female principle, Prakriti, on his head. When dancing with gopis, Krishna dresses up as a woman. Ramakrishna is categorical that as long as a man does not assume a feminine nature and attitude, he is not entitled to be with a woman and enjoy her company. But this can happen only after one realizes God, when the stage comes of seeing the Divine Mother in all women. It would be a mistake, however, to perceive Ramakrishna's anxiety to' overcome passion by assuming the attitudes of a woman as a way of coming to terms with one aspect of avidya alone. On the contrary, it offers an opportunity to look at three important strands in Ramakrishna's religious universe, one that Vivekananda would eventually reject or ignore. The first is to explore the ways by which an individual can conquer fear, shame and aversion. No spiritual gain was possible without transcending this triad of fear, shame and aversion. Equally significant, and this is the second strand, was to construct a vocabulary of transgression. Neither of these elements could be attained without a careful and judicious restatement of Tantra and Bhakti, and this constitutes the third element in understanding Ramakrishna's faith.

There are several instances of Ramakrishna reminiscing about what he called his period of 'divine madness', a period in which he followed the rigours of several spiritual disciplines and paths. The preliminary aim of these spiritual exercises was to overcome fear, shame and aversion in order to achieve the ultimate aim of seeing and realizing God. Those who had transcended difference and had conquered fear, aversion and shame had also realized that everything was the same Substance, the same Consciousness. Real sages who had the knowledge of Brahman, the purnajnanis, were 'mad', and they did not follow any social conventions.

The Hindu tradition of attempting link sexuality with the regeneration of India has remained on the political agenda of natonlist leaders. Unlike the nineteenth century European nationalist literature, which was either silent on the subject or celebrated sexuality, the emphasis on sexual self-discipline—at times bordering on puritanism—was a recurrent theme in its Indian counterpart.

Several nineteenth century Indian leaders contended that their countrymen had fallen prey to waves of foreign rule because they had become passive, effecte and devoid of energy as a result of their sensuous and self-indulgent life-style. They married very young, became physical and mental wrecks and lost interest in life by the time they reached adulthood, filled their empty lives with idle fantasies and were only fit to produce 'weaklings'. Some leaders even argued that the 'racial stock' had become degenerate and needed a radical eugenic programme. The terrorist literature at the turn of the century condemned homosexuality, masturbation and sexual excess and required young recruits to lead chaste lives. Vivekananda gave particular importance to sexual discipline as part of a comprehensive syllabus of moral and social regeneration.

Ramkrishna and Vivekananda shared these concerns. But Vivekananda was keen to harness sexual energy for political purposes and to transform the 'fire' of sexual passion into a 'fiery spirit' capable of 'igniting the masses'. However, he differed from the other leaders in several important respects. He placed far more emphasis on *brahmacharya* than almost all of them, and his prohibition of non-reproductive sexuality within marriage had no counterpart in any of their writings. With the exception of a few religious leaders, none of his contemporaries shared his mystical faith in their resistible spiritual power of a brahmachari either. Their concern to integrate man and woman and to become a whole person was also unique to him. Most nineteenth century religious reformers stressed masculine virtues and wanted Indians to become manly in the manner of their colonial masters.

But, if we ignore the ascetic tradition, Vivekananda's view of sexuality has no support in Hindu thought. For the Hindu sex is a necessary and beautiful impulse and occupies an important place among the four purusharthas. It is not just a means of procreation, nor a biological and psychological need, but a legitimate source of pleasure to be enjoyed without guilt during a specific period of life. In the Gita, Krishna declares on two occasions that sexual impulse is divine. Almost all Hindu gods, including divine incarnations, are married and the Puranas narrate the sexual adventures of some of them with considerable relish and joy. The Vedic gods had consorts and Indra was a notorious seducer of women. Prajapati, the lord of creation, split himself into two because he found no joy in being alone and desired company. The Kumara Sambavam of Kalidas, the greatest Indian dramatist, celebrates the union of Shiva and Parvati with great tenderness and offers moving descriptions of sexuality. The Gitagovinda of Jayadev and the devotional poetry of the Vaishnavites offer the most sensitive analyses of the structure and mechanism of the sexual impulse. In the absence of such cultural and religious legitimacy, Hindu writers would such have produced large body of literature on the subject of sexuality for over two millennia. Indeed, had the Hindus not perceived a close relationship between sexuality and religion, their artists would not have dared decorate some of their most sacred temples with erotic paintings and sculptures. Vivekananda's asceticism represented a relatively minor episode within the Hindu cultural tradition, and was largely a massive reaction to the debased Vaishnavite practices of his time. Vivekananda's attitude to woman and sexuality was differentiated by the Brahminical tradition regarding woman and sexuality.

In the Brahminical tradition, the female, whether divine or human, is inherently an ambiguous entity. The ambiguous female is anomalous, lying between categories, and is, therefore, essentially marginalised. Since the female is ambiguous, she is also dangerous and must be controlled. Such representations of female gender tap into more universal conceptions that are found in many different cultures. Feminine symbolism generally manifests a propensity toward polarised ambiguity and is represented in forms that are both utterly exalted and utterly debased. These forms are often exaggerated forms that do not lie within the normal range of human possibility and experience and are, therefore, 'other' than normal.

The female is not only 'ambiguous', she is also 'other'. Since the symbolism pertaining to female gender in Brahminical Hinduism represents femaleness as an ambiguous 'other', the social and cultural rules pertaining to this 'other' must be defined. Male gender is the measure by which social functioning is evaluated, whereas female gender is the 'other' gender that must be circumscribed. Whereas maleness is standard and, therefore, femaleness is different and is interpreted against this standard. Therefore, moral and ethical obligations for women are defined in relation to their gender, often as expressed in their sexual functioning, and are differentiated from those of men, whose moral and ethical standards in most situations have nothing to do with gender at all.

The representations and conceptions of female gender in Brahminical Hinduism provide both a theology and an ideology that ultimately can be used to support the repression of women. Because of her ambiguity and otherness, the female is interpreted as threatening to established societal and cultural norms and institutions and must, therefore, be carefully controlled. On the other hand, we may well ask whether the same representations and conceptions can be manipulated to promote change and enhance the position of women in Indian culture or, if women are to attain equality, whether all such representations must be rejected as male interpretations of female essence that are inherently restrictive by nature as a defining characteristic.

On the highest level, the representation of female gender in Brahminical Hinduism is embodied in the concept of a Great Goddess of whom different goddesses are represented as partial manifestations. Sometimes she is identified simply as the Goddess or the Great Goddess (Devi or Mahadevi); other times, a particular goddess who is important in a given textual environment is elevated to this status. Within Brahmanical Hinduism, the theology of the

Great Goddess is expounded in the Puranas, which are vast mythological works dating from about the fourth century BC.

The Goddess is identified above all with cosmogonic and cosmological principles that are unique and transcend the particular identity of individual divinities. The Goddess is described as the active dimension of the impersonal aspect of the Nirguna Brahman, that is, the creative power inherent within the Absolute. She is the impulse that mechanisms of the cosrnogonic process sets into motion and then sustains the universe once it has been created. In this capacity, she is called sakti, which means 'power'. The Goddess is also the principle of materiality that is the basis of the phenomenal—empirical world. As such, she is called prakrti, which means 'matter' or 'nature'. As prakiti, the Goddess is both an abstract principle, the very possibility for material creation to take place, and the embodiment of that possibility as matter itself.

Vishnu describes Lakshmi, his supreme sakti as absorbed within himself; the Siva Purana. asserts that Sadaivasa creates the Goddess, who is simply called sakti, by manifesting her from himself. In the next Nirguna stage, the Goddess is separated out from Nirguna Brahman and becomes an independent entity. She is now identified as the material principle of creation, prakti. As such, she is the immediate source of the manifest cosmos, which begins to evolve out of her. On a cosmic level, then, the essence of female gender is expressed as transcendental principles that are inherent .in the process of cosmogony and represent structures of creation. In most cases, the Goddess is subordinate to her consort, who is identified as Brahman. As sakti, the Goddess plays a creative role. But this role can be seen as both positive and negative. Sakti is often identified not only as a creative power but also as a power of illusion, maya. In this case, sakti is often seen to be negative. In the Narada Purana accounts of creation, sakti is equated with maya and is said to be of two natures: knowledge (*vidya*) and ignorance (*avidya*). As knowledge, it leads to God; but in its capacity as ignorance, which is that aspect of maya that leads to creation, it causes suffering and prevents the knowledge of God.

As pure sakti the Goddess is not only a cosmogonic principle but a cosmological one as well. She pervades creation and sustains it. As a force active in the world she is not only creative, but can also be destructive. This aspect of the Goddess is expressed in her many terrible forms that are associated with war, blood, death, destructions and illness, and can have either positive or negative connotations' Often, these terrible forms arise in context of the Goddess's role as the protector of the cosmos who destroys demons and who is therefore beneficial to creation. So the Goddess in her form as Devi is celebrated as the destroyer of demons, which is one of her main functions. In this capacity, she protects and maintains the cosmos by restoring order. Furthermore, in her destructive capacity, the Goddess is said to be the destroyer of ignorance. This function is performed above all by the goddess Kali, who is one of the Goddess's most terrifying and uncontrollable manifestations; she not only destroys demons but also devours them. Yet Kali's wild behaviour can be beneficial to those who seek to destroy their attachment to the world. Her raised and bloodied sword suggests the death of ignorance, her disheveled hair suggests the freedom of release, and her girdle of severed arms may suggest the end of grasping. As death or the mistress of death she grants to him who sees truly the ultimate boon of unconditioned freedom, release from the cycle of samsara, release from pain, sorrow, and ignorance.

In stark contrast to this celebratory attitude towards the manifest world, the ascetic and philosophical strands of Hinduism tend to adopt a much more negative attitude. Physical creation is viewed not as something to be honoured but rather as something that causes suffering and is therefore to be escaped. In these environments, the ultimate goal of human existence is to achieve liberation (*moksa*) from the world through various techniques, including ascetic practices that emphasise renunciation of the world. In the quest for liberation, prakrti represents bondage and is, therefore, that which one must escape. The Brahminical tradition regards the principles that the Goddess embodies with a great deal of ambivalence. First, as sakti, the, Goddess is the creative power that is needed for creation to take place, but she is also the power of delusion that prevents one from realizing Brahman.

The ambivalence towards the Goddess as sakti/prakrti is reflected on the human level in certain attitudes toward women. Since women are said to be portions of the Goddess, women, like the Goddess, are also embodiments of both sakti and prakiti. So the ambivalence expressed with respect to the principles that the Goddess embodies also applies to attitudes toward human women.

As an embodiment of sakti, a woman can be either creative, delusive or destructive; as an embodiment of prakriti, she can be either auspicious or inauspicious, liberating or binding. Thus, the Brahminical tradition is filled with tales of goddesses and women who act both as instruments of salvation and as temptresses who lure sages and ascetics away from their spiritual practices and impede their progress towards liberation. When left to her own devices, the female can go either way. And because she is ambiguous, woman, like the Goddess, is always capable of regressing into her least savoury aspects. In her regressive capacity, which is an inherent part of the female, she is dangerous. Danger is the essence of femaleness as it underlies Hindu religious beliefs about women.

The ambiguity and danger inherent within femaleness is a function of the intermediate position that the female occupies. Women are seen as dangerous by virtue of being closer to nature than men, who are more fully allied with the processes of culture. Women occupy an intermediate position between nature and culture and, therefore mediate between the two. The progressive tendencies of the female are expressed in those tendencies inherent in female gender that lead from nature, which represents disorder, towards culture, which represents order. Woman's regressive tendencies are those that lead in the other direction. In the Brahminical tradition, the intermediacy of the feminine is also reflected on the level of the divine in the transitional place of the Goddess in the process of cosmogony. Between the Absolute and the relative world lies the Goddess, who effects the transition. Since she lies between the Absolute and relative creation, she is the gateway to both. Therefore, she can conduce either to the realisation of Brahman and, thus, liberation (*moks*) or the snares of the phenomenal-empirical world, the continual cycle of birth and rebirth. Because the female principle is transitional, she is ambiguous. And because she is ambiguous, she is also dangerous.

The interpretation of female gender as a category implicates many dimensions of experience; the essence of the feminine as power and nature is expressed on the human level most strongly in female sexuality. Sexuality is, on one level, pure sakti, raw power, expressed as libidinal desire. The expression of this desire is seen as inappropriate for women and must be repressed. The drive of female desire creates a condition of inherent danger to social order, for a woman's desire for sex may lead her to engage in inappropriate sexual conduct, that is, to engage in sex outside of socially sanctioned circumstances. Such conduct, in turn, may lead to disastrous consequences.

In Brahminical Hinduism, the greatest danger with respect to female sexuality lies in the female's vulnerability to ritual pollution through sex, which in turn leads to disorder. This aspect of female gender can be attributed especially to her nature as prakrti, which is commonly described as the 'field' (*ksetra*) that is opposed to pure consciousness, purusa, which is the 'knower of the field' (*ksetrajna*) and is often allied with male gender. In a similar vein, women, who embody prakriti, are described metaphorically as the field in which men plant the seed during insemination. As the field, woman can become polluted, whereas the seed is not vulnerable to pollution in the same way. Therefore, for the female, sexual promiscuity is a sure road to pollution, for sex with different partners leads to exchange of bodily substance, which in turn leads to pollution of the 'field'.

The ideology concerning the duties and conduct of a pativrata emphasises not only the subordination of the woman to her sexual continence. A good wife is above all a chaste wife. A woman who uses her sexuality for any purpose other than providing for her husband's pleasure and bearing his children threatens not only the welfare of her husband but also the stability of society. Correct use of sexuality in marriage maintains order whereas any other use of sexuality leads to disorder. The powers of the chaste woman have no equal. Most critically, these are powers that are bound: they are powers that are built upon a culturally perceived morality, they are powers of order. The benevolent woman and the benevolent goddesses are those who maintain order and who are themselves regulated. Thus, for example, Sita the wife of Rama, who guards her chastity against the advances of a demon and remains faithful to her husband even when threatened with death, represents the standard for a good Hindu bride.

The Sudra Revolution

Vivekananda uses the term '*Sudra*' to mean the labouring classes, the common peasant and the artisan. In Bengal, for instance, Vaidyas and Kayasthas though among the most advanced in terms of education or professional mobility, were ritually still defined as

Sudras. This had resulted from changes peculiar to the province; as Bengal was successively overrun first by the Turko-Afghan armies and then by the Mughal, the local ruling elite had been reduced to a level of insignificance.

In the 1890s, the Hindu orthodoxy of Bengla often tried to counter Vivekananda's growing popularity by directing attention to his *Sudra* status. Such accusations not only caused him some social embarrassment but also threatened to undermine the very legitimacy of his mission. In general perception, the *Sudra* was still not a legitimate spokesman for Hinduism. When accused of being a *Sudra*, Vivekananda's characteristic counter-attack was to claim Kshatriya ancestry. In fact one of the few things that instantly provoked him was the reference to his 'low' ritual status and once, at Madras, he hit back at a group of Brahmins calling them 'pariahs'. One should also remember that in Vivekananda's case, identifying the Kayasthas with Kshatriyas was especially important as it upheld the ideas of courage and manly vigour.

Vivekananda also used the four-tier varna structure in his general analysis of Indian history. Historical change in India was seen to evolve through four well-defined stages, each corresponding to an equivalent stage in the varna structure. Thus the first of these four stages marks the hegemony of the priest and the law giver (Brahmin) and thereafter, successively passes through the regimes of the Kshatriya (warrior and statesman). Vaishya (trader and banker) and Sudra '(the common worker). Obviously, each of these stages had a distinctive character. The first, for example, was characterized by priestcraft and intense religious speculation, the second by war and aggrandizement and so on. More importantly however, each stage implied a rebuttal of the stage immediately preceding it. Thus the emergence of Kshatriya power was built upon a serious contestation of the Brahminical and likewise, political frontiers erected by centuries of war and aggression (Kshatriya rule) gradually dissolved before the emerging global networks of commerce (the rule of the Vaishya). Vivekananda quite convincingly characterized his own age as the heyday of the Vaishya even though he did not associate this clearly with the unique characteristics of modern industrial capitalism. The impending rule of the *Sudras*, Vivekananda prophesized, was to bring about the most momentous changes, overturning upper- class privileges and power and ushering in for the first time, the rule of the masses.

The agenda of a *Sudra* revolution would necessarily make it the most violent in character. The orders led by the Brahmin, Kshatriya and Vaishya had one thing in common - all of them thrived on the exploitation of the *Sudra*. This naturally gave all preceding revolutions an underlying unity of character; they were relatively more peaceful because they were also less radical in their aims. *Sudra* rule, because it was to dramatically bring the world closer to an equitable sharing of the fruits of labour, was to arrive through greatly conflicting claims and tumult. Here, it is difficult to say whether Vivekananda derived his conclusions from a critical understanding of history or thorugh some rare intuitive power, but some of the prophecies that he made are startling in their exactness. Long before they actually occurred in these countries, Vivekananda had predicted 'earth-shaking' proletarian revolutions in Russia and China.

At one level, the idea of a *Sudra* revolution was very precious to Vivekananda for in this he saw the rightful avenging of centuries of inhuman exploitation and injustice. Being cleverer and more resourceful, the upper classes had always been able to live off the labours of the common man. But at last the sleeping Leviathan had awakened, the *Sudra* was now more conscious than ever before, of his dignity and the economic value of his labour. The whole of Calcutta would be paralysed, writes Vivekananda, if the scavengers were to go on strike for a few hours and yet their work was considered ritually defiling and the people who rendered such useful service, socially marginalized. No work, however small or big, warns Vivekananda, could be demeaning. These ideas focusing on the dignity of labour that one encounters in Vivekananda were to later become important in the Gandhian movement.

Vivekananda did not envisage a free India to be the captive of the educated middle classes. 'A few thousand graduates do not make the nation,' he writes. The educated middle classes, in his opinion, were a spent force. Brahmins are sucking the life-blood of the people while millions live on Mahua flowers!' he cried. His soul cried out for the poor and the oppressed all around the world. He was in London when an event connected with the coronation of Tsar Nicholas moved him to tears. Apparently, hordes of poor Russian peasants had travelled many hundreds of miles to St Petersburg for the gift of an enamel glass that had been promised to them on this occasion, only to die later from police firing. In his concern and compassion for the poor, he saw the most sublime expressions of Vedanta: '... "the poor, the illiterate, the ignorant, the afflicted, let these by your God".

In trying to solve the long-standing problem of the *Sudra*, Vivekananda generally advocated the policy of positive non-discrimination. Inequities in nature had to be overcome by consciously creating equal opportunities for all. Even if they be equally poor, it was important that more money be spent on the education of the 'pariah' than on that of the Brahmin. Being the more ingenious of the two the Brahmin could educate himself but not the pariah. 'This is justice and reason as I see it', Vivekananda wrote. Towards the later stages of his life, Vivekananda apparently came to realize that the redressal of such grievances could not be achieved solely through education. In the context of Indian society, traditional parameters of reference were obviously no less important. A ritually degraded jati could not always rise in social esteem purely on the basis of educational advancement or professional ability. Mobility within the *jati* structure was no less important as was easily borne out by the proliferation of Sanskritizing recognition, Vivekananda advised conferring Dwija status on all members of the Hindu community. He suggests that the numerous Hindu *jatis* be restructured along the lines of the old Varna hierarchy and the ancient codes of Manu and Yajnavalkya brought back with suitable modifications.

How exactly this social restructuring would keep out older animosities, Vivekananda did not clearly confront. It is apparent that in trying to reconcile two mutually contradictory positions, the older *Varnashram* and visions of a modern, egalitarian society, Vivekananda ran into some difficulty. In his social Utopia, he would not depart too much from the *Shastras*. But the *Shastras* set tangible limits on social experimentation; while a host of upper and middle order jatis could be brought under the nomenclature of Dwijati, this was certainly not possible with the cobbler and the scavenger. One suspects that Vivekananda was only too aware of this and in essence, his idea of the ritual consecration of low jatis had more to do with his visions of an incipient 'Hindu' nationhood than with the abolishing of jati frontiers altogether. His passionate claim that the same blood ran through all - the cobbler, scavenger and upper-class

Bengali bhandralok-should likewise be seen as more of a political rhetoric. He was known to be against interfering with the institution of marriage and at best recommended marriages between various sub-*jatis* of the same *jati.* Marrying the ritually degraded muchi to the mahisya, a fairly respectable agrarian caste, was not his idea of brotherhood and social justice, far less so of his social Utopia.

Not with standing his critique of Hindu social order, Vivekananda would not agree to dissolve the institution of caste. 'Caste should not go', he writes, 'but be adjusted occasionally'. Also, in insisting that caste was entirely a social institution, Vivekananda seems to have overlooked the support and legitimacy it drew from religion. Among other things, he saw in the institution of caste, some kind of a buffer that would partly offset the consequences arising out of enormous disparities of wealth and social status. 'In caste', he thus argues, 'the poorest is as good as the richest'. Here again, Vivekananda failed to appreciate the complex interpenetration of class and caste, of economic power and the power born of ritual superiority. His argument that one form of labour was as good as any other was fundamentally just, humane and progressive. Unfortunately however, it was also to a great extent utopian and unrealistic. Even though he maintained this quite forcefully, Vivekananda must have known that when it came to accept social standards, the man who governed the country was by no means comparable with one who could do little apart from mending shoes.

It is possible that in devising the theory of the four-stage historical evolution, Vivekananda was somewhat influenced by the Hindu Yuga theory which also speaks of a four-fold division of time. Both theories furthermore believe in the idea of degenerative time, and both are preoccupied with the problems of women and Sudras, particularly in respect to the present Kali Yuga. Both regard the first of the four epochs corresponding to Brahminical hegemony to be the best and the last, that is *Sudra* rule, to be the worst in most respects. It is interesting that in Vivekananda's schema, *Sudra* hegemony, though fulfilling an important historical function, would lead to disorder, anarchy and a 'general lowering of culture'. In keeping with the Yuga theory, Vivekananda looked forward to the restoration of the ideal Satya Yuga when each man would have turned a Brahmin and all forms of oppression and inequality would have ended. It is obvious from Vivekananda's writings and speeches that he held the

Brahmin to be a symbol both of unjust exploitation and the embodiment of the highest human virtues. This paradox, interestingly, is resolved only in the light of what the Shastras themselves said about the Brahmin generally being the ideal of humanity but now fallen to his worst form in degenerate Kaliyuga, the last of the four Yugas.

It appears as though Vivekananda was somewhat uncomfortable with the possibility of the *Sudra* revolution unceremoniously throwing out the Brahmin. The Brahmin had done great things for India and was likely to do even more in future, and unfortunately, those who were to replace him in positions of leadership and power had neither his magnanimity nor his intelligence. Vivekananda supported mass education in the vernacular and yet held that no education would be complete without a knowledge of Sanskrit. 'Sanskrit and prestige go hand in hand in India', he remarked and his only complaint against the medieval Bhakti saints was that they neglected to take Sanskrit to the masses.

While accepting the inevitability of change, Vivekananda remained somewhat uneasy and apprehensive about the possible fallouts of the impending class struggle. 'We are to solve the problem of the *Sudra*', he once confessed in some anguish to Nivedita, 'but through what tumult, through what tumult!'. Vivekananda argued that in order to avoid motiveless violence, it was necessary that the upper classes themselves take the first step forward; rather than wait for the revolution to violently uproot them from their position, the privileged should voluntarily give the underprivileged their due.

Vivekananda accepted human society as a graded organization and like a true conservative felt that the more lasting solution to social inequalities was not the dismantling of privilege but the gradual elevation of the lower classes. In his schema significantly, educational progress was expected to produce a horizontal rather a vertical mobility. When once asked if the lower *jatis*, once educated, would not start behaving just as tyrannically as the upper classes, Vivekananda answered by saying that in their case, education was to lead to professional betterment and not to social or occupational mobility. The educated scavenger therefore was to continue in his traditional occupation but by the dint of his education, do the same job better. Effectively, this meant that education would raise the worth of the scavenger's work in his own eyes without necessarily producing corresponding changes in social attitudes towards such work.

In political matters as in the social, Vivekananda generally tried to stay within the boundaries of his own making, though this sometimes led to an acceptance of the status quo. His instruction to workers of the Ramakrishna Mission was to stay away, as far as possible, from sensitive state matters. Vivekananda was naturally upset on hearing the news of his brother disciple, Swami Akhandananda, incurring the displeasure of state officials at Khetri in his attempt to free some local people from beggar. In a letter of 21 February 1900 from California, he warned his brother disciple of the disastrous results that might follow such misdirected enthusiasm. Anticipating Gandhi, he said "leave the peasants and labourers to look to their own problem, to grapple with and solve it. But then you must not set up class strife between the poor peasant, the labouring people and the wealthy classes. Make it a point not to abuse the moneyed classes."

We need an intellectual and spiritual giant in our midst — like Vivekananda — who can restore to India the 'ancient nobility of temper' and the 'quiet content of her unacquisitive soul'. When social and cultural degeneration clouded the horizon in late 19th century India, Vivekananda's dynamic and rousing mission began to instil courage and confidence in the people. He declared, with passionate intensity: "Here is the same". India whose soil has been trodden by the feet of the greatest sages that ever lived. Here first arose the doctrines of the immortality of the soul, the existence of a supervising God, an immanent God in nature and man... We are the children of such a country".

To a superstitious people he exhorted: "Stand up and fight! You gain nothing by becoming cowards. You cry to 60 million gods and still die like mad dogs. This bending of the knee to superstitions does not befit you. You are infinite, deathless and birthless". His words of inspiration removed the diffidence caused by colonial rule, creating an atmosphere of self-respect and self-confidence. This spirit was later carried forward by eminent leaders like Gandhi and Tilak.

India today is a pale shadow of what she should have been. Instead of leading the world in life nurturing ideas, she is being led by materialistic forces. Her economy should have reflected the care and culture of her people; instead, it has been dehumanised by neomaterialism. She should have recreated and strengthened her tradition of upholding unity in diversity. Instead, the country has been torn asunder by conflict and confusion.

This has happened because India has failed to include the service oriented way of life based upon the highest principles of ethics and morality, as propagated by Vivekananda. Vivekananda gave importance to serving "the outcast Narayanas, the starving Narayanas and the oppressed Narayanas". He posed the question to his own class; "What have we done, we the socalled men of God, the sanyasis? What have we done for the masses?" Pointing to the main culprits, he thundered: "You, the upper classes of India, do you think you are alive? You are but mummies, ten thousand years old..... In the world of Maya, you are the real illusion. You merge yourself in the void and disappear. Let a new India arise in your place".

If Vivekananda were here today, he would tell to the present day social and political elites in the same tenor and tone. He would tell them: "You have betrayed the country. You have stifled the underlying inspiration for constitutional goals. You proceeded to set up political and administrative institutions, but failed to create the mind and motivation that would have given life and meaning to them. You built bodies without souls. You ignored the values engendered in the ideals of karmayogi, contentment, compassion and '*tyaga*' and '*tapasya*' and started worshipping the new gods of power and privilege. From the great storehouse of the past, you should have picked up the gems and thrown out the stones. You did exactly the opposite".

Bibliography

Ambedkar, B.R. 1970. *Who Were the Shudras?* Bombay: Thackers.

Ashby, Philip H. 1974. *Modern Trends in Hinduism*. New York: Columbia University Press.

Aurobindo, Sri. 1959. *Essays on the Gita*. Pondicherry: Sri Aurobindo Ashram.

Badrinath, Chaturvedi (2006), Swami *Vivekananda The Living Vedanta*, New York: Penguin.

Bakshi, Rajni (1994), *The Dispute Over Swami Vivekananda's Legacy: a warning and an opportunity*, Mapusa, Goa: Other India Press.

Ball, U.N. 1933. *Rammohun Roy*. Calcutta: University of Calcutta.

Banhatti, G.S. (1963), The Quintessence of Vivekananda, Pune, India: Suvichar Prakashan Mandal.

Banhatti, G.S. (1995), *Life and Philosophy of Swami Vivekananda*, Atlantic Publishers & Distributors, p. 276.

Basham, A.L. 1999 [1954]. *The Wonder That Was India*. Delhi: Rupa & Co.

Bharathi, K.S. (1998b), *Encyclopaedia of eminent thinkers: the political thought of Vivekananda*, New Delhi: Concept Publishing Company.

Bhupendra Nath Datta Swami Vivekananda—Patriot Prophet: A Study.

Bhuyan, P. R. (2003), *Swami Vivekananda: Messiah of Resurgent India*, New Delhi: Atlantic Publishers & Distributors.

Bowes, Pratima. 1977. *The Hindu Religious Tradition: A Philosophical Approach*, London: Rputledge & Kegan Paul.

Buhler, G., trans. 1886. *The Laws of Manu*. Oxford: Clarendon Press.

Burke, Marie Louise (1958), *Swami Vivekananda in America: New Discoveries*, Kolkata: Advaita Ashrama.

___ (1985), Swami Vivekananda in the West: New Discoveries (in six volumes) (3 ed.), Kolkata: Advaita Ashrama.

Chakrabarti, Tapan Kumar (2001), "Swami Vivekananda", in Arrington, Robert L., *A Companion to the Philosophers*, Blackwell Publishing.

Clarke, Peter Bernard (2006), *New Religions in Global Perspective*, Routledge

Dandekar, RN. 1967. *Some Aspects of the History of Hinduism*. Poona: University of Poona.

Dhar, Shailendra Nath (1976), *A Comprehensive Biography of Swami Vivekananda* (2 ed.), Madras, India: Vivekananda Prakashan Kendra.

Dutt, Harshavardhan (2005), *Immortal Speeches*, New Delhi: Unicorn Books.

Embree, Ainslie T., ed. 1972. *The Hindu Tradition*. New York: Random House.

Farquhar, J. N. (1915), *Modern Religious Movements in India*, London: Macmillan

Farquhar, J.N. 1967. *Modern Religious Movements* in India. Delhi: Munshiram Manoharlal.

Gambhirananda, Swami (1983) [1957], *History of the Ramakrishna Math and Mission* (3rd ed.), Calcutta, India: Advaita Ashrama.

Gandhi, M.K. 1950. *Hindu Dharma*. Ahmedabad: Navajivan Publishing House.

Georg, Feuerstein (2002), *The Yoga Tradition*, Delhi: Motilal Banarsidass

Gokhale, B. G. (January 1964), "Swami Vivekananda and Indian Nationalism", Journal of Bible and Religion (Oxford University Press) 32 (1): 35–42.

Gupta, N.L. (2003), *Swami Vivekananda*, Delhi: Anmol Publications.

Herman, A.L. 1976. *An Introduction to Indian Thought*. Englewood Cliffs, New ,1 Jersey: Prentice-Hall, Inc.

Hill, W. Douglas P. 1966 [19281. *The Bhagavad Gita* second edition. Madras: Oxford University Press.

Hopkins, Thomas A. 1971. *The Hindu Religious Tradition*. Belmont, California: Dickinson Publishing Co.

Houghton, Walter Raleigh, ed. (1893), *The Parliament of Religions and religious congresses at the World's Columbian exposition* (3 ed.), Frank Tennyson Neely.

Jackson, Carl T (1994), "The Founders", Vedanta for the West: the Ramakrishna movement in the United States, Indianapolis, Indiana: Indiana University Press.

Jones, Kenneth W. (1989), *Socio-religious Movements in British India*, Cambridge, England: Cambridge University Press.

Jordens, J.T.F. 1978. *Dayananda Sarasvati: His Lifr and Ideas*. Delhi: Oxford University Press.

Kotnala, M.C. 1975. *Raja Ram Mohun Roy and Indian Awakening*. New Delhi: Gitanjali Prakashan.

Lipner, Julius. 1994. *Hindus: Their Religious Beliefs and Practices*. London and New York: Routledge.

Mahadevan, T.M.P. 1960. *Outlines of Hinduism*. Bombay: Chetana Ltd.

Majumdar, Ramesh Chandra (1963), *Swami Vivekananda Centenary Memorial Volume, Kolkata: Swami Vivekananda Centenary.*

Marc, Seifer (2001), Wizard: The Life and Times of Nikola Tesla : Biography of a Genius, Citadel.

Marie Louise Burke: *Swami Vivekananda in America*: New Discoveries (4 vols, Calcutta, 1983)

Minor, Robert Neil (1986), "Swami Vivekananda's use of the Bhagavad Gita", *Modern Indian Interpreters of the Bhagavad Gita*, Albany, New York: SUNY Press.

Morgan Kenneth W., ed. 1953. *The Religion of the Hindus*. New York: The Ronald Press Company.

Mumukshananda, Swami, ed. (1995), *Vivekananda: The Great Spiritual Teacher: A Compilation*, Calcutta, India: Advaita Ashrama.

-- 1964, "Swami Vivekananda Centenary", Philosophy East and West (University of Hawai'i Press) 14 (1): 73–75.

Nikhilananda, Swami (1953), Vivekananda: A Biography, New York: Ramakrishna-Vivekananda Center.

Nirnjan Dhar's *Vedanta and Bengal Renaissance* (Calcutta, 1977).

Nivedita, Sister (1910), The Master As I Saw Him, London: Longmans.

O' Connell, Joseph T. 1976. "Caitanya's Followers and the Bhagavad-gita: A Case Study of Bhakti and the Secular," in Hinduism: *New Essays in the History of Religions*. Ed. Bardwell L. Smith. Leiden: E.J. Brill.

Organ, Troy Wilson. 1974. *Hinduism: Its Historical Development*. Woodbury, New York: Barrons' Educational Series.

Pande, Govind Chandra. 1994. Lfe and Thought of ankarts chatrya. Delhi: Motilal Banarsidass.

Pangborn, Cyrus R.; Smith, Bardwell L. (1976), "The Ramakrishna Math and Mission", *Hinduism: New Essays in the History of Religions*, Brill Archive

Paranjape, Makarand (2005), *Swami Vivekananda Reader*, Penguin India.

Pitt, Malcolm. 1958. *Introducing Hinduism*. New York: Friendship Press.

Prabha Dixit: 'The Social and Political Dimensions of Vivekananda's Ideology' in *Indian Economic and Social History Review*, 12(3).

Prakash, Vishwa. 1969. *Life and Teachings of Swami Doyananda*. Allahabad: Kala Press.

R.K.Dasgpta: *Swami Vivekananda on Indian Philosophy and Literature* (Calcutta, 1996).

Radhakrishnan, S. 1939. *Eastern Religions and Western Thought.* Oxford: Clarendon Press.

Radhakrishnan, S. 1967. *Religion in a Changing World London*: George Allen & Unyin Ltd.

Rajgopal Chattopadhyay: *Swami Vivekananda in India: A Corrective Biography* (Delhi, 1999)

Rambachan, Anantanand (1994), *The Limits of Scripture: Vivekananda's reinterpretation of the Vedas,* Honolulu, Hawaii: University of Hawaii Press.

Richards, Glyn (1996), "Vivekananda", *A Source-Book of Modern Hinduism,* Routledge.

Robinson, Richard H. and Willard L. Johnson. 1982 [1970]. *The Buddhist Religion: A Historical Introduction.* 3rd ed. Belmont, Calif.: Wadsworth Publishing Company.

Rolland, Romain (2008), *The Life of Vivekananda and the Universal Gospel* (24 ed.), Advaita Ashrama.

S.P. Basu and S.B. Ghosh: *Vivekananda in Indian Newspapers*: 1893-1902 (Calcutta, 1969).

Sailendra Nath Dhar : A Comprehensive Biography of Swami Vivekanan (Madras, 2 vols, 1975-6).

Saradananda Swami. 1952. *Sri Ramakrishna: The Great Master.* Madras: Sri Ramakrishna Math.

Sen, Amiya (2003), Narayani Gupta, ed., *Swami Vivekananda,* New Delhi: Oxford University Press.

Sen, Amiya (2006), *Indispensable Vivekananda*: anthology for our times, Orient Blackswan.

Sharma, Arvind (1988), "Swami Vivekananda's Experiences", *Neo-Hindu Views of Christianity,* Leiden, The Netherlands: Brill.

Sharma, Arvind, ed. 2002. *Modern Hindu Thought: the Essential Texts.* New Delhi: Oxford University Press.

Sharma, Benishankar (1963), *Swami Vivekananda: A Forgotten Chapter of His Life,* Kolkata: Oxford Book & Stationary Co.

Sharma, D.S. 1967. *Hinduism Through the Ages.* Bombay: Bharatiya Vidya Bhavan.

Sharma, Ram Sharan. 1958, *Sudras in Ancient India.* Delhi: Motilal Banarsidass. Sharma.

Sil, Narasingha Prosad (1997), *Swami Vivekananda: A Reassessment,* Selinsgrove, Pennsylvania.

Smith, Bardwell L. 1976. *Hinduism: New Essays in the History of Religions.* Leden, The Netherlands: E.J. Brill.

Sontheimer, Gunther D. and Herman Kulke, eds. 1989. *Hinduism Reconsidered*. New Delhi: Manohar.

Tagore, Rabindranath. 1967 [1931]. *The Religion of Man*. London: Unwin Books.

Tapan Raychaudhuri *Europe Reconsidered: Perceptions of the West in Nineteenth Century Bengal* (Delhi, 1988).

Trompf, G.W. 1976. *Friedrich Max Mueller: As a Theorist of Comparative Religion.*

Virajananda, Swami, ed. (2006) [1910], The Life of the *Swami Vivekananda by his eastern and western disciples...* in two volumes (Sixth ed.), Kolkata: Advaita Ashrama.

Vivekananda, Swami (2001) [1907], *Complete Works of Swami Vivekananda*, 9 Volumes, Advaita Ashrama.

Voight, Johannes N. 1967. *Max Mueller: The Man and His Ideas.* Calcutta: Firma K.L. Mokhopadhyay.

Von Dense, Christian D. (1999), *Philosophers and Religious Leaders*, Greenwood Publishing Group

Walker, Benjamin. 1968. *The Hindu World.* New York: Fredrick A. Praeger.

Yadav, K.C., ed. 1976. *Autobiography of Swami Dayananda Saraswati.* Delhi: Manohar.

Zaehner, R.C. 1962. *Hinduism*. London: Oxford University Press.

Index